Cultural Studies in the English Classroom

Cultural Studies in the English Classroom

Edited by
James A. Berlin
Michael J. Vivion

Boynton/Cook
Heinemann
Portsmouth, NH

Boynton/Cook Publishers, Inc.
A Subsidiary of
Reed Publishing (USA) Inc.
361 Hanover Street, Portsmouth, NH 03801
Offices and agents throughout the world

Printed in the United States of America.
93 94 95 96 97   9 8 7 6 5 4 3 2 1

Table of Contents

Introduction

A Provisional Definition

No one needs to be told that English as a field of study is in turmoil. Intense debates over what ought to take place in the English classrooms of colleges and schools, as well as what should be the objects and methods of scholarly research and graduate work, are a current fixture of academic life. These disciplinary disputes, furthermore, are not restricted to the professional membership. Rarely has the ideological role of English studies in the ongoing political life of the nation been more apparent in the popular press and media. Both *Time* and *Newsweek*, for example, have recently reported departmental disagreements over the literary canon in long pieces on "political correctness." The debate over the political content of a required freshman composition course at the University of Texas at Austin has meanwhile been covered in the *New York Times* as well as *Newsweek*. One of the ironies of these unmistakably political disputes is that one group of contestants — those representing the right — offer their transparently ideological judgments in the name of a transcendent, value-free commitment to "the best that has been thought and said." That this "best" is nothing other than an ideological designation — as its vociferous support by the likes of William Bennett and Gary Wills makes clear — remains unacknowledged. And this brings us to the subject of cultural studies.

Cultural studies is integral to the current uncertainty in English departments, acting as both a catalyst and a response. Most formulations agree that English studies can no longer treat literary texts as purely aesthetic documents transcending the realms of the political and historical, and rhetorical texts as mere transcripts of empirical and rational truths. The divergences among formulations, beyond these commonalities, are considerable, with representative voices ranging across a broad intellectual and ideological spectrum. Here the editors would like to discuss the notion of cultural studies we called upon in selecting the essays in this volume, a notion strongly influenced by the example of the Birmingham Center for Contemporary Cultural Studies. It should be acknowledged immediately, however, that no definition could hope to speak for so broad a group of cultural workers as are here represented. Indeed, after discussing our conception of cultural studies, we plan to explore its inadequacy in accounting for the diverse efforts offered here. In other words, we plan to consider the difficulties in formulating an adequate definition of cultural studies as well as indicate the open-ended nature of any formulation. Cultural studies simply cannot be easily pinned down.

The first issue in characterizing cultural studies is the definition of culture to be invoked. Since the eighteenth century, culture has commonly stood for a sphere of human behavior regarded as in some sense separate from the categories of the economic and the political. For certain orthodox Marxisms, this separation was merely apparent, a mystification of the truth. Culture was thus characterized as a reflex of economic behavior, as a totally determined and mechanically predictable sphere of dependent activity. In contrast, for institutional English studies in Britain and the United States, culture has usually been regarded as an autonomous category of experience manifested in an exclusive set of canonical literary texts and particular ways of reading them. These texts and readings were both regarded as completely free and independent of economic and even political activity. Both Marxist and British mainstream conceptions were strongly contested in the fifties by the work of Raymond Williams and Richard Hoggart. They argued that culture is more adequately portrayed as the entire lived experience of human agents in response to their concrete historical conditions, and that these responses are not simply reflections of economic and political behavior. Culture in their conception stands for a complex way of life that can never be finally reduced to a super-structural reflex of an economic base. At the same time, it cannot be seen as completely unrelated to the economic and political conditions of its creation. This formulation also breaks down the distinction between canonical and other cultural texts, arguing that cultural workers, such as English teachers, ought to consider noncanonical texts and forms of representation traditionally excluded from concern, such as film and television, advertisements, and oral histories.

This revised notion of culture was eventually challenged by the structuralist revolution in studies of language and society. Here cuture came to be seen as a set of representations with language, signifying practices, mediating and shaping all experience. Unfortunately, signifying practices and forms were initially posited to be as completely determinative of culture as was economic behavior in the old Marxist schemes. In time, however, culture conceived as signification was integrated with culture as lived experience by the workers at Birmingham, whose broader view had been influenced by Antonio Gramsci's conception of hegemony.

The editors here wish to forward the notion of cultural studies emerging out of the encounter between these two formulations. This notion regards culture both as the signifying practices that represent experience in language, myth, and literature and as the relatively autonomous responses of human agents to concrete historical conditions (see Hall, "Cultural Studies: Two Paradigms"; Johnson). One important corollary of this position, as shall be seen, is that culture always represents a conflicted field in which different representations and lived experiences are constantly competing for hegemony.

Our conception of cultural studies then must take into account the poststructuralist textual turn, most importantly in its reformulation of the subject of experience. We agree with Richard Johnson that "cultural studies is about the historical forms of consciousness or subjectivity, or the subjective forms we live by, or, in a rather perilous compression, perhaps a reduction, the subjective side of social relations" (43). Subjectivity here is not considered in the terms of liberal humanism, the Enlightenment stance of traditional literary studies. The subject is not taken to be the unified, coherent, self-present originator of experience. Instead, subjectivities are regarded as multiple social constructions, the effects of signifying practices. These signifying practices in turn make up the central activity of culture, or, as Johnson has it, "the structural character of the forms we inhabit subjectively: language, signs, ideologies, discourses, myths" (45). Cultural studies then becomes the study of the ways social formations and practices are involved in the shaping of consciousness, and this shaping is seen to be mediated by language and situated in concrete historical conditions. Signifying practices then intercede in the relations among material conditions, social arrangements, and the formation of consciousness. The important consideration is that the entire process is ideological: it is enmeshed in economic, social and political valuations that are always historically specific. In other words, discursive practices are never the mere reflections of economic categories; they are always negotiated in power and politics, and power and politics are always negotiated in discursive practices.

Cultural studies then deals with the production, distribution, and reception of signifying practices within the myriad historical formations that are shaping subjectivities. These range from the family, the school, the work place, and the peer group to the more familiar activities associated with the cultural sphere, such as the arts and the media and their modes of production and consumption. In other words, wherever signifying practices are shaping consciousness in daily life, cultural studies has work to do.

The central place of signifying practices and subject formation in this conception is perfectly compatible with one set of concerns found in traditional English studies: the preoccupation with ways of reading and writing. The two activities, however, are radically altered in cultural studies. Both composing and interpreting texts become overt acts of discourse analysis and negotiation. Writing and reading are regarded as culturally coded acts, discursive procedures which guide the production and interpretation of meanings, making a certain range of significances more likely to appear and others less probable. Nevertheless, writing and reading usually are negotiated acts of discourse analysis as the reader-writer attempts to locate the semiotic codes that are appropriate to the discourse situation at hand. This activity may result in a simple accommodation to hegemonic cultural codes, but it usually involves a negotiated transaction and even resistance. In other words, cultural codes are rarely totally predictable in their effects on lived experience. An advertisement, for example, usually evokes a range of responses in at least some consumers that was not intended or anticipated by its producers (Hall; Fiske). Thus, students may be instructed in the authoritative methods for reading and writing texts, but they will often negotiate these instructions, shaping texts in ways intended to serve their own purposes.

Certain features of this negotiation of cultural codes should be emphasized. As semiotic systems, these codes can function at a variety of registers and levels simultaneously. Thus, cultural codes usually endorse certain class, race, gender, age, and ethnic role designations, and usually a subject occupies more than one of these role positions simultaneously. At the same time, these roles form elements in larger economic, social, and political narratives, narratives that constitute a set of codes at a higher level of abstraction (e.g., "Only professional, middle-class men are suited for high political office" or "Women do not work as hard as men and so should be paid less." The important point is that cultural codes are never simply in the writer or reader, or in the text the writer produces and the reader receives. Composing and reception are both processes of production, requiring the active construction of meaning according to one or another or, more likely, a combination of these coded procedures; and the processes are never totally predictable, usually involving a complex web of negotiation and resistance. Thus, reading and writing are interchangeable because both are interpretive; that is, both are generative of meaning rather than simply activities in the transcription or reception of information.

This disruption of the reading-writing (passive consumption-active production) binary opposition leads to a further set of related disruptions in the usual business of the English department. These can be seen as organized around the poetic-rhetoric relation. As both Gerald Graff and Robert Scholes have argued, English studies in the United States has been grounded in the valorization of poetic texts and the corresponding devaluation of the rhetorical. The superiority of the poetic over the rhetorical has been expressed in terms of the preference for the disinterested over the interested, the private over the public, the contemplative over the active, and the creative over the imitative. The conception of signifying practices offered in the cultural studies described here contends that there are simply no disinterested uses of language since all discourses, both in poetic and rhetoric, are involved in ideological valuation. As Pierre Bourdieu and Raymond Williams have argued, aesthetic judgments are closely related to class distinctions, so that all texts are inevitably involved in political contentions. Similarly, the distinction between high culture and low culture, the cultivated and the popular, can be characterized as a further validation of the class structure, a distinction based on a hierarchy of texts created by a class forwarding its own interests. The social and communal nature of language means, in addition, the disappearance of the sharp distinction between private and public experience. Subjects are constituted by public discourse, although, as Paul Smith argues, each person becomes a differentiated site of converging discourses that enable agency and action. The subject as discursive formation acts as well as reacts, the private and public interacting dialectically, the two never altogether separate nor altogether identical. Neither the poetic nor the rhetorical text can thus be designated the exclusive province of the inside or the outside. The distinction between action and contemplation likewise collapses as we realize that all texts are involved in politics and power: all tacitly endorse certain platforms of action. Language, as Kenneth Burke has demonstrated, is always a program for performance.

It is important to note that the displacement of these oppositions does not mean that the distinction between rhetorical and poetic texts will be lost. It does mean that the distinction will have to be reconcieved, an effort that will mean a further re-thinking of the work of English studies, both in the objects of study and the methods pursued. The aesthetic code is a central element in literary production and interpretation, but it can only function in relation to other codes: it is never isolated and innocent. And it is never altogether absent from the rhetorical text. Cultural studies in the English department will address the distinguishing features of rhetorical and poetic texts, but it will do so on the basis of the writing and reading practices involved in each — the culturally indicated, historically specific codes deemed appropriate to each. Both are rich and complex, and both are necessary to the health of a society. The work of cultural studies within English departments will be to examine the discursive strategies involved in generating and interpreting each. English classrooms will thus provide methods for revealing the semiotic codes enacted in both the production and interpretation of a wide range of textual practices, practices including but not restricted to the medium of print. The codes considered, furthermore, will cut across the aesthetic, the economic, the political, the philosophical, and the scientific, preparing students to engage critically in the variety of reading and writing practices required of them as citizens, as workers, as individual sites of desire. English studies will then be interdisciplinary in methods and materials.

As mentioned earlier, all the essayists assembled here would not agree on this version of cultural studies in all its particulars. They would, however, probably concur that the classroom represents a site for working out the theoretical, practical, and political issues identified in the current debates over English and cultural studies. The classroom is a proving ground for a reformulation of the relationship between theory and practice, the two interacting dialectically in constant revision of each other. This relationship, furthermore, is inherently political. It is in the texts of culture, as broadly conceived here, that the ideological battles of the historical moment are fought. Thus, as Paulo Freire, Henry Giroux, Ira Shor, and others have argued, English teachers are engaged in a cultural politics in which the power of students as citizens in the democratic public sphere is at stake. The aim is to make them subjects rather than the objects of historical change. Both teachers and students then will engage in critique, in a critical examination of the economic, social, and political conditions within which the signifying practices of culture take place.

Some Provisional Practices

Having said all this, we must immediately indicate the variations in the conceptions and practices of cultural studies offered in this collection. These variations, we would argue, are necessary and inevitable. It is not just that there are so many different versions of cultural studies to choose from today, although this diversity cannot be denied. More important, for the participants in this collection cultural studies simply cannot be fixed and formalized, in the manner of an academic discipline, although there are some who would do so in order to more clearly stake out the disciplinary ground of *a* cultural studies. Thus, while cultural studies deals with signifying practices in their relation to subject formation within structures of economic and political power, its mode of operation is open-ended, positioning itself for revision and reshaping. This potential merits additional comment.

In the preface to *In Rethinking Culture*, an exploration of cultural studies in South Africa, Ntongela Masilela argues that cultural studies in his nation needs to assume an African focus, asserting that it is erroneous to assume that "cultural studies in South Africa is merely the continuation of English cultural studies on a different historical plane" (2). He further asserts that the "constellation of brilliant English

Marxists can only seriously be of assistance to us [in South Africa] in establishing cultural bridge-heads on the political terrain of our history." He goes on to call for a distinctly African version of cultural studies (1–5). We would argue that cultural studies in the United States, particularly cultural studies as curriculum and instruction, would do well to heed the premise that can be extrapolated from Masilela's remarks. In order for cultural studies to find an audience of U.S. teachers and students, workers in the area will need to construct programs and practices with a uniquely American flavor. At the recent Oklahoma conference, Crossing the Disciplines: Cultural Studies in the 1990s, Gayatri Spivak argued that we need to define an essentially American view of cultural studies, that Birmingham will not serve the aims of cultural studies in the United States. The question this consideration raises is whether English Marxism or its American descendant can provide middle-class U.S. students, or those aspiring to that condition, the critical structure essential to perform the kind of cultural critique that Stuart Hall and others call for.

Cultural studies as described in the essays in this volume thus tends to reflect the history and present of U.S. cultural values. Some of the essays explore the roles of the subject in relationship to First World culture. Others demonstrate how the methods of cultural studies work with traditional texts and within traditional courses. Many of them redefine the issues of power in ways that de-emphasize the importance of economic considerations. The nature of democracy in a variety of cultural contexts is frequently of concern. In short, the points of departure are varied, but all attempt in theory and practice to address the unique conditions of our time and place.

This book thus provides descriptions of cultural studies in practice, but even these descriptions imply attempts at definition, either explicit or implicit, and these attempts lead to questions. When we frame our classroom social investigations in terms of race, gender, sexual orientation, class, age, ethnicity, geocentrism, have we now formalized cultural studies? Is cultural studies a form of cultural activism or cultural archivism? Is cultural studies a formal discipline which needs a treatise nailed to a door at some professional meeting (as Cary Nelson decided at the Oklahoma conference)? Is cultural studies to be a U.S. extension of the cultural Marxism promulgated by the Birmingham Centre? Is cultural studies an academic frame providing yet another entry for marginalized academics seeking to develop credentials that will allow them to compete more fully within the highly stratified academic environment? Can cultural studies remain a loosely allied coalition of multidisciplinary professionals, or does it demand enough critical consistency to give it academic integrity? Do we need to spell Cultural Studies with capital letters?

Many of the essays in this collection reflect a concern with these questions. As one reads these articles it becomes clear that within cultural studies resides great diversity in approach, definition, and content. But one constant does emerge. The intense concern the authors have for coherent methods illustrates the error of calling any classroom practice that engages in cultural critique "cultural studies." When teachers in the sixties and seventies employed students in discussions about Vietnam, the Watts riots, drugs, social responsibility; when they read "Civil Disobedience" and "The Student as Nigger," they were not necessarily involved in cultural studies. Nor are programs which explore cultural diversity or popular culture necessarily cultural studies. The essays in this volume emphasize that cultural studies is not a prescribed content, but instead a method or various methods of making meaning and exploring how meaning is made — both an epistemology and a critique of epistemology. In a classroom, therefore, cultural studies as a way of looking at the world becomes inseparable from pedagogy. Students cannot learn *about* cultural studies: they can only learn to *do* cultural studies.

The language of cultural studies has recently become an issue. Its terminology, so often embedded in the vocabulary of Marxism and poststructuralism, has evoked resistance from many otherwise sympathetic practitioners, students, and teachers. The fear of some is that cultural studies will become an academic commodity, part of the university's cultural capital. The authors of the essays in this book largely avoid this form of linguistic exclusion, perhaps because when they write of students and classrooms they occupy subject positions quite different from the ones which shape their scholarship. Even this observation, however, must be qualified. These essays fall well within the bounds of traditional academic discourse, although they avoid needless technical terms and constructions. Academic discourse, at least within the university, still shapes the discourse of and about cultural studies, even as the practitioners of cultural studies question the privilege of canonical texts. Another reason for this compliance with academic genres may be related to the exclusions from this volume. We were not successful in our efforts to include colleagues from community colleges, although we know cultural studies programs thrive in certain of these schools. People of color did not choose to submit materials for consideration. We did not solicit essays from teachers in elementary schools. The silences created here speak loudly of a need to examine how we constitute ourselves as a community.

We would like to close this introduction with a further comment on resistance. Cultural studies in the classroom creates multiple forms of resistance: resistance from students who feel their values threatened; resistance from English faculty who see traditional content and teach-

ing under interrogation; resistance from teachers from other disciplines who fear the "politically correct" or who question the value of
post-modern rhetoric; resistance from the public who perceive as un-
American any kind of cultural critique. Much of this response results
from the abstract treatment of cultural studies in theoretical articles,
articles abstract both in vocabulary and in the absence of concrete
models of praxis. These treatments establish a new locus of privilege
and redefine the margins so as to exclude those who have been central
to work in English studies. Furthermore, although we must argue that
all teaching is political, there is clearly a difference between the politics
of critique that argues existing institutions must become part of the
dialectic of examination, and the politics of revolution that argues
existing institutions must be changed in preordained ways. When a
certain political stance situates itself beyond investigation, the critique
inherent in cultural studies is foreclosed. No position can be regarded
as immune from critical scrutiny. Thus, teaching students the methods
of critical inquiry peculiar to cultural studies while expecting them to
arrive at predetermined conclusions offers only the pretense of critique.

The authors of the essays presented here, aware of this tension,
invite readers to examine the programs and practices proposed as part
of the critical function of cultural studies. They offer this invitation in
language accessible to all engaged in English studies. They present
cultural studies in the context of graduate and undergraduate programs,
in composition and literature classrooms, in examining Shakespeare
and student texts. Their programs and practices are intended to be
suggestive of the rich possibilities of cultural studies, not just models
proposed for emulation. Teachers in English departments are offered
explorations of certain alternatives and invited to arrive at alterations
and alternatives best-suited to their institutional conditions. These
essays then represent the beginning of an ongoing discussion, not the
last word, in the intersections of cultural studies and English studies.

Works Cited

Bourdieu, Pierre. *Distinction: A Social Critique of the Judgement of Taste.*
    Trans. Richard Nice. Cambridge: Harvard University Press, 1984.

Burke, Kenneth. *Language as Symbolic Action.* Berkeley: University of Cali-
    fornia Press, 1966.

Fiske, John. *Introduction to Communication Studies.* 2nd Ed. London:
    Routledge, 1990.

Freire, Paulo. *Pedagogy of the Oppressed.* New York: Continuum, 1970.

Giroux, Henry. *Schooling and the Struggle for Public Life.* Minneapolis: Uni-
    versity of Minnesota Press, 1988.

Graff, Gerald. *Literature Against Itself: Literary Ideas in Modern Society*. Chicago: University of Chicago Press, 1979.

Hall, Stuart. "Cultural Studies: Two Paradigms." *Media, Culture, and Society* (1980): 57–72.

———. "Encoding/Decoding." *Culture, Media, Language*. Ed. Stuart Hall, et al. London: Hutchinson, 1980.

Hoggart, Richard. *The Uses of Literacy: Changing Patterns in English Mass Culture*. Fair Lawn, NJ: Essential Books, 1957.

Johnson, Richard. "What is Cultural Studies Anyway?" *Social Text* 16 (1986–1987): 38–80.

Masilela, Ntonga. "Establishing and Intellectual Bridgehead." *Rethinking Culture*. Ed. Keyan Tomaselli. Bellville, South Africa: Anthropos Publishers, 1989.

Shor, Ira. "Educating the Educators: A Freireian Approach to the Crisis in Education." *Freire for the Classroom*. Ed. Ira Shor. Portsmouth, NH: Heinemann-Boynton/Cook, 1987.

Williams, Raymond. *Marxism and Literature*. Oxford: Oxford University Press, 1977.

Cultural Studies Programs

Introduction
James Berlin

Cultural studies in the United States has been firmly committed to rethinking and reforming the relation of the work of English studies to larger societal commitments. Some prominent historical exigencies for this effort are considered in the lead essay by Michael Blitz and C. Mark Hurlbert, a piece that explores the contested definitions of culture that confront us today. The revisionary impulse in response to this conflict has led English departments at a number of important universities to structure themselves as departments of cultural studies. In this volume, the programs at Carnegie Mellon, the University of Pittsburgh, and Syracuse University are discussed in some detail, each account foregrounding the politics of the decision to alter dominant institutional conceptions of reading and writing practices. Alan Kennedy's depiction of Carnegie Mellon and Phillip Smith's depiction of Pittsburgh contrast efforts to unite text production and text reception in graduate and undergraduate study. Mas'ud Zavarzadeh and Donald Morton and James Zebroski respond to the program at Syracuse University, an effort program conspicuous in its separation of reading and writing practices. Once again the trajectories of these three projects display the diversity of cultural studies in theory and practice, as well as the struggles that attend their formation.

This section next considers the programmatic work of composition studies in responding to the concerns of cultural studies. Dee Schriner describes the reform of freshman writing at Northern Arizona University in response to the needs of Native Americans, a move that required an examination of established notions of culture. This effort underscores the constructed nature of subjectivity for both dominant and subordinate cultural groups. Christine Farris looks upon academic disciplines as cultural inventions, exploring the attempts of English studies to colonize other departments through the writing across the curriculum project. She subtly explores the struggle for hegemony in the academy in shaping the consciousness of students through the imposition of specific reading and writing practices in the different disciplines. Richard Penticoff and Linda Brodkey offer a description of the "Writing about Difference" freshman writing course at the University of Texas at Austin. This course became the center of a national debate conducted in newspapers and popular periodicals on the appropriate subject matter of a required composition course. The careful theoretical and practical work that was a part of the course's design is presented, offering in its concern for students and their critical capacities a marked contrast to the hysteria of those who opposed it. These three essays reveal the uses of rhetoric for cultural critique, disclosing the ideological processes surrounding the production and consumption of texts, as well as the attempts of those within and outside the academy to deny these processes.

This first section closes with a statement about the historical formation of cultural studies in England and the United States Anne Balsamo discusses the theoretical disputes that have attended the development of cultural studies, articulating the conflicting strands woven in its fabric throughout its history. She then provides an account of some common commitments of cultural studies that she has called upon to construct a series of undergraduate courses in cultural studies. As in all of the essays in the first section, theory and practice come together in concrete classroom practices, practices designed to figure students as agents of cultural production and change, not as mere passive consumers.

1

Cults of Culture

Michael Blitz & C. Mark Hurlbert

Eventually,
They're going to put you in a petri dish
And therein they're going to grow you.
Not all of you though. For instance
They're not going to grow your head
And they're not going to grow your body.
                              Edward Dorn, *Hello La Jolla*

"Culture this!"
                Wendy O. Williams (of the Plasmatics)

Escherichia coli, the most common species of intestinal flora, will confine its development and reproduction to the inscription any of us might make (i.e., with a stylus) in an agar medium. The rest of the culture-medium will remain virtually free of bacterial growth.[1] So why write *this* essay?

A quick review of the definitions of "culture" suggest that the university is, itself, a culture:

Noun

1. cultivation

2. the act of developing the intellectual and moral faculties by education

3. expert care and training

4a. enlightenment and excellence of taste acquired by intellectual and aesthetic training

4b. acquaintance with and taste in fine arts, humanities, and broad aspects of science as distinguished from vocational and technical skills

5

5a. the integrated pattern of human knowledge, belief, and behavior that depends upon man's capacity for learning and transmitting knowledge to succeeding generations

5b. the customary beliefs, social forms and material traits of a racial, religious or social group

6. cultivation of living material in prepared nutrient media (also a product of such cultivation)

This article is really a set of questions and explicit confusions. We thought to write a theoretical argument taking up the ideas of cultural studies, cultural critique, and the ideological implications of culturally pluralistic pedagogies, and so on. As we began to work, we found we could not get past the word "culture." We kept running out to find more and more texts in which we might discover a suitable definition or examination. Knowing something about culture became a literacy demand of a rather complicated order.[2] And yet courses, textbooks, and programs, committees and departments, and, of course, journal articles and books are proliferating (a culture in themselves). In our own English departments, we can see a growing interest in, and controversy over, the issue of whether and how to introduce multi-cultural approaches to writing instruction and cultural awareness into all course work. In other words, as universities across the land buy, wholesale, the imperative either to teach culture, to culture students, or to resist the encroachment of culture into the integrity of disciplinary scholarship, we become more and more entangled in what poet Don Byrd, referring to Descartes' cogito but also to self-consciousness, calls "a curious loop in grammar" (217). How will "the left" make certain *not* to turn culture into Culture 101? How will "the right" fence themselves off from culture so as to preserve the sanctity of traditional studies? And how will any of us avoid being drawn (written) into the cult of culture as it thrives "within" the university? And why is it necessary for us to even do so?

Higher education's operators believe that culture is "out there," as though, perhaps, it's a film or an object that can be understood, joined, examined, named, and formalized from and by the materials and personnel housed within the institution's walls. At the same time, the university must account for its own rich history as a *cult*-ural institution. (It is, in this sense, adoring of itself). But we are proposing, in this essay, that the university has failed to address its complicity in the culturing of culture as it presently manifests itself in social, economic, political, and sexual institutions. We typically make no distinction between cultural criticism and the (further) production of culture-information. We might go so far as to argue that discussions and critiques and textbooks addressing the idea(s) of culture, particularly within the academy, are frequently redistributions of information about culture already generated within and by the university, its documents, its publications, its pageantries. As anthropologist James Boon puts it, "Radically differing cultures [are] paradoxically inscribed in disarmingly similar books" (14). Thus, one role of cultural criticism as an academic enterprise (like other scholastic enterprises) is the production of readers — consumers — of the texts that academic scholars produce. Academics is a husbandry that grooms people to talk and listen to scholars within disciplines becoming so highly specialized that the failure of these apprenticeships would lead to the failure of the fields themselves.

We don't wonder that higher education has always attempted to mark off the lines of intellectual and cultural development, but we are deeply disturbed that higher education's institutions are fast becoming culture junkies, hooked on formal idea(l)s of culture which can be taught — Ramist topoi that, once learned, become the objective world. More and more departments boast of at least some courses in which the word "culture" appears. We, Michael and Mark, admit that one not-so-hidden agenda in this essay is to try to make the word "culture" difficult to say without feeling sick and tired of what Edward Said calls "thought-stopping abstractions." But our other purpose is to interfere with this abstraction, to make more visible some of the implications for the academicization of culture and for the culturization of academics (the people and the stuff). As Said argues, "Culture works very effectively to make invisible and even 'impossible' the actual affiliations that exist between the world of ideas and scholarship...and the world of brute politics, corporate and state power, and military force" (137).

An interesting, perhaps alarming, example of Said's contention is a two-page advertisement for the Fortune Education Series from the *New York Times Magazine*. David Kearns, chairman of Xerox Corporation, is pictured on the left-hand page, serious, toned by a kind of golden filter, with the caption: "*FORTUNE* Inside the mind of management." On the right-hand page is, presumably, a sort of concrete poem in which a large and bold-typed quote by Kearns is interwoven with the text (we can literally read between the lines) explaining Xerox's interest in education:

Education should

If 25% of all high school students drop out every year, what can American corporations do about it?

not compete with

To find out, Xerox has invested five million dollars in the Institute for Research on Learning. Using new national defense,

computer technologies and artificial intelligence, Xerox is creating education programs to train the so-called

the trade deficit,

untrainable. As the founder of the Education Summit for business, FORTUNE supports the work of Xerox and

drugs or AIDS.

other corporations, large and small, that are fighting the battle for literacy. Because when an education system

Instead, think of it

stops working, the rest of society stops working too. To learn more about what other companies are doing, write

as a solution to

James B. Hayes, Publisher, FORTUNE, Time & Life Building, Rockeveller Center, New York, New York 10020−1393.

those problems.

— David Kearns, Chairman of Xerox Corporation
(December 23, 1990)

This stops us cold. How, we ask, can education be seen as a solution to our nation's problems when literacy has itself been used to oppress those who suffer from poverty for racial and gender reasons (Stuckey)? If education is to offer us any kind of relief, teachers will have to achieve goals far different than the creation of people who work (for Xerox). Educators might, for instance, set themselves to the task of investigating *with* students Xerox's methods of influencing legislators, its environmental record, or its treatment of workers. And what does it mean to train the "untrainable"? Who decides who these people are? What are they to be trained to do? Just what is the corporate interest in literacy, and just what is this battle for it?

On Wednesday 23 September 1987, the Subcommittee on Education and Health of the Joint Economic Committee of the United States Congress began nine days of hearings entitled "Competitiveness and the Quality of the American Work Force." Congressman James H. Scheuer opened the hearings by citing the reasons for the government's interest in literacy education in this country: (1) the fear of a potentially bleak economic future — essentially tied to a fear to Japanese productivity — where businesses would be weakened or fail because of blue-collar illiteracy and (2) a fear of a future in which American foreign interests would be undermined by a military comprised of illiterate soldiers.

Scheuer concluded his remarks by stating that "the goal of these hearings is to develop a comprehensive legislative agenda which will enable the next Congress and the next [the Bush] administration to take the necessary steps to provide our industries with adequately trained and educated workers and to halt the deteriorating position of our nation in world commerce" (Part 1, 3). One of the chief means of accomplishing this goal, the witnesses testified, is through uniting American schools and American businesses in such a way that schools give students a core of competencies identified by business for success in the workplace. Owen B. Butler, a former chairman of the board of the Proctor & Gamble Company, defined these competencies this way:

> There are two essentials for employability, and only two...These two essentials are true literacy, the ability to speak and to hear, to read and to write the English language fluently and with true comprehension and true ability to articulate ideas. And included in that is the ability to communicate mathematical concepts because without that there is no true literacy.
>
> The other one which has not been mentioned in most of the education reform movement is work habits, attitudes, and behavior patterns. The attitudes and behavior patterns that a young person brings to the workplace are just as important and just as essential as the skills and we think the education community and the parents have in recent years largely neglected the impact of the invisible curriculum run by parents and schools to teach work habits. (Part 1, 152–53)

Other witnesses also spoke of this "core of competencies" that education should give and that every worker should have. Richard E. Heckert, chairman of the board of the DuPont Corporation, went so far as to equate this core with "trainability" — read "useability" — itself. According to Heckart, workers need "good work habits and attitude; and an understanding of American economic and social life. The essence of this is learning how to learn, and learning how to behave. These have always been the objectives to traditional education" (Part 2, 464).

> ...Entrants into the work force will need two fundamental characteristics.
>
> First, entrants must be trainable, now and in the future, because we envision a career-long process of on-the-job training and retraining for employees. Consequently, entrants should have basic educational, personal and interpersonal skills — the core competencies that are synonymous with trainability.
>
> Second, they should be compatible with the work environment, possessing the personal attitudes and attributes that are essential in

effective performance on the job. Among the most important of
these attributes are a positive attitude toward team objectives and a
willingness to work as part of a team. School sports can be very
useful preparation in this. Other essential personal qualities include
a clear understanding of an employer's fundamental requirements
and expectations, including consistent attendance and punctuality.
Again, these should be learned in school. (Part 2, 470)

If the schools are failing to do their part to culture America, the
military and the media aren't. Retired Navy Admiral James D. Watkins
testified that the Navy is doing its fair share to train the "untrainable."
It has been so successful, in Watkins' words — and all Americans should
be proud of this —

The Navy was rated by MONEY magazine a couple of years
ago as one of the 10 best large employers in the Nation. As a
consequence, the proclivity for sailors to stay in the Navy today is
the greatest we have ever known...But, most importantly, we took
70 percent of the youth-at-risk group, the same group that we are
still worried about — the disadvantaged, the impoverished, the illiterate... — and we brought them back into the productive workforce.
(Part 1, 45).

But what about professors? What are they doing for America?
According to Badi G. Foster, president of Aetna Life & Casualty
Company's Institute for Corporate Education, not much. In fact, Foster
warned the committee about university professors who research and
write articles (such as this one?), instead of "transmitting" "established"
knowledge.

In terms of the universities, we in the corporate world increasingly
need the knowledge that is generated in universities. But what's
happened over the last 40 years is that universities have become
decoupled from the needs of business and industry.
I'm not arguing that they should be handmaidens, but...*professors are rewarded more for, quote, "creating new knowledge" and
less for transmitting it...*education of the kind that we need is
always on the periphery. (Part 1, 281, emphasis added)

The witnesses knew the kind of education that business needs and
how far government and business are willing to go to get it. In fact,
Secretary of Labor William E. Brock spoke of what would happen
if education should ignore the voices of business and the military:

". . . We're going to leave our people without the kind of skills that are going to be needed to hold a job in the United States. If we don't change, we're going to have to import those people. . . ." (Part 1, 82). And Owen Butler went a step further. "The most profitable investment we can make to improve education for that [at-risk] group of children is to intervene early — ideally at conception. What happens to that child before the child is born has an immense impact on whether that child will ultimately drop out of school."

James Sledd has been warning us for years about corporate and legislative interests in education. But to see these interests played out so concretely sickens us. As Ralph Nader observes, "The university has long since sold its soul. It's just selling its soul now in more ways, for a higher price" (Magner). Yes, we suppose that the intentions of these witnesses were, in some cases, noble. Some of them even made valid calls for reform, such as the creation of more and better day-care facilities for parents who work and attend school. But good intentions do not change the ideologies of these statements and proposals: "Intervene at conception"? "Import people"? "Invisible curriculum"? What literacy demands led William Brock to talk about people in such dehumanizing terms? How could Owen Butler speak so casually about a woman's right to prenatal care and privacy? Or about the curricula we teach and don't acknowledge? Is it really the job of educators, we ask, to train students to be "willing and able" to do all that business demands of them — and "to behave" themselves while they are doing it? Is it really the job of educators to turn students into workers who are "compatible with the work environment," rather than able to change it? And what of the complaint that professors are rewarded for making new knowledge and less for transmitting traditional culture and skills? Our response is "If it were only so!" Beyond the smokescreen of Badi Foster's rhetoric is the sad fact that unversities seem less in the business of helping students to understand "American economic and social life," or of rewarding new knowledge-making, and more in the

In the cult of Culture, within academe, individuals are required to maintain a blind faith in the existence of a stable enterprise called "culture" from which texts, scholars, ideas, and actions come. The cult demands allegiance to an economic system which, despite liberal pedagogies to the contrary, consumes the educated masses into the machinery of mass consumerism. We note, with less irony than we might like, that "enterprise" also means "undertaking"; in an age of approaching nuclear catastrophe, eco-cide, overpopulation, AIDS, and the problems suggested by Mr. Kearns, above, the "solution" may very well be to prepare a generation of undertakers.

business of teaching students — and faculty — "to behave." If this were not so, surely students would not be behaving themselves as well as they are now! If this is the inherited wisdom that we, Michael and Mark, are supposed to be teaching, we opt for misbehavior!

Oh, but then, why write this article? Because we are not offering a theory against other theories or a counter argument. And we're not horsemen of the apocalypse. We are continuing our own work as educators and activists, friends and fathers and spouses, who want to figure out what we can do, locally and in a larger scene, to interfere in the sort of cynical surrender that paragraphs like the previous reflect. To do this, we began by trying to figure out what is really at stake in higher education: What are our roles in a culture that turns to universities for self-definition? How might we both complicate and understand differently the kinds of issues which still, at the close of the century, divide people into Cold War versions of "right" and "left" affiliations? What kinds of efforts can we make while working at universities which, as Said notes, work on "the principle that knowledge ought to exist, be sought after and disseminated in a very divided form" (141)?

As 1990 ended and 1991 began, the *Chronicle of Higher Education* featured a series of articles, "opinions," and letters on the idea of introducing cultural critique into everyone's favorite, most basic requirement, the writing class. At the epicenter of this controversy were a few individuals attempting to design courses and programs that reflect and explore social issues and a group of curators calling themselves the National Association of Scholars (as well as curator-locals at a number of institutions).

When Linda Brodkey proposed English 306, "Writing About Difference," a writing-intensive course to be taught at the University of Texas Austin, the storm found its eye. A collection of bizarre arguments began, ranging from Professor Alan Gribben's claim that "if you really care about women and minorities making it in society, it doesn't make much sense to divert their attention to oppression when they should be learning basic writing skills" to Maxine Hairston's announcement that as a "solid liberal...I absolutely abhor this idea of being politically correct, because I think it contradicts everything the academic world stands for" (Mangan). Of course, Hairston is correct — even politically correct — when she notes that the university has never stood for political correctness. But it has stood, and continues to stand, for correcting those politics which threaten to cast too critical an eye over knowledge-brokerage as embodied in or by universities. Oddly enough, Hairston's "strongest pedagogical objection to the proposed course is that racism and sexism are deep, complex psychological and social problems that cannot be understood or solved quickly and easily" (B1). Few could disagree that problems such as sexism, racism, homophobia, age-ism, and so on are "deep" and "complex." We would add that they are also economic, political, and, yes, cultural problems, as well. And of course they cannot be "understood or solved quickly or easily." But these seem to be precisely the reasons why such problems ought to demand our attention in the domain of the classroom.

A few lines later in her essay, Hairston cautions that "if such courses are to be taught responsibly, they must be taught by trained faculty members from disciplines like sociology, psychology, or cultural anthropology, not by English teachers." And the reason English teachers and composition classes are the wrong means by which students can learn about socio-anthropo-psychological problems in culture is that "we know students develop best as writers when they are allowed to write on something they care about. Having them write about other people's ideas doesn't work well." Perhaps Hairston views racism and sexism and homophobia as academic problems in which case she is, again, correct that they are better left to academic "experts." And perhaps if students really did not care about such issues, she would be right to speculate that students might not feel inclined to consider social and psychological and political problems. But discrimination on the basis of race, ethnicity, gender, physical challenges, age, sexual orientation, and so on are not academic problems, nor are they the exclusive domain of one or two groups of "experts." In fact, by ignoring or deliberately excluding these problems from our writing classrooms, (places where, according to Hairston, students are to "become critical thinkers by learning to articulate their ideas in writing"), we actually do require students to "write about other people's ideas," even as we decide what is and is not appropriate for their attention.

Gribben's remarks are telling in additional ways. We may infer that he sees Brodkey and others "like" her as not really caring about women and minorities because, in her political correctness, Brodkey is attempting to withhold "basic writing skills" from her students. His statement, then, bears witness to a sort of hegemonic loop in the preservative argument: women and minorities won't "make it in society" unless teachers stop forcing their own agendas on these students and start enforcing "the" language "laws." Perhaps Gribben meant to say that it does make sense to divert their attention from oppression to the basic skills. If women and minorities have any hopes at all of joining the culture at large, they are going to have to adopt the basic rules, the skills, the forms and practices of college writing without the contaminants of politically correct ideas. Culture will be unfriendly toward such ideas, whereas it will embrace those who have willingly, docilely absorbed not only the skills but the curricula of the traditional academy.

The understanding of culture, in these senses, seems absurdly narrow and habitual. In the rhetoric of those who would preserve academic integrity, that is academic "freedom," the National Association of Scholars seems particularly hostile to any but the most steadfastly traditional approaches to English studies. Theodore S. Hamerow, for example, wants to push this preservative approach still further — and more aggressively. As a member of the University of Wisconsin's local chapter of the National Association of Scholars, Hamerow has, according to Carolyn Mooney's article, made public statements in which he "sharply criticizes an ambitious university plan to hire more minority professors." As he puts it, "We have to be prepared to be dubbed racists, fascists, sexists and reactionaries" (A1). Yes, he does.

The growing anxiety about the loss of culture and politically correct indoctrination — as though classrooms were normally not the sites of indoctrination by the NAS's members — points up a problem of the debate itself. By allowing the camps — call them right and left, conservative and liberal, Great Books vs. Textual Diversity — to become a replica of a two-party system, we reify one of the great failures of United States culture. And the nearly wholesale adoption of culturally "diverse" textbooks as the new wave of pluralistic pedagogy looks like a shaky notion (especially when such texts are taught in conjunction with an old — or new — "reliable," expensive, grammar handbook). Ahistorical information about culture — not to mention ahistorical information about history — is not equivalent to culture(s). It does little to prompt inquiry and investigation into diversity (as if it were a thing itself) and the relations among people, groups, politics, economies, and histories. In other words, the culture-in-the-curriculum debate seems to be less an argument than a disgruntled disagreement about pedagogical purity and honesty. But the fact remains that the issue is a school issue, a scholastic debate, an academic — and moot — word-problem unless it is revitalized with a real inclusion of the people for whom the factions purport to struggle: students, their lives and families and works and problems. We are suggesting that the university's descriptions and formalizations of anything and everything cannot occur apolitically, nonideologically, a-culturally.

What are we asking our students to write? What are we writing? (What are we, Michael and Mark, writing?) What kinds of preparation do educators have with which to evaluate culturally diverse writings? What kinds of ignorances must we maintain to assign writing projects based on readings which, in the context of a particular textbook, are homogenizations, if not illusions, of difference? What does it mean when new textbook collections of ethnically diverse writings are part of a trendy method for trying not to alienate students, while the teacher works to get them to produce collegiate essays? Who are the editors of these books? What were the motives for assembling them? What does it mean when a textbook salesperson comes to our offices to show us new books which "combine lots of essays by people from all over the world and then set up suggested assignment sequences to get students to write about diverse ideas?" The new marketing research shows that cultural diversity/pluralism/hetero-geneity in a single, expensive container sells.

While the concern Professor Gribben (et al.) with "fundamentals" may make him a hero to some, to insist upon teaching grammar undistracted by the issue of oppression or freedom or poverty or gender or school is to maintain a kind of classroom decorum that is more decorative than humane. More to the point, the view, the cultic faith that our studies of texts, of writing techniques, of scientific prin-ciples, and of art forms, are nonpolitical is deluded. At the same time, the idea that cultural diversity in the classroom is a teachable school subject may be equally deluded, at least insofar as it remains subjected to heuristic "objectivity" and fairness. The New York State Board of Regents has, as Albert Shanker notes, detailed goals for "global edu-cation." One of them reads: "Each student will develop the ability to understand, respect, and accept people of different races; sex; cultural heritage; national origin; religion; and political, economic and social background, and their values, beliefs and attitudes" (E7). As Shanker cautions, however, teaching students to accept as simply different, values and beliefs that endanger people is an outrageous goal. As outrageous, perhaps, as teaching students that their own(ed) values are the best ones. Shanker reminds us that "it's important that we teach our children about each other's and other people's customs and values...But this does not mean teaching students that they need not hold other people's practices—and our own—up to moral scrutiny." What Shanker doesn't say is that moral scrutiny is itself part of the problem. By what standards can we measure someone's practices? How can we provide such standards without imposing them? How can we help our students to discover the kinds of measures by which to evaluate, and live in and on, the world? Is one way to pretend that anything can be taught in a school, regardless of its historical, social, philosophical, ecological consequences, relations, and circumstances? This is a rather arrogant approach to texts and learning and knowledge. Even the National Association of Scholars would have to admit that such an organization could only exist under particular, perhaps peculiar, socio-politico-economical and ideological conditions (some of which the NAS sees as its business to maintain and control.

One of us recently presented our students with copies of a hand-book for new English department faculty, particularly adjuncts. In the guidelines for the first-level developmental writing course, the description of "the" students included the statement that they "have great difficulty putting together correct sentences. Their command of English is almost entirely oral and their vocabulary is very limited...Many [of these students] are bilingual, though neither of the two languages they speak is standard...The written English of all [these students] is thus marked by errors." The students who saw this description were, not surprisingly, outraged. It was immediately clear to them (despite the fact that most had not passed a university-wide reading comprehension exam) that these guidelines were "scaring" new teachers and were, as one student wrote, "an insult to me and everybody else in these seats." Each student wrote his or her reaction to the descriptive passage about the students, and each also wrote a proposal for how he or she would change the document.

Reactions:

D: I can say I am angry. They have alot of nerve. They should of asked students what we was like. I can speak just fine and my writing is improving that's why I *took* this course.

M: This desciption is a dis [disrespect] to myself and my family! They should come to my project and they know they don't understand nothing there! Then we see who is who!

J: When the profesor told us what fluent means I got upset because I can speak and understand English. I am bilingual I can speak Spanish and English.

C: Bullshit! That's what I say. Where do these people come up with this shit? I am tired of people dissing [disrespecting] me because my accent or my background.

P: I guess the teachers who is going to read these thing will have alot of bad feelings about us. They supposed to teach to read and write but it sound like we can't do nothing but not talk so good in even my own langage.

A: I agree with the statement about students having trouble, putting their thoughts on a paper. The majorty of the errors are spelling or punctuation. The ideas and thoughts are their; but we are scearded of making errors. Some students feel embrasse of making an error by speech or writing about something. That makes the students self concious.

Proposed Revisions:

A: Many students do not speak what we call standard english. These students are here to learn a more diverse way of speaking and writing. This class is english speaking students and also bilingual. the students are here to perfect their writing and thoughts.

K: The English 099 student has not passed W.A.T. test with a proper score and so they have to take the class. They are intelligent but they did not pass a test.

L: Many English students are bilingual they should learn to speak standard English fluently. Even the native English speakers don't generally speak standard English there're should be a standard for the English language. The written English of all students in this course is thus marked by errors...

C: The students inn English class prepare to strength their writing and reading skill in which the english class are unfamiliarity with the standard english not set by the school district. In this case you fall into the school categories classes set by their standard english rule.

D: The students you will meet in this course lack many skills which you, the teacher, can give them. They are fluent in some ways but not in some others. They need you to show them the right ways of college so they can live within society.

D's reaction reflects a powerful understanding not only of the handbook description itself, but of at least one of the larger problems the document only points to. New teachers, like "old" teachers, can easily make the mistake of believing that students are just like descriptions of students. It doesn't take a summary of labeling theory to recall that if you call someone a "remedial writing student," you will teach something called remedial writing.[3] And just as *E coli* grows only where our stylus makes a pattern, students regarded as deficient and weak and lacking in things the university provides tend to develop — or fail to develop — along the lines inscribed by the university. And if one of those lines is the apolitical, a-cultural acquisition of skills, information, achievements, knowledge then anything not resembling those things will be as good as invisible (and as "bad" as bacteria, we suppose) in the culture-medium of the university. C's proposal attests to the fact that categorizations like these are common knowledge and suspect.

One does not teach students a brand of grammar (brand students with grammar?) divorced from the politics and ethics and cultural realities that have shaped their lives — and ours — and occasioned the practice of teaching composition. So why do educators maintain what amounts to a theistic ordering of knowledge and information? To train students to do the same? The students quoted above were outraged how the university situates them within the hierarchy of academia. They were upset by what was, to them, an offensive description of their language competencies. But it is also interesting to note that, except for D's reaction, the students did not object that they had been described. (That is, they had been unwritten from their own circumstances in an effort to normalize them as a group of remedial students.)

Indeed, even D, in the end, wrote a description which effectively replicates the university's. She even suggests that only by learning the "right ways of college" from "you, the teacher," can students hope to live within society.

Instead of insisting upon what constitutes knowledge, essentially, we might allow ourselves to wonder about how different kinds of knowledge function. Knowledge is not simply inherited information nor the legacy of methodologies for transmitting that inheritance. Knowledge is the engine of culture as culture(s) are the engines of knowing. But culture doesn't begin and then end (and then revive) in the university. Intellectual debates about course material may fuel interesting programmatic changes in curricula, but they don't typically result in very different classroom experiences for students. We say "typically" because while there are a number of fascinating experiments going on in classrooms across the country, the fact remains that universities are segmented into departments with inter-departmental competitions for course-territory (i.e., the traditional one between English and Theater departments, among the Social Sciences, between Literature and Writing programs, etc.). As the buzzwords "pluralism" and "diversity" ring louder in the public rhetoric of "the" profession, the institutionalization of those ideas thoroughly cements existing turf rites and the singularity (if not insularity) of academic compartments. What does cultural diversity mean in — and for — such circumstances?

Near the end of the fall semester of 1990 one of us asked an introductory literature class to read excerpts from the transcripts of the "Competitiveness and the Quality of the American Work Force" Congressional hearings, which we described above. We then asked the students to write a journal entry about them. Many students said that they agreed with what they read. They expressed the fear that America was indeed lagging behind as an economic world leader, that students today are underprepared for the workplace, and that American workers had just become lazy. But some of the other students saw through the testimony of the government's witnesses:

J: Richard E. Heckert said, "...a positive attitude toward team objectives, a willingness to work as part of a group..." Well, if this is really the goal, no wonder students are not living up to expectations! From the very beginning we are taught to compete with one another and to always worry about number one.

K: I honestly believe that what they are saying is that if a person in the United States can't read or write and are "dumb" or "stupid" that they don't belong and shouldn't be here.

C: I don't know whether uniting schools & businesses will help matters much. Many American businesses aren't exactly thriving, & I don't want power-hungry executives influencing my children.

William Brock's statement about having to import people puzzled me. Why does he think that *educated* foreign people will want to come here...?

F: Foster—Go and stuff it! There a lot of professors out there that are no good but those that "create new knowledge" are some of the best. They teach students to use their minds creatively...

C: I have problem with the fact that they are not asking the opinions and attitudes of the youth presently obtaining an education. Maybe some of us don't want to be merely trained to perform a skill.

S: The attitude that William E. Brock has of "If we don't change, we're going to have to import these people." gives me the idea that the government is not looking at the American people as Humans but as a Commodity.

J: The Navy and other armed forces are important for taking problem kids and turning them around. I know of a lot of kids who have taken this path and turned out allright. So long as there's no war. [One month later Dick Cheney announced, "America's liberation of Kuwait has begun."]

Reporting on the Brodkey controversy at the University of Texas, Austin, Katherine S. Mangan observes that "some faculty members remain convinced that students will feel pressure to conform to a 'correct' set of beliefs, including the basic assumption that Western civilization is inherently unfair to women, minority group members, and homosexuals." Well, yes! Students and faculty ought to feel some pressure, not to conform, but to acknowledge political realities as they might be studied, not simply as they have always been studied. How remarkable and indicative of a mutual inattentiveness that the NAS (and its "affiliates") and educators labeled as "politically correct" would both be concerned about students conforming or being indoctrinated! Actually, all educators—including ourselves—are challenged by the fact that students have always been indoctrinated to conform to a narrow range of possibilities for knowing what has happened in the world, what can be known of the world, and what ought to be learned. Inquiry, in the traditional sense within the academy, has always meant *in*-quiry: asking questions internally, within the inscription, protected from the "un-mediated" culture at large. We cannot afford to make culture a subject of composition courses or any other course work unless we prepare ourselves to acknowledge our teaching and our classes and ourselves as subjects of culture, of history, of eco-politics, economics, and ideologies.

Like most educators, we, Michael and Mark, know that our teaching doesn't achieve all that we struggle for. But we also know that we are at our best in the classroom when the students have helped to design the curriculum.

One of us recently asked the students in an introductory literature class to produce a book — a collection of their writings of their own design. After much class dialogue, the students decided to each photograph people on city streets and: 1) write a description of the people in the photograph and an imaginative projection about the occupations, values, and futures of the subjects; 2) write a description of the stereotypes and critical predispositions that they exhibited in their descriptions and projections; and 3) give their writings to another member of the class so that they could write a critical response to the first two writings. Each photograph and the accompanying three writings became the chapters of the book. For the book's conclusion, a Native American woman student quoted a suggestion for action from one of the chapters. "Next time you're filling out a job application and come to the box marked race, write in *Human*!" She also wrote:

> How would a Black person react to some of these chapters?...Some Blacks understand the white culture that has been rammed down their throats all these years. But they still demand the right to be themselves. Blacks will always be different than whites. Women will always be different than men...Out of all the chapters the white Businessman has the most going for him. In the real world he does. The rest of us: Blacks, women, elderly, can *never* fit into this value system because it wasn't designed for us...The authors of the chapters would have had a difficult time dealing with this [if they had realized it]. Many people in our class are white males...the rest of us had to exchange our papers with white males.

> If culture is to be a fluid medium in which we can make decisions, students will have to be able to take actions that are not simply oppositional to their own cultures, but which allow them to make insights other than our own in ways that may not be our own about our cultures. They must be allowed to show us our classrooms in ways we don't see them, to teach us how to re-green ourselves and how to collaborate on health and well-being. Being cultured, in this sense, is not to occupy positions, but to move through them.

If we educators are really serious about cultural studies, we will have to begin at home in culturally literate ways. We will have to connect critique and action. We will have to change oppressive circumstances, such as the way part-time faculty and students are successfully silenced within our own departments. We will have to investigate, with students, the ways they and we learn to be scared of not living up to a professor's or an administrator's conception of them/us. Christine Delphy tells us that "an institution that exists today cannot be explained by the fact that it existed in the past, even if the past is recent." (260). As long as we educators allow business, the military, government, or even other academics to prepackage, legislate, and articulate knowledge and culture for students, other teachers, or us, we will also continue to see students as devotees to us — the mentors, master teachers, master planners, *cult*ivators — and to our best styling, our most persuasive academic exoticisms, our most inviting cults of culture. As long as any of us pretends that our job is to bring about "enlightenment and excellence of taste acquired by intellectual and aesthetic training" (see the definitions of culture, above), we will continue to train students to be trainable, to be consumers of and in a culture — be it academic or corporate or "natural" — which promises less and less to an increasing number of us.

Cults of culture are not, then phenomena of "the" right or "the" left, but are cross words in a wrong-headed battle going on within increasingly soundproof institutional walls. As culture undergoes, along with other discrete and teachable notions, significant kinds of transformations, academic specialization, and pedagogical divisions, culture "at large" is, in some ways, sluffing off the very ideas of separation, division, and interiority. John Markoff, paraphrasing Jacques Attali, notes "as communications and computer technologies grow in power the notion of place will be fundamentally altered." So will our notions about *us*. We need new articulations, new vantage points for listening, fresh means of saying what and where we are — and where we are going. We might start by considering James Boon's question, "What subtleties of other cultures has the discourse of the normative monograph obscured?" (14). What set of pedagogies have we packaged and placed on line in an attempt to transmit a view of (our) culture which looks less and less like us — or like anybody?

> You, you look like the kind of guy
> The kind of inconclusive waste of space
> That we can use
> You, you've got just the right approach
> You've got this all-consuming, overpowering
> Will to lose
>
> The Bevis Frond

Notes

1. We owe this bit of information to musician-biologist Robin Reneé.

2. A "literacy demand" is a complex set of explicit and implicit institutional instructions for certain forms of literate behavior. For more explanation of this concept, see Blitz and Hurlbert, 1989; and Hurlbert and Blitz.

3. J. Elspeth Stuckey once told us that when she taught reading and writing in Africa in 1989, she began a "remedial" course by asking her students to try to write something in "remedial English."

Works Cited

Blitz, Michael, and C. Mark Hurlbert. "To: You, From: Michael Blitz and C. Mark Hurlbert, Re: Literacy Demands and Institutional Autobiography." *Works and Days 13: Essays in the Socio-Historical Dimension of Literature and the Arts.* 7.1 (1989): 7–33.

Boon, James A. *Other Tribes, Other Scribes.* New York: Cambridge University Press, 1982.

Byrd, Don. *The Poetics of Common Knowledge.* State University of NY Press, 1993.

Competitiveness and the Quality of the American Work Force. Hearings before the Subcommittee on Education and Health of the Joint Economic Committee. Congress of the United States, One Hundredth Congress, First Session. (23 September 1, 5, 21, and 27 October 1987). ERIC: ED295013–4 CE50200–1.

Delphy, Christine. "Patriarchy, Domestic Model of Production, Gender and Class." Trans. Diana Leonard. *Marxism and the Interpretation of Culture.* Eds. Cary Nelson and Lawrence Grossberg. Urbana: University of Illinois Press, 1988. 259–69.

Fortune Foundation Series Advertisement, *New York Times Magazine* 23 December 1990: 20–21.

Giroux, Henry A. *Theory and Resistance in Education: A Pedagogy for the Opposition.* South Hadley, MA: Bergin & Garvey, 1983.

Hairston, Maxine C. "Required Writing Courses Should Not Focus on Politically Charged Social Issues." *Chronicle of Higher Education* 23 January 1991: B1 and B2.

Hurlbert, C. Mark, and Michael Blitz. "The Institution('s) Lives!" *Marxism and Rhetoric.* Special issue of *PRE/TEXT.* Eds. James A. Berlin and John Trimbur. (forthcoming).

Magner, Denise K. "Nader Warns Universities of the Ethical Perils of Increased Links With Big Corporations." *Chronicle of Higher Education* 24 October 1990: A1 and A16.

Mangan, Katherine S. "Battle Rages Over Plan to Focus on Race and Gender in University of Texas Course," *Chronicle of Higher Education* 21 November 1990: A15.

Markoff, John. "Another Way to Get to the Global Village." *New York Times* 23 December 1990: E6.

Mooney, Carolyn J. "Academic Group Fighting the 'Politically Correct Left' Gains Momentum." *Chronicle of Higher Education* 12 December 1990: A1, A13, and A16.

Said, Edward. "Opponents, Audiences, Constituencies and Community." *The Anti-Aesthetic: Essays on Postmodern Culture.* Ed. Hal Foster. Port Townsend, WA: Bay Press, 1983. 135−59.

Shanker, Albert. "Multicultural and Global Education: Value Free?" *New York Times* 6 January 1991: E7.

Stuckey, J. Elspeth. *The Violence of Literacy.* Portsmouth, NH: Boynton/ Cook Heinemann, 1991.

2

Committing the Curriculum and Other Misdemeanors

Alan Kennedy

Positions and Purposes

Departments of English are positioned differently. Discussion of the place, or position, of cultural studies programs in English departments should also, therefore, be discussions of the placing or positioning of the departments in contemporary culture and society. In a general way, departments of English are currently positioned to do some substantial thinking about their purposes and constructions in relation to a general set of educational responsibilities of the university in a postmodern world. Unfortunately, debates about curricular development have in recent times tended towards political polarization and ideological entrenchment rather than towards the development of a vital and useful regeneration of the humanities.[1] What seems clear enough is that a growing number of intellectuals in English departments have begun to think of their task under the general rubric of "cultural studies," and that an increasingly strident group of traditionalists are preparing themselves to oppose any changes. We know well enough that the popular press is full these days of charges of the dominance of "pc," political correctness. It is subjects like curricular diversity that attract the epithet "pc," and however much we might dislike that fact, it may in part be attributable to the neglect by humanists of the necessity to develop a fuller description and justification of the purpose and function of cultural studies in educational institutions and in the world in general.

Rarely enough will a program in cultural studies be fully instituted in a department; the likely pattern for the near future will be one of accommodation as English curricula expand to include new options for students in cultural studies. While this is perhaps desirable in itself for a number of reasons, it risks simply substituting another set of objects for attention, a set of objects that could occupy the same un-reconstructed space of instruction that the canon itself occupied. We can see this possibility in debates that recur about the way that the new diversified curriculum threatens the canon and, supposedly, Western values. This binary conflict will continue to hold center stage just so long as the issue for curricular reform remains an issue of expansion without our having yet developed a full sense of the social purpose and value of either an English department or a program in cultural studies. It is easy enough to generalize and insist that we need to broaden our frame of reference, to say that we have been too narrow in our focus on particular elements of the canon or the literary tradition. But narrow in relation to what mission? one might ask. And broadened in the name of what mission?

We can talk about the place of cultural studies, and when we think of a place we can think of a function. The function, I'll argue, needs to be focused on a set of theoretical issues, issues of cross-cultural understanding and hermeneutics broadly conceived. Further, the issue of the place and purpose of cultural studies must, I am convinced, be addressed in the context of an institutional and programmatic commitment, where a department makes topics of cultural studies integral to its working. That is to say, there is an argument to be made for having the traditional curriculum of an English department transform itself sufficiently so that cultural studies is neither an add-on nor a matter of foreign relations with other departments, all of which still retain their own insistence on territorial integrity. Which is to say that we might consider the transformation of English departments so that it is unclear just what occupies their center; so that it becomes a matter, for a while at least, of indeterminacy whether or not we are looking at an English department with a cultural studies program in it, or a cultural studies department with an English program inside it.

For now Carnegie Mellon's English department houses a cultural studies program, and traditional literary studies have been decentered so far that the indeterminacy of what to call ourselves is real. The paleonymic "English" still has some work to do, and so I'll stick with that here. In fact, the English department at CMU has had a tumultuous recent history (recent meaning over the last dozen years or so). Immediately after World War II, the English department was a service department. By 1960, however, the department was providing the courses and curriculum for a substantial number of English majors in Margaret Morrison Carnegie College; and when the College of Humanities and Social Sciences opened in 1969, English majors constituted one of the larger groups in the entering class. It had a creative writing program, founded by Gladys Schmidt, that is now in its twenty-first year; in fact, the undergraduate major in creative writing is the oldest of the current programs in the department. In 1979−80 Richard Young, then head of the department, created a program in rhetoric. Young had to fight considerable battles to make this odd (then, and perhaps now) new degree win acceptance. The program remains one of the few in the country producing rhetorical theorists. One can say, then, that over ten years ago the traditional study of the literary canon was already displaced from the center of our curriculum in favor of a program focusing both on rhetorical theory in and on empirical research in the reading and writing processes (especially with reference to cognitive science and the paradigms of Herb Simon). One can recognize the really revolutionary move that represented for an English department. It mandated a theoretical concern with reading and writing processes, and with the social function of speech acts (production and reception of discourse) as a defining element of an English department. That move represented perhaps a much more radical possible transformation of our discipline than does the much contested appearance of cultural studies in our midst. The reasons for the failure of that model to be widely adopted deserve to be elaborated. Despite recent changes in the atmosphere, it is probably still the case that university English departments are characterized by a split between the elite study of literature (or the elite version of cultural studies, which stands to inherit much of the unpleasant side of the elitism of the old canon) on the one hand, and the underclass work of teaching writing on the other.

Let me hasten to make a practical clarification. A considerable number of the people employed by English departments are employed in nontenure track lines. Often they are part-time employees, with no job security, and with no access to regular benefit programs offered to full time employees. Most of these part-time people are women, and most of them teach classes in composition. Why should this be the case? I think it is not indirectly related to the operation of a certain value: that the content of literature is more important than the force of writing. The history of the dominance of a high-art concept of the literary object in the classroom is exactly coincident with the denigration of writing−including creative writing as a constructive contributor to humanistic and liberal education−and with the marginalization of a whole class of university instructors, condemned to second-class citizenship teaching composition classes. An imaginative reception of rhetorical theory at an earlier date could have cleared the ground sufficiently so that cultural studies would not now have to be the site of contestation that it appears to be.

With a Ph.D. program in rhetoric already underway, in 1982 our department moved to institute a new doctorate program in literary and cultural theory, a program that has attracted a certain amount of national interest. Now the two Ph.D. programs are well established, and the undergraduate curriculum of the department is moving to a deeper integration of these two unusual (in the sense of being non-traditional) programs, and to a deeper integration of creative writing as an essential part of our general educational mission.

I'll describe below some of the concepts that I think allow us to claim to the public that our curriculum has a real use in the world and at the same time fulfills what we want from it as a genuine intellectual introduction to our discipline. We are having to engage in thorough curriculum reform to be both purposeful as an academic department and relevant to society. We shall engage in a serious reflection on our upper level core classes in the coming year. During this past year we embarked on a major re-thinking of our first-year introductory classes. Briefly, we have hopes that our first-year classes will no longer break down into "comp" and "lit", the standard pairing of classes for the first year: one remedial class in composition and an introduction to literature. It has become increasingly necessary for us to construct a curriculum we can stand behind, be committed to. This need for curricular commitment is perhaps most strongly felt in the area of cultural studies, but if literature as an iconic object needs to be displaced to make room for cultural studies, then so too does the standard course in composition need to make room for a writing class rooted in rhetorical theory and at the same time amenable in its concepts to deep integration with cultural studies. With a general failure to benefit from the opening offered by rhetorical theory, and the appearance on the scene of a radical theoretical project in cultural studies, it is clearly time for us all to make some serious curricular commitments. In working through what can be done in practical terms in a curriculum, we encounter a material test of our ideals.

Misdemeanors

My title may prove disappointing if it leads to any expectation that I'll be producing a longish list of other misdemeanors, or crimes. I did want to focus attention, however, on the way in which the committed curriculum is thought by some to be wrong in an almost criminal way. Attacks from the irresponsible right do not seem to be abating, and at the time of writing this President Bush seems about to make an election issue out of the so-called political correctness movement. One might have thought that Roger Kimball's recent book, *Tenured Radicals: How Politics Has Corrupted Our Higher Education*, would have been the last salvo of silliness, but the recent entry of Dinesh D'Souza into the limelight of the popular press perhaps makes it clear that the inability of the humanities disciplines to define their mission adequately, in simple public language that sits atop complexity, leaves the door open for thoughtless political interference with the educational processes. We have to assume the absence of clearly articulated goals for humanities education creates an opportunity for some to insist that the curriculum must not commit itself to anything different from what will ensure a future for some elusive conception of national culture and identity. When we reject pressures of the kind being brought to bear on the curriculum by the descendants of William Bennett, we often do so merely with a negative critique of what they have to say. We are then constructed merely as naysayers, with little positive to offer except a doctrine that gets construed by the likes of Kimball as "ideological posturing, pop culture, and hermetic word games." When we are tempted to turn to some of our grandfathers, if that is now an acceptable way of thinking of the succession of intellectual generations since Derrida, we find some reasons to sympathize with the positivists. Derrida's recent essay, 'Some Statements and Truisms About Neo-Logisms, Newisms, Postisms, and Other Small Seismisms", which appears in David Carroll's book *The States of 'Theory'*, seems to argue that theoretical interventions need to keep pure their possibility for being interventionist (Derrida 1990). That keeping pure turns out to mean not moving to any finalized position but rather keeping open the possibility of yet more positions. Theories, he seems to suggest, are like jetties in a stream. They mark an intervention, they break the current and make it flow differently. But they are also ultimately *jêté*, flotsam and jetsam on the stream. We cannot risk conceiving of them as committed positions unless we want to risk the purpose of the whole theoretical enterprise. So it might be fair to say that there is a potential collaboration from different corners to keep us from committing a curriculum.

Nevertheless, as I've been suggesting, I think there is a double gesture of committal we are now called on to make. We need finally to declare our willingness to commit an old curriculum to the dustbin of history. History is littered with curricula, after all, so one more won't even be noticed. Secondly, we need to make some kind of commitment to a curriculum that we can believe will work, that will do some work. The principle of our commitment cannot merely be political (although what I say clearly indicates that it needs to be political). The principle of commitment must also, especially in our times, be seen to be doing some kind of productive work, which is a way of arguing a political contribution for a curriculum. We need to insist on a utility function for our curriculum. Or, we need to continue to make further reflections on the possible manifold "uses of literacy."

What is the curriculum we ought to commit to history? We ought to be in a position now to say that the study of literature will never again be thought of as the heart of an English department. It is time to make that commitment, or committal. Nowhere can you find these days a reasoned argument for the coverage model of literary study. The coverage metaphor is a particularly odd one, when you think of it, and it is intellectually embarrassing to think of oneself as having ever participated in such a weak concept of curriculum. It says: Just get through so much stuff and it will all be OK. It is a purely quantitative, and not at all qualitative, curriculum idea. While the study of literature dominated English departments, it clearly did cover the field, so much so that other tasks of a department were ruled out. Composition, creative writing, the theory of rhetoric, in general, were deliberately marginalized. So too were other cultural forms. A very narrowly defined field of objects, nations, and time became the naturalized focus of the "coverage". What we are now in a position to recognize is precisely the desperation lying behind the coverage model. What that model feared was a question about its worth, its value; precisely, its market value or utility in social terms. As the university has become more and more ensnared in the value system of our culture and society, more and more reliant on big business for funding, and more susceptible to curricular influence from such sources, the humanities have found themselves under more and more pressure to justify their implicit claim that to be beautiful is also to be useful. Engineers, I feel sure, don't particularly feel that their lives lack decorousness, and they at least do work. Humanists are faced with the charge that while they may indeed have succeeded in being beautiful (having followed Matthew Arnold too well), they are indeed, after all, useless. Coverage, lacking a real purpose or justification of its utility, desperately insists that it is doing everything, covering everything; it is exhaustive. Surely utility must be lurking somewhere in that exhaustion.

But if coverage is out, what takes its place? The answer seems to be cultural studies. We create problems for ourselves, it is worth noting, if we are really willing to make the first committal: literature is no longer at the heart. If we think that, we can readily get our universities to agree to let us substitute a form of cultural anthropology for what we have been doing. In fact, the move to cultural studies could readily degenerate into the old humanities. Indeed, the diversity movement that has been sweeping campuses in the last year or two has led to more and more demands (echoed by Lyn Cheney in her document, *50 Hours*) that the core curriculum include classes dealing with other cultures. Can we resist the temptation upper level administrators offer when they respond to our insistence that what we do is "cultural studies" by asking us to do a class "Understanding Balinese Dance," or asking us to offer a class for the business school that will make cross-cultural misunderstanding less likely to happen and so open new markets for our goods? If our curriculum has no more definition than the phrase "cultural studies" offers on the surface we may find ourselves giving a class called "Understanding Cultural Differences", the point of which is to subvert everything Said warns about in *Orientalism* and break down barriers of understanding so that American goods can more readily trade abroad[2]. The process we might find ourselves participating in is one that I like to call "global indifferentiation." The predicament of cultural studies is the one that James Clifford calls the predicament of culture. Clifford notes, with apparent lack of surprise, that the "exotic" is now next door. That little phrase of his does point to an aspect of contemporary reality: it reminds us of the need of electronic media, global capitalism, and its related political enterprises to blur boundaries, especially when those boundaries are the political boundaries of other countries. It also registers for us the imperialist tendencies of cultural understanding. At the very least, cultural studies owes itself the task of attempting to differentiate its own work from that of global market integration. What values does it work in the name of, and what products result?

I am clearly planning to co-opt the very language of business: work, product, exchange, and so might be charged with playing all too readily into the hands of the very forces I claim I would resist. What I am saying is this: The humanities have spent this century insisting that they are different, and their job is to offer an alternative to the world, especially if that world is the world of industry. People need circuses, we say; they need to be amused. So culture has become amusement, and the work it does is the very opposite of work. Culture and the humanistic studies associated with culture have allowed themselves to be assigned to the negatively stigmatized feminine role in our culture. Other folks do the hard work, and when they come home to us at the end of the day we scrub their backs, sing to them, and restore their souls. For which we get three squares a day and a bed at night.

Now some people will continue to be happy with that concept of culture. But what of cultural studies? What use does it have, other than serving as a kind of advanced *TV Guide* for the workers of the world? If culture has at least that much relation to productivity, what is ours? I think it is necessary to adopt the possibly threatening language of work and production, because I think it tells us more clearly than any other what world we live in. We live in universities that currently do more to reproduce the status quo than to change it. Universities are for the most part in the business of reproducing the means of production. I think we need to realize our situation.

I'll be more explicit, if perhaps less clear, by saying that I do think we have a responsibility to work in such a way as to help our students get jobs. We do nothing if all we can do is breed in them a fashionable (or possible out-of-fashion) alienation from their society. We ourselves have jobs and get paid. We have been trained for a job. We ought to recognize that our jobs include training others for jobs. If I say that my position in parts is summed up by Stein's advice to Lord Jim, "In the destructive element immerse," I don't want to be taken to be accepting the position of fashionable alienation. I do want to suggest, however, that we are indeed part of our society. And we contribute to it willy-nilly, especially if we do nothing to influence the way in which the values that surround us are shaped and reshaped. If the formula for work is force times distance, we can recognize that the result of work is that something is changed, transformed. If our work contributes only to the status quo then it is not work enough; it is a treadmill contribution just equal to the force of friction working against it.

I'm not, of course, going to be able to produce a finished and universal plan that insists that the curriculum ought to commit itself *here*, rather than *there*, in order to do the kind of work I'm talking about. If I could develop the line I'm now exploring, I would pursue the idea of change, and say that cultural studies deals with difference and that it faces a binary choice. It can, according to Said's analysis, eliminate difference by understanding it. Or, it can alienate itself from its own ground of understanding by going over to the other side — it can follow sixties pilgrims to Kathmandu or Kurtz into the heart of darkness. Or, it can attempt to find some position on the boundary between those two. Cross-cultural understanding is clearly important and necessary. The challenge is for it to allow for some osmotic crossing of border lines without eliminating those borders. If our under-standing eliminates lines of difference, then it eliminates the political, since the political will continue for some time to be concerned with the way in which space is shared amongst us. I would say the work of production for cultural studies is not understanding difference; perhaps it can be thought of as the "production of difference." Difference, of course, is in itself nothing and cannot therefore easily be produced. It is an odd kind of product, and so an odd kind of work will be necessary to produce it. That odd kind of work is the work of cultural studies. I mean that our work will of necessity involve us in producing the contradictions inherent in ideas like culture, self, and so on. It will not do, of course, merely to have everyone work to be different. That would merely reproduce the self-centered bourgeois individualism that makes it so hard for us really to deal with difference. I have in mind a kind of applied deconstruction that works at the fissures in cultural materials, but does not give up on political commitment. The old humanistic universalism made claims for a universal human nature. It insisted that underneath we are all the same. That means that local differences, of politics, culture, economy, did not count. From the point of view of the dominant culture, it is satisfactory to insist that others are like us. We don't have, then, to remember how they differ in their real material conditions. It is satisfying for a liberal male hegemony to insist that we are all equal. Real differences—that is, differences that occupy material positions, that inhabit political and economic boundaries—do need to be produced. They need to be made visible.

Histories and Values

But let me return to the question of the different position that English departments now occupy, which is, I believe, a result of the impact of post-structural theory. My contention is that English departments revitalized in large part because of the influence of what I will here, loosely, deliberately, vaguely, and provocatively, call deconstruction[3]. Why deconstruction and post-structuralism in general should make people so angry, is something that ought to be studied closely. I suspect there is some general tendency abroad to want to close down a line of inquiry because it is believed to be bad. Deconstruction is certainly upsetting, disturbing. It stirs things up; stirs up sediments in otherwise clear waters. It does this by pointing to the complexity of textual objects, and of history, which is largely constructed out of texts. I think it can be argued that the positive legacy of deconstruction will be two principles: History is what there is, and ethics is a fundamental concern of theory. Derrida brings our attention again to the fact that change is what constitutes our lives. Forms, structures, systems, are constructed in time, they change in time and evolve into other forms systems and structures. If we cannot engage our students in the lifelong process of beginning to understand change and difference, we will do nothing of significance in our curricula. When we come to see that judgements about forms, values, and structures are not timeless, are not the acts of gods, but are rather time-bound, historically positioned, we became capable not only of studying cultural objects from inside but also of considering the history of the ways in which we study such things.

In working more and more closely into the grain of textuality—a process analogous to theoretical physics when it deals with subatomic particles—post-structuralism made some interesting and disorienting discoveries about the way in which language represents the world. Briefly, deconstruction pointed out that a principle of indeterminacy is at work in the subatomic world of language, just as in physics. De Man problematizes the relation between grammar and rhetoric, and confronts us with the need to live with a rhetoricized grammar and a grammatized rhetoric (3–19). Similarly, both de Man and Derrida, in developing aspects of J.L. Austin's speech act theory, elaborate the mutual interference of the performative and the constative.[4] If we can determine exactly what is being said, or meant, then we cannot also determine exactly what the force of that meaning will be. If we can, on the other hand, determine the force of what is said, we cannot at the same time make a match with what is in fact being said. Truth and Force are not always on the same side, to put it at its simplest. A deconstructive account is so far from being nihilistic that it always and inevitably deals at least with two value systems—here the value of Truth on the one hand, and the value of Force on the other. Deconstructive accounts show the world to be constructed by mutually interfering systems of value; a truism we are all comfortable with in our daily lives, in fact (Kennedy). It can be shown, I think, that the central principle of deconstruction is an ethical one, although a somewhat esoteric ethical one. It argues that values themselves depend on the ability to differentiate values. If there were no differing value systems, there would be no basis for evaluating at all. With the disappearance of difference, we would witness the disappearance of value. So deconstruction, or deconstructive critics, cannot simply assert value. Instead deconstruction works at a lower level of atomic specificity: Lead our students into a comprehension of difference, of differentiating, and they will then have the tools out of which all value systems are constructed. They will not be victims of indoctrination, nor will they be subject to a curriculum that is inherently nihilistic. They will learn that there are different, and often contradictory, value systems in the world. But they will not necessarily learn therefore that all values are worthless.

By focusing on the sub-atomic structure of language (performative vs. constative) we turn our attention to the force of writing as much as to its meaning. If we think that we can simply teach our students the content of great works, and ignore the way in which writing is forceful, if we think we can give them stuff without introducing them to the complexities that come with thinking through issues of process, then we are mistaken. Rather than think of the work of literary art as a container of great truth, we can focus instead on the ways in which, in particular situations, forceful writings take on particular historical importance. We can direct our attention to the ways in which cultures and societies invest certain practices with importance, which is one way of saying that cultural objects always occupy positions, that they are rhetorical. And we need also to direct our attention to teaching students how they themselves can become the producers as well as consumers of culture.

Teaching Conflicts?

Let me for a minute come closer to home to talk about the commitments that are beginning to take shape in my own university. We have had several models, or slogans, attached to our work. Gerry Graff has acted as an external reviewer for our department on a couple of occasions. That has led to a mild recurrence in our ranks of the belief that we should be "teaching the conflicts" in our discipline. Gary Waller has given us a lot of publicity by claiming that we have "the first poststructuralist literary curriculum" (6–12). Thirdly, we are taken to be engaged in what Waller has called a "polylogue."[5]

What about the conflict model? How does it work in practice? What seems to happen is that people who represent different sides of the conflicts entrench themselves further in their positions and rigidly defined divisions continue to develop. It leads to further conflict of a small p political kind, and is not at all pedagogically interesting. If you think about it, a narrowly conceived definition of the conflict model is pluralistic, relativistic, and again somewhat despairing[6]. It seems to suggest that all we can do is continue in conflict. To be sure, it perhaps also suggests that any clash of ideas will lead to new ideas and new understanding. We might think that this is somewhat idealistic, especially if we recollect how conflict tends to get materially embodied in actual institutions with actual individuals and groups that tend to become possessive of the ground they occupy. The problem on the one hand is discovering just how to "teach" the conflicts. But there is an over-riding problem: What is the purpose that lies beyond the teaching of conflicts? If we do not agree about what is fundamental to our discipline, we might want to teach the conflicts in it. Our students, however, will be asking themselves disturbing questions about the point of this discipline; questions about its payoff, its purpose, and goal. Why do I need this particular line of study? they could well ask. If we could persuade them that the goal of learning our subject is worthwhile, then we might persuade them that immersing themselves in the conflicts inherent to the subject is important. If we cannot articulate a teleology for our discipline, it would seem impossible to be able to persuade anybody that learning about the conflicts in it were a valuable way of spending time. Indeed, an inability to articulate a full purpose for a discipline would, after all is said and done, seem to be deeply disabling.

Now, it is true that other disciplines, even engineering, cannot altogether make definitive sense of their curriculum. But none say that they do not know where to go at all, are so lacking in purpose that they have to teach their students the confusions. If the work that the conflict model achieves is to convince students that they merely have to commit themselves to one camp or another, and that it doesn't much matter which since there is no clear intellectual basis for choice, we are in fact training our students in nihilism, cynicism, and relativistic power politics.

What about the poststructuralist/postmodern curriculum? Well, I think that idea also needs to be committed; it needs to join those other curricular ideas which are littering history. The prefix "post-" doesn't in itself convey anything very precise. It represents us as being after something instead of before something. It suggests to some that we are circus clowns in the service of anything but the truth, since the truth doesn't exist. Even more than the conflict model, the word "postmodern" conveys a debilitating sense of liberal relativism. What kind of work does postmodernism do? What contribution to our shared lives does it make? And the answer is not forthcoming. It is after something, but it is not for something, or for anything. The idea of the polylogue is similarly bankrupt. If the voice of authority says let a thousand flowers bloom, they start trying to bloom, but they all tend to be heliotropic. They all try to bend themselves to the way in which they think the sun of authority will be shining. There is no genuine polylogue anywhere I know of. If an institution of higher learning, supported by public money and defined as operating in the service of that public, says, effectively, let every voice sing its own song in polyphony, then there can be no comeback when that public demands some closer accounting and control.

Now clearly I don't want to be taken as saying that alternative voices shouldn't be heard. Part of what I am saying is that our work is the production of difference. I am saying that the idea of the liberal polylogue hides a power relation. Similarly, I don't want my critique of poststructuralism to imply that we do not need a theoretically based curriculum. We do. We need to work at refining our thinking about the ways in which theory works both in the graduate and undergraduate curriculum.

Rhetoric, Writing, and Cultural Studies

A pedagogy needs to include a principle of change and development. Maxine Hairston has argued that students write best about those things they are interested in (Hairston). She argues that writing courses "should not focus on politically charged issues" and positions herself in opposition to the contested class at the University of Texas at Austin, English 306. Her position begs a number of issues. It depends, for instance, on some subjective estimation of what a political issue is, as opposed to a nonpolitical one. It requires some ability to discriminate when an issue is "charged" and when one is not. Perhaps a degree of charged-ness is to be measured by the extent to which it is getting current coverage in the popular press? One can understand why Hairston might want to separate substance from the craft of writing. She is possibly anxious to protect the discipline of writing instruction, which has fought to achieve some degree of respectability, from inroads of mere topicality. That position, if it is one she would make, would be at odds with her belief that "students develop best as writers when they are allowed to write on something they care about." That position links an ability to improve one's writing, a capacity to benefit from the science of writing instruction, to a predisposition to the topicality of the issue being addressed — if topicality can be taken to mean that the subject has a personal investment in the issue. Hairston insists that "having them write about other people's ideas doesn't work well."

What is at stake in that claim, perhaps, is the issue of who owns ideas. Are there ideas that are not those of other people? Are there ideas that are exclusively my own, ones that therefore I take a greater interest in and therefore write better about? Does such a claim entail the belief that writing about ideas is not a way of acquiring those ideas? That I have to be in possession of an idea and claim it as uniquely my own before I can write well about it? Such a separation between writing and thinking processes seems to be at odds with what a lot of thinkers about the issue would believe. Hairston's position seems to be based on a simple notion of interest. If students are interested, they will write better. How, though, to lead them into a development of new interests? How get them to "take" an interest? How to persuade them that there are issues in the world that have in interest *in them*, and that it would be to their interest to develop an ability to write and think well about such interesting and interested (possibly "changed") issues? A pedagogy that does not take developmental change into account, that cannot claim to be attempting to help students engage in a change of thinking, cannot really be making a claim to educate students at all.

Having recognized that our first-year curriculum at Carnegie Mellon was probably not doing the job any better than any other curriculum, we have decided to embark on a process of reconstruction. We are uprooting the classes we have, and our assumptions about them. We are asking ourselves hard questions about how to structure a first-year curriculum so as to best use the time we have to influence our students' language abilities. I have charged my colleagues to produce a class that will best represent the discipline, as we conceive of it at Carnegie Mellon University, and also provide the best service to the university community. The marginalization of composition and rhetoric by the focus on literature had deep-seated and serious negative consequences. It will be hard for us to overcome them and to avoid falling back into the dichotomy. We do seem, however, to have continued to make congenial space for creative writers, rhetorical theorists, and people in literary and cultural theory. We relate like three legs of a triangle, each leg meeting the others at the corner, with nothing dominating the center. That lack of a center makes it possible for us to have an extremely wide range of options for our students. They can do a degree in creative writing while taking classes in cultural studies, feminist studies, film studies and professional writing. They can take a class in journalism, while doing one in Shakespeare, another in advertising, and another dealing with the way in which the portrayal of the erotic in film has been influenced by the discourse on AIDS. What is perhaps most striking, is that a program in professional and technical writing can live side-by-side with programs in literary and cultural studies, and there be no real hierarchy of privilege established. If anything, our professional writing students perhaps feel themselves the most privileged, because they are the most readily employable. Students with a B.A. in professional writing can get starting salaries at least equivalent to those earned by Ph.D.'s in literary studies.

We ask ourselves what utility is served by a degree in English, and more broadly, what utility is served by the humanities. It seems easy enough in the case of composition. We teach them to be better writers. But little of what passes for common wisdom in the teaching of writing is based on real research into the nature of the writing and reading processes. If you counted the number of doctoral programs in literary studies, you would soon tire of counting. If you tried to count the number of institutions producing theoretical rhetoricians and so promoting a research-based understanding of writing, you wouldn't even need all the fingers on one hand. So it is not easy to say what writing skill is, nor how to teach it.

Positions, Argument, Interpretation

In trying to answer the general question of utility the word "position" often comes into play. What do we want? We want our students to be able to understand the idea of position. We want them, of course, not to be disabled from getting positions in the world. We want them to be capable of occupying responsible and demanding positions. We want them to understand competing positions in world affairs. We want them to recognize their own positions, and be able to compare their positioning to that of others perhaps more or less fortunate. We want them to have positions, and be capable of comprehending the positions of others, and to be able to take a position when necessary. Now, that doesn't do the whole job, but it does enough by way of outlining a set of goals for the humanities. With such goals, how choose strategies for a curriculum?

It isn't enough just to ask your "comp" people to teach students to write better. What does that mean after all? Does it mean spell correctly, know punctuation? And if it does, does anyone seriously believe that we should be teaching such subjects at the university level? In our case, when we looked over our curriculum, we found that we had an alternate first-year writing class in place, called "Reading and Writing Arguments." We began to realize that we could use that argument class as a model. It is based on the pedagogical system elaborated in the book *Arguing From Sources* (Kaufer, Geisler, and Neuwirth). (Two of the authors, Kaufer and Neuwirth, have been the instructors for the class.) This past year the class has focused on a set of about ten readings on the issue of literacy. Students are led towards an ability to isolate those parts of the text that develop an argument. First they are asked to summarize a single author's position. They discover that summary is different from repetition, that summary is in fact a transformation of the text. Summary turns out to be an interpretation or representation of a text. A summary can be seen as a theory of a text. Next students are asked to synthesize several different arguments on the same topic by different authors. They construct issue trees, and note which of the various authors take which positions on the range of issues. They begin to recognize that an author's positioning on a particular issue will be related to his or her silence, assent or dissent on other issues. They learn quickly that so-called authorities differ with each other, and that the world of discourse and choice is made up of interpretations, arguments, positions. Students begin to recognize that the world is multi-positioned, and that there are complex conversations being carried on around them. They begin to feel themselves part of a community of people concerned about issues. They begin to learn how an argument is constructed and they learn how to make arguments and take positions themselves. They learn that summarizing a text is a way both of recognizing the argument of the text, and a way of interpreting and appropriating it.

A third stage in the process is analysis. Part of this process involves students bringing out of their personal experience some piece of information that relates to the cases at issue. Here they find that they can write about what they care about, their own experience, but that they do not merely have to bare their souls for the sake of writing an essay that has apparently no other purpose. Their production of a personal narrative is now seen in the context of the issues they have become engaged with. Their personal experience is not just personal any more, but can be seen as a "case of" something, as addressing a problem situation. The final stage in the pedagogy of argumentation is that of making one's own contribution. By making a contribution to an ongoing conversation, students learn something about their own agency, and also something about the nature of engagement with issues of interest. Having seen already that authorities take different positions, there is no necessity for students to feel that they have mastered the situation and are giving the final word on the topic. At the same time, there is no reason for them to feel that the position they take is merely personal and of no interest to any other readers.

Since our department also houses a theoretically based program in cultural studies and theory, we have asked one of our professors of cultural studies, Kris Straub, who is an eighteenth-century scholar and a theorist of gender issues, to work with Neuwirth to make a new first year class that will mix issues from "Reading and Writing Arguments" with issues from cultural studies. And on top of that we have asked them to make sure that creative writing plays a role in our introduction — a tall order perhaps, but clearly the element of narrative offers a natural point of entry.

We asked our cultural studies people to say briefly how their approach to texts differs from the traditional way, and to say what skill students acquire from a cultural studies approach that they couldn't get from, say, a new critical approach. The new critical approach turns students into, if anything, reactive consumers, into passive appreciators, into people who are positioned below the great works looking up to their authority. Hardly the best description of what we want from an engaged democratic population. A poststructuralist approach to texts sees them, in short, as positioned. It sees literary objects, or films, or TV ads, as more or less what Kenneth Burke called "equipment for living," some of the equipment works better than some of the rest perhaps, but it is clearly the case that both an ad for a new toothpaste and a novel by Jane Austen can be regarded as in some way equipment for living. Texts have historical positions, economic and social and cultural positions, positions that often change as history unfolds. From those positions they make claims on us; they persuade us, cajole us, deter us, exhort us, encourage, calm, and recompense us. All of the things traditionally claimed, in fact, for art. All we add is the claim that in occupying positions, works of art, including the artifices of TV advertising, are engaged in some argumentative way with us (and a concept of ideology is thereby easily brought into play). They occupy positions that can be metaphorically considered as arguments. So instead of saying to our students: Isn't that beautiful? — and requiring them to say yes or risk failure — we ask, What kind of argumentative claim does this film (*Do the Right Thing*, for instance) or that play (*Hamlet*) make on you? So we ask our students equally, to summarize, interpret, and position themselves with regard to cultural objects. In doing so, we seem to be extending rhetorical principles to cover writing on the one hand, and the study of culture on the other. We will be doing so under the guiding ideas of timeliness and constructedness, and issues of argumentation and positioning.

We expect to be able to develop a vocabulary that will help us to bridge a gap that has been evident on occasion between rhetoric and cultural studies. When students learn in one class that a summary is a theory of a text, it is easy enough to ask them in a theory class to worry about issues of representation. Indeed, when we instruct them in the nature of summarizing, we can use some of the terminology in the first paragraph of *Arguing from Sources*. There writing is compared to setting out on an exploration of new territory. The traveller first consults all the available maps, travels to the country and makes a new map on the basis of experience. The traveller may think the new map is an improvement, but would be unwise to think that this is the final map that will ever be made. So a contribution to an ongoing discourse, when the issue is presented in an argumentative framework, need not produce an atmosphere of agonistic confrontation. Argumentation and interpretation can be seen as the necessary poles of our responsible membership in any community. When one thinks of maps as representations, it is possible to move from an argumentative strategy into the realm of cultural studies with relative ease. Cultural studies programs that are theoretically based will need to pay attention to issues of representation, and will need to help students understand that the language of representation is not transparent. When students are taught to summarize other positions, they can be led to understand that their representation of somebody else's position is first of all a representation, and not that other position in itself; and secondly, they can be led to understand that their own map is in fact a representation of representation(s). A host of educational possibilities opens up with that recognition.

Much remains to be done in our thinking about this class and related curricular issues. But it does seem to be the case that we have found ourselves with a certain freedom to engage in curricular revision. There are probably many reasons that account for our access to this freedom. Amongst them we have to count living without a center of literary icons, which has enabled us to consider a radical restructuring of our department, a restructuring based on rhetorical and cultural studies theories. The new theoretical approaches we are using seem astonishingly like common sense, at least to me. But it takes a great deal of sophisticated theoretical thinking to become capable of seeing how models that are now proving to have been inadequate have had a grip on our thinking. We have been in the grip of polarized cliches, and still find ourselves surrounded by a lot of sloganeering. The time is ripe for universities to engage in some real work of curricular development. The political position that urges that we return to the past and enshrine old values, both misreads the nature of current theoretical thinking and puts our whole educational enterprise at risk. In sum, in rethinking the humanities under the guise of new theory, university professors, and administrators are called on to be intellectual again. If they think they need a purpose, which they do, then I would suggest that this is their purpose: to begin to try to design a humanities curriculum that has a purpose, a utility, rather than mere coherence.

Conclusion

I have been arguing that a mere move to cultural studies does not yet address the real problem of what our curricula are for. I am not trying to give any kind of metanarrative answer that is intended to produce a plan for all occasions. Indeed, I suspect that curricular planning, a theory in practice, will always have local material determinants, and that there are no longer any readily exportable models for core curricula, If, however, we ask of cultural studies the question that once was only asked of composition, What skills can you teach?, I think we are now in a position not to be absolutely tongue-tied, or merely negative about other proposals, or vaguely humanistic or liberal in suggesting that we can "broaden" minds. We can respond by saying, without having to feel ourselves threatened by mere jargon, that cultural studies begins by recognizing difference and the need for interpretation. It starts from the recognition that there is a hegemonic move by global capital to produce a kind of cultural integration, one that is not different indeed from a deep cultural disintegration or elimination of deep cultural differentiations. At the same time there is a recognition that the modern world and the modern self are fragmented and incoherent. If we accept as a possible condition that cultural fragmentation characterizes the postmodern scene — accept that as a starting point, but not an end point — then we commit ourselves to developing a curriculum that deals with boundaries of differentiation. We recognize that there cannot any longer be a fixed set of cultural objects around which we organize our teaching. We make a commitment to theorize our curriculum in a thoroughgoing way precisely because it begins to be clear that only a theoretical focus on problems of interpretation and argument broadly conceived, can usefully address differences in understanding. a theorized curriculum, with an eye on real problems in world cultures can make a claim to a genuine utility in pedagogical and research terms.

In answering the question about skills attendant on such a theoretical curriculum, we can respond that cultural studies teaches lateral thinking because of its insistence on contexts, on drawing students' attention to the situatedness of cultural objects. Because contexts are never saturated nor exhausted, and times change as do perspectives, the useful task of reinterpreting will never be over (Derrida 1982). Cultural objects, like selves, occupy multiple positions. A program in cultural studies, allied with rhetorical theory, ought to be able to begin to develop a curriculum that deals with the multiplicity of positionings that occupy our lives and our students' lives. Students do occupy positions, but we do not always do what we could be doing to make them understand that fact. If we could develop a curriculum that helped them to see just how they are already put in their place, and do this by leading them into a rhetoric of argumentation that gave them systematic access to the comprehension of argumentative positioning, we would be doing something useful. Once having recognized a position, or possible positions, students are set to become players, or agents. So a principle of difference, that makes one aware of the need to deal with contexts and changes of contexts, and a principle of arguing from a position, might be one model for a new program in cultural studies, one that stands to overcome at least some of the costly neglect of the humanities in our time.

Perhaps it needs again to be emphasized that by focusing on the work that the humanities can do, we would be entering deliberately into the debate that is currently being developed around the issue of political correctness. One bad reaction to the charges of political correctness would be to deny that we teach values in our classes. Equally, it would be unsatisfactory simply to return to a liberal human-istic claim to be able to teach the eternal values. Values are in conflict. We can teach the conflict of values, and claim that there is value in that. Further, we can insist that cultural studies is a useful broadening of the traditional literary curriculum, a broadening that keeps a respon-sible eye on the contexts in which our students live and will live. Studying culture, it can be said, is a matter of studying all of the aspects of current contexts. Such a claim, of course, makes it all but impossible really to define or delimit cultural studies. It seems to include everything. And, clearly, one cannot leave out the political and the historical, or theories of race, class, and gender, when one "studies culture." But one might usefully remind oneself from time to time that the real object of study is culture, or cultural production and reception. We might again insist that not enough weight has been given yet, even in cultural studies circles, to the study of production, except in a theoretical manner. Wouldn't we benefit by extending ourselves really into the problems that go with trying to be producers as well as receivers? Wouldn't we benefit by attempting to teach our students something of the work of being producers or contributors?

It might be worth thinking of English departments as institutions dedicated to all aspects of the speech act. We could then claim that cultural studies deserves to be fully instituted in a university because one of its purposes is to make a contribution to knowledge. One of the ways it might make such a contribution would be by questioning the ways in which institutionalizing, and the establishment of a disciplinary structure for knowing, shape knowledge. But that would be different from claiming that cultural studies has no knowledge to contribute. That latter kind of claim would in fact be a claim that cultural studies does not really belong in a university. Not a good move for a movement that might want to make a change in universities. We could further claim that not only does cultural studies impart knowledge, it imparts what we might as well call skills. Recalling our earlier discussion of writing, however, we could also call it force. To claim that the humanites have more to teach than mere knowledge might fly in the face of a dominant scientism in our universities. It would, nevertheless, go some way to restore some of the meaning of an educational experience that really ought to help a citizenry find out how to live by trying to provide them "equipment for living."

If we teach our students something about the ways in which they can responsibly engage issues of their society—that is, we teach them the arts of becoming producers of significant speech acts—we could perhaps restore a sense of direction for ourselves. Merely to know what is the case, in scientific studies, or in cultural studies, is not enough. People need to be capable of acting once they know. It is that extension of our knowledge into areas of social practice that is a central domain of the humanities. To fear moving into that area because we do not want to be thought to be teaching values, or because we are cautious about admitting that our curricula require commitment, would be, at least, a misdemeanor. The humanities have lingered too long in the belief that "understanding" is enough. We need to add doing. What we can do is to develop a curriculum directed towards the production of responsible speech acts. Doing and learning in the humanities involve political commitment. There can be no escaping that fact.

Notes

1. I use the word "humanities," as the expression "English department," with a keen sense of the value of paleonymy. The old name might serve us if we recognize that there is no way back to the old Renaissance concept of the humanist and the associated ideas of the "humanities" subjects. The name still suggests an area of educational discovery and associated values. One must, of course, be wary of the way that a conscious and strategic paleonymy could too readily turn itself into some recurrent reification of old and ossified patterns of pedagogical choice.

2. See Hall, Edward T., and Mildred Reed Hall, *Understanding Cultural Differences*, (Yarmouth, Maine: Intercultural Press, Inc., 1990) 196. The Halls are unabashed about the purpose of cultural studies: it will explain other markets to American producers of consumer culture and so open up the world to "our" goods, for our profit.

3. The point I make in the text needs further emphasis: I use the word "deconstruction" provocatively and in order to be able to stipulate under its name some useful changes that have taken place in the general intellectual climate of English departments as a result of the "theoretical" project of the last decade or two.

4. Crudely put, the constative is the content conveyed by what is said and the performative is done by what is said. So while it is possible — conceivable — that the content of a statement contains reinforcing information ("Saddam Hussein is an intelligent man"), the force of the statement might be such as to function as a warning rather than a compliment.

5. Just how far representations can get from what is the case can be seen by considering the attack made on CMU curriculum by Donald Morton and Mas'ud Zavarzadeh in *Theory / Pedagogy / Politics: Texts for Change*. Although they were invited to come see for themselves just what the actual practices are at Carnegie Mellon, they seemed satisfied to attack Waller's representations, which may well deserve a better critique than the one they provide, and in that attack presume that they have somehow got to the reality of what we are trying to do.

6. It is not necessarily the case that Graff's model is crude in its conception. All I am claiming here is that it may be more difficult to put into practice than Graff is willing to admit.

Works Cited

Austin, J.L., *How to Do Things With Words*, second ed. (Cambridge, Mass.: Harvard University Press, 1975) 169.

de Man, Paul, "Semiology and Rhetoric," *Allegories of Reading*, (New Haven and London: Yale University Press, 1979) 3–19.

Derrida, Jacques, "Some Statements and Truisms About Neo-Logisms, Newisms, Postisms, and Other Small Seismisms," *The State of Theory*, ed. David Carroll. (New York: Oxford University Press, 1990) 63–64.

Derrida, Jacques, "Signature, Event, Context," *Margins of Philosophy*, trans. Alan Bass (Chicago: University of Chicago Press, 1982).

Hairston, Maxine, *Chronicle of Higher Education*, 23 January 1991.

Hoggart, Richard, *The Uses of Literacy: Changing Patterns in English Mass Culture* (Fair Lawn, N.J.: Essential Books, 1957).

Kaufer, David S., Cheryl Geisler, and Christine M. Neuwirth, *Arguing From Sources: Exploring Issues Through Reading and Writing*, (New York: Harcourt Brace Jovanovich, 1989).

Kennedy, Alan, *Reading Resistance Value*, (New York: St. Martin's Press, 1990).

Said, Edward, *Orientalism*, Vintage Books ed. (New York: 1979) Random House.

Waller, Gary F. "Working Within the Paradigm Shift: Poststructuralism and the College Curriculum." *ADE Bulletin* 81 (1985): 6–12.

3

Composing a Cultural Studies Curriculum at Pitt

Philip E. Smith II

No, we have to do here with something different, the curriculum not as a canon but as a work of art. We must think here of a change like that which post-modernism brought to the visual arts, a change from static to dynamic, from contemplative to interactive, from curriculum as canon to curriculum as participatory theatre, as a happening. The modern university curriculum is too varied, and our professional lives, both students and professors, too intensely idiosyncratic, to lay down an externally guided curriculum. We must provide internal guidance, a curricular compass, or perhaps better, a gyroscope, for our students....The canonical or "Great Books" curriculum finally sought to present the humanities curriculum as a stable, finished work of art. The curriculum I have tried briefly to sketch can be thought of as a work of art too, but a work of post-modern art, unstable, unfinished, interactive, not a certified canon of revealed cultural truth but a participatory drama in which the student must take part, a drama which is set on a stage but not set in concrete, with dialogue which is there to revise and a plot which licenses us to collaborate with chance — all these together aiming to teach not only knowledge but the way knowledge is held. — Richard Lanham, "The Rhetorical Paideia: The Curriculum as a Work of Art" (140−41).

Lanham's distinction between a static, canon-based curriculum that certifies revealed cultural truth and a dynamic, postmodern curriculum that interrogates knowledge and ways of knowing can stand for two models of English curricula that our department began to talk about as early as 1977. Within a year, talking led to committee work that initiated more than a decade of reconfiguring Pitt's English literature and composition curricula from an accreted collection of period, genre, theme, and theme-writing courses into undergraduate and graduate programs in cultural studies.

In the process we revised our identity *away* from the traditional belletristic English department; in 1986 we instituted our new Ph.D. program under the name of "Cultural and Critical Studies." We redefined the "coverage" model of aestheticized literary study by confronting it with recent developments in canon revision and in theory (literary, cultural and feminist), pedagogy, film, media, and popular culture, by including the global dispersion of literatures in English as well as the special discourses of gender, race, and class, and by developing the graduate study of composition, literacy, and instructional history. Our revisions seem to be attractive: in 1991 applications to our graduate programs increased by 288 percent over the previous five years, while the increase in applications to the Ph.D. was 547 percent.

We chose what Lanham would call the postmodern option for change, electing to determine our new curriculum as much by theory and praxis (literary and pedagogical) as by the textual object of study considered in historical context. We no longer felt ourselves limited to the traditional canon of "high" literature set against its introductory-lecture, two-dimensional historical backdrop. We explicitly embraced texts usually marginalized by their unorthodox associations with class, race, gender, and institutional positions; that is, we included courses in working-class, African-American, ethnic, women's, immigrants', popular, and other nonstandard literatures and in presentational modes such as melodrama, television, and film. We explicitly affirmed our commitment to teach with student writing as a textual and focal center in the classroom. We adopted a pedagogy of problem-posing for our principle of internal guidance, Lanham's curricular "gyroscope." We wouldn't all name it that way, but most of us would recognize the process, which had been developing and flourishing particularly in our composition program.

As the process of curriculum revision developed, it required discussion, compromise, adjustment, revision, and reassessment. We have not finished it; and, because we anticipate continuous modification, we have promised ourselves that it has no "final" pre-imagined form. The process has presented the occasion and focus for a revitalization of our faculty interested in professionally developing pedagogy and curriculum at the same time that it has served as a laboratory for training graduate students. As the changes have taken a direction towards what we name cultural studies, they have been importantly shaped by a nexus of influential discourses: our new program has grown out of our encounters with literary, cultural, and social theories as well as the teaching practices and theories of composition.

Several overlapping stages have led to the present (1991) form of our undergraduate and graduate curricula. In brief, our discussions in the late seventies produced a revision of the undergraduate literature curriculum, completed in 1979. Then, as part of a college-wide curricular reform of general education requirements in 1983, we revised our composition courses and developed a new set of introductory, writing-intensive literature courses for nonmajors. The first revisions to bear the name "Cultural and Critical Studies" were the Masters degree and doctorate programs, which accepted new entrants and transfers from the old "four-area comprehensive" Ph.D. program in September 1986. Since then, we have continued revising: for example, in 1989 we changed the M.A. examination considerably from its previous comprehensive coverage model to reflect two lists of about 15 changing texts and films. One of them changes slowly, at the rate of two or three texts per year, and the other is completely reset each fall to reflect the year's seminar offerings. Both lists include representations from composition and film as well as literature, criticism, and theory.

I write this account not to prescribe a process of revision for anyone or any department; instead I would like to describe what has worked for us at Pittsburgh, given where we started, who we are, and who our students are. I'll proceed from the general to the particular in profiling our department and its curriculum revisions. I want to give some idea of our size, of the process and its principles, and of a few courses and individuals who helped define and shape our practice.

We are a large group; our constellation in the spring of 1991 reflects the disproportionate minority of tenure-stream to nontenure-stream faculty characteristic of most state-financed universities: fifty-two full-time faculty, eighty-three part-time faculty, and eighty graduate teaching assistants. Given the size of our teaching staff (215 faculty and graduate assistants) and our undergraduate teaching mission (to provide composition and literature courses not only for 9,300 students enrolled in Pittsburgh's College of Arts and Sciences, but also for another 4,000 undergraduates spread across the evening College of General Studies and the Schools of Nursing, Pharmacy, and Engineering), it should be no surprise that we proposed and generated new courses before attempting to legislate widespread reforms. We made changes through "bottom-up" participation of all interested department members, including part-time faculty and graduate-student teachers, who met in committees to draft and propose ideas to the whole department. Significant changes thus occurred relatively slowly because our departmental by-laws call for ratification by the department as a whole. We are constitutionally unwilling to produce the swift, radical revisions characteristic of "top-down" academic management. That is, we continue to redefine a curriculum that, from undergraduate introductory courses in composition and literature to advanced graduate seminars, project work, and dissertations, accords serious recognition to pedagogy, literary theory, and theoretically informed historical study of literary, visual, and critical texts.

Given our adoption of a pedagogical principle of internal guidance, the process of curriculum reform implicitly called for further and better integration of programs and areas of study: of composition with literature and film, graduate study with undergraduate; and for blurring of the lines of disciplinary study within programs — more reading in composition courses, more writing in literature courses, more theory in literature and composition courses, more teaching of both kinds of courses by faculty and graduates from literature, film, composition, and creative writing programs. The ferment of ideas generated by this commitment to integration produced a lively series of meetings, talks, presentations, and publications that continues to help us redefine and revise. It stimulated new courses in cultural studies, literacy, and pedagogy that bridge former disciplinary boundaries among literature, film, and composition in undergraduate and graduate studies. There are important traces of our curricular discussions in my colleagues' publications on pedagogy, composition, and cultural studies, some of which anticipated and most of which were generated by this ferment. They are traces of the ways that our curriculum change benefited from and contributed to debates within the profession of English studies over methodological and theoretical questions. Jean Ferguson Carr, for example, describes cultural studies in terms of the disciplinary shift that has informed our curricular changes:

> Cultural studies is not a single position or set of behaviors, but rather a cluster of interests that comes from theory, from teaching, and from social concerns. The shift from literary to cultural studies marks a change that draws on work in many different areas of the humanities — feminist criticism, minority studies, composition and pedagogy, the history of the book, textual editing, reception theory, popular culture and media, literacy and instruction. The shift emphasizes the changed understanding of "literature" and its relationship to society. Cultural studies moves away from "history of ideas" to a contested history of struggles for power and authority, to complicated relations between "center" and "margin," between dominant and minority relations. (25)

Changing the Undergraduate Major: Pedagogy and Principles

My rhetorical perspective is what Kenneth Burke might call "consubstantial." To tell the story of how we developed our internal principles of guidance I need help from my colleagues' voices and from writers whose work helped us explain ourselves to one another.

My starting point is one in a series of theory-based general education courses we inaugurated in 1983, "Introduction to Critical Reading," which doubles as our required introduction to English studies for majors. Originally designed for honors students by Paul Bové, it was revised by Mariolina Salvatori and Marcia Landy as a sophomore-level course not limited to beginning majors so it would satisfy a college general-education requirement for a first course in literature.

Salvatori has written about the critical reading course in "Toward a Hermeneutics of Difficulty." She makes a crucial distinction between *pedagogy* and *didactics* that underlies not just her own work, but much of our new curriculum and our focus on theoretically informed teaching methods. She puts the distinction this way:

> Because I would like to reclaim pedagogy as a philosophical science, as the theory and practice of knowing that "makes manifest" its own theory and practice by continually reflecting upon and deconstructing it, I will call *didactics* any approach to teaching that shuns the teacher's and the student's critical reflexivity on the act of knowing and promotes the reduction of somebody else's way of knowing into a schematization of that method. Whereas didactics sets up "models" and dictates procedures that will make the approximation of those models possible, pedagogy inquires into the prehistory of those models, and analyzes and assesses their formation. The radically different epistemological assumptions at the basis of didactics and pedagogy determine radically different teacher/learner relationships, classroom activities, projects, and curricula. (93)

The implication for her teaching is profound: "Our pedagogical imperative should be consciously and consistently to make *manifest* the rules and practices of interpretation we have acquired from institutional training, and to teach all students—remedial as well as mainstream, undergraduate as well as graduate—the very methods we practice in the classroom and use to produce the texts that grant us professional status" (81). She accomplishes this in the context of an introductory course based on "in-depth and recursive readings of three classic (canonical) texts—*King Lear*, *Madame Bovary*, and 'The Waste Land'—and a set of professional critics' readings of these texts" (82).

Salvatori's pedagogy depends upon close work with student papers generated in response to their reading of canonical texts and critics. A founding principle for her pedagogy and for our curriculum reform is the recognition that students' written texts, no matter how problematic or naive in their attempts to produce critical readings, must be taken as beginnings worthy of serious attention and revision. They must be respected by teacher and students and must be seen individually and collectively as embodying the product and purpose of the class. Students are not enrolled to worship the canonical texts or to imprint and reproduce the critical methods of the skilled "insiders" who decode hidden meanings. Salvatori's purpose for having students read professional critics is not for their "'canonical interpretations' which readers can only contemplate/imitate/emulate"; rather, critics are "studied, and critiqued, as examples of some of the strategies expert readers use to gain autonomy, to negotiate power away from a text's/writer's authority. Not to do so, to offer them instead as inscrutable, hermetic models, risks magnifying students' insecurity about their own critical abilities and producing yet more uncritical docility or uncritical rebellion" (83).

After redefining the idea of "critical" reading and writing for students, since their ordinary language definition has to do with negative and censorious "tearing apart," Salvatori proceeds with her difficult but rewarding method which combines "two reciprocally monitoring techniques":

> a self-reflexive "hermeneutical" critique and a "deconstructive" one. The hermeneutical critique posits the necessity for the knower/reader to understand herself in the act of understanding: thus it demands that the reader reflect on the motives, prejudgements, and preunderstandings that can both foster and impede interpretation. ...The deconstructive technique posits the necessity for a reader/thinker to expose a text's fissures which are to be examined and studied less as symptoms of "flaws and imperfections" in the theoretical system that has produced the text than as indications of "that system's possibility."... In the congruence of these two critiques I see the possibility of enacting a process with which a reader can negotiate her autonomy as "knower" from the silencing influence of "uncritically" accepted authority (the text's/author's/teacher's authority or the authority of the prejudices that can blind her to the question a text, an author, a teacher is trying to raise)—an autonomy, however, which self-reflexively she must always keep in the making, subject to scrutiny and revision (81–82).

Salvatori's problem-posing method seriously encounters student work, attempts to demystify the professional practices of readers, critics, and writers, and teaches students that significant work of their own can begin with the very texts and commentaries that have been canonized, worshipped, and uncritically accepted in other curricula that do not set as their principle-of-principles the empowerment of students.

The phrase "problem-posing" comes from the Brazilian educator, Paulo Freire, to name the education that problematizes knowing and acting upon knowledge, in contrast to the education based on uncritical, passive transmission and reception of texts that he calls "banking" Banking, to continue the metaphor, makes students and faculty feel secure, as if they have properly deposited and protected their assets. This security, however, can breed a static and fatalistic view of the human condition by embalming as forever fixed the relationships of

people to the world they inhabit. This is education in the most conservative and reactionary sense: it says to a student, learn the immutable
ways of the world, be satisfied in your place, don't try to change
things. Freire describes the oppositions between banking and problem
posing this way:

> Banking education (for obvious reasons) attempts, by mythicizing
> reality, to conceal certain facts which explain the way men exist in the
> world; problem-posing education makes them critical thinkers. Banking
> education inhibits creativity and domesticates (although it cannot
> completely destroy) the *intentionality* of consciousness by isolating
> consciousness from the world, thereby denying men their ontological
> and historical vocation of becoming more fully human. Problem-
> posing education bases itself on creativity and stimulates true reflection
> and action upon reality, thereby responding to the vocation of men as
> beings who are authentic only when engaged in inquiry and creative
> transformation. In sum: banking theory and practice, as immobilizing
> and fixating forces, fail to acknowledge men as historical beings;
> problem-posing theory and practice take man's historicity as their
> starting point. (248)

Historicity, for Freire, means looking at the human condition in
the "here and now," recognizing ourselves as beings in the process of
becoming; because we can think of ourselves thinking, we have the
power to study and intervene in our individual and collective histories
(248–49). Historicity, for our curriculum revision, became an important
concept, especially for those many courses in precontemporary literature
that bring students to confront texts from historically remote contexts —
and for many of our undergraduates that means anything written
before 1980.

Freire's problem-posing education was not an *a priori* model that
we set for ourselves in designing a curriculum. Rather, along with
Salvatori's emphasis on pedagogy, it helps to describe what has emerged
out of our collective efforts since 1977 when the project of reevaluating
the curriculum began. Our department carried over from the 1960s an
aesthetic formalist curriculum that might have been drawn from the
pages of Northrop Frye's *The Anatomy of Criticism*. When I arrived at
Pitt in 1970, the curriculum existed as if it were natural and permanent:
there were no documents or rationales to explain it, and whatever
discussion might have taken place at its creation survived only in the
memories of the longest-serving members of the faculty. It pivoted
upon generic divisions, with lower-division introductory courses in
poetry, drama, and narrative that prepared students for upper-division
courses like "Modern Poetry," "Major British Drama," or "Development of the Novel." The teaching assistants, who were largely responsible for instruction in the lower division courses, enrolled in graduate

seminars in the teaching of poetry, prose, and drama, and went on to take masters comprehensive and doctoral qualifying examinations organized around the same three genres. Usually they answered questions by citing the works they taught to undergraduates. As my colleague Jim Knapp describes it, "The department was not only providing a particular shape to undergraduate education, but making a commitment to reproduce itself within a profession that would presumably continue to be concerned first of all with questions of literary form and aesthetic tradition" (1987, 3).

Knapp was one of the leaders in the discussion of how we might replace unselfconscious formalism with pedagogically self-aware historicity in the curriculum. In the literature curriculum, the revisions began at the level of individual courses, and gradually, through discussion and mutual reeducation, gained the support of a consensus of faculty concerned with effecting evolutionary changes. For example, Knapp designed an upper-level literature survey course called "The Medieval Imagination" that modeled the department's concern to shift its attention from literature as artifact of aesthetic form (in the older version of the course, called "Epic and Romance") to literature as a product of culture and history. Knapp describes his method and design this way:

> Invoking a conventional phrase [Medieval Imagination] which already suggested broader "cultural" approaches which included art, music, philosophy, etc., that course then set out to deconstruct the notion of "imagination," looking at medieval ways of knowing (or "discursive practices") which ranged from the archaic remainders of prehistoric Celtic myth to the sophisticated hermeneutics of high medieval literary theory in John of Salisbury, Dante and Boccaccio. Assuming that medieval discursive practices acted to mediate the enormous social, political, and cultural changes which occurred during those centuries, the course, for example, examines the contest of Christian and pagan cultures in the early Middle Ages as that contest was inscribed in texts such as Bede's *Ecclesiastical History of the English People*; or with regard to a later period, the Twelfth-century re-writing of heroic culture into the new—and in many ways subversive—language of romance by writers such as Marie de France. (1987, 3–4)

The department adopted Knapp's course as the first of seven in a core of period surveys for majors that begin with early British literature, include American literature to 1860, and finish with a pair of courses that consider late 19th and early 20th century literature written in English from two perspectives, "Modernist Tradition" and "Realist Tradition." Like "Medieval Imagination," both modern survey courses were designed to pose the problem of how we understand and interpret the texts and self-constituting discourse of a "tradition." Separating the modern survey into two synchronic courses also was a curricular gesture suggesting that any single survey, however constituted, was the creation of professional critics and literary historians and, just as students come to demystify the opinions of professional critics in Salvatori's "Critical Reading" class, any literary survey course should be demystified to counter our profession's tendency to reproduce an uncriticized, "natural" history of literature or culture. The faculty committed itself to a concept of "historicity" like Freire's: rather than memorize and deposit in final-examination bank accounts the chronology of major and minor texts and authors in the English and American canons, as survey courses once required, we proposed to study not only the texts and their place in contextual discourses but also the problems of accounting for them in a historical narrative that had meaning for a student in the "here and now." As in other courses in our new curriculum, the new surveys called for the serious integration and study of student-written texts along with the assigned readings for the course. Only by taking seriously the students' attempts to learn how to negotiate their own critical responses to literature could we be said to practice a pedagogy of problem-posing.

General Education Courses

The time for integrating this pedagogy with a programmatic revision of lower-division courses arrived in 1982 when we began to design new general education courses to meet the reformed requirements of the College of Arts and Sciences. We gradually phased out the old genre-based courses (which did not require students to compose any papers, though most instructors used at least midterm and final examinations). We designed a new series, known in our department by the shorthand of numbers as "The Thirties" and we wrote a programmatic statement for these courses, setting goals for their development that reflected our revisions of the curriculum for majors.

> These courses will introduce students to literature by exploring funda-
> mental issues in the production and reception of significant texts.
> Their distinguishing feature will be a commitment to sustained inquiry
> into the informing values, concepts, and methods of literary practice
> and critical study. In keeping with the College of Arts and Sciences
> guidelines, they will focus mainly on "works of abiding literary value";
> in doing so they should seriously consider the reasons or purposes a
> text is deemed to be "of abiding literary value." Likewise, the training
> they offer in "techniques of literary analysis" should entail some
> reflection on the values and assumptions embedded in their interpretive
> approaches. The courses should show students how the basic concerns
> of literary study are actively and essentially contested, and are always
> open to re-definition and further elaboration. They should seek to

enable students to participate in this interpretive and evaluative process.

All the 30s courses, in keeping with our sense of necessary historicity, were to be culturally and historically situated; all would require a significant amount of writing and revision, enough to satisfy the college's new "Writing Across the Curriculum" requirements, but more to the point, enough to provide student writing its rightful place in the pedagogy of problem-posing. As they were developed and taught, some courses continued to address subjects associated with traditional genres. Others addressed the issue of interpretation by making it the center of the course; for example, English 37, a course entitled "Literature and Ideas," frames canonical and noncanonical literary texts together with works like Plato's *Phaedrus* and Freud's *The Question of Lay Analysis* that offer the student powerful ways of reading discourses and oneself. The course description written by Steve Carr and Mariolina Salvatori highlights the relationship between interpretation of literary texts and of students' work:

> The content and pedagogy of the course are based on two related premises: we assume that reading and writing are reciprocally inter-active interpretive processes, and we emphasize the power of language to transform even as it represents. The difficulties of reading and writing, of marrying text and idea, are treated not simply as problems of disruption or of imperfect communication but as ways of opening up interpretive possibilities, as enabling opportunities to revise, extend, and/or renew previous forms of understanding. Students learn to read their own writing with the same intense scrutiny that they devote to literary texts, to question the fundamental assumptions of an essay, to play off its various underlying metaphors, to explore and revise its acts of disclosure and closure.

In English 37 the goals of a problem-posing pedagogy are adapted to the needs of a general-education introductory literature course whether the texts to be read are Melville's *Benito Cereno* or *Moby-Dick*, Gilman's *The Yellow Wallpaper*, Hurston's *Their Eyes Were Watching God* or Blake's *Songs of Innocence and Experience*, all of which, and many more, have been required over the last five years. Ten to twelve sections (limited to twenty-two students each because of the writing component) are offered each term, and they are taught by faculty and graduate students who meet together weekly as a staff to discuss their pedagogy and the progress of the course. Instead of the diffusion and loss of focus that happens when ten or twelve teachers of a course do their own thing as independent entrepreneurs, the staff's reflective consideration of the course's goals and methods has resulted in the constant revision and evolution of English 37. Most of the teachers previously have taught freshmen and sophomores in our composition program where a similar problem-posing pedagogy operates (indeed, many 1991 sophomores who enrolled in "Literature and Ideas" or in "Introduction to Critical Reading" had read and written about the Freire essay in their composition courses the year before).

Another of the 30s courses, "Literature, Tradition, and the New," situates its problem-posing pedagogy in the curricular space that used to house the introductory "Great Books" course. Jim Knapp's memorandum to the teaching staff exemplifies several of the characteristics of our revised curriculum. In the foreground are the institutional setting and goals of the course: the memorandum includes a course description, history, rationale, and constraints for teachers; it briefly explains how and why the course was approved by a college curriculum committee.

Knapp's memorandum to teachers of English 30 suggests basic texts that teachers should read to understand the post-structuralist theoretical underpinnings and contexts for historical and textual issues raised by the course. It also describes the sequence of writing assignments and gives a sample full-length assignment on the Breton *Lais* of Marie de France. As in other courses in our revised curriculum, English 30 makes student writing a central focus for pedagogy: "Student papers will be discussed in class, and those student-generated texts will serve to focus our discussions by bringing together the acts of reading and writing. An important assumption will be that reading and writing are both activities which produce (not simply absorb) knowledge" (3). Knapp's language here, as in his statement of the course's goals, is deliberately straightforward and not like much technical vocabulary associated with high theory. But a reading of the goals should convince anyone who questions the applicability of critical theory to introductory undergraduate teaching of literature that there are serious and approachable issues at stake for students and teachers:

1. To have students read a variety of important literary works from several historical periods and cultural traditions.
2. To stress precise reading of complex verbal texts.
3. To make students aware of the power of literature to interpret, and in part to constitute, the symbolic systems which enable both social change and social stability.
4. To let students see themselves as active participants in the process by which a cultural tradition is reproduced over time, and in doing so to address questions which many students will ask in a required course such as this: why are these works of literature important? what do they have to do with me? (1984, 2)

My final example of problem-posing pedagogy is "General Writing," one of the courses that satisfies our college's composition requirement.

Over fifty sections of twenty-two students are offered each term. Like many of the 30s, this is a staff-taught course; the first teaching position for entering graduate teaching assistants is one section of "General Writing". All first-year teaching assistant's attend both the weekly staff meetings and a twice-weekly teaching seminar, a sort of meta-General Writing that introduces them to the theoretical positions and debates that undergird our pedagogy and this course. The undergraduate students complete a recursive set of assignments that have them reading and writing about, in 1991 for example, John Ruskin, John Wideman, Adrienne Rich, Clifford Geertz, and Annie Dillard. The designers of the "General Writing" assignment sequence, David Bartholomae and Tony Petrosky, address their students in a way that embodies our largest pedagogical goals and expectations:

> The sequences allow you to participate in an extended academic project, one in which you take a position, revise it, look at a new example, hear what someone else has to say, revise it again, and see what conclusions you can draw about your subject. These projects always take time — they go through stages and revisions as a writer develops a command over his or her material, pushing against habitual ways of thinking, learning to examine an issue from different angles, rejecting quick conclusions, seeing the power of understanding that comes from repeated effort, and feeling the pleasure writers take when they find their own place in the context of others whose work they admire. This is the closest approximation we can give you of the rhythm and texture of academic life, and ... its characteristic ways of reading, thinking, and writing. (17)

"General Writing" each year has a new sequence of assignments; some equivalent composition courses now in development have been added, including a Women's Studies version and a course that brings together reading, writing, and film studies. We are adding upper-division courses in literacy and the history of instruction and new topical courses in composition.

The revision of our department's undergraduate curriculum and major will continue in parallel with revision of our graduate program and with a conscious effort to further integrate faculty and programs in theory, literature, and composition. We remain committed to a programmatic integration in English Studies empowered by a pedagogy of problem-posing, of teaching reading and writing of texts and images in a theoretically and socio-culturally self-aware way. That self-awareness is aimed for in the composition courses we teach for all students in the college, just as in our introductory course for the major and in the capstone senior seminars. All Pitt undergraduates, we hope, not just English majors, will enter their chosen areas of study with a sense of what it means to write and revise a reading that honors complexity and enables strong individual responses, that values self-awareness and difficulty in texts and in their interpretation. We try to exemplify this awareness as a faculty committed to the revision and furtherance of a problem-posing pedagogy, and we are training our graduate teaching assistants to teach literature and composition from these principles.

A Pedagogy of Critical and Cultural Empowerment: What We Talk About in Graduate Teaching Seminars

One of the founding principles of our cultural and critical studies program commits us to reflect about our disciplinary assumptions and language — our educational ideologies and rhetorics — as we train graduate students to be university teachers of English. For more than a decade it has been an ongoing programmatic concern of ours to provide a location in our graduate curriculum for discussion of professional and pedagogical issues that relate directly to the teaching, writing, and research projects of our teaching assistants and teaching fellows. To make plain our commitment to a foundational principle that "advanced study in language, literature, and media can offer intellectually powerful kinds of cultural criticism," and to counteract institutional forgetting by remembering and foregrounding the debates that accompanied our program's conception, we constituted it according to a statement of its goals and a rationale recognizing the importance of both traditional work and of new professional developments. Therefore, our graduate program is based on commitments to:

1. ground its teaching and research in a continuing process of self-scrutiny made possible by serious engagement with the theoretical and critical debates of the time;

2. understand literary texts as historical productions, with the corollary that "high" literature may be read in conjunction with texts traditionally seen as marginal or as not "literary" at all (popular literature, texts by women and minorities, film, discursive writing, student writing, etc.);

3. bring together areas of scholarly inquiry which have, for largely institutional reasons, been kept apart: primarily, composition research and pedagogy dealing with the social constitution of writing; literary and intellectual history; and theoretical inquiry into the power of language's relationship to social order and social change. (21)

These three promises to ourselves and our students suggest our positions on current professional issues such as the value of theory in graduate curriculum, the vastly widened scope of canonical and noncanonical texts available for teaching and research, and the need to bridge gaps — to bring together the teaching, study, and practice of reading and writing with social, historical, and textual studies. These founding principles of our pedagogy of critical and cultural empowerment are tested and revised through practice by every incoming class of graduate students.

In September each academic year at Pitt about twenty-five first-year teaching assistants and teaching fellows begin work as instructors of "General Writing," the composition course most Pitt undergraduates take. This mixed group is composed approximately of thirds studying for the three degrees we grant, the M.A., M.F.A., and Ph.D. Along with their teaching assignments, they begin a year's training program including a summer workshop, weekly staff meetings, several observations and follow-up conferences about their own teaching, and a two-semester sequence of required seminars. We require the two seminars in the first year of teaching, when a teaching assistants load is one section of "General Writing" per term; thereafter they teach three sections per year. The seminars are *not* concerned with recipes or first aid for new teachers; instead, over the course of the year, graduate students investigate the intellectual assumptions behind the course they teach as well as their own location within the institutional structure of the department, the university, and the history of English studies. They read, discuss, and write about reading and writing, about theories and methods of pedagogical practice, drawing upon books and articles concerning teaching, rhetoric, the history of the profession, literary and composition theory, and cultural criticism. In these two seminars we lay the foundations for the connections between reading and writing, for the definition of intellectual positions about teaching and theory, that are built upon as graduate students proceed to advanced seminars and to their Ph.D. projects and dissertations.

Both seminars emphasize the pedagogical concerns for strong reading and writing, revision, and students' intellectual empowerment that center the "General Writing" course. The fall "Seminar in Teaching Composition," as developed in the 1980s by Dave Bartholomae, and taught at various times and in teams of two by Bartholomae, Paul Kameen, Joe Harris, and Mariolina Salvatori, is focused through readings in contemporary theory and pedagogy from writers such as I.A. Richards, Italo Calvino, Michel Foucault, Ann Berthoff, Stanley Fish, and Robert Scholes. The seminar invites consideration of how writers and teachers imagine the field of reading and writing, how their attempts to conceive theories — of composition and teaching, of interpretation and writing — constitute a discourse that new teachers need to learn and enter. The winter "Seminar in Teaching English," as Joe

Harris and I have developed it, contextualizes the teaching of "General Writing" in larger institutional and professional settings: in the fields of composition and English studies as they have developed out of past and present debates over the principles, social missions, and utility of cultural education. Drawing upon texts from writers such as Plato, Matthew Arnold, T.S. Eliot, I.A. Richards, the Leavises, Raymond Williams, Ursula Le Guin, Kenneth Burke, Milan Kundera, and Gerald Graff, as well as anthologies of writings about the profession like Graff and Warner's *The Origins of Literary Studies in America* and *the South Atlantic Quarterly*'s issue on "The Politics of Liberal Education", we attempt to create the seminar's dialectic of discussion and, thereby, to empower individual stances towards teaching, reading, and writing.

Our model of teaching as problem-posing offers our new teachers a context for understanding the responsibility and authority they need to claim in their daily work. We offer our student-teachers more questions than answers about institutional history and pedagogy: that is, we wish to open and introduce problems, not foreclose them by imposing solutions or directions. As Joe Harris writes in the course description, "We will try to find a way of talking about teaching that allows us to act with some sense of mission and confidence and yet does not pretend to solve once and for all the problems of language — to avoid talking, that is, as if the difficulties of reading and writing might be made to disappear by following a certain method or adopting a particular stance or ideology."

In the sense I have used it above, the word "empowerment" might be taken, on the evidence of its wide use in instructional materials and its adoption in 1989 as a Conference on College Composition and Communication theme, as naming an ideology for English teachers. However, we have talked about empowerment in our teaching seminars at Pittsburgh for several years, and I want to present some of the positions developed by graduate teachers. Because our program has committed itself to consider student writing, undergraduate and graduate, as serious texts for study, I offer our graduate students' work as an example of their engagement with pedagogical issues of present concern and debate across the profession. The selections I have chosen come from papers written in the second term of the seminar. The assignments asked writers to discuss their teaching in relation to the goals and dialectic of "General Writing," and in relation to their own agendas or missions as teachers.

Marianne Davis, writing a second paper in the 1986 seminar about her goals as a teacher, saw problems in accepting empowerment, understood as the creation of a self through writing, as in itself sufficient for her "General Writing" class: "I want to believe that working at writing can enable a person to enact 'tentative selves' (Richard Lanham), to imagine new worlds, but...even at its ideal level the notion of empowering the self fails to address certain practical and political concerns" (2/26/86).

I consider Marianne's passage as doubly significant in relation to the idea of empowerment: First, in her concern with why and for what purpose she teaches students, she recognizes a problem with self-creation when it is only self-regarding and not part of a social and political matrix. Just as importantly, however, she takes a step towards developing her own teaching stance by recognizing her indebtedness to others and the need to address concerns they do not.

Therese Parks, writing a year later, also mentions some of the rhetorically charged terms teachers used about "General Writing." Like Marianne Davis, Therese produces a critique of the course's goals and language; she also wants to understand the value of empowering students as potentially greater than therapeutic self-realization:

> In General Writing, learning what is expected of a university student in terms of reading, thinking, and writing is mediated by a host of constructed concepts of the self, of the practice and value of writing, and of the teacher's role in the process. It invokes such ideas as the "sovereign individual" and "recovery" in order to suggest a kind of liberatory rhetoric which would have the student believe in the active role s/he is to play in transforming her/his knowledge. I would argue that, instead, the possibility for a mode of action which would position the student as a self-determining agent (rather than as a "literary self") in her/his own learning is an illusion in General Writing. While I recognize the value of making a dominant form of discourse available and accessible to everyone, I am concerned about the appropriation of writing, a potentially very empowering act and medium. (1/20/87)

The distinction between "literary self" and "self-determining agent" was well taken; but in this paper Therese did not follow up her concerned statement about the appropriation of writing. In naming it as "a potentially very empowering act and medium," she honors a rhetoric without giving a reason or relating it to a purpose or motive.

In 1988 another teacher in seminar spoke about her understanding of empowerment. There had been changes in the structure and readings in the "General Writing" course, not least because of critiques like those of Marianne and Therese. Donna Dunbar-Odom, then, reflected a revised classroom and assignment sequence, one that represented itself less in terms of a "literary self" and more in the spirit of Donna's remarks on empowerment:

> To become empowered is to become able and willing to question authority—all authority—in order to see what subtexts may lie underneath the surfaces of declarations, explanations, and exposition.

> This means [students] will know what kind of power language has...If my students are ones on the margin, I want them, through the power of their reading and writing and thinking, to find ways inside; if they are already inside, I want them to understand that those on the margins are coming in. If no one questions authority — on the written page, in the classroom, wherever — and if students do not recognize the power within them to ask these questions, the status quo, which has excluded too many for too long, will remain. (1/25/88)

I read Donna's paragraph as an answer to both Marianne's and Therese's concerns for what empowerment could mean to undergraduates in composition classes. How might we at least talk about English "empowering" students to participate in their own social and political destinies as "self-determining agents," using language that had not already been appropriated (even though language is in some general sense "always already appropriated")? The power comes from informed questioning based in reading and writing, questioning that discounts rhetorics of power and authority, and in that act asserts the agent's and the language's counteraction, power, and authority.

I will end the series by quoting a seminar paper written in 1989, not to close off the issue, but to exemplify a direction in our recent discussions. The writer, Richard Miller, taught a "General Writing" section using texts from popular culture as a test run for an assignment sequence. His stance toward empowerment recalls Donna Dunbar-Odom's description and implicitly proposes an answer to Marianne Davis's and Therese Parks's concerns: "My hope is that by learning how to read their own readings of culture, by learning how to ask better questions, by coming to use their writing to push rather than to terminate their understanding, my students will leave my classroom better prepared to recognize and negotiate the cultural conflicts that define the world we mutually occupy" (2/22/89).

Richard's passage expresses a pedagogical position about empowerment without the need for the god-term itself; he envisions critical conversations about reading cultural conflicts, and sees student writing as a way of pushing understanding, of shaping and negotiating conflicts. His recommendation for teaching honors the pedagogy of problem-posing and exemplifies the intersection of composition and cultural studies enacted by graduate-student teacher.

If we grant empowerment (without taking it for granted) to our students and ourselves, then how might we negotiate our study of reading, writing, and interpretation in ways that speak to the questions and hopes of the four teachers I have quoted? As an ideological term like "empowerment," "negotiation," in this special sense of a culturally and critically informed intervention in the affairs of the world, also has to come under scrutiny in our seminar discussions. If this critical term, or any unexamined theory or pedagogy, develops an orthodox following of pious worshippers, they will have defeated the principles upon which we have based our programmatic reforms. The strength of our principles must lie in our abilities to critique and revise them as we carry them out.

When teachers and students discuss these questions and their relation to literary texts, when students write about them, revise and refocus their work, and subsequently confront the same problems posed about different texts, then I think our new pedagogy and curriculum have accomplished important changes in English studies and undergraduate education in the humanities. The most relevant contemporary critical debates about textual production and interpretation help shape the general education curriculum, upper-level study for majors, and graduate studies and help produce self-aware readers and writers who will, we hope, go on to greater creative independence as they learn to negotiate the professional discourses of the subjects they study.

Some Consequences

Our department has received some recognition in news stories, journal articles, and institutional histories as one of several pioneering the development of cultural studies curricula and programs (Heller A16; Simpson 16; Graff 258; Brantlinger x). Although we have negotiated our way differently than the others, our shared participation in the disciplinary and curricular shift towards cultural studies will continue to frame our department's intellectual development over the coming decade. Two consequences, among many, are worth noting at the end of this paper.

First, we expect that the preparation of our undergraduate and graduate students will differ markedly from past and present norms. Our undergraduates who choose to attend graduate school in English studies will bring a different kind of critical literacy than was developed by the coverage model of study. Our graduates who look for teaching jobs in the 1990s will have very different expectations of the profession, experience in teaching, and specialized knowledge than did their predecessors.

Second, in selecting new graduate students and new faculty for our department, we will seek those who have interests in cultural studies. Not only have we increased the number and quality of our graduate applicants, we have also made significant junior and senior appointments. We have advertised and filled positions in English, American, and minority literatures and cultures, in composition and cultural studies, literacy and the history of instruction, and film and cultural studies. Our new hires have arrived with enthusiasm for turning their research and teaching interests towards cultural studies. Since they arrive without the experience of our curricular development, they also present us with the opportunity to raise and discuss again the rationale and history of our revisions, to continue composing the cultural studies curriculum at Pitt.

Note

This essay grew from talks given at a 1988 meeting of the Ohio College English Association and the 1989 CCCC and it presents curricular revisions in effect through June 1991. Subsequent revisions include the addition of an upper-level course in "Global English," focusing on texts in English produced outside the Anglo-American mainstream, which replaces one of the period surveys required of majors. We have hired a new faculty member to teach and develop undergraduate and graduate courses in this area and to advise about the appropriate inclusion of representative texts across our curriculum.

I am grateful to colleagues and students for permission to quote from unpublished essays, course materials, and papers.

Works Cited

Bartholomae, David and Anthony Petrosky. "Introduction: Ways of Reading." *Ways of Reading: An Anthology for Writers.* New York: St. Martin's Press, 1987. 1–17.

Brantlinger, Patrick. *Crusoe's Footprints: Cultural Studies in Britain and America.* New York: Routledge, 1990.

Carr, Jean Ferguson. "Cultural Studies and Curricular Change." *Academe* 76.6 (1990): 25–28.

Carr, Steve and Mariolina Salvatori. "English 37, Literature and Ideas, Course Description." Unpublished document. Department of English, University of Pittsburgh, 1983.

Freire, Paulo. "The 'Banking' Concept of Education." *Ways of Reading: An Anthology for Writers.* Ed. David Bartholomae and Anthony Petrosky. New York: St. Martin's Press, 1987. 237–52.

Graff, Gerald. *Professing Literature.* Chicago, IL: University of Chicago Press, 1987.

"Guidelines for English 30's." University of Pittsburgh, Department of English, 19 May 1982.

Harris, Joseph. Course Description, English Literature 286. University of Pittsburgh, Department of English, Winter 1989.

Heller, Scott. "Some English Departments Are Giving Undergraduates Grounding in New Literary and Critical Theory." *Chronicle of Higher Education,* 3 August 1988: A15–A17.

Knapp, James F. "Cultural Studies and the English Department." Unpublished essay, 1987.

Knapp, James F. Memorandum to Literature 30 staff. University of Pittsburgh, Department of English, 13 December 1984.

Lanham, Richard. "The Rhetorical Paideia: The Curriculum as a Work of Art." *College English* 48.2 (1986): 132−41.

"The Ph.D. Program." *Graduate Student Handbook, 1986−87*. (Pittsburgh: English Department, University of Pittsburgh, 1986), 21−27.

Salvatori, Mariolina. "Toward a Hermeneutics of Difficulty." *Audits of Meaning: A Festschrift in Honor of Ann E. Berthoff*. Ed. Louise Z. Smith. Portsmouth, New Hampshire: Boynton/Cook, 1988. 80−95.

Simpson, David. "Teaching English: What and Where Is the Cutting Edge?" *ADE Bulletin* 98 (1991): 14−18.

"The Politics of Liberal Education." *South Atlantic Quarterly* 89.1 (1990).

4

A Very Good Idea Indeed:
The (Post)Modern Labor Force and Curricular Reform[1]

Maśud Zavarzadeh
Donald Morton

1

Taking its cue from the conservative students, faculty, and administrators of the English department, the Syracuse University student newspaper, *the Daily Orange*, published a feature article (see Appendix) on the newly instituted curriculum in English and Textual Studies (commonly known as ETS). The article, "ETS Delivers Non-Traditional Approach,"[2] hailed the new curriculum as — in the words of the current (spring 1992) English department chair — a "more complete transformation" than similar "new" curricula developed in other universities (McIntosh 28). (The article is reproduced at the end of this essay.) What the chair calls *trans*formation is, however, a mere *re*formation of the English curriculum. A reformation, it should be noted, made necessary by the radical historical shifts in the U.S. labor force — which makes the new curriculum complicit in (post)modern capitalist practices, and not, as its proponents would like us to believe, the result of "progress" produced by "enlightened" debate.

In fact, the history of the development of the new curriculum is marked by the suppression of radical debate. The reformist character of the new program is nowhere more clear than in the way in which it has so easily and perfectly fit into the existing structure of the academy and its supporting knowledge industry. One might expect that a program which is advertised as a radical transformation — and thus as contrary to the dominant practices — would run into some resistance from the dominant power structure. However, the ETS program has not only been approved by New York State educational authorities, but has also been commodified, with great success, and sold to high schools in the northeastern United States (under Syracuse University's Project Advance) as the latest educational innovation. It is a transformation, in other words, which does not transform anything: it simply meets the existing educational needs of the emerging (post)modern labor force of late capitalism. This is a labor force which needs a more comprehensive grasp of the abstract concepts that provide the matrix of the digital culture of today's transnational capitalism. In this essay, we would like to address some aspects of the "success" of this seemingly new curriculum, indicate its imbrication in capitalist economies, and discuss the politics of curricular reform and reformist practices in the academy in general.

The reform of the humanities curriculum in the last two decades or so has been a response to the changes in postwar economic relations and to the corresponding change in the labor force. The emerging (post)modern economies were heavily dependent on high-tech knowledges. These new economies needed a new kind of labor force: a labor force which, unlike its predecessor, was more capable of "abstract thinking" — of conceptual operations which had become fundamental to the business culture of computers and allied technologies and new modes of management. It was in recruiting for this new labor force that the main weaknesses of the humanities and social sciences curricula became most clear. In the late 1960s and early 1970s — the time in which Japanese as well as German industries began to outperform U.S. industries — the conceptual naiveté of the available U.S. labor force began to take its toll on the national economy and showed itself in the much-discussed loss of "excellence" and the much-publicized inability of U.S. industry to match "foreign competition."

During this period, it became evident that the students who were trained in the humanities were simply unable to deal with the growing complexity of the new forms in which capital was being deployed throughout the world. The literacies they had been taught were the linear and concrete literacies more appropriate for low-tech industrial societies, which justified themselves by the appeal to such traditional (humanist) notions as individuality, certainty, rationality, progress, family, heterosexuality, and a firm belief in the superiority of European intellectual practices. The literacies they had been taught were linear: they were based upon the notion of time as it was formalized in Cartesian philosophy and translated into the high industrial, assembly-line practices of early twentieth-century Taylorism. The Taylorization of the labor force broke down work tasks into their absolute minimum units and thus produced a laborer who, with minimum (pseudo)skill, could perform the job. Taylorism, needless to say, was a fetishization of empiricism and a reification of the concrete and the tangible. All the "linear" laborer had to do was to manipulate objects. Even the managers Taylor introduced to the factory floor in order to safeguard the assembly-line system were merely managers of the already linearized. These linear, concrete literacies were therefore more appropriate for a labor force whose work skills and managerial skills gradually became useless as the industrial base shifted from low-tech to high-tech. It was the gap between the flexible and agile high-tech labor force that was needed and the low-tech labor force actually being produced by the traditional humanities program that created what came to be called the "crisis in the curriculum."

The rising labor force required mental skills which could go beyond the linear and the empirical and produce in workers an understanding, no matter how elementary, of systems operation in general. We have referred above to contemporary culture as "digital." Digitalism, in our analysis, is used not as the cause of changes in contemporary capitalism and labor force.[3] It is, rather, deployed here more as a mediating concept that, in a rather economical manner, points to the shift in the superstructural discourses and practices which are involved in constructing (post)modern subjectivities and "consciousness skills" needed for the rising labor force of late capitalism. The primary reasons for the shift in the labor force (which we shall discuss shortly with the example of the processes of typing and word-processing) are changes in the material base of (post)modern society—shifts in the mode of production and exchange and in the prevailing forms of social relations (class struggles).

The class character of the changes in the curriculum we are describing here become partially clear if we bear in mind that the changes we are marking are taking place not in all U.S. universities and colleges but only in the "elite" ones; that is, in those universities and colleges which, for the most part, produce the managers for the advanced high-tech labor force. The traditional curriculum remains in effect in the universities and colleges which, in the social and academic division of labor, continue to supply the workers of that part of the U.S. labor force still deployed in more traditional (and, in terms of labor skills, backward) industries. As the new mode of production and exchange becomes the dominant mode, the curriculum of these colleges will also change. (The specific form of the U.S. academic hierarchy and its relation to the social division of labor is not the immediate subject of our discussion here.) We are, in other words, using the notion of digitalism to describe an uneven development in contemporary capitalism.

The academy has always played an essential role in the production of the labor force: not only by teaching practical skills (engineering, medicine, pharmacy, law, etc.) but also by producing the appropriate subjectivities for the labor force. In the social division of labor of capitalism, it is the "job" of academic intellectuals to serve capital by providing the practical and theoretical skills it needs to reproduce itself. However, the focus of our attention here is not so much on the (class) role of intellectuals in producing and disseminating theory, as on the historical necessity of theory itself for the training of the rising (post)modern labor force.

To return to our narrative: On the most primitive level, the abstract knowledge needed for the rising labor force is taught (to the lower-echelon workers who are not college graduates) by such skills as computing. Even though these skills are often taught together today in high-school courses in "keyboarding," there is nevertheless a funda-mental difference between the high school students who are taught typing (the trope of the linearity of low-tech industry in which all you had to do was press the keys) and those who are taught "computing." Computing is radically different from typing. Although he or she knows far less than a programmer, the computer keyboard operator needs to know not only the concrete skill of how to press the keys, but also to some degree the abstract pattern of software systems. Our focus here, however, is not so much on the level of the labor force produced in high schools as on the level which is produced in universities.

In universities the higher echelons of the labor force (the managerial levels) were introduced to abstract knowledges through the discourses of "theory." It is helpful here to bear in mind that the function of the humanities, both in high schools and universities, is to develop the *affective* makeup of the labor force: to produce in the labor force the kind of (ideological) consciousness which situates the subject of labor in a manner necessary for the reproduction and maintenance of the existing social relations.

In other words, the humanities curriculum, at any given historical moment, structures the consciousness of the labor force: it teaches the labor force at all levels how to respond to the world in the "right" way. It legitimates the feelings one should have, the emotions one should experience, the vision one should cultivate — in short, it teaches how to interpret the world in the "correct" way. What is proposed as correct, of course, is that interpretation needed for the reproduction of the dominant relations of production. It is the humanities curriculum that teaches the subject of labor what to take seriously and what to laugh at; what to accept as a joke and what to ridicule. In other words, the humanities curriculum formalizes and institutionalizes (in terms of interpretive practices) the appropriate ideological responses to "reality" and inscribes the subject of labor in the "immutable" values promoted as the basis of a "meaningful" life.

The new discourses of theory generated since the mid-1960s have helped to produce the consciousness necessary for the rising labor force: they have put in question the traditional empiricism and positivism that provided the justification for the existing curriculum and argued for a more conceptually self-reflexive and interdisciplinary mode of inquiry redefined ("retheorized") as "reading"—the skill upon which the entire humanities curriculum was founded.[4] It must not be forgotten that the humanities curriculum does not simply produce liberal arts majors and provide graduate training in the humanities. What makes the humanities curriculum so important to the constitution of the labor force is, we repeat, the *affective skills* it teaches. At every historical moment, affective skills are taught that are appropriate to the prevailing mode of production and to existing class relations.

Not surprisingly, then, the first object of inquiry of the newly emerging theory was reading—the operation through which the subject of labor is taught how to produce the experiences necessary for the "natural" continuation of the dominant labor relations. In the new theoretical discourses, reading was no longer regarded as an activity aimed at recovering the meaning placed in the text by the author, but as an operation whose main purpose was to analyze the very processes that produce meaning itself. Reading as an empirical practice, in other words, was replaced by reading as a philosophical and speculative inquiry into the conditions of signification and meaningfulness. At the core of the new practices of reading were no longer the ideas of beauty, coherence, harmony, and so forth, but the differential movement of the sign that fractured the text and marked its difference not simply from other texts (the ideal of "low-tech" reading practices) but from itself. Reading, in short, was no longer an act of mimesis (reproducing the already constituted text), but a demonstration of the impossibility of representation. Reading lost its "concreteness" and became a highly "abstract" and "conceptual" activity—even while it argued against conceptuality itself (for further clarification, see our discussion of textual studies below). Thus, in this new moment of the introduction of theory, reading was shifted from the level of discourse to the level of metadiscourse.

Unlike traditional interpretation (a practice which allowed for the full range of the reader's self-expressiveness and therefore legitimated the text as empirical object, the reader as free individual, and the imagination as supreme), reading was understood as an operation which went beyond the mere connection of the network of reader-text-imagination. Thus reading became an abstract process in which the issue was not the creation of meaning by the individual reader but instead the condition of possibility of meaning itself. With the advent of reading, the reader's individuality was problematized into a very elaborate notion of the "decentered subject," and the text was rearticulated as a very subtle and complex movement of what Derrida calls "différance." The text was no longer a representation of the world, but an allegory of reading — an articulation of the impossibility of any reliable knowledge which can extend beyond the differential movement of the sign. In short, the mimetic knowledge (realism) which had served market capitalism and low-tech industry could not cope with the increasing complexities (abstraction, nonlinearity, binarism, cyberneticity) of high-tech culture. Thus, in the wake of the new theory, there emerged what might be very broadly described as an anti-mimetic, anti-representational humanities.

Suppressing the connection between curriculum and economics, U.S. universities celebrated changes in the curriculum as a sign that the academy is an "enlightened" institution which constantly "examines" itself and produces "new" and "better" knowledges. By relying on this narrative, in short, U.S. universities have suppressed the recognition of the material base and political forces which have made the reform in the humanities curriculum historically necessary in order to preserve capitalism. At the core of the new reform was the introduction of theory to the curriculum. Theory, it was argued, would produce the abstract thinking needed by the new work force of the age of simulation. "Undecidability," "supplementarity," "discourse," the "anagrammatic," and the "differend" were substituted for "harmony," "ambiguity," and "beauty." Likewise, "semiotics," "psychoanalysis," "tropology," and "deconstruction" took the place of "literary history." And, of course, the "texts" of Hegel, Derrida, Heidegger, Freud, Lacan, and others displaced the "work" of novelists, poets, and playwrights. The simulacra of Jean Baudrillard were found to be more relevant to the required managerial skills in the age of simulation and exchange value than the humanist pieties of Saul Bellow. "When the program was first conceived," the *Daily Orange* article quotes a faculty member as saying, "it was assumed that theories such as feminism and deconstruction would be intrinsic parts of the curriculum" (McIntosh, 28).

Under the new regime, the "classics" were read "differentially" and the contemporary fictions that became part of the theoretical canon were either deeply influenced by theory (Kathy Acker) or, in their technomanic textuality, foregrounded high-tech thematics (Thomas Pynchon). Writers such as Acker and Pynchon were not only theoretical in their discourses but also had the additional virtue of providing newer examples of what de Man had defined as the "literary" — the space of rhetorical slippage and epistemological negation. Not only did they teach theory, but they also "resisted" it. They not only offered exemplary sites for the rebirth of the subject that thought abstractly, but they also defended the nomadic self of the "feeling" and "tasting" ludic subject. The old (Cartesian) self, which was killed in the early structuralist thinking, was now reborn in the more advanced texts of (post)structuralism, which was much more responsive to the ideological needs of multinational capitalism.

2

In the Syracuse University English Department, as elsewhere, the recognition of the economic and political base of the crisis for curricular change was also suppressed. Taking into account the shifts in the labor force (and mode of production), we ourselves attempted in the 1980s to produce a humanities curriculum at Syracuse which did not simply produce employees for the new labor force, but also new subjects of knowledge — *critique-al* subjects aware of the historicity and situatedness of their knowledges and their own relation to economic forces. Such critique-al subjects of knowledge are aware of their place in the relations of production and know the close relation between knowledge and various social forces, especially class. In its general articulation, such a curriculum, we ourselves argued in the Syracuse English Department exchanges, would evolve around, for example, a mode of materialist ideology critique which is capable to writing back the process of production (the extraction of surplus labor as the basis of capitalist exploitation) into the naturalized commodity world of the bourgeois university and its underlying knowledge industry. Needless to say, our proposals were defeated.[5]

Instead of offering such a materialist pedagogy, what the new curriculum actually offered was mystified as a sign of the department's intellectual flexibility, agility, and up-to-dateness. However, if one looks at the maneuvers that the Syracuse English Department has gone through from the early 1980s to the present time in order to cope with this curricular crisis, it becomes clear that what is represented as "progress" is in fact a mode of containment and what is advertised as a radical curriculum is basically a calculated reform designed to contain and manage the crisis (by mystifying the connections of theory to economics) and to rob it of its socially progressive potential (of allowing students to see that connection and to intervene in their own production as workers).

The Syracuse Program in English and Textual Studies is the outcome of contestations among traditionalists and theorists, on the one hand, and — most importantly — between the theorists themselves, on the other. In contestations between the theorists, the political economy of the curriculum became foregrounded in a fashion that was not at all clear as long as the battle was seen to be taking place between the theorists and the traditionalists.[6] We would say that the battle between the theorists and traditionalists was in fact over before it began. The humanists (not only at Syracuse but at all other Western universities) did not offer any sustained resistance to theory at all; that is, they did not offer rigorous counter-theories. Instead they retreated into nostalgic (and theological) views of the humanities and of individuality (see, for instance, Steiner), into views that were no longer credible even in the culture at large. The emerging labor force had no use at all for the values which the traditionalists advocated.

However, even though it did not need the notions of the free individual or the idea of interpretation or the theory of a free-standing text, the emerging labor force nevertheless still needed *all the ideological effects* of these concepts. In other words, in order for the new labor force to be created so as to remain cooperative, that force still has to be produced in such a way that it still believed in its own autonomy. This is to say that the ideological effects of humanism had to be reproduced for the creation of the emerging labor force, even though the founding principles of humanism itself had to be abandoned.

Although the emerging labor force did not need a "free" individual in the sense of a coherent, unitary, sovereign individual, it nevertheless still needed a subject who would recognize and acknowledge itself as *not* coherent, *not* unitary, *not* sovereign. In other words, the new labor force needed an individual in a new sense, one that could think of itself as a split subject because a new labor force was itself a split labor force: a dispersed labor force which was appropriate to the new, pluri-central, late capitalism.[7] What the emerging labor force needed was a new subject that no longer thought of itself as an organic whole, but knew it was the effect of complex cultural mediations. What had to be saved was the notion of the subject itself (a viable self in some way separable from social collectivity) — only the way it was made intelligible had to be changed. This new knowledge, nevertheless, still permitted the new split, fragmented, dispersed subject to think of itself as "free." In fact, some (post)structuralist philosophers found a new basis for this freedom which was just as "organic" and as "natural" as that promoted in the organicism of the traditional curriculum: Michel Foucault, for example, anchored the new, split, post-individual subject in the body. If the new subject did not have a "free" consciousness, it still had a "free" body.

This new subject was no longer anchored in the idea of the indivisibility of consciousness (not in the principle, "I think, therefore I am"), but in the undeniability of the body (in the principle, "I feel, therefore I am"). Hence, the crucial battle in the English department was not over the difference between the traditional individual and the new subject, but rather over how the new subject had to be articulated. The contestation was, in other words, over the difference of "difference." Was "difference" simply the effect of the Lacanian "symbolic order" — the post-Oedipal triangulation articulated in cultural prohibitions; the Derridean idea of différance — the disappearance of the securing "transcendental signified" and thus the everlasting slippage of representation and the unavoidable condition of "undecidability"; the Lyotardian order of the "sublime" — the apprehension of the "real" as an endless series of incommensurate "language games"? Or, was it to be articulated as the difference of labor — the difference of private property as the effect of surplus labor? Is difference the difference of a body free in its libidinal playfulness, or is it a body at work — that is, a body as the producer of surplus labor?

It was in this space that those who argued for a materialist (rather than pleasure-alist) understanding of the subject were excluded from the debate and the new curriculum was formulated through the consensus formed between some of the theorists, the pro-(post)structuralists, and some of the traditionalists, who had joined these theorists to reconstitute a new, departmental power center and to exclude proponents of a materialist curriculum. The new curriculum, called English and Textual Studies, is the outcome of this coalition between the traditionalists and the (post)structuralist theorists. What happened at Syracuse was paradigmatic of the widespread maneuver one might call "conservation through renewal." Since we believe that this reconfiguration of the departmental power center teaches a lesson in political struggle, we want to dwell on it a little longer.

3

Bourgeois institutions are highly flexible and have immense powers of endurance. They obtain their flexibility and their staying power by constantly absorbing the elements of culture which oppose them; that is, by reducing critiques to various types of reform. In other words, bourgeois institutions, such as universities, always maintain the ideological practices needed to preserve the hegemony of the ruling classes by constantly adapting to, and adopting, whatever opposes them. Among the most important strategies for absorbing the opposition and maintaining the system is the strategy of inclusion: the institution adopts (and thus adapts to its purposes) the discourses of its adversaries. As a result, reforms take place which manage to defuse the pressure for revolutionary change involving the total structure. It was this strategy that was deployed to ward off radical change in the Syracuse English Department. The adversarial discourses were absorbed, reforms were made, and those radical faculty members and students who insisted on producing discourses that resisted recuperation and thus transgressed the boundaries of the "reasonable" were excluded. They were excluded because their "extremist" knowledges were marked as "nonknowledge," "propaganda," "dogmatic," and "doctrinaire" — in short, as "illiberal."[8]

Of course, we have to explain these tactics for exclusion of the radical more fully because in the university, as in all other liberal bourgeois institutions, nobody is *formally* excluded. In fact, these institutions acquire their legitimacy by claiming total inclusivity (the liberal claims never to exclude any point of view). What happened in the Syracuse English Department happens all the time: the radical thinker is situated on an axis of alternatives such that he or she has the "choice" either of working from within the system or being marked as an extremist who can therefore be legitimately excluded because she can be regarded as "self-excluding." In other words, the options come down to either accepting that existing structures and working within them or finding that there is no space for radical change.

The maneuvers we have just described in the Syracuse English Department have not gone unnoticed on the national scene. Writing in the *Chronicle of Higher Education*, Scott Heller, referring to the "Marxist professors" at Syracuse University who were resisting the reformist project, wrote: They "ultimately refused to work on a committee that drew up a statement of purpose about the new curriculum [that is, "Not a Good Idea"]" (A17). Our concern here is to point out how the refusal to serve on committees is construed, in bourgeois institutions, as the mark of "unreasonableness," "irresponsibility," "extremism," and even as a form of "terrorism." If professors decline to serve on committees and thereby refuse to go along with reformism, such refusals are interpreted as a sign of their absence, as a failure or collegiality and citizenship, rather than as a protest against the existing terms of "collegiality" and "citizenship."

We want to argue that in order to produce any radical change of the system, one has to maintain the notion of an "outside" to the existing system's "inside." This notion is necessary if critiques are to avoid being readily absorbed by the status quo and if certain practices are not to be simply added onto (tolerantly included side-by-side with) existing practices. One way to mark the outside is to invoke the notion of "disparticipation." Of course, existing institutions have no place for political disparticipation — a concept which marks the illegitimacy of the existing system by a refusal to "play the game" according to its present, oppressive, and exploitative rules.

To indicate how dominant groups in the university manage to render disparticipation unintelligible by equating any political practice which is not reformist with the absurd and the ridiculous, we can draw upon our own most recent experience. In January of this year (1992), we wrote a letter to the English department's Chair Slate Committee (which was preparing for the election of a new chair) proposing a new model for the chairship. In place of a unitary singular chair (which, in the English department of Syracuse University and many other departments, has usually meant a white, Euro-American male), we suggested a collective leadership of three persons who would articulate contesting positions in the department.

To our proposal, we received from the current department chair (spring 1992), a response that was both stunning in its personalizing tone and highly revealing in its politics. His response not only ridiculed the model we proposed as a committee of "clowns" and "stooges" (and indeed as a model that could only be proposed by persons who are themselves clowns and stooges), but — most importantly — tried to completely discredit our proposal on the grounds that it came from people who do not "participate" and are not "team-players." His response implies that our absence from committee meetings completely disqualifies our proposal from being taken seriously. In other words, the current chair's letter rehearses the position that change can only be brought about by participation in the dominant system and the games it engenders as "legitimate"; that is, in games which in no way threaten the existing system. Of course, at the core of these games (participation in committees, etc.) is the game of voting, but what is mystified here is the politics of voting as a device of system maintenance. When one votes, whether one votes for or against, one has — above all — accepted the legitimacy of the system of voting. In other words, one is regarded as reasonable only if one accepts the fundamental frame of *participation from within*. The Syracuse English Department chair's rejection of the idea of disparticipation in the dominant games is nothing but a repetition of Roger Kimball's notion of the "tenured radical" as an unacceptable member of the academic community. A "good" academic, on this logic, is a powerless and vulnerable (that is, nontenured) person who is thus subject to the whims of administrators and unable to offer any resistance to the pressures to play the academic game. Somehow, tenure is reserved for "team players."

4

Thus far we have indicated (a) how the crisis in the curriculum is not an internal crisis of the academy but the effect of a shift in the labor force in advanced industrial democracies; (b) how the change in the curriculum is not a radical change but in fact a reformist change within the existing system in order to make it more responsive to the need for a labor force appropriate for late capitalism; and (c) how within universities (including Syracuse's English department), radical proposals and radical forces are, in a subtle "democratic" manner, excluded by completely erasing (as Foucault and Derrida do) any "outside" to the system. In such a climate, as we have indicated, the only legitimate critique is immanent critique — critique from within.

We would like to conclude with a brief discussion of "Not a Good Idea," the statement of purpose for the ETS program mentioned above, which has become the semi-official account of the new Syracuse curriculum written by those who support it.[9] This statement has been widely distributed throughout the American academy as offering a model of change that might be adopted elsewhere, and it is frequently quoted in local articles about the new curriculum. We wish to show how the new Syracuse curriculum inscribed by the program in English and Textual Studies is in fact a very oppressive version of the old curriculum, how its newness is only another version of old, familiar, reformist strategies.

In order to do this, we must first elaborate more fully than we have done above on the broad shift in humanistic inquiry which has been under way in the American academy in recent years. The shift away from humanist traditionalism has moved, on the one hand, in the direction of the new textual studies promoted by those under the strong influence of (post)structuralism, and, on the other hand, in the direction of the new cultural studies promoted by those who oppose pan-textualism, the limiting of cultural analytics to questions of signification, and the consequent erasure of the political economy of knowledge. Unlike (post)structuralists who deny that any difference is "decisive," we believe that there are decisive differences between the two forms of study. While both were produced under the pressure of (post)modern thought, they have quite distinct preoccupations and political implications.

Textual studies is a superstructuralist mode of analysis in which writing — as the trope of intelligibility — is taken to be an autonomous practice: it is non-representational and differential, and it works not according to a social logic but in terms of its own immanent logic. Although textual studies rejects the notion of an intentional consciousness and the associated philosophical vocabularies, it is in the end an argument for the independence of human consciousness. It is, in Bakhtin's words, an analytics that posits that "the word [consciousness] gives birth to the thing [the world]" (182). Thus, textual studies is an attempt to occlude the social production of ideas and feelings in order to produce the (post)modern subject as autonomous, that is, free from class and class struggle. Cultural studies, on the other hand, attempts to write the social back into consciousness and relate its products to the material base, not simply to the materiality of language. Cultural studies is, therefore, an attempt to demonstrate that "it is not the consciousness of men that determines their existence, but their social existence that determines their consciousness" (Marx, 21). Ultimately, what is involved in the academy in the contestation over the cultural logic of intelligibilities between textual studies and cultural studies is the role of mode of production and class relations in capitalism.

To expand the distinctions: Textual studies is concerned with the mechanics of signification (the relation of signifier to signified; thus the emphasis on Saussurean linguistics in the new Syracuse curriculum), while cultural studies is concerned with the production and maintenance of subjectivities; that is to say, with language as a social praxis and not merely a formal system of differences. Textual studies puts in question the validity of cultural studies by proposing a theory of textual *différance*. Because of the effects of *différance*, culture is not available in any reliable way, according to textualists; through language-as-representation, culture is itself subject to the laws of *différance*. But the results of these textualists moves for a political agenda must also be elaborated. Textual studies basically defines politics as those reading activities that delay the connection of the signifier to the signified. Deconstructive politics, in other words, is the interruption of the easy trafficking of meaning in culture (the disruption of *concept*uality by *text*uality). Although it takes the materiality of signification into account, cultural studies, by contrast, in its focus on the politics of the production of subjectivities rather than on textual operations, understands "politics" as access to the material base of power, knowledge, and resources.

The story of recent developments does not end here, however. Under the impact of current academic/intellectual politics, cultural studies has itself split into two opposing modes, a critical and an experiential mode. The dominant form of cultural studies today, which is exemplified by the theoretically updated work of writers such as John Fiske and Constance Penley, must be called "experiential cultural studies." It "describes" various emerging, suppressed cultural groups, and its goal is to give voice to their previously un- or little-known "experience," to let them "speak for themselves." Against this dominant form stands "critical cultural studies," which is a reaffirmation in the (post)modern moment of the concerns of classic cultural studies and which, even in the wake of the (post)structuralist disruption of conceptuality by textuality (the disruption of the signified by the signifier), still privileges conceptuality while accounting for textuality. Critical cultural studies takes as its radical political project the transformation of the very social, political, and economic structures which have suppressed those groups in the first place and prevented them from speaking.

Unlike experiential cultural studies, whose mode is descriptive and whose effect is to give the bourgeois student of culture the pleasure of encounter with "exotic" others, the mode of critical cultural studies is explanatory, and its effect is to alter the settled and exploitative relations between the bourgeois reader and her or his "others." The point of critical cultural studies is not simply to witness cultural events, but to intervene in them; that is, to produce socially transformative cultural understandings. It does so by refusing to take experience (either as the sensations of empirical traditionalism or as the recognition of the signs of a supposedly antiempirical textualism) as a given. To do so is to accept a highly restricted and restricting understanding of the "materiality" of culture; that is, to see the material as what a given subject experiences. In its efforts to produce social *trans*formation (a radical redistribution of wealth and power) rather than *re*formation, critical cultural studies investigates the production and maintenance of subjectivities in relation to the ideologies of class, race, and gender — and the related ongoing struggles over access to power and economic resources.

These modes of knowledge — textual studies, experiential cultural studies, and critical cultural studies — promote (as we have suggested) distinct and competing understandings of the political, the historical and the material, although today's renovated U.S. academy (under the dominance of textual and experiential cultural studies, in close collaboration) is making a strenuous effort to occlude the differences, specifically the difference of critical cultural studies.

To begin with, the reformist character of "Not a Good Idea" is immediately discernible in the program's title, which clearly suggests an unproblematic grafting of traditional English studies (humanism) onto the new textual studies (the new theory). In other words, nothing is displaced; the "new" is simply included — in the manner of bourgeois institutions — with the "old." The document's bourgeois reformism is also evident in its uncritical blending of textual studies with cultural studies. While not a part of the new program's title, the appeal to the concern of cultural studies (with subjectivities) is evident in the document's narrative by which part of the impetus for the kind of change it represents is such movements of the 1960s and 1970s as the Feminist movement, the movement against the Vietnam War, and the Gay and Civil Rights movements (Cohan, et al., 1) — that is, those movements that called the dominant and normative subjectivities (white, middleclass, heterosexual, patriotic, male, etc.) into question in the name of their marginalized others. It refers to these movements as elements of "recent American experience." Alongside this impetus, the document mentions — as the basic ground for its endorsement of textual studies — the impact of (post)structuralist theory. In other words, what "Not a Good Idea" proposes for the new curriculum is actually an eclectic and untheorized mixing of "subjectivities," "experience," and "textuality" — an indiscriminate blending of the categories which lie behind textual studies, experiential cultural studies, and critical cultural studies. This blending is itself an instance of the bourgeois institution's method of absorbing opposition that we described above: the resistant difference represented by critical cultural studies (which moves beyond both experientialism and textualism to connect changes in the curriculum to changes in the labor force) is occluded rather than revealed in "Not a Good Idea."

"Not a Good Idea" also offers a quite self-serving narrative of institutional history which pivots climactically around the hiring (in the mid-1980s) of a new chair from outside the university, whose arrival is seen to coincide with the arrival of "theory" itself and whose first year in office is described as a time of "nearly constant flow of memoranda and position papers" (Cohan et al., 2). What is occluded by this narrative is the fact that the flow of memoranda and position papers had preceded the arrival not only of the new chair but also of quite a few of the others who signed the document. Of its eleven signatories, only a few were at Syracuse when its curricular contestations were begun and of those few, only one or two played any sustained role in those exchanges, a fact which gives the document a distinctly opportunistic and career-istic air.

More important, the writers of the document take great satisfaction in stressing the openness and "publicness" of the exchanges about the new curriculum (they describe it proudly as "the product of the *agora*, the public meeting place" [Cohan et al., 2]); in other words, they shore up the liberal university's claim to "inclusiveness." However, they nowhere mention that they blocked the publication in book form of those memoranda and position papers, which would have made the materiality of the contestations inscribed in them truly public. As excuse, they cite their unwillingness — as one put it, in the best tradition of common sense — "to launder dirty linen in public." However, there was no dirty linen in those exchanges, unless, of course, they meant those strong critiques that did not find their way into the consensus document they have written.

What inclusiveness means, in other words, is the inclusion of those willing to be included in the structures of the status quo. For this political game, the key maneuver is "coalitionism": the dominant group's coalitionist politics proposed the department not as a collective whose general interests are to be theorized but as a set of factions (each supposed to represent, more or less, a single issue) which have to be united by consensus. This is how the limits of theory are set: the pragmatic politician suspends the pressures that theory can put on the various positions in the name of "getting things done." Theorizing stops and the work of the "real world" begins; and by "real world" here we mean the existing world, which is to say the world "as it is."

(In defending theory we do not mean a set of formalistic and merely cognitive processes but an analytics of praxis, taking praxis to mean a grasping of the world historically for the sake of transforming it in a collective fashion). By postulating departmental politics (and intellectual exchange) as basically factional and single-issue politics, "Not a Good Idea" works specifically to block any effort to articulate the curriculum in terms of the kind of global theory promoted by critical cultural studies and finally localizes issues to the extent that the new curriculum itself becomes, in our view, just a set of local topics — history, theory, politics.

While the document tries to pass itself off as the result of a compromise made between departmental factions, it actually represents the coalition that has recently formed in the dominant academy between traditionalists and (post)structuralists — in other words, between "experientialists" and "textualists" — the political aim of which is ultimately to occlude the politically directed agenda of a (materialist) critical cultural studies. At several points the document stresses that "no one is satisfied" with the new curriculum (Cohan et al., 3, 5), as if this were a result of all the compromises made in order to arrive at a consensus. Actually, the text celebrates (quite cannily) the uncertainties of "satisfaction" and underwrites the department's pragmatism with characteristic deconstructive moves. If the new curriculum is "Not a Good Idea," we need not worry since — as (post)structuralism teaches — there are no "good" (in the sense of "autonomous") ideas, for ideas are inseparable from their discursive production. As for the three basic categories used as the "template" of the new curriculum (history, theory, politics), "Not a Good Idea" has this to say: "Each may claim dominance, but their necessary intersection can only undermine such claims" (3). In other words, the categories behave in approved (post)structuralist fashion: they are reversible and emblemize the unending "play of signification." If the curriculum is uncertain and does not know what it is teaching, it then fits quite nicely that notion of pedagogy as "teaching ignorance," which Barbara Johnson, among countless others, has so effectively promoted (see Johnson). Rather than offering a global theory and politics, the new curriculum is merely a renovation and rescuing of the old from the theoretical interventions of critical cultural studies.

"Not a Good Idea" ultimately reveals its strong humanistic streak — in the midst of its supposed (post)modern theoretical sophistication — by tending to write the history of the department in terms of "personalities" rather than "discourses" and "ideologies." As we have already noted, it attaches great significance to the arrival in the mid-1980s of a new department chair (to shifts in *personnel*, not shifts in *discourses*). However, far from heralding the advent of theory at Syracuse, the arrival of the new chair signaled instead the time when, since the vigorous and ongoing theoretical inquiries seemed to be "getting out of hand," attention had to be shifted from theoretical questions to the pragmatic business of putting together a consensus curriculum, a direction that has only increased under the present (spring 1992) departmental administration, whose anti-intellectualism and pragmatism are marked by the current chair's response to our proposal for a new model for the chairship.

From the beginning, our essay has paid special attention to the article in the campus student newspaper, the *Daily Orange*, because we see its appearance as one mark of the bringing-to-completion of the process of institutionalization of the ETS curriculum as an intellectually "up-to-date" and "transformative" curriculum of which the institution can be "proud." However, the reformist character of the new curriculum (and the theoretically and politically regressive character of current local discussions of it) is made quite clear in the *Daily Orange* article, where the "radicalness" of the new curriculum is equated with nothing more than its avoidance of the conventional canon and with a desire for an unspecified and undirected "constant change" (McIntosh 28). That the allegiance of the new ETS curriculum is to *re*formation rather than *trans*formation is clearly captured in the historically and politically freighted slogan, summarizing the effects of the program, with which the article begins: "Literature is dead! Long live literature!" (28). Even more politically telling is this statement: "The ETS curriculum... teaches you to critique responsibly" (28). In the light of what we have said here, it should be clear that "responsibly" is ultimately a code word for "reform." The lesson that such a proposition teaches is ultimately that the only legitimate and acceptable kind of critique is the safe and unthreatening critique that comes from within, the critique that plays the games of existing institutional structures.

Appendix

ETS Delivers Non-Traditional Approach

New Method for Studying English Aims to Avoid Conventional Canon

By Scott MacIntosh

Literature is dead! Long live literature!

Syracuse University's new program of English and textual studies

(ETS) breaks from a traditional approach to teaching English.

The program does not believe that "coverage of a canon is the goal of an education in English," according to a proposal titled "Not a Good Idea; A New Curriculum at Syracuse."

The "canon" often refers to a set of "great books" predominant in traditional English curriculums.

The proposal also says the program seeks to produce not "the traditional 'well-read' student, but a student capable of critique — of actively pressuring, resisting and questioning cultural texts."

The curriculum evolved, according to associate professor Steven Cohan, co-author of the proposal, when professors began offering special topics courses, showing "there was a need in the curriculum" for a different kind of study.

A new leader

In the mid-1980s, a new department chair, Steven Mailloux, was hired for the express purpose of developing a new curriculum, Cohan said.

The ETS program was then developed and finally installed as a major program in 1990. Mailloux continued as a professor, but the department is now chaired by professor John Crowley.

The curriculum is divided into lower- and upper-division levels. The lower division consists of two introductory courses, ETS 141 and 241.

In the upper division, there are three groups of study — history, political and theory. This changes the curriculum from one "organized by chronological period...to a curriculum organized by modes of inquiry," according to a 1990 issue of *The English Newsletter*.

ETS majors are required to take courses in all groups.

Crowley said the ETS program is a "more complete transformation than others."

"We're labelling the approach that we're taking."

"Once you change the categories, you change the way in which knowledge is perceived. Knowledge itself is constructed. It is not natural.

"Every discipline goes through an evolution. Even the most traditional departments have changed."

Constant change

Kenneth Rosen, a visiting professor from the University of Southern Maine, agreed with Crowley. "All departments are in flux," Rosen said. "Few are willing to be museum custodians."

"Statues stand in the park and collect bird droppings. The change is a good thing."

Associate professor Patricia Moody expressed the same idea. "Language is not artifactual," she said. "You don't just study the written word."

"Reading is an ongoing transaction. It can never be finished. The artifactual page and the student's mind are both culturally produced."

Moody said the ETS program brings to the forefront the fact that "there are other countries, other genders, other races. It's more aware of difference. It creates a greater consciousness."

According to Cohan, when the program was first conceived, it was assumed that theories such as feminism and deconstructionism would be intrinsic parts of the curriculum.

Rosen, who considers himself a relatively traditional professor, nonetheless approves of courses in these theories.

"I like ideas," he said. "I'm stimulated by ideas. I'm enriched and rewarded by colleagues who make ideas their business."

Rosen said students who take courses in theory "bring new insights to the texts I teach in my class."

Against the canon

Critics of programs like ETS claim there is too much theory and not enough stress placed on the literary canon.

But Moody questions this criticism, claiming the canon is explored sufficiently by her students.

"It's possible that a student could go through the ETS program and not read some major works, but I believe that my students don't read just in the classroom," Moody said. "I expect that they read on their own."

"The ETS curriculum is empowering," she said. "It teaches you to critique responsibly. The ETS student is going to understand more about less, and that's a fair trade-off."

Joann Blaszczak and Deborah Hepburn teach the introductory ETS class to seniors at Clinton Senior High School in Clinton, N.Y., as part of SU's Project Advance.

They had to "relearn" English to accommodate the ETS program. They originally learned English according to a chronological order of great works and authorial intent, they said.

"I want an integration of both traditional and theory," Blaszczak said. "To ask a student to read a work from a different point of view is great."

Gretchen Murphy, a junior ETS major, agrees. "Literary theory is more important politically than teaching traditional literary canon," she said. "The program should have literature survey classes built into the system."

"We should read books from the literary canon, but we should read them from a different perspective."

Hepburn feels the ETS curriculum is an imposition of beliefs that she would not normally teach in her class.

Moody agrees that "there's a danger of being just as oppressive and blind as the old which it seeks to replace," she said.

Hepburn said the ETS program tends to create an elitist class where "if you learn the discourse, you can join the club."

However, Blaszczak said even though they don't teach the major works implicitly, the application of theories to these works is important to the teaching of English.

Notes

1. In our title we have in mind the title given to the final articulation of the new Syracuse English and textual studies program: "Not a Good Idea: A New Curriculum at Syracuse." As will become clear below, the point of our title is that, far from being "not a good idea," the ideas embodied in that document are very good indeed — that is to say, they fulfill the historical function of producing subjects of labor suitable for transnational capitalism in the moment of the ludic (post)modern.

2. See McIntosh.

3. For a different understanding, see Poster.

4. For a discussion of the role of empiricism and positivism, see Zavarzadeh and Morton, *Theory, (Post)Modernity, Opposition*, especially chapters one and two.

5. Most of our own writing on the need for such a radical shift in the curriculum was done in the 1980s in the form of memoranda to the Syracuse University English Department. Next year (1993) a collection of these memoranda and the responses they provoked will be published as *The Memo Book*.

6. See Cohan, et al. For further articulations of the maneuvers in the struggle between these groups, see Zavarzadeh and Morton, *Theory, (Post)Modernity, Opposition*, especially chapters one and four.

7. One of the major sites of struggle over the new labor force is in Paul de Man's reading of Proust in *Allegories of Reading*. For a detailed examination of the politics of de Man's putting in question metaphor and privileging metonymy as tropes of the early industrial labor force and emerging late capitalist labor force, see Zavarzadeh, "Pun(k)deconstruction."

8. For a discussion of this exclusion, see Heller.

9. For a somewhat more expanded articulation of our critique of "Not a Good Idea," see Morton and Zavarzadeh, *Theory/Pedagogy/Politics*, pp. 23ff. For a parallel discussion of the differences between experiential cultural studies and critical cultural studies, see Zavarzadeh and Morton, *Theory, (Post)Modernity, Opposition*, preface.

Works Cited

Cohan, Stephen, et al. "Not a Good Idea: A New Curriculum at Syracuse." Syracuse, NY: Syracuse University Department of English, 1988.

Heller, Scott. "New Curriculum at Syracuse University. Attacked by 2 Marxist Professors." *Chronicle of Higher Education* 3 Aug. 1988: A17.

Johnson, Barbara. "Teaching Ignorance: *L'École des Femmes. Yale French Studies* 64 (1982): 165–82. (Special issue on "*The Pedagogical Imperative*")

Kimball, Roger. *Tenured Radicals: How Politics Has Corrupted Our Higher Education.* New York: Harper Perennial, 1991.

Marx, Karl. *A Contribution to the Critique of Political Economy.* New York: International Publishers, 1981.

McIntosh, Scott. "ETS Delivers Non-Traditional Approach." *Daily Orange.* 3 February 1992: 28.

Morson, Gary S. *Bakhtin: Essays and Dialogues on His Work.* Chicago: University of Chicago Press, 1988.

Morton, Donald, and Mas'ud Zavarzadeh. *Theory/Pedagogy/Politics: Texts for Change.* Urbana and Chicago: University of Illinois Press, 1991.

Poster, Mark. "Foucault and Data Bases." *Discourse* (Spring-Summer 1990): 110–27.

Steiner, George. *Real Presences.* Chicago: University of Chicago Press, 1989.

Zavarzadeh, Mas'ud. "Pun(k)deconstruction." *Cultural Critique* (forthcoming, Spring 1992)

Zavarzadeh, Mas'ud, and Donald Morton, *Theory, (Post)Modernity, Opposition: An "Other" Introduction to Literary and Cultural Studies.* Washington, D.C.: Maisonneuve Press, 1991.

5

The Syracuse University Writing Program and Cultural Studies:
A Personal View of the Politics of Development

James Thomas Zebroski

The Syracuse University Writing Program is not a program in composition and cultural studies. Nonetheless, because of a peculiar combination of historical and institutional factors, the question of composition and cultural studies is one that is presently of importance to a large number of teachers in the Writing Program. In this essay I will describe the new writing curriculum at Syracuse, briefly problematize one of its underlying concepts — that of development — and show that composition taught as cultural or ideological critique *alone* may have its own attendant contradictions.

This has been a tricky essay for me to write since it will be relatively easy for a reader to focus on one part in isolation and misunderstand the point I am trying to make. So let me begin by saying I am not writing against the idea of development; it has proved to be a generative and humane instrument for thinking about our students, their writing processes and practices, and our studio courses. Nor am I arguing against cultural studies per se; cultural studies has the potential for sharpening our concepts by historicizing them and tracking their political and economic effects. Cultural studies also potentially can make our everyday life with all its contradictions and possibilities for transformation, the subject of our courses and our field.

What I am asserting is that it is increasingly popular to see "development" (and the related concept of writing as "process") in isolation studies, or even as opposed to cultural studies. To disconnect the concepts, to reduce one to the other is dangerous since it reinforces the reigning dichotomy of the "individual" versus the "social" when it is precisely that idea, and the function and structure of the dichotomizing mentality in our historical and cultural milieu, which needs to be critiqued.

The Writing Studios

"Like a studio in painting or design, a writing studio is a place for students to practice a skill and learn an art. In a studio, writers explore the uses of writing as a communication tool and also as a means of discovering what they know" (Temes 1990, 2).

The Writing Program at Syracuse has been in place since 1986, and since that time writing studios for each year of the undergraduate experience have been created. The Writing Program itself is not in the English department, though faculty and teaching assistants often have contractual ties with English. The Writing Program is a semi-autonomous unit located in the College of Arts and Sciences and serving the entire university community. As Louise Phelps has noted, "Writing is perhaps the most pervasive common activity on a university campus — and the irony is, no one notices it. Like the air we breathe, it is a medium we live in — transparent and invisible" (6). One of the goals of the writing studios is to take this commonsense notion of writing and problematize it and support the development of writing in a variety of ways within and outside of the writing studios.

There is purposely a great deal of range in the topics studios examine, though all studios are expected to have a "topic of inquiry" in which teacher and student co-investigate and write from a variety of perspectives on a single issue. This range makes it possible for individual teachers to select topics of inquiry that may arise in cultural studies and that deal with issues of language and power.

Further, teachers are expected to select from a variety of reading, writing, and discussion studio practices. By the end of their writing experience, all students should have as much experience as possible with practices like peer reading and editing of texts, collaborative writing, groupwork, writing heuristics like freewriting, brainstorming, or writing to read (including reading journals and responses) and the writing of reflective essays about the development of reading and writing processes.

What follows is one description of the writing studio courses drawn mostly from my personal experience teaching the studios. This scenario is meant only to suggest what I have done when I taught the studios. It is not meant to be an official account of what all or many teachers do or should do.

Studio I

This freshman course focuses on "writing to learn" and attempts to introduce students to many informal and formal writing practices. Students are asked to look at the full spectrum of writing forms and functions — everything from ordinary genres like lists and notes to journals and academic prose. I have taught this freshman course around the topic of "working," having students investigate (a) working in the world, (b) the work of school and schooling, and (c) the writer's work. Students write about and discuss personal working experiences and compare these with readings from Karl Marx on "Estranged Labor," Erich Fromm on "Work in an Alienated Society," Studs Terkel on *Working*, among others. Students interview people outside of class about work/working and do ethnographic essays on the topic. Finally we read writers on writing and compare their work with ours over the term. We also examine the "work" writing does to locate the writer in a certain position, to place her or him in a certain discourse, in a certain discourse community, in a certain social structure.

Studio II

This sophomore course is a "contrastive rhetoric" course that focuses on reading and writing more complex texts that are concerned with issues of language and power. By contrasting rhetorical acts of and in writing, the class examines discourse communities and the power relations that shape them and their writing practices, and the writer. Using the topic of inquiry of "literacy/literacies," the class reads selections from Tillie Olsen, Richard Rodriguez, Min-zhan Lu, Malcolm X and others to raise questions about the power relations involved in literacy. One issue that arises is the way literacy can empower or silence, depending on one's class location in the social structure. The course addresses what counts as writing in which communities and why, and often gets into the issue of what counts as convention and creativity in writing. Students end the course by doing primary research on local language issues, like racist or class or gender bias in the student newspaper or in textbooks in a discipline.

Studio III

This course for juniors or seniors in an advanced art of writing is a "rhetoric of _____" course. The studio emphasizes a developing expertise in rhetorical practices, rhetorical awareness, and intellectual abilities in specific discipline(s) of expertise. I have taught a "rhetoric of process" course in which I introduce students not only to the idea and experience of writing as a process, but also ask students to do research that puts "process theory" in composition into a historical and ideological context. Students are asked first to experience process and then to situate and problematize the concept of process. Students then go on to do projects that track ideas of creativity or process elsewhere, in other disciplines or other communities or cultures attending especially to the relations in effect between language, power, and knowledge. I have also concluded it is extremely important to provide students a chance to do research writing on whatever topics they find especially interesting, so that students can place their own authentic experience with process among the varied views of process.

Studio IV

I haven't taught this junior/senior course on the writing of professional cultures. The studio asks students to reflect on the writing they have done over their undergraduate career and to consider the postcollege writing they will do. The course provides an opportunity for students to look at the rhetoric of writing in nonacademic settings. Some teachers in the program ask students to investigate aspects of the history of scientific or organization writing, while others look at the power relations in effect in organizations (and government) that affect and define writing products, processes, and situations in those cultures.

Development

The Syracuse curriculum clearly and explicitly privileges the concept of development — the development of student writing practices, the development of teaching practices, and the development of the curriculum as a whole. By "development" we do not mean the more usual idea in composition of remedial or basic writing. Instead development when used to describe the Syracuse curriculum emphasizes contextually sensitive attention to the emerging writer and writing. As Louise Phelps argues, the development orientation "rejects ideas of literacy as a set of limited skills that children learn in component steps and master once and for all. Instead we see written language as profoundly implicated in intellectual and social development; writing and reading abilities grow and adapt to new contexts and needs over the life span" (37). Development then highlights process and reflection on process so that writers know what they know and understand that knowledge is socially constructed and that they are part of and positioned in that social construction of knowledge. Development in the Syracuse writing studios privileges change across time and place, and therefore is often highly comparative.

Development helps us to create writing studios that contrast with more typical freshman composition courses that focus on set-piece themes and formalistic readings that are oriented around modes or aims or patterns, but make little place for the student. Yet while it has been helpful in putting the student and the student's experience at the center of the curriculum, development is also associated with theories from psychology like those of Piaget and Kohlberg that are clearly culturally bound, but also function to reinstate, legitimize, and naturalize ideologically charged concepts. For example, the idea of an autonomous, private, rationalistic, monologic, monolithic, free self is often assumed by development theorists when in fact this postulate needs to be made into a problem for investigation. Such concepts of self play a key role in an ideology of self-help that supports the existing inequitable social and economic structures.

Development theory also has tended to reinforce the concept of a linear notion of time that always seems to place the ruling class and their abilities, whether cognitive or moral or linguistic, at the top of a temporal ladder, implying in that process a "natural" bottom of that ladder. Over and over again developmental theory "discovers" that members of oppressed and marginal communities and cultures perform at a lower ability level than those from privileged groups in society. Edward Sullivan, in a little booklet titled *Kohlberg's Structuralism*, provides one of the most incisive critiques of this use of development, demonstrating that according to Kohlberg's linear schema Martin Luther King's words and deeds fall at the bottom categories for moral development. In using a linear notion of time, development theory too often presses capitalist notions of inevitable progress into service. Also, by viewing time as linear, development theorists privilege a present time that is the end result of past development. History produces this present and therefore legitimizes its existence. Developmental theory by privileging the present as a singular result of the past affirms the ruling structures and groups of this singular present moment.

Further, a developmental perspective has also traditionally excluded any explicit mention of, let alone discussion of, the politics of the ends of development. Such a thinker sees politics as social and development as individual and hence a discussion of the political ends of development and developmental theory can be seen as a digression, as a tangent, as something additional or external to the subject at hand. Such a developmental theorist might see politics as being dragged into the composition classroom instead of being inherent in the very categories we assume and use in our everyday life as teachers.

Finally the uses of language that a developmental perspective may encourage, while on some level attractive because they are so different from positivistic perspectives, sound suspiciously like a description of the emerging high-tech, multinational corporate world that we live in and that is supposedly replacing the outdated industrial milieu. For example, what does a developmental curriculum do when it emphasizes abstraction, reflection, frequent — almost continuous — revision? When plasticity and malleability are seen to be the primary character of language? All of these traits seem to fit nicely with the needs of a late twentieth-century commodity culture to constantly reprocess itself, to present the people supposedly with the "new" and "improved" product and a plethora of consumer "choices," which are then equated with freedom but ultimately reduce our freedom and the potential for transforming our world, if in no other way, by distracting us with the trivial and inconsequential.

Cultural Studies

Still, this does not mean development should be abandoned as soon as possible for cultural studies. Development provides a means of acknowledging the student's experience and affirms the student's ability to reason things out given a supportive context. Cultural studies as I have observed it practiced among a few teachers at Syracuse and elsewhere has too often meant a reversion to old notions of knowledge and its place and function in the classroom. I think some place needs to be made for the student and her or his interests and needs, and in too many culture studies classrooms, despite the recuperation of popular culture as a topic of study, I observe a denigrating of the student's culture and values, and most importantly, her or his ability as a member of a community to produce knowledge.

While the subject may be Bruce Springsteen's concert or 2 Live Crew or Nike pumps, students sometimes find the approach (and language) of cultural studes to be as alien and arid as New Critical formalist analysis was to an earlier generation. Too often, the student may discover that what matters is learning (reproducing) the knowledge (the subject matter and analytic technologies) the teacher (banker) presents (deposits) rather than considering the possibility that all peoples are always already creating knowledge, knowledge which may not be valued by the elite or even may not seem to be knowledge, but knowledge nonetheless. It seems strange that some teachers who came of age at a time when universities paid lip service to the idea that the subject matter of courses should be relevant have little difficulty imposing their relevance on a new generation that may or may not see this as relevant at all. It would be a terrible irony indeed if cultural studies functioned to reinstate (or reproduce) the banking model of education.

But, regardless of whether the class sits in a circle or square or trapezoid or parallelogram and writes on *Eraserhead* or Public Enemy, the key consideration is, in what position do the classroom relations place the student. Is the student seen to be capable of knowledge production? Is the teacher able and desirous of engaging in *dialogue* with the students?

Dialogue is key to the success and ultimate importance of cultural studies to composition and to English studies. It is not possible or desirable to pretend that politics does not exist in the very pores of the classroom, the curriculum, and language studies. Language is not neutral. If it were, it'd be dead. The issue for me is whether I can present questions of language and power in a way that both involves and respects the students. I do not believe that teaching is about indoctrinating the student, either into the ruling-class ideas of the time or into the teacher's position, no matter how correct that view may be. Rather, dialogue potentially creates a space where I can go into the writing classroom and put my commitments and positionings on the table and invite the students to understand these positions, but also to challenge them and to work on making new structures and positions, developing new knowledge about and perspectives on language and power that I can learn and take hope from. I think that in the composition classroom, where cultural studies is most effectively taught, this is what happens.

Paulo Freire in his *Pedagogy of the Oppressed* more than twenty years ago worked through these very issues. He asserts:

> Those who authentically commit themselves to the people must re-examine themselves constantly. This conversion is so radical as not to allow ambiguous behavior. To affirm this commitment but to consider oneself the proprietor of revolutionary wisdom — which must then be given to (or imposed on) the people — is to retain the old ways. The man who proclaims devotion to the cause of liberation yet is unable to enter into communion with the people, whom he continually regards as totally ignorant, is grievously self-deceived. The convert who approaches the people but feels alarm at each step they take, each doubt they express, and each suggestion they offer, and attempts to impose his "status," remains nostalgic towards his origins... To achieve this praxis, however, it is necessary to trust in the oppressed and in their ability to reason (47, 53).

Works Cited

Buck-Morss, Susan. "Socioeconomic Bias in Piaget's Theory: Implications for Cross-Cultural Studies" in *Psychology in Social Context*, ed. Alan Bruss. (New York: Irvington Publications, 1979).

Freire, Paulo. *Pedagogy of the Oppressed*. (New York: Seabury, 1970).

Phelps, Louise Wetherbree. "Making Writing Visible at Syracuse" in *Connections: Ideas and Information from the College of Arts and Sciences*. 3 (Syracuse: Syracuse University, 1987): 6.

Phelps, Louise Wetherbee. "The Spiral Curriculum" in *The Writing Program Sourcebook*. (Syracuse: Syracuse University Writing Program, 1990): 37.

Sullivan, Edward. *Kohlberg's Structuralism*. (Toronto: Ontario Institute for Studies in Education, 1977).

Temes, Delia. *Writing Words: Bulletin of the Writing Program at Syracuse*. Spring 1988. (Syracuse: Syracuse University Writing Program, 1988).

———. *Writing Studios: A Description for Students*. First edition. (Syracuse: Syracuse University Writing Program, 1990).

Zebroski, James. "Writing as 'Activity': Composition Development From the Perspective of the Vygotskian School." Dissertation. Ohio State, 1983.

6

One Person, Many Worlds: A Multi-Cultural Composition Curriculum

Delores K. Schriner

Stark, wind-carved deserts; sharply rising monoliths; sandstone canyons of imperceptible depth and scale: the landscape of the American Southwest is one of vast, elemental forces that overwhelm the understanding and defy classification. No less rich and deeply variegated are the people who have settled this region. Like the Indian Paintbrush, Columbines, Sego Lily, and Larkspur, which blossom in spite of extremes in climate, the people who inhabit the Southwest are of amazingly vibrant variety. Shards of pottery, and petroglyphs carved into the red rocks are a ghostly record of the ancestors of the Navajo, Hopi, Apache, Zuni, and Pai tribes who today struggle to maintain their communities and heritages on vast reservations in the area. More recently, Mexicans, Anglos, and other racial and ethnic groups have come to occupy this region, each bringing with them a different way of seeing the sky and of naming the gorges that split the earth. Today, as always, these groups of people radiate in a dozen different directions like the turbulent rapids of the Colorado River, yet all hang together in a tenuous kind of cultural composition.

Situated within this rare and magnificent array of land and people is Northern Arizona University. As a major site of higher education in the Southwest, the university has long held a dominant place in the societal ecology of this region. Although the university has made efforts to be responsive to the richness and intricacies of the population it serves, a disproportionately high number of students from minority groups unfortunately continue to leave or fail from the university.

Data from 1987, for example, show a 90 percent attrition rate among
Native American students. (Northern Arizona University enrolls one
of the largest populations of Native Americans of any institution in this
country.) Other data demonstrate that difficulty with the discourse
conventions of the academy is a primary factor in these high attrition
figures. The university thus turned to the English department's
Composition Program to create a new composition curriculum that
would provide for more effective literacy instruction and hopefully
lead to greater equity in educational opportunities among students
from all racial and ethnic groups.[1] In emphasizing the priority of literacy
instruction, the university gave important recognition to the fact that
"problems with access of knowledge" are inseparably intertwined with
"levels of literacy" (Scribner, 76).

The relatively new phenomenon of integrating cultural studies with
composition seemed to offer great promise and direction as we set out
to develop a new curriculum for English 101, the first semester composition course which is required of all students. Among the numerous
reasons that support such an integration is the fact that language and
culture have an integral and reciprocal relationship: "The form of
language influences the form of culture; the form of culture influences
the form of language and language change" (Gleeson and Wakefield,
v). Our hope was that a conflation of composition and cultural studies
would not only take our students' cultural variations into account and
provide them with opportunities to explore and reflect on the richness
and variety in their experiences but would also better enable students
to make the immediate transition into the academy and its "book
culture" (Scribner, 76). The factors that influenced our particular hy-
bridization of composition with cultural studies are offered here, as
well as a summary of the features of the curriculum and issues relating
to the teaching of it.

For us, the process of developing a curriculum that incorporated
composition with cultural studies began with a careful examination of
the concept of culture. Obviously, how one chooses to define culture
directly reflects underlying ideologies that will determine both the
theoretical ends and pedagogical shape of such a program. There is in the
literature a veritable sea of definitions of culture, encompassed by
extremes in which the interactions of the individual and society are
portrayed. The classic or traditional view objectifies culture as hermeti-
cally sealed, static entity with measurable, fixed characteristics that
enfold and direct the actions of its members. However, as Jerome
Bruner and others have argued, this timeless societal portrait is "a
fiction used to...legitimate the subjugation of human populations"
(Rosaldo, 42). Anthropologists, sociologists, and others, therefore,
have recently rejected this view and have come to see culture as a

"porous array of intersections where distinct processes crisscross from within and beyond its borders" (Rosaldo, 20) and as malleable, since the members who constitute any given culture are its creators and recreators.

Several factors argued strongly that we also reject the classic definition of culture. For one, the context of our student population clearly supports Mary Louise Pratt's observation that "people and groups are constituted not by single unified belief systems, but by competing self-contradictory ones" (228). Native Americans, for example, are often considered to be one of this nation's most highly self-contained and homogeneous cultural groups and, to some degree, there is truth in this conception. However, while there are certainly distinct cultural practices and ideologies shared by Native Americans, which distinguish them from other cultural groups, it is also shortsighted to generalize that the Native American experience is somehow uniform and fixed. There are great differences not only between tribal nations, but also within these nations. Simply stated, there is no such thing as a singular "Native American experience," just as there is no such thing as a singular "Anglo-American experience."

Additionally, research in the field of ethnic and cultural studies has demonstrated that accepting the classic definition of culture can result in pedagogical practices far removed from the political and social urgencies that initially led to the formation of ethnic and cultural studies. Multi-cultural or cross-cultural curricula based in an objective definition of culture often result in "presenting students with ethnic stereotypes of how they might expect members of Culture X to act under certain clinical circumstances" (Vasquez, 30) or in recognizing minority groups only in terms of their difference or distance from dominant social groups (Perry and Pauly, 17). At its worst, that is, presenting culture objectively can further entrench and perpetuate stereotypes and provide for greater segregation among groups by ignoring the "processes that lead to sexism, racism and the conditions that make for the continued oppression of people" (Macedo, 2). At its best, this approach is one-sided in that it leads students merely to a simplistic understanding of how one belongs and fits into groups, without considering the subjectivities that work to create cultural experience and practices. Thus, this approach denies the processes by which one both fits into and becomes creator of cultural groups, processes which are not mutually exclusive: "Indeed, the interactions of fitting and creating are the essence of our contradictory lives" (Irby, 2).

In the spirit of Paulo Freire, who states that "culture is just as much a clay doll made by artists who are his peers as it is the work of a great sculptor, a great painter, a great mystic, or a great philosopher; that culture is the poetry of lettered poets and also the poetry of his own popular songs. . .culture is all of human creation" (403), we decided to develop a curriculum around an expansive and porous conception of culture. In adopting such an approach, however, we faced a dilemma similar to that which caused Renato Resaldo to speculate, "If we envision a world where 'open borders' appear more salient than 'closed communities,' one wonders how to define a project for cultural studies" (45). We began by deciding that our curriculum must first recognize all students as being multi-cultural and all as having experience moving between and within communities of open rather than closed borders. We then decided that the curriculum must provide students with opportunities for examining the movement across these borders, as well as opportunities to explore and understand how they are both creators of and created by their multi-cultural social realities. Central to this exploration are the ways in which practices of accommodation, resistance, and opposition (Giroux) work to promote or deny individual subjectivities in a social world. Such explorations, we hoped, would provide the basis from which students could begin to "politicize their lived situatedness in dominant or subordinate cultures" (Macedo 1), while also helping them gain insight into and a measure of control over their immediate transition into the university.

"One Person, Many Worlds"

In our quest to translate this theoretical foundation into practice, we decided upon a generative theme for the course which recognizes all humans for having multi-cultural social realities: "One person, many worlds." The reading and writing assignments that evolve around this theme provide for the exploration of an individual's interplay with his or her social and cultural worlds. Students, that is, are asked to consider the various worlds that they live in and the ways in which they make transitions between these worlds. We chose to use the word "world" because it refers more broadly to all "forms through which people make sense of their lives, rather than more narrowly to [culture as] the opera or art or museums" (Rosaldo, 26). Using "world" rather than "culture," in other words, allows students to look at a broad range of human experience which may or may not seem "cultural" in the classic sense of that word.

In practice, the curriculum is comprised of fourteen sequenced assignments. Seven assignments concern the readings and seven are personal writing assignments.[2] These assignments are clustered into three series. Each series spans approximately five weeks. The first asks students to consider notions of individuality and the ways that individuals control and direct their experiences. The second series asks students to consider the social and cultural factors which also work to control and direct experiences, and the third asks students to reflect on the intersections between individuality and society. In addition to prompting reflection on these issues, the assignments are designed to foster critical thinking and the development of interpretative abilities. As it is conceptualized and formulated in this curriculum, however, critical thinking does not equate with the more familiar term, "thinking skills," which is generally articulated outside of an experiential context. In the sense that we use it, critical thinking takes place in the act of composing itself, in the engagement of reader and text, and in the act of self-reflection. Thus, this form of inquiry is founded largely through the struggles for interpretation and making meaning of both text and personal experience.

In Our Time by Ernest Hemingway and *Double Yoke* by Buchi Emecheta are the two texts for the course. This selection of texts has not gone without criticism; the most vocal opposition contended that using a novel by an African feminist and another by a traditional Anglo-American male is blatant tokenism. These texts, however, were selected for their dialectical interaction with each other. Each presents highly divergent ways in which characters from different eras and cultural milieu confront the interplay between individuality and society.

Assignment Series 1: Defining Individual Experience

We begin this assignment series by asking students to describe a change in "worlds" that they have undergone:

Personal Writing Assignment No. 1

As new college students, you have had to leave behind a world that is familiar to you for the unfamiliar, new world of the university. For this assignment, we'd like you to write about this or another change in "worlds" that you have had to make recently. Choose a transition that has somehow altered your life, your sense of self, or the way you go about certain things. Reflect on the circumstances that prompted this change. Describe the experience as completely as possible.

The wording of this assignment, as well as the others which follow, is intentionally vague, thereby allowing for responses as diverse as the students themselves. While many students chose to write about making the transition into the academic world, others wrote about the births of their children, marriages, and religious or cultural ceremonies marking their transition into adulthood. A large number of students wrote about overcoming alcohol and substance abuse, adjusting after a divorce or a death in the family, and of suicidal thoughts or attempts. These vastly divergent responses set the stage for highly rich classroom dialogue in which students began discussing disjunctions and connections between their individual stories. They also began discussing what their cultural heritages consist in and came to see that culture is something more than formal, fixed events or observable structures, such as ceremonies. Many Anglo students reached the surprising revelation that they, too, "have culture."

Since personal experience in itself is blind (Eagleton) and it is only through the struggles of interpretation that experience comes to have meaning (Giroux), the next assignment in this series asks students to begin to interpret and make critical sense of the experiences that they addressed in the first personal writing assignment. In other words, while the orientation in the first assignment is descriptive or "information-driven" (Hunt and Vipond 1986, 1987), the second switches to a "reflective" orientation (Lavery and Straw 1986). The second personal writing assignment, then, asks students to consider their roles as individuals in controlling or directing their change in world.

Personal Writing Assignment No. 2

In your first personal essay, you described a turning point in your life. Making such a change necessarily involves making decisions and taking action. For this assignment, we'd like you to return to this situation and think about how you responded to it. When confronted with change, what kind of decisions did you make and why? What kinds of action did you take and why?

The third assignment in this series asks students to detach themselves as much as possible from their understanding of their change in worlds and to adopt what Britton refers to as a "spectator stance." Students are asked to envision other perspectives and alternatives, and to speculate about how a decision to act differently than they did in regards to their world change could have transformed the nature or outcome of this experience. Here students begin to become aware of the ramifications of choosing one option over another and of how one decision necessarily obviates other potential outcomes.

Personal Writing Assignment No. 3

You may have heard people say, "If only I knew then what I know now..." Return to personal writing assignments #1 and #2 and ask yourself, "If I could do it all over, how would I respond to this transition in my life?" Write about how you might meet this challenge differently. Then tell us why you would change your approach. Speculate on the outcomes of this new approach. Would things now be better for you? Why or why not?

While students are writing about these themes in terms of their own lives, they are concurrently considering similar issues in three parallel assignments concerning *In Our Time*. These reading assignments, as well as the others which follow, are intended to complement the personal writing assignments by encouraging students to use personal associations as a means of entering and exploring the text. The first reading assignment asks students to describe a character that they find particularly interesting and to look at different facets which comprise the world of this particular character; to consider, that is, the variety of complementary and contradictory circumstances that create this character's experience.

Reading Assignment No. 1

For this assignment, we'd like you to focus on one of the characters in *In Our Time*. Pick a character you find interesting or relevant and then tell us as fully as you can: Who is this character? In what world does this character find himself or herself? That is, what are the particular sets of circumstances (time, place, way of life, codes of conduct, etc.) surrounding the character? Next, write about why this particular character stood out for you. Did you associate with the character and his or her situation? Why?

The next reading assignment asks students to focus on a story about *In Our Time*'s main character Nick as a youth or adolescent and to understand Nick in terms of how he is challenged by the circumstances of his particular world and the ways that he meets these challenges. The third assignment focuses on Nick as an adult and how he confronts the problems or complications posed by his adult world. Students are encouraged to consider how his decisions and actions as an adult compare with his decisions and actions as a youth, moving beyond superficial conclusions, which point merely to the fact that Nick acts differently because he is older, to the underlying experiences which have caused him to make certain decisions and act in certain ways. By looking at the ways Nick changes through different phases in his life, we hope to reinforce the notion that changes in worlds are an essential part of the development of one's identity and that we carry frameworks for knowing from one experience to another.

Assignment Series 2: Exploring Social Forces

The purpose of this series of assignments is to move students towards what Fiore and Elsasser call "literacy in its most profound sense," by using reading and writing as a means to make the links "between their own lives and larger social contexts" (291). In these assignments, students begin to investigate the relationships that exist between individuals and their social worlds; to consider more fully, that is, the social contexts that envelop individual experience. At the heart of this series of assignments is an exploration of the ways in which the processes of accommodation, resistance and opposition (Giroux) function in the interplay of personal subjectivities and social values and ideas.

These assignments cast students' notions of individuality, which they explored in the first assignment series, into a rather foreign and often uncomfortable light since most embrace a Western ideology which glorifies the individual experience.

The series begins with reading assignments about *Double Yoke*, which tells the story of undergraduates at a Nigerian university who must confront the conflicting demands of the modern world (represented by the university) and their traditional, tribal worlds. In the first reading assignment, students are asked to choose a character that they find particularly interesting and to consider how this character must accommodate himself or herself to either the modern or tribal worlds. Accommodation, according to Giroux, refers to instances in which individuals must adjust, reconcile or compromise themselves to certain conventions, often without fully understanding or questioning these conventions.

Reading Assignment No. 4

Throughout the novel, characters find themselves being pulled in various directions by the expectations of the tribal and modern worlds. Within each of these worlds there are differing expectations about marriage, family, the roles of men and women, etc. In this assignment, focus on one of the characters that you find interesting or relevant. Then describe a way in which the modern world or the tribal world affects this character's behavior. How, in other words, is the character bound or constrained in what he or she can do or say by the demands and expectations of this world?

This fourth reading assignment created highly charged discussions in which students asserted that in Africa, perhaps, individuals must accommodate, but not in America, the land of the free. Students, in other words, initially resisted the idea that they had at some point in their past, or may at some point in the future, display accommodational behaviors, and they often blamed such behaviors on weaknesses or character flaws. Their resistance to this idea, however, led perfectly into the next assignments. For the next two assignment on *Double Yoke*, students are asked to consider issues of resistance and opposition. Opposition refers to deviant behaviors that run against the grain and prevent or block learning or societal progress (Chase, 14–15). Resistance also refers to opposition but "redefines the causes and meaning of oppositional behavior by arguing that it has little to do with the logic of deviance, individual pathology, learned helplessness (and, of course, genetic explanations), and a great deal to do, though not exhaustively, with the logic of moral and political indignation" (Giroux, 107). We ask students to first consider how certain characters display oppositional or resistance behaviors when they refuse to simply order their lives around the terms set forth by the tribal or modern worlds. They are then asked to consider what happens when characters go against the stream and if their behaviors threaten or enhance the traditions and values of the tribal or modern worlds.

Reading Assignment No. 5

In the previous assignment, we looked at how characters in *Double Yoke* were confronted by conflicting demands of the modern and tribal worlds. If we stopped here, it might seem that the role of the individual is minimal. In fact, however, there are many instances in the book where the characters display their individuality and refuse to order their lives in terms of their tribal or modern worlds. For this assignment, we'd like you to consider what happens when a character tries to break with the demands or expectations of the tribal or modern worlds. That is, how does this character assert his/her individuality and go "against the stream?" Next, consider what happens to this character as a result? What are the ramifications?

In the final assignment on *Double Yoke*, students are asked to consider the interplay among accommodation, resistance and opposition. Can the conflicting demands of an individual and his or her society be resolved or reconciled, and what is gained and what is lost in this resolution?

Reading Assignment No. 6

In the last two assignments you looked at characters caught in a "double yoke." For this assignment, look specifically at ways that these double yokes are resolved. That is, how do the characters incorporate these conflicting demands into their lives? What part of the modern or tribal world do they accept? What part do they reject? Do you agree with the choices these characters make? Why or why not?

Three personal writing assignments run parallel and concurrent to these reading assignments. In the first, students consider the degree to which they were constrained in intervening in their social environment and were either forced to or chose to accommodate as they made their transitions in worlds. In the second, they consider if they displayed any oppositional or resistance behaviors as they made this change.

Personal Writing Assignment No. 4

In the last assignment, you considered what you might do differently in terms of an event that has changed your life. For this assignment, we'd like you to think about that same event but now consider those things that you wouldn't have been able to change — even if you could go back and try to do it all over again. That is, how were you constrained or restricted to act in ways that you might not have wanted to? Why?

Personal Writing Assignment No. 5

Once more, return to the "world change" you have been writing about since the beginning of the semester. Analyze yourself as you have analyzed a character in *Double Yoke*. How did you assert your individuality in the situation that you were faced with? How did you break away from the demands or expectations of your world. Why did you choose to go against the stream? What were the consequences?

The final assignment in this series asks students to analyze the ramifications *of displaying oppositional or resistance behaviors*. In this sense, they come to understand how resistance or opposition can be a means of asserting one's individuality, but also that these behaviors may bar them from acceptance into a community. On the other hand, this assignment also encourages students to see that these behaviors can work to appropriate the expectations and demands of one's social world to one's own needs.

Personal Writing Assignment No. 6

Once more, return to the change you have been writing about since the beginning of the semester. Analyze yourself as you have analyzed a character in *Double Yoke*. How did you attempt to break away from the demands or expectations of your world as you made this transition? How did you choose to go against the stream? How did you ultimately, if at all, end up resolving this conflict?

Assignment Series 3: Perspectives and Insights

In this final series of assignments, students are asked to reflect on and merge all of the work they have during the semester, and to take a new critical stance towards the events they have been writing about. In other words, this assignment attempts to move students beyond the simple act of reproducing what they have already produced into further development of their stories. This paper not only serves as a synthesis of the variety of interpretive strategies students have learned during the semester but works as a presentation of students' new ways of understanding and seeing their movement between worlds. This assignment is carried out through three drafts over a three-week period.

Personal Writing Assignment No. 7

We have spent the semester thus far reading, writing, and talking about crossing from one world into another. In the process, we have reflected on the ways such transitions are made, and the tension that often exists between the expectations of the world around us and our own individual expectations. For this assignment, we'd like you to refer to all of the previous assignments, and to tell us what you have learned about yourself and the transitions you have made from one world to another.

This assignment is, in essence, a major revision of everything you have done in this class throughout the semester. It will require that you carefully review everything you have written, read and discussed, and then assess the significance of this material. We want you to do more than retell the stories you have already told. Now ask, what does it all mean? How do the facts add up? What have I learned about the world that I live in? What have I learned about myself as a member of many different worlds?

Following Bartholomae and Petrosky's lead, these term projects are bound by a local copying center into a collection in much the same way that "course-paks" are produced. Students are informed at the beginning of the semester that this collection of term projects is a required text, which they must purchase. Thus, the students' own texts are taken as seriously as any of the other published texts they are required to read. According to Donaldo Macedo, having the class read the collective term projects and to ground methods of inquiry into the students' own texts "is a Freirian emphasis, and an excellent one at that...which brings together lived histories and critical reasoning" (2).

The final reading assignment asks that students synthesize the variety of experiences reflected in this collection. Although synthesis is the goal of this assignment, we caution students to avoid presenting simple universals and thus falling into the trap we hoped to avoid as we created this curriculum — the trap of objectifying culture and making stereotypical comments about cultures and cultural interaction.

Reading Assignment No. 7

You have now read the final essays of students in your class. For this assignment, we'd like you to consider if there are any patterns that emerge from this collection. That is, /Are there themes or similar experiences that run through the essays? Are there similarities in the ways students dealt with the situations they faced? Are there commonalities in the conclusions and generalizations the students have reached? Look next at differences. Consider an essay that seems decidedly different. Compare the differences you note to the patterns or similarities. How do you account for these differences? Do the differences invalidate any conclusions you may have drawn? Why or why not?

Teacher Training

As described earlier, our reasons for conflating composition with cultural studies were complex and numerous. Since the approach to teaching composition which arose from this conflation is somewhat out of the maintream, it was necessary to develop a teacher training program that would familiarize instructors with the pedagogical aims and goals of this curriculum as well as its theoretical underpinnings. This proved to be no small task since this curriculum was to be used program wide by forty graduate teaching assistants responsible for eighty sections of composition. The training of these instructors was carried out in two phases. First, they were required to attend a weeklong summer workshop. The curriculum and a sixty-page supplemental teaching handbook developed specifically for this curriculum were sent to these instructors well in advance of the workshop. Although the teaching assistants arrived at the workshop familiarized with the program through these materials, instructors were nevertheless confused and concerned, as well as excited, about the prospect of teaching composition from this strange and different angle. Paradoxically, experienced teachers were often the most confused and concerned, as their prior experiences were so greatly distanced from this pedagogy. New teachers, with no framework within which to place the curriculum, more quickly adapted themselves to its agendas and approaches.

The first two days of the workshop focused on discussing the theoretical framework that informed the curriculum. We then addressed three primary areas in relationship to the teaching of it: generating and maintaining class discussions; grading and commenting on papers; and cultural awareness or sensitivity. The foundation laid during this workshop was extended and built upon throughout the fall semester in a required seminar for which the instructors received three graduate credits. This seminar provided the setting for further exploration of the theories which inform the curriculum and additional ways in which these theories might be translated into pedagogical practices. Bartholomae and Petrosky's *Facts, Artifacts and Counterfacts: Theory and Method for a Reading and Writing Course* was a required text and provided teachers with a thorough overview of the program at the University of Pittsburgh, upon which this curriculum was based. A "course-pak" containing most of the readings listed in the bibliography to this chapter was also required.

Central to this two-part training prograam was familiarizing the instructors with notions and practices of creating a dialogic classroom. Here we were informed by the work of Paulo Freire, who explains that dialogue is at the heart of critical reflection, and by theories of the social construction of knowledge which hold dialectical reasoning as the foundation of its thought (Bruffee; Bizzell; Meyers). What this meant in terms of training teachers was moving them from familiar lecture and teacher-centered practices to discussion and student-centered practices. Substantial time was devoted during the teacher training sessions to ways of creating dialogue in the classroom, particularly through a workshop approach to evaluating student papers. Borrowing once again from Bartholomae and Petrosky's model for teaching composition, workshopping student papers is a central pedagogical feature of this course. Each day, at least one student is required to workshop his or her paper in class. All discussions about issues raised in the assignments and the readings are to originate from the students' texts.

The concept of dialogue as central to critical reflection is, of course, not limited to classroom practice. The assignments in this curriculum, which may appear repetitive to some degree, are intended to have students entertain multiple points of views, arguments and counter-arguments, and to come to see the many ways of reading their experiences. Their texts, then, are considered to be dialogic in nature, and through them students should become more aware of their own positions and feelings. The dialogic and personal nature of these assignments place special demands on teachers in their roles as evaluators and graders. Here, Jan Armon's work provided us with direction in helping teachers to understand their role in evaluating and commenting on personal writing. Since the assignments are geared toward helping students to probe deeply into the meanings of their experiences, the teacher should provide comments that help students move beyond mere reporting of events into constructing and reconstructing these events. In addition, teaching personal writing "requires more frequent and directed encouragement from the instructor" and "the personal nature of the writer's commitment may require a comparable commitment in response" (Armon, 176). This means, in part, that the teacher should offer to her students what their texts have meant to her and how she may have connected the students' experiences with her own (Armon, 178). In other words, this curriculum requires that teachers reconsider their relationship to their students. We envisioned what Paulo Freire called a "teacher-student, student-teacher" relationship in which the teacher becomes an integral member of the classroom community rather than acting as an individual outside that community.

Because this curriculum is geared towards looking at issues which are culturally driven and because the students at Northern Arizona University are so diverse, we devoted a large amount of time in the workshop and seminar to issues of cultural sensitivity. Our discussions centered on how teacher attitudes, which all too frequently have generated remarks at Northern Arizona University such as "Native American students don't read by nature," can trigger resistance to the educational process and destroy student's self-concepts. Such comments and attitudes may also be one of the most important factors contributing to the high percentage of minority students who leave school, "only later to be profiled by the same system as drop-outs or poor and unmotivated students" (Macedo, 3). One highly successful approach that we used to address these issues, involved panel of individuals from a variety of cultural and social backgrounds who discussed the positive and negative aspects of their educational experiences.

At the same time that we provided our instructors with a standardized curriculum and attempted to orient them towards it, we also strongly invited them to deconstruct this pedagogy as they learned about and taught it. We asked that teachers, like their students, become critical and reflective of not only their past experience but of their present situations and roles in the university setting. Although we had created a curriculum that we hoped was somehow immune to perpetuating the status quo, we also realized that all institutionalized curricula, by definition, work to legitimize dominant values. Without ongoing interrogation of the values embedded in curricula, teaching methods may continue to negate the history, culture, and language practices of many students. As Donaldo Macedo explained to us, "Teachers who are unreflective and uncritical act as agents to perpetuate the status quo and reproduce the dominant normative values which, by and large, work against the very students they teach." Encouraging teachers to critically analyze the curriculum as well as their role as teachers in the university educational setting led to some exciting and unexpected results. Many innovative pedagogical modifications were developed throughout the semester in response to the particular needs of various classes—far too many to list or discuss here. In addition, the teaching assistants began questioning the terms and conditions of their employment and their marginalized status within the English department and they set processes into motion that resulted in a pay increase and graduate student representation on departmental committees.

Conclusion

It would be greatly pleasing to conclude with an array of tables and charts and other data that prove beyond a shadow of a doubt the great success of this program; however, because it has been used for three semesters thus far, only preliminary data is available. Essay tests scored by trained readers before and after the program do demonstrate a statistically significant improvement in the writing abilities of those students enrolled in this course, compared to those who took a traditional composition course based upon the modes of writing. Of course, students in this new curriculum wrote and read substantially more than students in the traditional course, which is probably at least a partial explanation for the increased scores. Follow-up research also indicates that there may be a slightly lower attrition rate among the students who were enrolled in this program over those in the traditional course. Of course, we cannot say that this course alone accounts for this difference.

There is no instrument sensitive enough, however, to measure what is really important about this program: Have students become more aware of the way they as individuals interact with their worlds, and have they taken greater control over their social contexts? Although we do not have statistics in regards to these questions, we do know from reading scores of students' texts and from the subjective impressions of the instructors that many of our students seemed to have had profound insights into their past experiences and that they are turning these discoveries into practices which provide them with greater control over their present day realities, as the following excerpt from a student text illustrates:

> It seemed like the reality of living life on the reservation would limit my abilities. I wondered for a long time what it would be like to go back to school, what kind of competition I would face. I had no idea how I would pay for my school and I did not know if it was too late for me to get an education. I had frightening feelings because I had no answers to these questions and yet I was determined to become a teacher.
>
> My imagination of becoming a teaching originated from weaving rugs. Weaving involves a great deal of preparation, discipline, time and energy before a rug can become a finished product. Much like the process of weaving, in order for my dream to become a reality, I had to go through preparation. Now, I have moved from the reality of living on the reservation as a weaver to my imagined goal of coming here and becoming a teacher. My will power created this dream and now my will power will produce the reality.

From the instructors, reactions to teaching this course ranged from favorable to profoundly favorable. While there is an apparent rigidity in the structure of the program, it in fact allows teachers great freedom to incorporate themselves and their own agendas. Working from a common curriculum also helped the teachers to develop a sense of community and a shared "mission." They also came to develop a healthy critical attitude towards the teaching of composition, which in turn helped to make them more powerful teachers and scholars.

While we have taken a stance to teaching composition that is quite distanced from the norm, we have not done this merely as an attempt to be radical or different but as a means of best addressing the context of our particular student population. Toward this end, we remain constantly critical of this curriculum and are currently looking towards ways to revise it. We hope that others who are interested in the curriculum presented here and who may be thinking of trying it in their own classroom would do the same. That is, we don't expect the same outcome from this curriculum if it were simply transplanted to rural Nebraska or urban Detroit; rather, we would encourage a careful exploration of the context in which it would be applied. As Paulo Freire explains, every educational program should be contextually specific and should be designed with careful critical analysis of the needs of the student population in mind.

Notes

1. This project was funded by a grant from the Ford Foundation and Northern Arizona University. I would like to thank the many people who have helped to move this project from a conception to a reality. First and foremost, I would like to gratefully acknowledge the invaluable contributions of my colleagues Victor Villanueva, who collaborated with me in writing the curriculum, and Matthew Willen, who helped me prepare this text for publication. The Ford Foundation made it possible for us to invite David Bartholomae, Susan Benally, Patricia Bizzell, Lynn Bloom, Donaldo Macedo, Harvey Kail, and Anthony Petrosky to Northern Arizona as consultants and evaluators of this project. I would like to thank them for their comments, advice, and encouragement. Many other colleagues at Northern Arizona University also played an important role in various phases of this project, including Paul Ferlazzo, William Grabe, John Paddison, Deirdre Mahoney, Jeannette Deschenie, Loma Ishii, Ingrid Estell, Joel Daehnke, Speed Campbell, Dean Hargrave, Richard Hight, Newman Clark, and Carol Rodriguez.

2. The influence of David Bartholome's and Anthony Petrosky's approach to teaching composition, which is detailed in *Facts, Artifacts and Counterfact: Theory and Method for a Reading and Writing Course* can be found throughout this curriculum. I would like to thank David and Tony for serving as consultants to this project and for encouraging the liberal adoption of their methods.

Works Cited

Armon, Jan. *Functions of the Personal, Reflective Essay as Academic Writing.* University of Michigan: Unpublished dissertation. 1988.

Bartholomae, David and Anthony Petrosky. *Facts, Artifacts and Counterfacts: Theory and Method for a Reading and Writing Course.* Upper Montclair, NJ: Boynton/Cook, 1986.

Bizzell, Patricia. "College Composition: Initiation in the Academic Discourse Community." *Curriculum Inquiry* 12 (1982): 191–207.

Britton, James. "Viewpoints: The Distinction Between Participant and Spectator Role Language in Research and Practice." *Research in the Teaching of English* 18 (1984): 320–31.

Bruffee, Kenneth A. "Social Construction, Language, and the Authority of Knowledge: A Bibliographic Essay," *College English* 48 (1986): 773–90.

Bruner, Jerome. *Actual Minds, Possible Worlds.* Cambridge: Harvard University Press, 1986.

Chase, Geoffrey. "Accommodation, Resistance and the Politics of Student Writing," *College Composition and Communication* 39 (1988): 13–22.

Emecheta, Buchi. *Double Yoke.* New York: George Brazziler, 1982.

Eagleton, Terry. *Literary Theory: An Introduction*. Oxford: Basil Blackwell, 1983.

Fiore, Kyle and Nan Elsasser. "Strangers No More: A Liberatory Literacy Curriculum." *Perspectives on Literacy*. Ed. Eugene R. Kintgen, Barry M. Kroll, and Mike Rose. Carbondale: Southern Illinois University Press, 1988. 286–99.

Freire, Paulo. "The Adult Literacy Process as Cultural Action for Freedom and Education and Conscientizacao." *Perspectives on Literacy*. Ed. Eugene R. Kintgen, Barry M. Kroll and Mike Rose. Carbondale: Southern Illinois University Press, 1988. 398–409

Giroux, Henry A. *Theory and Resistance in Education: A Pedagogy for the Opposition*. South Hadley: Bergin Garvey, 1983.

Gleeson, Patrick and Wakefield, Nancy. *Language and Culture: A Reader*. Columbus: Charles E. Merill Publishing Company, 1968.

Hemingway, Ernest. *In Our Time*. New York: Charles Scribner's Sons, 1958.

Hunt, R.A. and D. Vipond. "Evaluations in Literary Reading." *TEXT* 6 (1986): 53–71

——— "Aesthetic reading: Some strategies for Research." *English Quarterly* 20 (1987): 178–83.

Irby, Charles. "Ethnic Studies in the Twenty-First Century: A Proposal." *Explorations in Ethnic Studies* 11 (1988): 2–11.

Macedo, Donaldo. Letter to the author. 31 March 1989.

Meyers, Greg. "Reality, Consensus, and Reform in the Rhetoric of Composition Teaching." *College English 48* (1986): 154–74.

Perry, Robert L. and Susan Mae Pauly. "Crossroads to the 21st Century: The Evolution of Ethnic Studies at Bowling Green State University" *Explorations in Ethnic Studies* 11 (1988): 13–22.

Pratt, Mary Louise. "Interpretative Strategies/Strategic Interpretations: On Anglo-American Reader Response Criticism." *Boundary* 211.1–2 (Fall/Winter 1982–83): 201–31.

Rosaldo, Renato. *Culture and Truth: The Remaking of Social Analysis* Boston: Beacon Pres, 1989.

Scribner, Sylvia. "Literacy in Three Metaphors," *American Journal of Education* 3 (1984): 6–21.

Vasquez, Jesse. "The Co-opting of Ethnic Studies in the American University: A Critical View." *Explorations in Ethnic Studies* 11 (1988): 23–36.

7

Giving Religion, Taking Gold:
Disciplinary Cultures and the Claims of Writing Across the Curriculum

Christine Farris

Under the banner of an alliance between cultural studies and composition studies, I would like to do two things. The first is to share some conclusions my colleagues and I have reached from an investigation of student writing in disciplinary cultures. Our study indicates that the extent to which students were able to engage in critique in their writing was shaped not so much by their capacities to think critically as by the belief systems of particular disciplines and individual instructors. In the uses that were made of student writing and the classroom practices that informed it, we witnessed a power struggle between students and instructors. Despite the potential of writing to initiate students into critical practices, the rhetoric operating in most of the classrooms we investigated upheld the discipline's foundational knowledge and status quo (Farris).

Consequently, I would also like to interrogate not only the assumptions that underly the discursive and pedagogical practices of disciplines but the assumptions of the writing across the curriculum movement as well. It is my hope that an English studies link with cultural studies will move us beyond the global claims about commonality and difference, made so often by interdisciplinary studies and writing across the curriculum, toward the accumulation of more local knowledge of the actual classroom cultures where students, teachers, ideology, and disciplinary norms intersect. While a link between cultural studies and composition studies offers a hopeful look at what *is possible*, such a link must also involve what *is practiced* in the culture, that is, cultural studies *of* composition.

It is perhaps inevitable that cross-disciplinary writing specialists whose origins lie in English departments will always be "colonizers." In our dealings with non-English disciplines, what we are doing is constructing an "other" that is either a methodologically sophisticated ideal of ourselves or an inferior version of ourselves in need of completion.

Writing Across the Curriculum, in theory, assumes (1) fields not unlike our own are already inviting initiates to join interesting "disciplinary conversations" and engaging in the sorts of practices *we* hope to foster; or (2) after colleagues are "converted" in writing across the curriculum workshops, writing in their courses will function in the ways *we* want it to: as a mode of learning or as a social behavior characteristic of a particular discourse community.

Those of us in composition studies who have turned our efforts toward writing-intensive courses in other disciplines don't want to think of ourselves as "colonizers." We would never admit to perceiving differences between our approach to writing and those of other disciplines in terms of superiority and inferiority. We would probably never say publicly that we know best how people think, read, and write or that textual interpretation is strictly *our* business. Nor would we want to be accused of merely projecting our own values on other disciplines in order to insure that the work of English departments remains relevant: "Oh, look, biologists keep journals; economists revise; anthropologists and physicists interpret. They are hermeneut beings just like us."

In *The Conquest of America*, Todorov accuses Christopher Columbus and all colonists since of being alternately guilty of these attitudes toward the colonized—either projecting their own values on the natives or viewing them as inferior. Both, says Todorov, are attitudes that grow out of their desire to convert and ultimately exploit—give religion and take gold and land in the name of the king. What is denied in both attitudes, he says, "is the existence of a human substance truly other, something capable of being not merely an imperfect state of oneself" (42). These are attitudes grounded in an egocentricism that writing across the curriculum, like interdisciplinary studies, as Stanley Fish maintains, can never escape (19). In the case of writing across the curriculum, as with the missionary conquistadors, it is an identification of our own values with values in general, "of our *I* with the universe—in the conviction that the world [or at least the curriculum]...is one" (Todorov 42).

I may be stretching the analogy here, but I think it is an appropriate one if we consider that, like Columbus', writing across the curriculum's spiritual expansion may also be linked to material conquest. In our zeal to tally up disciplinary evidence that would legitimize writing across the curriculum's claims, gain converts, or even extend the borders of English departments, we are often guilty of reading into disciplines what we want to be there, or *not* be there. We may take advantage of current efforts to "blur genres" and disrupt what cultural and inter-disciplinary studies now consider the artificially constructed, self-contained systems that are "disciplines." Too often we assume that we are in some sort of unmarked position that allows us to encourage faculty to help students critique the very terms of analysis in a discipline that serves as its foundation. To what extent is it possible for English-trained academics working in cross-disciplinary writing programs to acknowledge how disciplines and their discourse are "*not* like us," but different, perhaps even something "truly other"?[1] How might acknowledgement of this otherness help us move writing across the curriculum into what Charles Bazerman has called its "second stage," beyond the successful institutionalization of an idea to an investigation of "the roles written language actually takes in disciplines and disciplinary classrooms" (209).

Now that I've acknowledged the difficulty if not the impossibility of true interdisciplinarity, let me say that I'm not a nihilist, but rather intend to carry on as if different disciplines could speak to one another and struggle together at making the curriculum responsive to change. Because we do want, dare I say, converts, and we want to keep cross-disciplinary writing programs alive at large research universities as well as at small colleges, it is my hope that even as we work out of our commonality, we will respect the differences among disciplines, among individual members of those disciplines, and differences among the different discourses they produce.[1]

Now I will admit that many of us who voyage across the curriculum to consult with faculty on their uses of writing do not find in other departments streets paved with the gold writing across the curriculum promised. Along with the treasure, we often find ways of approaching material or reading texts that arrive at right and wrong answers, close off conflict, and fly in the face of many of WAC's claims. In short, they do not always do it "the way we do at home." We encounter the biologist who is more concerned with grammar and correctness than anyone in English ever was. For every Hayden White there is an historian who is only interested in the correct facts, and for every Clifford Geertz there is an anthropologist who has no intention of sharing the construction of the terms of analysis in his field with his students. For every window of possibility we find for students to write their way toward critique we find a colleague who limits students to regurgitating information, sometimes in the guise of "analysis," so that the instructor's or the critics' analyses must become that of the students.

While it may be unfair to imply that what writing-across-the-curriculum people really do is "give religion and take gold," what if we discover writing in our disciplinary explorations that has no intellectual consequences for the student? What if we don't see writing playing an active role in the construction of knowledge? What if we see that, aha, the natives are not yet converted? Are we able to shrug and say, "It is truly other," and not jump in to remedy by force what is "an imperfect state of oneself"?

As soon as English-trained people start thinking we just plain "know better," that is the point at which we should attempt to work against the "colonizer" mentality and investigate further how thinking, reading, and writing function epistemologically and ideologically in those instructors' courses and disciplines. Though Stanley Fish is probably right that we can never transcend the paradigm of our own discipline, cross-disciplinary writing program staff should at least make an attempt to "get inside," to get local knowledge of how this particular culture functions for these citizens. If for no other reason, we need to find out from where students get their impressions of what constitutes "truth" or the "right answers" in the course along with their perception of the criteria that will be used to evaluate their writing.

In an effort to "get inside," my colleagues and I designed a three-year study to take a closer look at what we were learning from students in the writing lab and from interviews with faculty who had taught their courses as writing-intensive for one semester. We were particularly interested in investigating one of the claims programs make for writing in the disciplines—that it enables and strengthens the site for critical thinking. We wanted to know what really went on behind the classroom doors of those colleagues who had agreed to make their courses writing-intensive: Does what *they* practice have anything to do with that *we* preach?

We combined ethnographic "thick description" of classroom practices with two other lines of investigation, oral interviews with students before and after taking a writing-intensive course and an examination of those students' papers written in the course. Both the student interviews and the papers were rated on scales of critical and reflective thinking derived from the work of William Perry, Mary Belenky, Carol Gilligan, Karen Kitchener, and Patricia King.[3] Thick description of the full social, rhetorical, and political context in which writing-intensive courses were taught helped us determine why the level of critical thinking displayed in the writing was not consistent with the level students seemed capable of in the oral interview. Our research team studied at close range for a full semester writing-intensive courses in journalism, art appreciation, and human and family development.

Space does not allow me to report all of our findings from this study. Suffice it to say that my colleagues and I are certainly more realistic and reflective writing-across-the-curriculum advocates for it. We have a better sense of how instructors' classrooms actually function as interpretive communities. We have evidence of pedagogical strategies that seem to encourage or discourage independent thinking and writing. We have observed on a daily basis the extent to which writing is tied to inquiry and integrated with course goals in the way it is assigned, shared, analyzed, and evaluated. We are able to say, finally, that the degree and type of critique students are permitted to engage in their writing is contextually determined and includes students' responses to the assumptions of the discipline, the belief systems of the instructors, and the extent to which those instructors have reflected on these in planning and carrying out class assignments and activities.

Two excerpts from our case studies will illustrate the kind of things we now know more about. This was not the sort of knowledge that we would have been able to come by simply from interacting with faculty in large workshops or even from meeting with them one-on-one to talk about writing in their courses.

Journalism: Point/Counterpoint

Professor Walker views his discipline, journalism, both philosophically and technically. For him, journalism is a too-often maligned profession responsible to a democratic society, as well as a set of writing skills and rhetorical strategies to be mastered if journalists are to reach and keep an audience. At first it appeared that these dual allegiances would result in contradictions. Early in the course he testified as to the importance of writing-intensive courses ("They make you think"). He underscored his belief that journalism belonged as much in the liberal arts as in a professional school and that many of the issues they would discuss in class would pose "tough ethical questions" to which there would be no right answers.

However, as the semester progressed, and the course took on its flesh of definitions, conditions, categories, causes and effects, contradictions faded and it became apparent that Professor Walker's approach to critical thinking was consistent with the approach generally taken in his field. Students were to master the "Principles of Journalism" (a title he prefers for the course to the one in the catalog, "Mass Media and Society") and apply, rather than critique, those principles in their research and reporting by converting subjective opinion into contextualized, well-documented, objective journalism.

As very-soon-to-be-technicians, his journalism majors do not have the liberal arts luxury of critically examining the sources of their subjective responses to the issues under discussion, nor, in his view, do they have the need to analyze competing theories or viewpoints for the purpose of committing themselves to one. He repeatedly told the class, "We don't care what *you* think in these papers on ethical issues."

Professor Walker raises questions for discussion (and for potential paper topics as well) by having students consider two sides of a polarized issue and provide a balanced view of the world. In doing so, he replicates the way in which journalism both mirrors and constructs the values of a democratic society with a two-party system for arriving at justice. The course focuses primarily on issues of the First Amendment and the implicit belief that truth will emerge from a diversity of viewpoints argued fairly. Controversies that surround standards and practices in journalism are raised in class discussion, for example: "Should the names of rape victims be published in the newspaper along with those of alleged rapists?" Our research assistants came to refer to this phenomenon as "the ghostbuster effect" — issues were introduced in class, they floated in the air for discussion, were labelled tough questions, and then zapped back out of existence.

The terms of analysis, the assumptions behind, say, the ten functions of the press in society or the five major criticisms of the media remained intact ("list-making," according to our observers), and were reinscribed on multiple-choice quizzes and exams. Those disciplinary assumptions were only occasionally brought to bear directly on a new problem or challenged by a student's position on an issue.

Professor Walker's only class remarks about the two major papers, other than that they were to objectively address two sides of an issue in journalism, stressed form and stylistic matters, outlining, and proper citation and footnoting. He warned against the use of the first person because, "Remember, we don't care how what you think or how you feel." While this caveat is intended primarily to address matters of style, it affects more than pronoun choice. In the concluding paragraph of one of the assignments, students were asked to reveal what they "think is the best thought on the subject at this time," but ratings on many of the papers reveal their lack of personal engagement.

At first it might have seemed like Professor Walker was inconsistent — that he failed to model a socio-political or ethical analysis of a research issue that is unsettled in order to arrive at an informed, reasoned, and committed critical position. But this was not contradictory at all if one considers that Professor Walker's brand of journalism, whether he is having students write *in* it or *about* it, is more a technical, if not a sophistical, rhetoric than a philosophical one.

Art Appreciation: "I Know What I Like/I Like What I Know"

The art instructor we observed, Professor McLean, like Professor Walker, had some difficulty clarifying to herself and to her students what role their own "thinking" about art was to play in their response to her writing assignments. In applying to make her course writing-intensive, she had designed a series of assignments that she hoped would engage students in interesting rhetorical approaches to the course material she had been teaching for a number of years, via large lecture, some discussion, and quizzes and exams.

In this first run-through as a writing-intensive course, however, the sequence of assignments was not very well integrated with the purposes for the course that she retained from years past. Like Professor Walker, she felt that students needed to master certain foundational principles, in this case, of art, that would enable them to appreciate and understand differences in style and technique. The bulk of her course, as might be expected, provided definitions of the basic tools: form, mass, line, color, realism, and expressionism, and illustrated these through slides shown apart from any historical or cultural context.

One of Professor McLean's stated goals for the course, not unlike Professor Walker's, was that students be aware of multiplicity — that there is no one, right interpretation in art, and that they too can come to "know what they like" and support their preference by demonstrating some formal understanding. "The assignments," she said, "make room for many ways of thinking, but we do have standards by which we can talk about visual arts and defend our thinking." Early in the course she presented students with a modification of Bloom's taxonomy as the "Steps to Art Criticism": observation, description, analysis, interpretation, evaluation. She gave the initial impression that her approach to course material and the tasks that students would be encouraged to perform in the writing assignments would follow this scheme.

It was the perception of the research team, however, that this scheme was not successful in eliciting writing that would presumably move students through analysis in the direction of informed and committed evaluation of art. Unlike Professor Walker, who could justify the absence of subjectivity as part of journalism students' "fluency in the discipline," Professor McLean's goal of wanting to validate students' subjective response to art finally conflicted with her desire that students master the "objective" principles, "the knowledge base," as she often referred to it. And the principle site of this conflict or failed integration was the writing assignments.

Most of the assignments as they were described in the syllabus required that students create a persona and an "audience" for their supposed analysis: "Describe a visit to the campus museum to your best friend." "Convince your roommate with whom you are decorating an apartment that there are merits to nonrepresentational art." "Imagine you are Edvard Munch explaining to two visitors to your studio what it is you are trying to achieve in painting *The Scream.*" In class, when she would provide hints for writing the papers, McLean would make adjustments: "Even though you are speaking to your friends, I want you to actually write to me or your teaching assignment, someone learned in the visual arts, so you will want to use your class notes and textbook to write formally and intelligently, using the concepts we have covered so far: medium, implied surface texture, color, line, space, shape, mass, and so on."

Most students approached the assignments in one of two ways: they took their cues solely from the affective dimension in the course, as demonstrated in certain segments of class discussion ("How does this make you feel?" "In this painting by Rousseau, where do you think the lion is sleeping in relation to the woman?") and figured, if there are no right answers, then one interpretation is as good as another. Or, they played it safe and cut-and-pasted their lecture or quiz notes into a received pseudo-interpretation that relied primarily on technical description, not genuine analysis, for support.

It was the sense of the research team that the latter may have reflected the more accurate assessment of Professor McLean's real objectives. Despite the playful "mindset," as she called it, which would make the assignments more "personally relevant," writing for her was still the act that takes place *after* learning has happened. Papers, even supposed informal ones, were not exploratory or even attempts to support a gut response with reasoned analysis, but *fait accompli* interpretations sanctioned by the critics.

How did students get this message? Not only from direct discussion of criteria for the papers, but also from her approach to her subject. When first presenting a slide of a painting—for example, *In the Cafe*, by Emil Nolde, the German expressionist—she would ask that they use the deductive method to analyze. "What's the general impression, and then we'll move to particulars." She would solicit responses until a student provided the one she was looking for: "Sinister? Yes, that's what the critics say...Yes, that's what we feel. Now you are becoming intelligent observers."

In implying that "intelligent observers" agree with "the critics," Professor McLean is validating a correct response (or at least the *idea* of a correct response) that frames the interpretation that a culture presumably shares, effacing the complexities of potential individual responses—gender, class, race, history—not to mention differences among individual critics or competing theories of art.

If I were to say that Professor McLean was not yet able to conceive of the role writing might play in students' development and refinement of a critical perspective on art or that she has only begun to consider the variety of ways that writing might be used to extend or critique that foundational "knowledge base" characteristic of an introductory course, I fear that I may have to return to Todorov's analysis: I am as guilty as Columbus in conquering the Indians. After all, Professor McLean had implied more than once that the reason one took an art appreciation course was not to be able to write one day for *Art Forum* but to avoid the charge of cultural illiteracy at cocktail parties.

Of course, as an ethnographer I am not merely describing and interpreting custom. Ethnography once looked out at a clearly defined other — the primitive, the preliterate. Now ethnography, James Clifford reminds us, "encounters others in relation to itself, while seeing itself as other" (23). Certainly, we have learned more from our disciplinary "subjects" about what it is we "do" (and can't claim that we do) in writing across the curriculum than they will ever learn from us. But, as Vincent Crapanzano has put it, the ethnographer always in a provisional way comes to terms with the foreign and "renders it familiar while preserving its foreignness at the same time" (52). This acknowledgement of foreignness, of difference, while rendering it familiar and arriving at a final interpretation is also the job of writing-across-the-curriculum specialists. And yet, they must do even more than the ethnographer. They are charged with transforming that culture, getting it to change in some way, exploiting it.

Our ethnographic studies of the cultures of particular courses has made it clear that our colleagues across the campus don't always view inquiry in their disciplines in the ways we had imagined. We don't always agree with faculty on the changes that could be made when writing plays a bigger part in a course. We don't always agree on how much of a voice students should be encouraged to have in the disciplinary conversation. Our research has enabled us, however, to discuss our differences from an informed position and the writing program staff to do a very specialized kind of consultation with the instructors we have investigated. In several cases, the writing program was able to award instructors like Professor McLean summer stipends to work on re-conceiving the connection between writing and other aspects their courses in light of what we all learned from the study. In the end, however, instructors make the changes they want to make, changes that very likely yoke writing to *their* theory of the role language plays in the construction of knowledge, changes that tie writing more closely to *their* course goals. These are theories and goals we now understand much better, however, having immersed ourselves in their course culture. Professor Walker's assignment that calls for two sides of an issue will probably always conflict with our original hope that students in writing-intensive courses will generate a committed position that drives the analysis of an unsettled issue. But we now understand the place of that assignment in Walker's world view and the profession into which he believes he is initiating students. Eventually, he did agree to have teaching assistants hold conferences with students for work at the invention stage so that, rather than choosing from a stock list of topics, students might at least identify an unresolved issue in journalism that was of interest to them.

The most successful writing-across-the-curriculum programs, the ones that endure and grow beyond the-people-like-us are those that finally relinquish some colonizing in favor of more faculty ownership of the changes that the incorporation of writing will make in courses and in pedagogy. It is my sense that the writing-across-the-curriculum programs that will last will be not only those that convince faculty to "understand the rhetorical nature of their own work and make conscious and visible what was transparent," as David Russell has urged (300), but those that take their own advice on "revision," that are willing to continually re-see and readjust their training materials and claims in terms of the actual disciplinary student and instructor practices they encounter every day.

Hope for tying writing to learning, critical inquiry, and meaningful change lies in dealing with it as locally and as discipline- and professor-specifically as possible. We must maintain a dialogue between locally produced classroom knowledge and global theoretical knowledge if we are to continue to explore meaning-making and discursive practices throughout the university. Those of us from English may forever be the original "colonists" (there will always be an English), but an effective writing-across-the-curriculum program, if it wishes to keep operating into the nineties, must gain the trust and the disciplinary familiarity that only the "natives" can give.

Notes

1. Writing across the curriculum will forever be caught in a paradox: the rise of the university allows for specialization and difference that generates writing embedded in specialized knowledge communities, but in isolating a reason to use writing, WAC advocates must work from some vision of schooling: a belief in a developmental learning scheme, a faith in curriculum reform permitted by writing, or an idealization of those "other" discourse communities whose paradigms and reflexivity English emulates and hopes to reproduce in writing across the curriculum. None of these can ever be the same as a disciplinary insider's inquiry which the outsider simply cannot fully know or enact.

2. In order to resist reinscribing the unified liberal arts ethos or a too-easy interdisciplinarity that ultimately privileges English and to increase our chances of dealing with other disciplines on their own terms, I believe that we should house WAC programs outside of English departments.

3. I would like to acknowledge my co-investigators on this project: Raymond Smith of Indiana University and Douglas Hunt and Phillip Wood of the University of Missouri.

4. Perry, William J, Jr., *Forms of Intellectual and Ethical Development in the College Years: A Scheme*, (New York: Holt, Rinehart and Winston, 1970); Belenky, Mary Field et al., *Women's Ways of Knowing: The Development of Self, Voice and Mind*, (New York: Basic, 1986); Gilligan, Carol, *In a Different Voice: Psychological Theory and Women's Development*, (Cambridge, MA: Harvard University Press, 1982); King, P.M., et al., "Sequentiality and Consistency in the Development of Reflective Judgment: A Six Year Longitudinal Study," *Journal of Applied Developmental Psychology* 10 (1987): 73–95.

Works Cited

Bazerman, Charles. "The Second Stage in Writing Across the Curriculum." *College English* 53 (1991): 209–212.

Belenky, Mary Field, et al. *Women's Ways of Knowing: The Development of Self, Voice and Mind.* New York: Basic, 1986.

Clifford, James. Introduction. *Writing Culture: The Poetics and Politics of Ethnography*, edited by James Clifford and George E. Marcus. Berkeley: University of California Press, 1986. 1–26.

Crapanzano, Vincent. "Hermes' Dilemma: The Masking of Subversion in Ethnographic Description." In *Writing Culture: The Poetics and Politics of Ethnography*, edited by James Clifford and George E. Marcus. Berkeley: University of California Press, 1986. 51–76.

Farris, Christine, Raymond Smith and Phillip Wood. *Final Report on Critical Thinking in Writing Intensive Courses.* Office of the Provost, University of Missouri, September 1990.

Fish, Stanley. "Being Interdisciplinary Is So Very Hard to Do." *Profession 89.* New York: MLA, 1989. 15–22.

Gilligan, Carol. *In a Different Voice: Psychological Theory and Women's Development.* Cambridge: Harvard University Press, 1982.

King, P.M., et al. "Sequentiality and Consistency in the Development of Reflective Judgment: A Six Year Longitudinal Study." *Journal of Applied Developmental Psychology* 10 (1987): 73–95.

Perry, William J, Jr. *Forms of Intellectual and Ethical Development in the College Years: A Scheme.* New York: Holt, Rinehart and Winston, 1970.

Russell, David R. *Writing in the Academic Disciplines, 1870–1990: A Curricular History.* Carbondale: Southern Illinois University Press, 1991.

Todorov, Tzvetan. *The Conquest of America: The Question of the Other.* Translated by Richard Howard. New York: Harper and Row, 1984.

8

"Writing About Difference":
Hard Cases for Cultural Studies

Richard Penticoff
Linda Brodkey

Some twenty years ago, James Kinneavy introduced *A Theory of Discourse* with a formidable catalogue of the institutional barriers facing composition:

> Composition is so clearly the stepchild of the English department that it is not a legitimate area of graduate study, is not even recognized as a subdivision of the discipline of English in a recent manifesto put out by the major professional association (MLA) of college English teachers, in some universities is not a valid area of scholarship for advancement in rank, and is generally the teaching province of graduate students or fringe members of the department. (1)

That composition dismantled many of these institutional defenses in a remarkably short time is a testament of sorts to the virtues of scholarship. Composition is now a legitimate area of graduate study at many state universities, recent MLA "manifestos" declare composition to be a field, and at many state universities, at least, scholarship on writing counts for tenure and promotion. That improved conditions for scholars does not necessarily extend to teachers is nowhere more evident than in the Wyoming Resolution's critique of the continued institutional misuse of graduate students and part-time faculty to staff most college writing courses (see "Statement of Principles and Standards").

Far too many composition teachers still work under appalling conditions, even in those institutions where there are graduate programs in writing and where research on writing is grounds for tenure and promotion. They teach too many courses and too many students a term, and they are neither paid well enough nor prepared well enough to teach writing. Most of the professoriate can justify treating writing teachers as guest workers in the academy, for most probably imagine writing pedagogy to be much as Ian Watt once represented it, simply a matter of doing "all the hard and often unpleasant work of reading and correcting a lot of student papers week after week," even if they do not also share his conviction that composition research and English handbooks alike "spy upon the obvious" (14). Composition *is* pedagogy. But pedagogy can be reduced to correcting student papers only if you imagine yourself to be the writing police, for those who make a fetish of grammar or style also imagine themselves to be protecting the literate from the illiterate who threaten the powerful homology of one nation/one language/one culture, without which such prescriptions would be revealed as the self-interested protection of privilege that they are.

"Students' Right to Their Own Language," the resolution adopted by the members of the Conference on College Composition and Communication in 1974 and reaffirmed several times since, publicly denounces ill-informed and self-serving language policies as "false advice for speakers and writers, and immoral advice for humans" (see preface to "Students' Right to Their Own Language"). The syllabus drafted for "Writing about Difference" at the University of Texas may not address precisely the same issues as the 1974 resolution, but opposition to the syllabus is curiously reminiscent of the political climate in which the resolution on language was drafted and ultimately adopted. Whether the controversy is about dialect or difference, it seems, opponents just say "No," perhaps because difference and dialect alike challenge "many long held and passionately cherished notions about language" ("Students' Right to Their Own Language," 1).

As it has come down to us from poststructural language theories, difference tries to account for the practice of defining by negation, of accentuating the positive, so to speak, by distancing the positive from the negative term in a pair or set and hence affirming the positivity of the preferred term at the expense of that from which it "differs." That we can make these distinctions in language is a tribute to the human intellect, except when we forget that we must then take responsibility for the consequences of defining real human beings as different. Unlike diversity, a word that recognizes variety without attempting to analyze the part language plays in making distinctions among people, difference challenges the culturally and socially sanctioned practice of imputing extraordinary human value to some people by diminishing the worth of others. In other words, "ability" and "dis-ability" may be an arbitrary linguistic pair, but the legal and educational consequences of being defined as "disabled" or "abled" are not arbitrary (see Brodkey, "Transvaluing Difference" and "Articulating Poststructural Theory in

Research on Literacy"). It matters a great deal whether you are the unmarked (normative) or marked (deviant) term in such pairs as white or black, Anglo or Hispanic, American or Asian American, male or female, straight or gay, young or old, monolingual or bilingual. Such binary oppositions are more than theoretically interesting examples of human cognition, for the processes of defining by negation are sometimes used to justify the political and economic practices of exclusion.

Among other things, difference falsifies the analytical and pedagogical fiction that form is literally separable from content. To our minds, it is a fiction that serves the interests of neither students nor teachers, if only because most students believe that teachers talk form but mean content, and good teachers worry that students may be right. Yet when writing teachers assume the right to assess the content of student writing, they disturb the order of things, notably, the common sense belief that grammar, style, and rhetoric are independent of the production and reception of knowledge. Language conveys ideas or reality or even truth, but plays no critical part in their construction. Writing programs which attempt to institutionalize the rights of teachers and students to assess the content of writing risk being deemed presumptuous, the more so if that right is claimed on behalf of graduate students and lecturers. For what amounts to a right in "content areas" is likely to be seen as unwarranted privilege — a license to indoctrinate students or an open invitation for instructors to impose a particular political bias — in a first-year writing class. No matter how unjustified the charges, they are believed because many believe pedagogy to be a matter of transmitting culture by precept and correctness to be the reigning precept in writing pedagogy. According to this logic, composition teachers, themselves a marginalized cohorts whose intellectual work with students remains marginal to the institution, may legitimately transmit lessons on grammar, style, and rhetoric, but transgress disciplinary boundaries if they raise questions about the quality of the assertions writers make.

The syllabus for "Writing about Difference" celebrates students and teachers by inviting them to conduct sustained rhetorical inquiry into a topic troubling many people in this country — difference. And to our minds, any writing course that positively values the intellectual labor of students and teachers goes a long way toward celebrating the field of composition itself. An ad hoc group of faculty and graduate students worked on the syllabus during the summer of 1990. Membership in what become known as the Ad Hoc Syllabus-Writing Group was open to anyone scheduled to teach the course in 1990–91 and consisted of the director of Lower Division English (Linda Brodkey), four other faculty members of the Lower Division English Policy Committee, which proposed implementing a common syllabus on the topic of difference for one year (Susan Sage Heinzelman, Sara Kimball, Stuart Moulthrop, and John Slatin), and six graduate-student assistant instructors (Margaret Downs-Gamble, David Ericson, Shelli Fowler, Dana Harrington, Allison Mosshart, and Rick Penticoff). We make a point of mentioning these names because our weekly, sometimes twice-weekly, meetings produced the syllabus as well as experience of collaboration akin to what we hoped to recreate in the course itself. The collaboration not only shaped the syllabus, but continues to shape the intellectual issues raised by the syllabus and ruthlessly ignored by administrative fiat on 1990 July 23, when the dean of Liberal Arts sent the English department a memo announcing his decision to postpone the implementation of "Writing about Difference" to address "misunderstandings about the course expressed within the university community" (Meacham).

I

As the title suggests, "Writing about Difference" is a course with a focused topic, *difference*. Writing about and discussion of the topic are oriented by four kinds of readings: essays which discuss the issue of difference (e.g., Martha Minow's *Making All the Difference*); U.S. District, Circuit, and Supreme Court opinions on cases involving disputes over specific kinds of difference (race, gender, physical ability, bilingualism, sexual orientation); essays which discuss issues raised in court opinions (e.g., freedom of association); and federal laws invoked in the court opinions (e.g., the First and Fourteenth Amendments to the Constitution; Title VII of the Civil Rights Act of 1964; Title IX of the Education Amendments of 1972). In a series of linked reading and writing assignments, student as well as professional texts sustain rhetorical inquiry into the topic of difference.

"Writing About Difference" is a syllabus written for English 306, the first-year writing course at The University of Texas at Austin. Credit for English 306 is required of all students at the university. More than half the entering students (about 3,000) take the course each year. Others take an equivalent course elsewhere or place out by passing a standardized grammar and usage test. Students in the course generally come from the top 25 percent of their high-school classes. Most are white and middle class; there are slightly more males than females. Despite long-standing and wide-spread local suspicion, English 306 is neither a "basic" nor a "remedial" writing course, as those who teach Open Admissions students would understand the term (see Shaughnessy). Special sections of English 306 are offered only to those students, generally foreign nationals, for whom English is a second language. Fifty-plus sections of English 306 are offered during each of the two regular semesters of the academic year (some 20 more during the summer); about 95 percent of these sections are taught by graduate-student assistant instructors, who must take a full load of courses (three every semester) in order to be employed. English 306 is the first course most graduate students teach in the department, and few begin their service with any teaching experience, let alone knowledge of composition research or pedagogy.

We provide these details to give some picture of the institutional context out of which "Writing About Difference" emerged. The department has a responsibility not only to the undergraduates who take the course but also the graduate instructors who staff the vast majority of sections. Responding to the needs and desires of these sometimes conflicting constituencies required some compromises in the syllabus design. For instance, we decided against portfolios on the grounds that we could not reasonably expect graduate student teachers to increase their work load at precisely the same point that their own course work is due. Even so, we aimed for solutions that would be pedagogically sound and intellectually defensible for students and teachers alike at The University of Texas. No doubt the problems and solutions would be different at other institutions.

Most graduate student instructors of English 306 study literature. The syllabus for "Writing about Difference" attempts to build on the strengths that literature majors are likely to bring to the classroom while at the same time inviting them to participate in teaching composition as an intellectual enterprise in its own right. It positively values their abilities as close readers, yet asks them to work with texts outside their usual purview. Though not literary analyses, court opinions work very like interpretations, and literature students will likely find themselves in familiar territory, since both jurisprudence and literary studies are founded on intertextual interpretive practices. Yet to think like a writer—so shift from reception to production—is to accept that the consequences of writing texts are different from those of reading them, which includes taking responsibility for the potential violence of words. Michael Calvin McGee, for instance, argues that rhetorical acts which aim at persuading inflict a kind of violence because the persuasive act aims at changing people's thoughts, attitudes, or behavior. Legal opinions strike us as excellent illustrations of this kind of rhetorical power and violence. As Robert Cover so eloquently puts it: "Legal interpretive acts signal and occasion the imposition of violence on others: A judge articulates her understanding of a text, and as a result, somebody loses his freedom, his property, his children, even his life" (1601). We take Cover to mean that the language used by the court invariably changes people's lives. We mean that the language used by students and teachers in classrooms and essays is, if not equally consequential, as potentially violent, and want students and teachers to learn that what they say to one another and what they say about texts matters.

Some current work in literary studies will make it easier for students of literature to recognize in the writing of court opinions what rhetoricians know as invention, a process of finding or discovering materials for topics. Jerome McGann's work on textual studies, for instance, though focused on publication, opens up the issue of textual production by questioning the notion of an author's "final" intentions. McGann argues that authors' intentions toward their texts can best be seen as a social process of interaction and negotiation with editors, publishers, copyists, and readers. In jurisprudence, legal briefs, court transcripts, and discovery evidence, each contribute material to the court's opinion, visible testimony of a public and protracted invention process. These legal texts also make available a more expansive, ontological view of rhetorical invention — the view that language constitutes social reality. This is a view that James Boyd White argues for in his discussions of both literary and legal texts. From this perspective, one might argue that every decision handed down by the courts, and the Supreme Court in particular, invents democracy anew. In this sense, then, even we who are not judges but citizens who read and interpret and evaluate legal opinions are writing commentaries in the margins of American history.

Many teachers of English 306 are new to composition as well as teaching. New teachers often question the source of their classroom authority, and some deal with their uncertainty by resorting to pedantry. The course intentionally channels interest and enthusiasm for current literary theories into a pedagogy fairer to students than most inexperienced teachers are likely to create on their own. Difference is a notion familiar to most graduate students and dear to some, but the syllabus requires instructors and students alike to examine difference critically, allowing a forum for neither *ex cathedra* pronouncements based on theories unknown to students nor conclusions based on unverifiable personal experiences. The syllabus, with its common reading and writing assignments and methods of evaluation, initially shifts authority from individual teachers to the program. Hence responsibility for the topic, materials and assignments is returned to the institution, leaving relatively inexperienced teachers some much needed time to learn how best to teach writing practices — inventing, drafting, evaluating, revising, editing. Finally, the detailed syllabus lessens instructors' anxieties about whether they "know" enough to teach writing even as it encourages them to acquire a common body of knowledge — lore, research, and scholarship—to be generated, applied, and transformed by teachers themselves (See North). Instructors thereby contribute to a larger intellectual enterprise, at the very least one more productive to them and students than the more usual exploitative one in which they are virtually forced to rationalize teaching writing on the side while building up capital for a later, more respectable, life teaching literature.

Similarly, the syllabus seeks to build on the strengths of the undergraduates who take the course. Most eighteen-year-olds come to college hoping to leave high school behind; older students enter or re-enter college already considering high school a closed chapter in their lives. This being the case, we can see no reason to treat any of them as thirteenth graders. "Writing about Difference" breaks decisively with high school by, among other things, using Stephen Toulmin's language in *The Uses of Argument* to talk about writing. While similarities between thesis and claim, evidence and ground enable students to bridge their high school and college discussions of writing, Toulmin's notion of warranting leads most of them into uncharted, but crucial, intellectual territory.

In addition to building on undergraduates' desire for intellectual challenge, the syllabus resituates ongoing campus conversations. Racially directed incidents involving several fraternities during both the spring and fall 1990 semesters, detailed proposals for curricular and administrative reform from both African-American and Chicana/o student groups, and "coming-out" rallies on the part of gay and lesbian groups have established difference as a topic of conversation and, on occasion, shouting matches. Local violence amplifies a national intolerance of difference. Consider the voter showing on behalf of David Duke in Louisiana or the anti-affirmative action ads that Jesse Helms ran in the last weeks of his 1990 re-election campaign. One way or another, people are talking about difference—at home, in the dorms, and on the streets as well as in voting booths and on talk shows—and most of the talk suggests a deep, layered, and conflicted consciousness of the issue. "Writing about Difference" attempts to take an issue in which there is already heated interest and make it an occasion for intellectual inquiry rather than forensic spectacle.

Finally, many students enter the classroom with a desire for an experience more participatory than is usually afforded by the standard lecture hall with 100-plus students and an instructor pronouncing from on high, behind a lectern. The syllabus puts writing groups of four to five students at the intellectual and logistical center of the course. Each group is responsible for teaching its court case to the rest of the class. Scholastic success relies on the collective as well as individual work of students. We are betting that these intellectual interactions will, in some instances at least, foster friendships outside the classroom and hoping they will counteract the fragmenting and alienating experiences that seem increasingly to characterize undergraduate life at large state universities, of which The University of Texas of Austin is one (see Wilson).

Such are some of the local circumstances which influenced the formation and design of the syllabus for "Writing about Difference." We tried to take account of the fact that two of the most vulnerable groups at the university, first-year students and first-time graduate-student instructors, are most affected by this course. We tried to be responsible foremost to them in meeting the already stated curricular goals with a common syllabus that supports teaching writing. Our initial goal is to engage students and instructors in intellectual inquiry. The topic of difference poses some risk to this goal, for it is a "hot" issue. But we think it a risk well worth taking because students and instructors need to learn how to discuss political issues in pedagogically and intellectually responsible ways. Teachers and students live outside as well as inside classrooms, and many feel keenly their responsibilities to their families and communities. To the extent that writing classrooms are sometimes also constituted as communities, however temporary and fragile, we do not see difference as an incidental means of engaging in written inquiry, but as a positive way for students and teachers to contribute to civic life.

II

Scholarly inquiry does not arise out of a historical, social, or political void, but is instead generated and sustained by published texts, many of which will exert near-canonical power over most students and some teachers. Yet teachers must afford student texts the same privileges as professional ones in writing classes if they expect students to see their own writing and that of peers as contributions to ongoing intellectual conversations. Efforts to value student and professional texts equally, however, more often than not create conflict between intellectual and pedagogical imperatives. Making professional texts the center of a classroom is often taken, by teachers and students, as a sign of fealty to the intellectual tradition represented by the text. Making student texts the center of a classroom is taken as a sign of the teacher's commitment to writing pedagogy. When intellectual imperatives pre-dominate, there is the temptation to offer professional texts as models: of stylistic features, of structural or rhetorical principles, or of proper moral or political content. In our view, the pedagogy of imitation sets up a textual hierarchy in which student texts are invariably devalued. When pedagogical imperatives predominate, there is the temptation to ban professional texts altogether from the classroom. The ostensible rationale is that students will find their own voice or discover their most creative thoughts only if the more powerful, and hence oppressive, published texts are absent.

We have tried to balance the intellectual and pedagogical imperatives in our syllabus by putting student and professional texts in conversation and contention with each other. "Writing about Difference" begins by trying to interrupt the authority of published texts. We don't ask students to directly model or imitate any of the professional texts in their own writing, but we do create situations in which students can themselves gain sufficient scholarly authority to "talk back" to laws, court opinions, and academic essays. We focus on a common topic for the semester because we reasoned that the more familiar students are with a set of published texts on a topic, the less likely they are to assume that publication itself guarantees that any argument is invulnerable. We also reasoned that students are more likely to gain sufficient scholarly authority to challenge professional texts when they are not repeatedly required to build up wholly new knowledge bases, as they must when topics change with each writing assignment. We teach students scholarly practices — analysis, research, synthesis — which build expertise. And we set up classroom situations in which expertise gained by an individual can be shared with the group. We expect that by the end of the semester whatever intellectual home the professional texts may have offered initially will be rebuilt or abandoned by students and teachers who work from the pedagogical blueprints offered by the syllabus.

What complicates our attempt to achieve reciprocity between student and professional texts, between intellectual and pedagogical imperatives, is the topic: difference. The topic, and hence the texts representing it, are disturbing. The texts provoke because they sometimes question received wisdom. For example, Judge McMillian's dissent to the majority opinion in *Chambers v. Omaha Girls Club, Inc.* casts doubt on the very idea of a role model. Some texts may also provoke because they ask us to consider the lives and views of people different from most students and instructors at The University of Texas. Peggy McIntosh, in "White Privilege and Male Privilege," for instance, notes homologies between the privileges males have in relation to females and those white people have in relation to people of color. The syllabus asks students to perform a similar imaginative exercise for themselves in relation to those who are vision or hearing impaired.

No doubt, the topic will make some students uncomfortable, particularly those who were taught to believe that laws literally prevent discrimination or that privilege is necessarily deserved. Other students may see raising the topic as a violation of a politeness convention; that is, problems may exist but polite people don't talk about them. We have staged an educational scene which may well distress some students. While writing classrooms need be safe places for students, we take that to mean safe from gratuitous judgments of their writing, not from intellectual life. It is at least arguable that intellectual discomfort gives point to writing in a way that intellectual comfort cannot.

When confronted with reluctant or rebellious students, instructors often resort to "explicating the text" in order to ensure that students "get the message." Instructors can then claim they have at least done right by the text (or the message or the author or the group represented by the author), if not the students. In a writing class, resorting to explication seems both unfair and antithetical to the aims of pedagogy. Learning to teach writing is learning to do right by the texts students write. No text, professional or student, can be treated as sacred. The syllabus for "Writing about Difference" discourages students from making pro-nouncements about issues based on personal experience (which is what most first-year students have to go on), and teachers from making pronouncements about texts based on theories (which is what most graduate-student teachers have to go on). Pronouncements from either quarter stifle the pedagogy of writing as inquiry. Rhetoric of inquiry relies on students and teachers talking with rather than talking at one another.

III

Many students have been taught that finding a position *is* the intellectual task in a writing course. For these students, once a position is stated there's really not much interesting work left to do beyond marshalling the requisite three pieces of evidence smartly on the page. We hoped to interrupt this version of argumentation on parade with Stephen Toulmin's language of claims, grounds, and warrants. One of the singular advantages of Toulmin's terms is that they encourage us to examine the positions we take as claims. Claims make it easier to treat positions as partial and provisional statements about the world, rather than as unarguable and immutable truths with which readers either agree or disagree. And when the conversation shifts from thesis state-ment to claim, we become less concerned about the position as a position and more interested in where an argument for it would position us — in relation to both other people and other arguments. In other words, Toulmin's lexicon offers students and teachers alike a view of argumentation as a prologue to further inquiry, which we see as an antidote to viewing arguments as debates, performances that invariably end with winners and losers, and, ultimately, silence.

In Toulmin's model, argumentation begins with some claim made about a problem or a state of affairs. A writer asserts that such and such is the case. When a reader responds to this initial claim with the question, "What do you have to go on?", the writer offers some data as grounds for the assertion. Just offering these grounds, however, may be insufficient to make the assertion convincing. One might well ask, "How do you get from here to there, from ground to claim?" That is, how well is the relation between ground and claim warranted? Further, one might challenge the particular rule, principle, custom, or law that is used as a warrant. One may ask, in other words, about the grounds for the warrant itself by asking whether the backing for the warrant is sufficient.

The concepts of claims, grounds, and warrants have a number of features important to our pedagogical aim of generating and sustaining inquiry in writing. Claims are provisional statements, a way of staking out an intellectual territory. In *An Introduction to Reasoning*, Toulmin, along with co-authors Richard Rieke and Allan Janik, compares making a verbal claim to "staking a claim" for mining rights (30). Territorial claims are subject to dispute and need defending, certainly legally, but often times physically as well. We are less concerned here with the analogy drawn beween physical and intellectual property, and more intrigued by the notion of territory or position. Any claim stakes a position in an intellectual field, which then circumscribes the kinds of arguments that can be made from that position. By way of example, some readers of *Fricke v. Lynch*, a case in which a male high school student sued to overturn his principal's prohibition against bringing a male escort to the prom, may claim that homosexuality is wrong. These readers will find, however, that such a claim positions them in an intellectual field not considered by the court. The plaintiff argued that the principal's prohibition was a violation of his First Amendment right to free expression; the defendant argued that the prohibition was made in the interest of public safety. Homosexuality itself is not an issue for either the litigants or the court. To make it an issue, one has to shift the grounds of the dispute from civil liberties to personal conduct, and, on some states, from civil to criminal law.

The provisional nature of claims can be seen in the way the issue is, in fact, framed in *Fricke v. Lynch*. One could say that two acknowledged rights are in conflict: the right of free expression and the right to enjoy public order and safety. Historically, federal courts have defined neither right as absolute. Students may well find during their inquiries that the courts shift position on the issue of free expression. A district court argued for the primacy of this right in "Fricke," but the Supreme Court denied its supremacy in *University of Pennsylvania v. Equal Employment Opportunity Commission*, unanimously finding against the university's claim that confidentiality is necessary to protect the First Amendment rights of those who write tenure reviews. Students may not readily accept our assertion that claims are provisional, but the writing assignments developed for the syllabus require all of us to make public the grounds on which we state such and such to be the case.

For purposes of pedagogy, the key concept in Toulmin's model is warranting. Warrant is complex because it refers both to things (principles, rules, customs, laws) and actions (warrants *license* the relation between claims and grounds). The chief feature of warrants is that they are field-dependent. When warranting the relation between a claim and ground, at least three conditions must be met:

1. the grounds must be relevant to the claim;
2. the grounds must be sufficient to substantiate the claim; and
3. the argument must be rhetorically appropriate to the situation.

The criteria of relevance, sufficiency, and appropriateness link argumentation to the contingencies of context and loosen its connections to the determinant laws of logic.

The notion of warranting is particularly useful when assessing the merits of majority and dissenting opinions — especially so in *Chambers v. Omaha Girls Club, Inc.* Crystal Chambers, a single, black woman employed as an arts and crafts instructor by the Omaha Girls Club, was fired when she became pregnant. The defendant argued that employees were expected to be role models for the predominantly "minority" members of the club, that pregnancy outside marriage is a harmful behavior to model for this membership, and therefore that Chambers' pregnancy was grounds for dismissal because it modeled harmful behavior. In this chain of arguments, one strand that becomes an issue amongst the judges is as follows: claim — girls will emulate Chambers' behavior and get pregnant; ground — Chambers is a role model for the girls; warrant — people will emulate the behavior of role models. The majority opinion accepts this chain of reasoning as valid. Judge McMillian's dissenting opinion, however, takes issue with the warrant:

> The district court, and now this court, accepts without any proof OGC's [The Omaha Girls Club's] assumption that the presence of an unwed pregnant instructor is related to teenage pregnancies...OGC failed to present surveys, school statistics or any other empirical data connecting the incidence of teenage pregnancy with the pregnancy of an adult instructor. OGC also failed to present evidence that other girls clubs or similar types of organizations employed such a rule. OGC instead relied on two or three highly questionable anecdotal incidents to support the rule. (707)

The dissent disputes the backing for the warrant; in other words, the evidence used to support the behavioral law or principle which predicts that people emulate the behavior of role models. Note that the dissenting opinion does not question the ground of the argument, that Chambers was employed to function as a role model, but challenges instead the relevance of the ground to the claim. McMillian reasons that if there is no empirically verifiable evidence to support a necessary cause-effect relation between the behavior of a role model and that of her clients, then Chambers cannot be fired on the grounds that she was a negative role model. Being a role model might be a part of an employee's job description, but in this case, one cannot say, if one's test is empirical evidence, that the job either is or isn't being done.

This example illustrates how context-dependent or field-dependent, to use Toulmin's language, warranting is. The judges writing the majority opinion are willing to accept anecdotal evidence for the efficacy of role models because, we presume, it is common sense and customary knowledge that such a relation exists. In fact, the majority is even "uncertain whether the role model rule by its nature is suited to validation by an empirical study" (702). The dissenting opinion, by contrast, takes a view of the role model principle more characteristic of what one has come to expect in, say, experimental psychology; namely, that an assertion can only be applied generally as an explanation of human behavior if it has been empirically validated. The opinions in "Chambers" are thus arguments drawing warrants from two competing fields — custom and science. We realize that the very notion of warranting is highly complex precisely because it is field- or context-dependent. One obvious reason to make it a critical part of the course, however, is that we see warranting as a way of teaching students that providing three pieces of evidence does not "prove" a claim, if only because data are themselves problematic.

Seen in terms of pedagogy, Toulmin's terminology also gives us a way to make the daily activities of the course internally coherent to students and teachers. Claims, grounds, and warrants are the terms in which all readings are analyzed as well as the invention principles by which all writings are generated. Toulmin would not himself argue that these analytical terms generate arguments, since formal logic, unlike rhetoric, is not concerned with invention. But standard heuristics, such as Young, Becker, and Pike's tagmemics or the adaptations of Burke's pentad, which focus on gathering data, are by themselves not sufficient for invention because they do not easily transform data into information. Data cannot be seen to ground a claim without an explicit procedure for determining their relevance to a particular argument. The criteria for warranting allow us to sift through raw data and "find" those that are relevant, sufficient, and appropriate to the argument at hand. Students can use Toulmin's language to analyze and evaluate their own arguments as well as those they read. As may already be apparent from the discussion of warranting, Toulmin's language redefines form and content as mutually implicated in argumentation, making it apparent that both must figure in evaluation. Organizational and stylistic choices in a text are taught as part and parcel of warranting. This means that organization and style are treated as intrinsic features of a particular argument, crucial for judging its effectiveness, not as empty and interchangeable containers into which content is poured.

IV

We designed "Writing about Difference" to encourage students to conduct intellectual inquiry in writing. For those of us who worked on the syllabus, such inquiry is made possible in the academy by sustained intellectual dialogue in which positions are grounded by research and warranted by relevant, sufficient, and appropriate arguments. Teaching inquiry is not simply a matter of providing students with tools: scholarly texts and strategies of argumentation. Nor is it a matter of putting the tools to work through assignments which ask students to reproduce what they read. Such approaches employ students and teachers alike as day-laborers in academia, who produce piece-work in return for the academic equivalent of a paycheck—grades for students, credentials for graduate-student teachers. The very possibility of intellectual inquiry entails imagining students and teachers as intellectuals, fully capable already of doing, or developing the ability to do, independent intellectual work. To this end, we designed the syllabus with two structural principles in mind: (1) the course activities had to be both sequential and cumulative; and (2) the course activities had to revolve around a common topic for all participants through the entire semester.

The first structural principle animates the teleology implied by our notion of intellectual inquiry. In other words, what students write at the end of the semester depends on what they have written throughout the term. We see the syllabus as differing from similar writing courses we are familiar with mostly in terms of ends rather than means. We are not trying to influence cognitive or psychological maturity (see Flower; Axlerod and Cooper). Nor are we trying lead students through a process of self-creation (see Coles). While we wouldn't necessarily exclude these other ends, we view students as intellectuals, and hoped that the course might even encourage some students to see themselves as transformative intellectuals, people who, in the words of Stanley Aronowitz and Henry Giroux, can make "the pedagogical more political and the political more pedagogical" (36). We are perhaps not as convinced as Aronowitz and Giroux that transformative intellectuals are necessarily in opposition to a "dominant" society, since our understanding of a democratic society—as individuals and groups whose multiple and sometimes contradictory interests intersect differentially—

suggests that the hegemony of those in power is vulnerable to internal as well as external critique. We wholeheartedly agree, however, that intellectual activity is potentially transformative, personally and socially. We hoped, then, that after a semester of reading and writing arguments about discriminatory employment and educational practices, students would come to see themselves as reasonably well informed on the topic of difference and entitled, therefore, to participate in the ever more public debate about civil rights.

The teleological structure is premised on four conceptual nodes. In the first node, Toulmin's language of argumentation frames the topic of difference. Students read from Martha Minow's *Making All the Difference* and are asked, in several informal scripts and one formal essay, to identify a central claim she makes and the grounds she offers in support of it. They next read Peggy McIntosh's essay, "White Privilege and Male Privilege," and are asked to use it as a springboard for library research into stereotypes (these stereotypes come from the court cases considered later in the course). Minow's conception of difference as relational rather than inherent underlies both McIntosh's insight into the nature of privilege and students' understanding of stereotypes. The relational notion of difference also helps open up the practice of argumentation by showing that intellectual positions are not fixed to immutable truths encased in prefabricated structures but are constructed for particular purposes from local materials.

The second node of the course uses the Supreme Court opinion on *Sweatt v. Painter* and "The Spurs of Texas Are Upon You," a chapter from Richard Kluger's *Simple Justice*, as a practice case that the whole class does together. We chose *Sweatt v. Painter* in large part because it is a local case. In 1946, under the separate but equal ruling, The University of Texas law school refused to admit Heman Sweatt, a black male. He sued and lost at all three state court levels, but eventually won the case in the United States Supreme Court in 1950. The writing assignments ask students to compile a class lexicon of legal terms (used in this and subsequent cases) and to distinguish and analyze the arguments made by the plaintiff, defendant, and court in the published opinion.

The work of the third node relies on student writing groups. Each group reads a court opinion and a scholarly essay discussing some issue of difference relavent to the case. Group members write a "review" of the scholarly essay and an analysis of the court opinion. But here, instead of just identifying and summarizing claims and grounds, students also evaluate arguments in the article and opinion. Evaluating arguments, in this course, means evaluating warrants. Assessing warrants invoked or implied by the court, litigants, and scholars in their respective texts is also likely to require students to unpack notions of difference at work in these texts. The time set aside for each group to present issues and arguments raised by their case to the class is critical, for taking the time publicly values the reading, thinking, and writing students do in the course.

In the last node, students take a set of materials—legal briefs and laws—and write an "opinion" finding in favor of either the plaintiff or defendant in the case. This is obviously a cumulative assignment because it asks students to use what they have learned from analyzing and evaluating judicial opinions, and from the group presentations, to write their own. Semester-long experience with the topic and terms and opinions and essays teaches student writers the absolute value of giving due attention to the arguments made by plaintiffs and defendants, which is after all the basis of our faith in law and argumentation alike.

The second structural principle, a single topic, supports the implementation of the cumulative syllabus. We realize, nonetheless, that single-topic writing courses have an uneasy relation to the rest of the university as well as to the history of rhetoric. Historically, rhetoric (and written composition as a branch of rhetoric) has most often been viewed as a methodological study, codified in ancient Greek theory as a *techne* or art. As Aristotle put it: "Neither rhetoric nor dialectic is the scientific study of any one separate subject: both are faculties for providing arguments" (1356a 30; Roberts translation). There have been periods, however, when learning rhetoric was considered almost an end in and of itself because eloquence was thought to define the telos of human social existence. For Gorgias and Isocrates in Greece, Cicero and Quintillian in Rome, and Petrarch and Salutati in Renaissance Italy, civic life or paideia *was* the topic of rhetorical study. But this formulation of rhetoric, where technical proficiency cannot be distinguished from a person's civic or social identity, is abandoned when the state prevents citizens from having an effective voice in its affairs or when academic disciplines artificially rationalize the study of language—segregating language users from language use, form from content, intentions from effects, grammar from rhetoric, rhetoric from philosophy, and philosophy from social life.

Modern English departments, formed in the late nineteenth century around the study of literature, retained responsibility for one branch of rhetorical instruction—the teaching of writing. And so long as English departments have been responsible for it, writing has been largely conceived of and taught as a methodological and instrumental art. This conception of writing has proven to be the source of many conflicts because English departments must forever fret about whether they should teach writing as a service to the rest of the university or as a service to their own discipline. In the university service model, writing is usually taught as instrumental to the discovery and propagation of knowledge. Instruction focuses on formal features, whether considered "universal" (e.g., organizational patterns or punctuation) or particular to a discipline (e.g., research proposals or technical manual as genres). In the intradisciplinary service model, writing is taught as the instrument of literary style or as the conveyor of literary content through textual explications. When writing is taught as a university service, one can ask why composition necessarily "belongs" to English departments. When it is taught as a service to English majors, one can ask why students across the university are required to learn it. Neither conception of composition makes a persuasive case for the practice of writing in and of itself.

"Writing About Difference" is grounded in an alternative conception of rhetoric which reconfigures disciplinary boundaries. In our version of rhetoric, which some scholars have already labeled "The Rhetoric of Inquiry" (see Nelson, Megill, and McCloskey), form and content jointly construct social reality and topics are hardly incidental to learning and teaching. Despite recent reconceptualizations of rhetoric embodied in such programs as the University of Iowa's Project on Rhetoric of Inquiry, a topic-driven writing course remains problematic in the modern university because it is presumed that topics, with their established content and approved methods for studying them, already "belong" to some discipline. Topic-focused writing courses make discipline-oriented academics anxious because students will not be learning the disciplinary representations of those topics. As David Bartholomae and Anthony Petrosky point out in the introduction to *Facts, Artifacts and Counterfacts*, students in these kinds of writing courses "can only approximate the work of professional academics; they can only try on the role of the psychologist or anthropologist or sociologist. They will not 'get' the canonical interpretations preserved by the disciplines, nor will they invent that work on their own" (38). Despite these limitations, they go on to say, students can "learn something about what it means to study a subject or carry out a project" (38). Along with Bartholomae and Petrosky, we would argue that topic. Topic-driven writing courses, ours included, which refuse an instrumental relation, either to the English department or the university as a whole, require students and teachers to actually "invent" a discipline.

Inquiry invents disciplines. To paraphrase John Dewey, inquiry transforms an indeterminate situation into a determinate one. The purpose of inquiry is to construct "warranted assertions" about a disturbed, troubled, ambiguous, confused, conflicted, or obscure "existential situation" (Dewey, 108). What could be more disturbed, troubled, ambiguous, confused, conflicted, or obscure than existential situations evoked by difference? It is inquiry then, more than the acquisition of any content or skill, no matter how valuable, that justifies the subject matter and pedagogical activities of "Writing About Difference." It may seem that the course is about law, given that most of its texts are laws, court opinions, or articles framed by legal issues. But the course is only incidentally about law. It may also seem that the course is about writing as rhetorical skills, given that the writing and reading assignments teach traditional rhetorical strategies. But the course is only incidentally about rhetorical skills. When students explore in writing an indeterminate situation like difference in writing, they transform seemingly determinate disciplines like law and composition into new, yet-to-be-determined disciplines. Inquiry thus secures students both the right to enter "disciplinary" conversations in the classroom and the right to contribute to public debate — as citizens whose authority to speak out rests less on having an opinion than on being willing and able to lay out a case in support of it.

Every writing program articulates a project. If a project is meant to be intellectually transformative, however, it must deal with what law sometimes calls hard cases. Hard cases in law complicate a court's ability to reach facile rulings because human contingencies prevail over legal precedents. Difference is one of those contingencies. At the University of Texas we hoped to use law's hard cases to foreground some hard cases for writing pedagogy. A hard case for students is learning to use writing to conduct rhetorical inquiry. In turn, the hard case for teachers is teaching themselves and convincing students that learning to conduct rhetorical inquiry takes precedence over learning to produce more examples of what Janet Emig once called the "Fifty-Star Theme" (97). Hard cases for students and teachers add up to a hard case for research in composition, namely, how to study what is taught and learned about writing arguments in courses where rhetorical inquiry into difference grounds writing pedagogy.

Theory can generate a syllabus, but theory only imagines what can happen rather than what does happen to students and teachers. It's research that links theory and practice, for it interrupts the excesses of theorists and practitioners alike by asking the hard questions, what might be called the *cui bono* questions. We hoped "Writing about Difference" would interest more students and teachers than other courses teachers might have designed and taught. And we hoped that their interest would be justified by what they learned about writing during the semester. While we had good common-sense reasons to think a single topic would be a more viable approach to writing pedagogy than changing the topic with every assignment, our reasons for teaching argument as rhetorical inquiry are more theoretical than practical. Yet, whether one reasons from experience or theory, only a full-scale empirical study could have even begun to broach the kinds of pedagogical issues we hoped to redress with the syllabus.

To the extent that classes can be seen as mounting cultural scenes at which students and teachers stage cultural events, a writing class would be the site at which students and teachers produce literacy. What does and does not count as literacy is played out in a series of literacy episodes in the course of a semester. The syllabus for "Writing about Difference" stipulates a definition of literacy which is premised on rhetorical inquiry. Defining literacy as largely a matter of exploring arguments by identifying, analyzing, and evaluating their claims, grounds, and warrants leaves little room for what students call personal opinions. While personal opinions may be based on reasons, the reasons are usually of considerably less interest to the claimant than the claim itself. In this course, however, we hoped to shift attention from claims to the ways grounds and warrants qualify the opinions. Research could tell us something definite about what happens to students and teachers whose literacy scripts narrowly define writing and reading in the classroom along these lines and expressly prohibit more familiar scripts that count for a good deal elsewhere.

The syllabus discounts personal opinions as irrelevant to the practice of conducting rhetorical inquiry, however important they may or may not be in a writer's own experience. No writing assignment, for instance, solicits a personal opinion or personal narrative from students. This was a deliberate decision made in the interests of pedagogy. Given that some students and teachers understand "everybody has a right to their own opinion" to be the sine qua non of classroom democracy, however, it's hard to imagine that some would not see the privileging of argument as a violation of free speech. Like the courts, we do not believe free speech to be an absolute right and consider it instead to be contingent on other rights and responsibilities in the classroom. We take seriously the potential violence of language, and so would encourage students and teachers to state claims they do not intend to argue.[1]

The decision to prohibit personal opinions comes from practice, specifically from remembering that displays of personal opinions too often preface a decision among students *not* to argue, commonly signalled by the invocation of "everybody has a right to their opinion." Yet, had we taught the course and conducted surveys and interviews and observations and talk-aloud protocols indicating that our injunction against personal opinions was inhibiting the writing of arguments, we would have revised the syllabus to accommodate those findings. In the absence of data, however, the theory and practice out of which we produced the syllabus for "Writing about Difference" stand aloof from any but the most speculative criticism about our understanding of writing and writing pedagogy or our motives for asking students to read and write about difference or for selecting discrimination suits or for assigning particular essays.

The course was designed to study legal decisions as literate events at a time when many people profess to believe that discrimination is a thing of the past. The court cases testify that not everyone believes this to be so, and the decisions clarify, as little else would, that the arguments in court opinions are profoundly contingent on circumstances. We can think of no more important dimensions of culture to study than laws prohibiting discrimination and the strategies of argumentation employed in suits brought before the courts. Law is one of the few places in this society where arguments are evaluated as arguments. We would like to think the academy is another. But convincing students and teachers that the academy is such a place requires that pedagogical conditions transform classrooms into cultures wherein people use arguments to raise more interesting intellectual questions than they resolve. Only when these conditions obtain will we have a society as worth inhabiting as studying.

Notes

1. Patricia Bizzell, following Mina Shaughnessy, characterizes this assertion of a right to personal opinion as "the ethos of the 'honest face'" ("Ethos", 353).

Works Cited

Aristotle. *Rhetoric. The Complete Works of Aristotle*. Ed. Johnathan Barnes. Vol. 2. Princeton: Princeton UP, 1984. 2152–2269.

Aronowitz, Stanley and Henry Giroux. *Education under Siege: The Conservative, Liberal and Radical Debate over Schooling*. South Hadley, MA: Bergin & Garvey Publishers, 1986.

Axelrod, Rise and Charles Cooper. *The St. Martin's Guide to Writing*. 2nd ed. New York: St. Martin's, 1988.

Bartholomae, David and Anthony Petrosky. *Facts, Artifacts, and Counterfacts: Theory and Method for a Reading and Writing Course*. Upper Montclair, NJ: Boynton/Cook, 1986.

Bizzell, Patricia. "The Ethos of Academic Discourse." *College Composition and Communication*. 29.4 (December 1978): 351–55.

Brodkey, Linda. "Articulating Poststructural Theory in Literacy Research." *Multidisciplinary Perspectives on Literacy*. Ed. Richard Beach, Judith L. Green, Michael L. Kamil, and Timothy Shanahan. Carbondale: Urbana: National Conference on Research on English; Urbana: National Council of Teachers of English, 1992. 293–318.

——— "Transvaluing Difference." *College English* 51 (October 1989): 597–601.

Burke, Kenneth. *A Grammar of Motives*. Berkeley: University of California Press, 1969.

Chambers v. Omaha Girls Club, Inc. 834 Federal 2d 697. (8th Circuit, 1987).

Coles, William E., Jr. *Seeing Through Writing*. New York: Harper and Row, 1988.

Cover, Robert M. "Violence and the Word." *Yale Law Journal* 95 (1986): 1601–29.

Dewey, John. *Logic: The Theory of Inquiry. John Dewey: The Later Works, 1925–1953*. Vol. 12: 1938. ed. Jo Ann Boydstone. Carbondale: Southern Illinois University Press, 1986.

Emig, Janet. *The Composing Processes of Twelfth Graders*. Urbana: NCTE, 1971.

Flower, Linda. *Problem-Solving Strategies for Writing* 2nd ed. San Diego: HBJ, 1985.

Frick v. Lynch. 491 Federal Supplement 381. (1980).

Kinneavy, James L. *A Theory of Discourse: The Aims of Discourse*. New York: Norton, 1971.

Kluger, Richard. *Simple Justice: The History of "Brown v. Board of Education and Black America's Struggle for Equality*. New York: Vintage Books, 1975. 256–84.

Minow, Martha. *Making All the Difference: Inclusion, Exclusion, and American Law*. Ithaca: Cornell University Press, 1990.

McGann, Jerome J. *A Critique of Modern Textual Criticism*. Chicago: University of Chicago Press, 1983.

McGee, Michael Calvin. "A Materialist Conception of Rhetoric." *Explorations in Rhetoric*. Ed. Ray E. McKerrow. Glenview: Scott, Foresman, 1982. 23–48.

McIntosh, Peggy. "White Privilege and Male Privilege: A Personal Account of Coming to See Correspondences through Work in Women's Studies." Copyright 1988, Peggy McIntosh. Wellesley, MA: Wellesley College.

Meacham, Standish. "Memorandum to the English Department." 23 July 1990.

Nelson, John S., Allan Megill, and Donald M. McCloskey. "Rhetoric of Inquiry." *The Rhetoric of the Human Sciences: Language and Argument in Scholarship and Public Affairs*. Ed. John S. Nelson, Allan Megill, and Donald N. McCloskey. Madison: Univeristy of Wisconsin Press, 1987. 1–18.

North, Stephen M. *The Making of Knowledge in Composition: Portrait of an Emerging Field*. Upper Montclair, NJ: Boynton/Cook, 1987.

Shaughnessy, Mina P. *Errors and Expectations: A Guide for the Teacher of Basic Writing*. New York: Oxford University Press, 1977.

"Statement of Principles and Standards for the Postsecondary Teaching of Writing." *College Composition and Communication* 40 (October 1989): 329–36.

"Students' Right to Their Own Language." *College Composition and Communication* 25 (Fall 1974): 1–32.

Sweatt v. Painter. *U.S. Supreme* 629 (1950).

Toulmin, Stephen. *The Uses of Argument*. Cambridge: Cambridge University Press, 1958.

Toulmin, Stephen, Richard Rieke, and Allan Janik. *An Introduction to Reasoning*. 2nd ed. New York: MacMillan, 1984.

University of Pennsylvania v. Equal Employment Opportunity Commission *United States Law Week* 58 (1 January 1990): 4093−98.

Watt, Ian. "On Not Attempting to Be a Piano." *Profession 78*. New York: MLA, 1978. 3−15.

White, James Boyd. *Heracles' Bow: Essays on the Rhetoric and Poetics of the Law*. Madison: University of Wisconsin Press, 1985.

Wilson, Robin. "Undergraduates at Large Universities Found to Be Increasingly Dissatisfied." *Chronicle of Higher Education* (9 January 1991): A1, 37−40.

Young, Richard, Alton Becker and Kenneth Pike. *Rhetoric: Discovery and Change*. New York: Harcourt, Brace, and World, 1970.

9

Cultural Studies and the Undergraduate Literature Curriculum

Anne Balsamo

Cultural studies, in its most recent and most contested form, is a cultural formation in its own right. It is *defined* in one sense by a set of institutional and academic practices that take culture as an object of study. Yet at the same time, the various narratives of its historical development protest that it can not be, and indeed must not be defined at all, least of all by such an objectivist notion of culture. For some critics, cultural studies takes shape as a generalized political response to the postmodern, while for others it emerges more specifically as a response to the crisis in the humanities—a crisis first identified in Britain in the late 1970s and then more recently in the United States (Widdowson; Batsleer, Davis, O' Rourke, and Weedon; Grossberg; Hall; Brantlinger). Whatever the conditions of its origins—an issue I will come back to later in this paper—by the late 1980s cultural studies had become a spectacle in a local economy of names, commodities, and academic discourses. I say "local" because its status here in the United States is not the same as it is in the United Kingdom, or even in Australia. Although certain tendencies are similar across cultural contexts, the institutionalized space of cultural studies in the United States seems to be of a different sort. The focal issue of this essay—the elaboration of a series of undergraduate courses in cultural studies— emerges within a convergence among several strands of cultural analysis that form the context for cultural studies in the United States. These cultural discourses include not only the various narratives of identity of cultural studies but also the set of critical reflections on the intellectual history and blindspots of literary studies, as well as the debates about the politics of academic work and of multi-culturalism. In this essay I will briefly consider the contribution of these discussions to the development of a curricular agenda for cultural studies, and then describe a series of courses that addresses that agenda. The broad purpose of this essay is to call attention to the institutionalization of cultural studies now going on in English departments in the United States.

The Turn to Cultural Studies

Several essays reprinted from the *ADE* and *ADFL Bulletin* during the 1980s called for a rethinking of the disciplinary identity of literary studies. Sometimes this impulse was to address the issue, or the impossibility, as Stanley Fish would have it, of interdisciplinarity; in other essays it was to reflect on the place of literary *theory* in the undergraduate curriculum (Lipking; Prince; Peck). In other instances though, scholars have called for the expansion of literary studies to include broader cultural topics — such as discussions of the power relations that ground the discipline of literary studies itself or the history of the institutionalization of literary discourse (Carby; Winkler). One way that departments of English are beginning to respond to these thoughtful demands is to advertise for entry level positions requiring some background in cultural studies, cultural criticism, or cultural theory. But in some announcements the cultural studies position also called for an expertise in a traditional period specialty. Taken together these moves articulate a rather ambiguous desire on the part of some departments: a desire for scholars who could at once work beyond the currently established disciplinary boundaries of literary studies, but who could, in a funding pinch, I suppose, still deliver traditionally defined courses in period literature.

Behind these more administrative discussions are those that have innervated scholars about the practice of literary study "after the New Criticism." In one controversial volume titled *Re-Reading English*, Peter Widdowson and others elaborate how the "crisis" (in Britain) in English studies suggests certain questions about the academic orientation of the discipline. These questions are not about differences among interpretive approaches but rather are "question[s], posed from within, as to what English *is*, where it has got to, whether it has a future, whether it *should* have a future as a discrete discipline, and if it does, in what ways it might be reconstituted" (13). Other essays in the book consider the ways that British cultural studies — most notably work associated with the Centre for Contemporary Cultural Studies at Birmingham and the Open University — has been "profoundly instrumental" in challenging the disciplinary conventions of English studies by foregrounding how its intellectual history is also a political history and how literary pedagogy often functions as a "vehicle for [the] ideological transmission" of class-based knowledges and values. According to these essays, cultural studies does two things vis-a-vis the discipline of literary studies. On the one hand, cultural studies elaborates the ideological work of English departments by provoking a discussion of the manifest purpose of the development of such a field called English studies. On the other, cultural studies offers a model for a transdisciplinary approach to the type of questions that have come to be associated with English studies: namely, questions about readers, writers, texts, and practices of interpretation. What is also abundantly clear from these essays is that the two fields have been entangled throughout their histories, so that although it may *seem* like a radical move on the part of some literature faculty to assert a relationship between them, it is actually the case that the two fields have been mutually determining from their murky beginnings. The question I'd like to address in more detail concerns the way in which cultural studies can contribute to the reconstruction of literary studies curricula in the United States.

In an essay in *College English*, Mary Poovey argues that popular postmodern phenomena, such as rock and roll and MTV, offer a reconceptualization of art that will nudge literary criticism in a new direction — a direction she believes is determined by the same forces that operate on the domain of the popular. In thinking through the changes in the object of literary criticism, Poovey also rethinks the role of institutionalized literary studies. As Poovey rehearses the elaboration of cultural studies offered by Stuart Hall, revising it in keeping with her commitments to feminist poststructuralist theory, she makes explicit what is often only implicit in the discussions mentioned earlier: the turn to cultural studies is seen as a way out of an impasse that literary studies finds itself in between an aesthetist formalism on the one side and a sociological historicism on the other. Poovey elaborates a "three-tiered enterprise" of "cultural criticism" that would involve the following projects:

> the study of culture as an independent set of institutional and informal practices and discourses; the study of the traces this larger social formation produces in individual texts; the study of the role our own practice plays in the reproducing or subverting the dominant cultural formation. (620)

Here Poovey lays out the basic project for cultural studies as she reconceptualizes it from within the domain of contemporary literary studies. First, it will be first concerned to identify culture in terms of practices and discourses, not objects and texts; "concepts are seen as the effects of representations and institutional practices, not their origins" (621). Secondly, the individual text is decentered as the focal object of cultural criticism and the process of textual analysis is refashioned accordingly to focus on the effects of broader social formations. And finally, but not inconsequentially, this revitalized form of cultural criticism requires the examination of "the conditions of possibility of our own classroom practices." This last point is not a simple call for enhanced self-reflexivity among literarure teachers, although that is probably a necessary moment in such a transformation. Here Poovey argues that we must understand both the way in which our teaching and scholarly practices are determined by broader social forces and the way in which they are also in need of wide-scale revision. All in all, Poovey's model of cultural criticism raises several issues about the construction of cultural studies courses within a literary studies curriculum: the emphasis on cultural practices, the textual circulation of meanings and interpretations, and the institutionalization of cultural studies as an academic enterprise. For now I would like to consider in greater detail the issue of the name of such cultural criticism or, rather, the contest over the claiming of cultural studies.

Narratives of Identity and the Rush to Colonize Cultural Studies

Although there is relatively wide consensus on the identification of the founding figures of cultural studies (i.e., Williams, Hoggart, and Thompson), there is less agreement about other key figures and important developments. And for the most part, this lack of agreement is considered to be one of the abiding strengths of cultural studies as an anti-discipline of sorts. In his 1980 article, "Cultural Studies: Two Paradigms," Stuart Hall begins by stating unequivocally

> in serious, critical intellectual work, there are no absolute beginnings and few unbroken continuities. Neither the endless unwinding of 'tradition,' so beloved in the History of Ideas, nor the absolution of the 'epistemological rupture,' punctuating thought into its 'false' and 'correct' parts, once favored by the Althusserians, will do. (57)

In this essay, Hall identities cultural studies as a "problematic" that emerges at a particular historical moment — in this case the mid-1950s — that was in part constructed by two books of cultural theory: Hoggart's *Uses of Literacy* and Williams' *Culture and Society*. From here, Hall then offers one possible narrative of the development of cultural studies in light of its organizational and intellectual affiliations with the Centre for Contemporary Cultural Studies (CCCS) in Birmingham and the scholarship that is marked by the publication of the first seven years of *Working Papers in Cultural Studies*. Ironically, by the end of the 1980s this very same article had itself been written into the narrative accounts of the development of cultural studies as a foundational essay. For example, in an article published in 1989, Lawrence Grossberg offers a more chronological account of the history of cultural studies as a problematic, in which he narrates how cultural studies changes through its engagement with poststructuralism, feminism, psychoanalysis, and postmodernism ("The Circulation of Cultural Studies" 1989). In offering this account, though, Grossberg stresses the importance of Hall's initial disclaimer: cultural studies must not be "reduced to a singular position or a linear history" (114). But, as Grossberg goes on to argue, neither should cultural studies "be dispersed into a set of unrelated differences" (114). Grossberg is responding here to what he describes as a set of "potential dangers" in the recent "turn to cultural studies" on the part of some literary scholars in the mid-1980s. He worries that in the gold rush to claim cultural studies as a new academic speciality people would "fail to recognize its history" and in so doing would empty it of its theoretical and, more importantly perhaps, its political specificity.

In part, Grossberg's apprehensions that the history of cultural studies would be lost or obscured have been waylaid. In two of the most recent books on cultural studies — Graeme Turner's *Introduction to British Cultural Studies* and Patrick Brantlinger's *Crusoe's Footprints: Cultural Studies in Britain and America* — the authors take pains to discuss its historical antecedents in work by Williams, Thompson, and Hoggart. But from here their stories differ dramatically. Taken together, these two books illustrate one of Grossberg's main assertions about cultural studies: namely, that its identity is "constantly renegotiated as it is repositioned within different political and intellectual maps" ("Formations," 115). Where Turner emphasizes the media focus of cultural studies by addressing its organizing principles and sites of investigation (subcultures, audience, media), Brantlinger narrates the identity of cultural studies through and in relation to the field of American studies — a discipline that Turner, or others for that matter (Alexander; Becker; Carey; Punter), never mention. In doing so, Brantlinger demonstrates how the story of cultural studies changes as it is framed through different disciplinary lenses, but he also comes the closest to enacting one of the dangers Grossberg feared most: that cultural studies would be emptied of its explicit political critique.

Brantlinger chronicles in greater detail (than does Turner or any other account) the stormy relationship between cultural studies and literary studies, especially, as he describes it, how the focus of cultural criticism shifted from literature to culture to ideology. But in this description Brantlinger keeps the issue of politics at an arm's length. In a chapter titled "Class, Gender, Race," he describes the explicitly politically informed intellectual work going on at the CCCS as "work on the question" or the "politics" of representation. This recoding of the politics of cultural studies is readily apparent in his account of the feminist work going on at the CCCS. He fails, for example, to describe two key issues brought forward by feminist scholars at the Centre at the time he writes about (the time of the publication of *Women Take Issue*): that intellectual work can never be divorced from ideological determinations; and, relatedly, that the institutional context of scholarly work calls into question the political effectiveness of any ideological critique inherent in the Centre's academic work (Balsamo). According to other accounts of the development of cultural studies (notably Stuart Hall 1992), the discussion of these issues that were initially raised by feminists irrevocably changed the nature of cultural studies.

> For cultural studies...the intervention of feminism was specific and decisive. It was ruptural. It reorganized the field in quite concrete ways. First, the opening of the question of the personal as political, and its consequences for changing the object of study in cultural studies, was completely revolutionary in a theoretical and practical way. Second, the radical expansion of the notion of power, which had hitherto been very much developed within the framework of the notion of the public, the public domain, with the effect that we could not use the term power...in the same way. ("Theoretical Legacies," 282)

In overlooking the historically specific feminist intervention into cultural studies and reducing the self-reflexive political critique to a matter of the "politics of representation," Brantlinger disseminates a narrative account of the development of cultural studies that glosses over its commitment to interrogate its own institutional position and to critique its own role in the dissemination of dominant ideologies. This becomes a critical oversight in the recent turn to cultural studies in the United States where the multiplicitous identity of cultural studies is celebrated to the exclusion of its concrete historical specificity.

Cultural Studies Courses

My purpose in the first section of this essay was not so much to tease out the contradictions among various narratives of identity of cultural studies as to identify some of the foundational commitments of cultural studies that should be taken into account when constructing undergraduate courses in cultural studies. At a broad level, the project of cultural studies is to analyze cultural formations or articulations. This implies two dialectically intertwined domains of study: cultural texts and the social arrangements that constitute them—both the "what" that is said, and the social relations that allow or disallow something to be expressed. In his essay titled "What is Cultural Studies Anyway?" Richard Johnson (director of the CCCS after Hall) develops a detailed model and social theory of the production and circulation of meanings that schematizes the changes in the problematics of cultural studies identified by Hall and Grossberg. In so doing, he delineates three broad cultural studies projects: text-based studies primarily concerned with cultural products; studies that focus on the production of cultural forms, and studies that focus on "lived culture" (including ethnographic studies), especially studies of "reading" — of the way that elements of mass culture are appropriated. In the following section, I describe three undergraduate courses that each address one of the central preoccupations of cultural studies as elaborated by Johnson. At the introductory level, the "Reading and Writing Culture" course focuses on the constructedness of cultural texts and establishes the centrality of the productive act of "reading." At the second-year level, the "Popular Culture" course investigates what people do with those texts and how popular cultural forms are appropriated in the construction of subjectivity. A third course, simply identified here as "Introduction to Cultural Studies," provides an overview of the historical development of cultural studies tied to changes in its theoretical problematics and its multidisciplinary identity. These courses require not only the refashioning of curricular offerings, but, probably more importantly, the rethinking of actual classroom practices. To the extent that cultural studies also directs critical attention to the conditions of the production of knowledge, it requires, much like feminist studies does, what we do many things differently in our classrooms, in our professional lives, in our scholarship. A fuller account of the pedagogical commitments of the cultural studies teacher is the topic of another paper (Balsamo and Greer, forthcoming); suffice it to note here that discussions of pedagogy are crucial for any consideration of cultural studies courses and are already in process. (See especially: Nelson; Giroux, Shumway, Smith and Sosnoski; Giroux and Simon).

"Reading and Writing Culture"

One of the first courses I teach in cultural studies focuses on forms of reading appropriate for cultural texts that do not come in familiar literary form. For one opening exercise, I used a clip of the "CNN Headline News" video sequence that served (up until late 1989) as the station's visual and audio trademark. Although the clip only lasts nine seconds, it works well to illustrate how tele-visual meterial is formally constructed and as a demonstration of the practice of reading a visual text.[1] For this exercise in the practice of "reading culture," students transcribed one segment of a news program that I previously videotaped and put on reserve for them. Using the instructions I provided, they worked in pairs to produce a visually annotated transcript of one short segment. I collate all transcriptions, and redistribute an annotated script for the entire half-hour program, including commercials. For the next phase of the assignment, students prepared a content and visual analysis of their segment of the show in relation to the entire thirty-minute news program. I asked them to examine its formal aspects, such as the format of the program, how the program moves from segment to segment, the purpose of different segments, and the form of audience address. From here we moved first to a discussion of Stuart Hall's essay, "The Narrative Construction of Reality," then to an elaboration of the role of the media in the construction of "the news," and finally to a consideration of the relationship between the news, narrative, ideology, and culture.[2] For their first paper assignment students were instructed to identify and elaborate one of the narratives that this news program constructs about contemporary United States culture. They were instructed to refer back to the visual and content analyses they produced to support their interpretations.

The "Reading and Writing Culture" course is organized around the study of the construction of meaning and dissemination of knowledge through different forms of cultural expression. The emphasis here is on discovering the "constructedness" of cultural knowledge (Raymond Williams) through a close examination of cultural texts. Throughout this course, the notion of a text is broadened to include nonliterary forms of communication, such as news reports, advertisements, popular magazines, electronic bulletin boards, and subcultural practices. Of equal importance is the investigation of what's involved in reading different types of texts, including those presented visually, tele-visually, aurally (music and speech), spatially, and bodily.

Theoretically, this course is grounded in an understanding of culture as an ensemble of signifying practices; following this, the course is *process oriented* in that the exercises, lectures, and reading material elaborate the ways in which reading and writing are productive cultural *practices* of meaning construction. We move from exercises in seemingly objective methods of analysis (such as content analysis and semiotics), to a discussion of different practices of interpretation (structuralist, feminist, psychoanalytic). In a similar way, we move from the consideration of seemingly objective cultural texts, such as news programs and documentaries, to more interpretive and expressive cultural forms, including special interest magazines, films, and popular fiction. In a broad sense, this course moves from a reflection model of culture to a mediation model, in which culture is understood to be produced through the interactions among texts, formal characteristics, reading, and writing practices.

The objectives for students in this course include: (1) to understand the constructedness of cultural texts and, relatedly, the different ways in which culture is written; (2) to understand how popular media participates in the social and narrative construction of reality; (3) to gain basic familiarity with notions of semiotics, signification, codes, and conventions; and (4) to investigate what's involved in the practice of reading different types of cultural texts. This course lays the foundation for upper-division cultural studies courses that continue to study different types of texts, and, more importantly, begin to elaborate the process of constructing cultural criticism.

Configured in this way, the "Reading and Writing Culture" course could probably fit into a number of disciplinary curricula. The outline I offer here is for a course that was designed to fit into a literary studies curriculum, positioned conceptually between a "Writing Across the Curriculum" course and introductory literature courses. The second course I describe follows from the first but is specifically designed to address a second preoccupation of cultural studies: the focus on popular cultures and the culture of everyday life. This second course builds on the objectives of the "Reading and Writing Culture" course in that it relies on a broader notion of what counts as a text and defines culture as a complex system of signifying practices, textual dissemination, and productive reception. But in the "Popular Culture" course, the focus shifts to a consideration of the kinds of knowledges that are often subjugated (in Foucault's sense) in the academy—knowledges that can't be generalized or easily determined in advance—the knowledges of pleasure in the consumption of popular culture. In so doing, this course explicitly rejects an elitist definition of culture in favor of a notion of culture as "the expressive practices and involvements of everyday life" (Willis, "Art or Culture?").

"Introduction to Popular Culture."

In the "Popular Culture" course, I expand the definition of culture to include the practices of everyday creativity that give shape to the process of identity formation. In this course, students are instructed to think critically about the connection between personal identity and popular culture. The framework for such an analysis of youth subjectivity and identity comes from lectures and readings about the subculture work of British cultural studies.[3] Here I introduce the notion of ideology, drawing on James Berlin's elaboration of a social-epistemic rhetoric. As he describes it: "the material, the social, and the subjective are at once the producers and the products of ideology, and ideology must continually be challenged so as to reveal its economic and political consequences for individuals."[4] My ideological aim in this course is to instruct students about the production of cultural criticism as it is developed through a close analysis of subcultural practices and popular cultural texts.

For their first exercise students contruct a media autobiography that describes their relation to various forms of popular texts/media, as well as their experience or access to material media culture: Do they own a television? Do they buy music? What kind? What form? What kind of media devices do they use? What signs, symbols, and products do they use to establish an identity? How does a person construct an identity? I ask them to reflect on the forms of popular culture they enjoy and describe the kinds of identities it promotes. From here we move to a discussion of how identity is itself a cultural construction, of the biological, the material, the social, and the popular. As in the first course, the focus here is on the productive act of reading culture in which identity itself, a fiercely individualistic notion, is understood to be a symbolic and creative but no less culturally determined construction.

In the second part of the course I present lectures on the conventions and formal elements of various media and popular cultural forms (music, television and film, dance, and visual art). We discuss the construction of representations of gender, ethnicity, and race, and how these representations are, in turn appropriated, performed, and reproduced. I present background lectures on methods of media studies including encoding/decoding studies and subculture ethnographies.

In the final section of the course, the group project challenges students to critically engage a popular cultural issue. Some of the more successful topics from past courses include: "Whitewashing America: Race and Ethnicity in the Media," "Gender Advertisements: Buying and Selling What," "Media Terrorism: Scandals, Spectacles, and Ethics," and "Selling Science: From Sputnik to Star Wars."[5] The focus of the course now shifts from teacher-centered discussions to student performances and discussions. These projects not only require that students get together outside class, but more importantly that they actively engage their own popular culture and begin to develop investigative research techniques. For many students, these reports often represent breakthrough understandings of what it means to talk about the social construction of something. For other students, the group project offers an opportunity to critically reflect on their own cultural pursuits and to consider what they take to be intensely individual tastes or opinions as determined by broader economic and social relations.

Although the first two courses I've described here focus exclusively on contemporary culture and popular media, I must stress that cultural studies inherits from Marxism a more specific interest in the study of historical forms of subjectivity and material life. As Richard Johnson argues, "All social practices can be looked at from a cultural point of view, for the work they do, subjectively. This goes, for instance, for factory work, for trade union organization, for life in and around the supermarket, as well as for obvious targets like 'the media'" (45). To offset two common misunderstandings about the study of popular culture, namely, that it is either inherently resistant, or the converse, that it is totally determining, I begin this course with a lecture on the history of mass culture, the construction of the notion of "the popular," and the place of the popular in the academy. The point of this lecture is to historicize the contemporary shape of mass culture and to establish the objective for the rest of the course, which, broadly conceived, is to investigate the ways in which media institutions, personal identities, and "experiences," are subtly shaped but not fully determined by ideology. The next course I describe attempts to lay out the broader history of cultural studies, to show how the focus on contemporary culture is only one moment or site of cultural criticism.

"Introduction to Cultural Studies"

In keeping with the main point of the opening section of this essay, I must reassert that there are as many ways to organize an introductory course in cultural studies as there are narratives about the identity of cultural studies itself. The course I describe here though is intended to fit into an undergraduate literary studies curriculum where the history of the discipline of English studies is not taught.[6] Clearly, any course design would have to take account of the curricular offerings already in place, especially those courses that introduce the variety of contemporary literary criticisms or the range of contemporary interpretive theories.

This course demonstrates two objectives that I think are of importance for an introductory course in cultural studies. Firstly, such a course should elaborate the *specificity* of cultural studies including its historical development out of British literary studies, the formation of the field of study that self-consciously takes the name "cultural studies," and its grounding in Marxist, feminist, and postcolonialist political critiques. The point here is that for all its fluidity and multidisciplinarity, "Cultural Studies" nevertheless names an identifiable set of critical projects. In this sense it is important to show how cultural studies emerges (as a "problematic," in Hall's terms) from a set of debates about the relationship between literature and society such that early issues included discussion about literacy, class identity, and national education. Furthermore, it is important to explain that cultural studies is concerned to elaborate the historically specific relation between forms of culture and the articulation of class, gender, racial and ethnic identities, struggles and domination. Secondly, the course must also represent the *heterogeneity* of various cultural studies projects, not only the early projects of Birmingham but also the more recent ones coming out of different disciplinary contexts (i.e., in anthropology, rhetoric, film studies). This is the point at which the foundational commitments of cultural studies work against its easy codification in an undergraduate program of study. Although there are recognizable founding figures and some agreement on the importance of certain issues and key debates, they cannot be stitched together as a progressive narrative of development. In short, the introductory course in cultural studies must not only relay the specific history of a set of practices, it must also explain how that history is constructed, institutionalized, and most importantly, contested.

This version of the "Introduction to Cultural Studies" course is organized around a set of historical topics. The first section describes the rise of modernism and the development of the concept of mass culture. The broad historical context of the development of cultural studies is elaborated in terms of a set of questions or problematics: how to describe the historical and economic changes of modernism, how to evaluate the rise of consumerism by which a large majority of society gains access to products of culture, and how to assess the role of the media in the production of hegemonic consent. In a broad sense these issues establish the two charges of cultural studies: to contribute to the critical analysis of everyday life and to engage a series of intellectual debates with literary theory, European social and political philosophy, and feminist and postcolonialist theory. In an effort to make this set of issues more concrete, the second section of the course presents the early history of the development of cultural studies in Britain. Here it is important to describe how the Centre for Contemporary Cultural Studies in Birmingham was organized, in particular as a way of describing in greater detail the issues, essays and debates that were produced by the working group on "Literature and Society." Thus this section would include an overview of different approaches to the study of the relationships among literature, society and culture that could begin, for example, with Raymond Williams' book *Culture and Society*, or with the essay "Literature and Society: Mapping the Field" written by members of the CCCS working group in "Literature and Society." From that point, the course could turn to a discussion of how the relationship between literature and culture has been conceptualized within different traditions of scholarship. This sets the stage for discussions about the process of institutionalization in general, and, more specifically, of literary criticism in the United States. The third and final section of the course presents overviews of the different projects of cultural studies, including those that originated in Birmingham and those that have been initiated more recently in different places in the United States: encoding/decoding studies, subculture ethnographies, media studies, new historicism, symbolic interactionism, ethnomethodology, cultural anthropology, popular culture, American studies, and feminist cultural studies. In a broad sense, this course organization follows Brantlinger's description of the move from literature to culture to ideology as a way to account for the changes in the preoccupation of cultural studies over the past thirty years.

The structure of assignments depend upon the level and the institutional context of the course, but one of the assignments that has worked well in the past is a modified group project where students work in small groups to investigate the way that culture is studied within different traditions of schorlarship. Working from one major text, students use bibliographic research techniques to describe a cultural studies project. The cultural anthropology group, for example, began by elaborating the model of culture implied in *Writing Culture*, by James Clifford and George Marcus, and then identified other people in the field who conceptualize their work as being informed by cultural studies. Another group delineated the differences between various approaches to the study of culture by describing an essay from each of the following approaches: dramaturgical, Marxist, post-structuralist, and feminist.[7] In both cases, the point of the assignment is to facilitate student engagement with cross-disciplinary scholarship and, relatedly, to require them to formulate an account of the central questions or issues that animate other traditions of cultural studies. A related objective for this assignment directs students to identify journals in other disciplines that could inform their own work in literary studies. The assignment could be limited to a description and analysis of only one such project or could function to get students started on their own projects. In this case, the final assignment for the course could require them to present a proposal for a critical cultural investigation of their own design and political investment.

The courses I have described here are only suggestive of the type of cultural studies courses that could be developed within a literary studies curriculum. The construction of a program or emphasis in cultural studies would be best served by taking advantage of other courses that are already in place, such as film studies, women and popular culture, introduction to postcolonialist literatures, the history of rhetoric, survey of contemporary interpretive theory, or literature and the history of ideas. Another important project is to coordinate efforts with other disciplines and programs, to elaborate the connections between cultural studies and traditional departments — communication and media studies, sociology, anthropology, and history — and interdisciplinary programs in women's studies, science and culture, and multi-cultural studies. One of the key issues that this raises concerns the organization of the English department and the process of disciplining knowledge or scholarship. In the introductory course, as well as in graduate seminars, the first item on the agenda considers the institutional place of the course itself, how it is determined, how it is policed, and how it is contested. This would be one way to provide a space in the organizational structure of the department for the kinds of discussions that Gerald Graff argues are critically important for the ongoing revision of the discipline. In one essay, Graff argues that "the university should subsume literary studies under cultural studies and cultural history, conceived not as a privileged approach but as a framework that encourages ideological dialectic while retaining enough chronological structure to keep focus and continuity from being lost ("Taking Cover" 42). In this sense, Graff's model for the reorganization of literary studies recalls Mary Poovey's description of cultural criticism. Both call for a new organization of the curriculum to foreground the set of institutional practices and discourses that organize and discipline knowledge in the humanities. The emphases here, as well as in the cultural studies courses I've described, are on cultural practices, social and literary formations, and the conditions of possibility of intellectual work itself. Changes in organizing structures, however, do not necessarily guarantee changes in classroom practices; clearly another front of analysis and revision must address the pedagogical practices of cultural studies teachers. The question remains how such changes will be enacted.

Strategies and Tactics

I address the practical issue of curriculum construction for several reasons, but I will only elaborate one here now. Feminist teachers, who are already in the academy, must begin to think *strategically* about how to introduce undergraduate students to feminist, antiracist, postcolonialist cultural studies in more formalized ways than through ad hoc writing projects, chance lectures, or serendipitous elective courses. This issue, of course, is related to the question of the institutional context of cultural studies. As a multidisciplinary project, cultural studies could probably fit into a number of departments. Certainly in the last five years a range of disciplines have made claims to some sort of project of cultural analysis in the name of cultural studies, so that in the United States the name identifies a space of cultural contestation among traditional disciplines. Upon closer inspection, we can see how cultural studies is caught in a crosscurrent of institutionalizing forces. Among other things, institutionalization involves strategies of identity formation and reproduction that involve countervailing forces: one of dissemination and dispersal and another of centralization and codification. On the one hand, cultural studies is marked by diffuse boundaries that attest to its theoretical commitments to the *trans*-disciplinary production of cultural criticism. But on the other, the construction of a narrative of identity is important to legitimate cultural studies as a distinct academic enterprise for purposes of funding, hiring, course design, and curriculum construction.

Given the current set of institutional arrangements, it seems likely that the near future of cultural studies may best be played out in departments of English. But these departments are only one of several possible places for cultural studies. Even though these other places are yet to be determined, no doubt they will be located within institutional networks, which is to say that although they may not be so *centrally* academic (i.e., critical journalism, new social movements, or new art formations), they will still be institutionalized in some way. Within the current configuration of capitalist disorganization, spaces entirely outside of institutional relationships seem to be utopian fantasies. If the current form of hegemonic struggle requires that we take up institutional positions where we can, once there we must work to elaborate the specificity of cultural studies so that it is recognized as distinct from traditional disciplinary programs — that cultural studies is about doing things differently. And yet, the call for specificity, even when offered as part of such open-ended accounts of the commitments of cultural studies, are often taken up as part of the disciplinary and the *disciplining* apparatus of U.S. academic departments in such a way as to produce a deleterious unintended consequence: the formation of a canon of sorts of cultural studies — of popular forms of cultural expression or of certain authors, texts, or practices. In this case, the disciplining of cultural studies produces a palpable tension when a heterogeneous collection of critical cultural projects becomes homogenized by certain practices of institutionalization. I hope I have shown that cultural studies isn't simply accomplished by replacing so-called "elite" objects of study with "low-brow" texts, nor even by the study of the context of classic texts. Furthermore, to "do" cultural studies is not simply to "do away" with the study of literature. If, in one sense, it is about the study of the production, reception, and circulation of cultural texts, it is also about working-class culture and the production of cultural criticism and hegemonic struggle.

When cultural studies is "done" within the confines of a department of English, it is in fact enacting a *tactical* maneuver to infiltrate the "proper" disciplines. By complicating the reproduction of disciplinary knowledge, it works to open a space for the production of cultural criticism. Furthermore, with its critical focus on the texts of everday life, it also works to intervene in the reproduction of hegemonic consent. We know that domination is not won for all times, for all situations, but must be continually reproduced over and over in opposition to forces of dispersion and creative resistance — forces that threaten to destabilize organized consent. Our aim through cultural studies is to amplify such disruptive forces.

Notes

1. The nine-second sound track begins with three electronic blips, continues with a music interlude, and ends with a deep male voice-over that says, "From Turner Broadcasting System, this is the Headline News Network." The clip visually and aurally establishes a sense of urgency and criticality through the rapid rhythm of edits, the inward movement of the camera, and timbre of the voice-over. The rows of TV monitors symbolize the different "feeds" or sources of information that CNN draws on. These also symbolize the multiple points of surveillance that CNN deploys. The understanding then, is not only that CNN is connected (cybernetically) to the rest of the information world through its many communication channels but that it also has multiple lenses focused on that world, so that the entire world could be said to be under its watchful gaze. The viewer, too, is plugged in to the same cybernetic network. Through the use of a point-of-view shot looking at news copy, news-in-process, symbolically, *CNN Headline News* connects the viewer with a larger, global communication and information network; a network that is signified not as a "global village," with its connotations of simplicity, community, and cohesion, but rather a network that is high tech, up-to-the-minute, that comes to us as a visual reality in virtual space. CNN is our technologized eye and ear on the world; the current — at this moment — world, the "news" world of multinational modernity. The decision to have students watch CNN is not arbitrary, of course. Although some people claim that the news is a high form of masculinist discourse, with the attendant problems of objectivity, rationality, and the different valuation of the public from the private, it is also a broadly available discourse that students are familiar with in some form. There are few other such popular discourses that all students have familiarity with — not so with popular music, fashion, skateboarding, film, or even television programs. The focus on CNN becomes even more interesting lately considering that Saddam Hussein is reported to rely on the Cable News Network as his "sole source of information" about U.S. military deployment (reprinted in the *Chicago Tribune*, 24 August 1990).

2. Other readings for this course are taken from several books in the Methuen series "Studies in Communication" including: *Key Concepts in Communication* (Tim O'Sullivan, John Hartley, Danny Saunders, and John Fiske 1983); *Introduction to Communication Studies* (John Fiske 1988) *An Introduction to Language and Society* (Martin Montgomery 1986); and *Film as Social Practice* (Graeme Turner 1989). Other reading selections come from: *Reading the Popular*, by John Fiske; *Gender Advertisements*, by Erving Goffman; *Image-Music-Text*, by Roland Barthes; and *Female Desires: How They Are Sought, Bought, and Packaged*, by Rosalind Coward.

3. Key texts for this course include *Subcultures: The Meaning of Style*, by Dick Hebdige; Angela McRobbie's critical response to the British subculture work, "Settling Accounts with Subculture: A feminist critique"; *Popular Culture:*

The Metropolitan Experience, by Iain Chambers; *Understanding popular Culture*, by John Fiske; and the anthology, *Making Face, Making Soul: Haciendo Caras*, edited by Gloria Anzaldua.

4. The kinds of questions that Berlin enumerates as part of his elaboration of the social-epistemic rhetoric are similar to the questions I use in the *CNN Headline News* analysis in the "Reading and Writing Culture" course: "Who benefits from a given version of truth? How are the material benefits of society distributed? To whom does our knowledge designate power?" (489). But in the "Popular Culture" course, students confront more explicitly the way in which they are situated and determined by larger social and economic forces (Berlin).

5. Other topics that have stimulated interesting group reports include: "Feminist Media Watch: Transgressions and Transformations," "Women, Technology, and the Future," "Television Ethnography," "Spectator Sports: Bodies in Slow Motion," "Nukespeak: National Security and Imperialism," "Cyberpunk: Postmodern Science Fiction." The reader I prepare for the course includes at least two articles on every topic that I assign as background reading for the rest of the class. The articles also help the students get started on their research and also to allow me to influence the critical angle of the project.

6. In an essay titled "Critiques of Culture: A Course," Jon Cook describes how one such cultural studies course, offered through the School of English and American Studies at the University of East Anglia, was organized "in terms of an unresolved question about the relation between English and European resources" and took up the issue of the state of national culture. This essay is included in a book edited by David Punter, called *Introduction to Contemporary Cultural Studies* (London: Longman 1986) that includes several other essays addressing the problems that arise when teaching cultural studies in Britain. As Punter elaborates in his introduction, although all the essays in this volume address British contemporary culture (after the Second World War), they also cannot avoid reference to historical and international influences.

7. One book that offers an overview of all these approaches, with the notable exception of feminism, is *Culture and Society: Contemporary Debates*, edited by Jeffrey C. Alexander and Steven Seidman. The issue of the relationship between feminism and cultural studies is addressed in my essay "Feminism and Cultural Studies."

Works Cited

Alexander, Jeffrey C., and Steven Seidman, eds. *Culture and Society: Contemporary Debates*. Cambridge: Cambridge University Press, 1990.

Alexander, Jeffrey C., ed. *Durkheimian Sociology: Cultural Studies*. Cambridge: Cambridge University Press, 1988.

Anzaldua, Gloria, ed. *Making Face, Making Soul: Haciendo Caras*. San Francisco: Aunt Lute Foundation, 1990.

Balsamo, Anne. "Feminism and Cultural Studies." *Journal of the Midwest Modern Language Association* (Spring 1991): 50–73.

Balsamo, Anne and Michael Greer. "Cultural Studies, Literary Studies, and Pedagogy: the Undergraduate Literature Course." *Changing Classroom Practices: Resources for Literary and Cultural Studies*. Ed. David Downing. Urbana: University of Illinois Press, forthcoming.

Barthes, Roland. *Image-Music-Text*. London: Fontana, 1977.

Batsleer, Janet, Tony Davis, Rebecca O'Rourke and Chris Weedon. *Rewriting English: Cultural Politics of Gender and Class*. London: Methuen, 1985.

Becker, Howard S., and Michal M. McCall, eds. *Symbolic Interaction and Cultural Studies*. Chicago: University of Chicago Press, 1990.

Berlin, James. "Rhetoric and Ideology in the Writing Class." *College English*, 50, 5 (September 1988): 477–94.

Brantlinger, Patrick. *Crusoe's Footprints: Cultural Studies in Britain and America*. Routledge: New York, 1990.

Carby, Hazel. "Civilization's Discontent: An Interview with Professor Hazel Carby on Canons, Curricula, and Change." *Village Voice* (24 January 1989): 3–4.

Carey, James W. *Communication as Culture: Essays on media and society*. Boston: Unwin Hyman, 1989.

Chambers, Iain. *Popular Culture: The Metropolitan Experience*. London: Methuen, 1986.

Clifford, James, and George E. Marcus, eds. *Writing Culture: The Poetics and Politics of Ethnography*. Berkeley: University of California Press, 1986.

Coward, Rosalind. *Female Desires: How They Are Sought, Bought, and Packaged*. New York: Grove Press, 1985.

Fish, Stanley. "Being Interdisciplinary Is So Very Hard to Do." *Profession 1989*: 15–22.

Fiske, John. *Introduction to Communication Studies*. New York: Methuen, 1988.

———. *Reading the Popular*. Boston: Unwin Hyman, 1989.

———. *Understanding Popular Culture*. Boston: Unwin Hyman, 1989.

Giroux, Henry A., David Shumway, Paul Smith, and James Sosnoski. "The Need for Cultural Studies." *Teachers as Intellectuals: Toward a Critical Pedagogy of Learning*. Ed. Henry Giroux. Massachusetts: Bergin and Garvey Pub, 1988.

Giroux, Henry, and Roger I. Simon, eds. *Popular Culture, Schooling, and Everyday Life*. Massachusetts: Bergin and Garvey Pub, 1989.

Goffman, Erving. *Gender Advertisements*. New York: Harper Colophon, 1976.

Graff, Gerald. "Taking Cover in Coverage," *Profession 1986*: 41–45.

———. "How to Deal with the Humanities Crisis: Organize It" *ADE Bulletin* 95 (Spring 1990): 4–10.

———. "Teach the Conflicts," *South Atlantic Quarterly* 89, 1, (Winter 1990): 51–67.

Grossberg, Lawrence. "On Postmodernism and Articulation: An Interview with Stuart Hall." *Journal of Communication Inquiry*. Special issue on Stuart Hall. 10, 2 (Summer 1986): 61−77.

———. "The Circulation of Cultural Studies: 'Birmingham' in America." *Critical Studies in Mass Communication* 6, 4 (December 1989): 413−21.

———. "The Formations of Cultural Studies: An American in Birmingham." *Strategies* 2 (1989): 114−48.

Hall, Stuart. "The Narrative Construction of Reality: An Interview with Stuart Hall." *Southern Review* 17 (March 1984): 33−40.

———. "Cultural Studies: Two Paradigms." *Media, Culture and Society* 2 (1980): 57−72.

———. "Cultural Studies and the Centre: Some Problematics and Problems." *Culture, Media, Language*. Eds. Stuart Hall, Dorothy Hobson, Andrew Lowe, and Paul Willis. London: Hutchinson, 1980. 15−47.

———. "The Emergence of Cultural Studies and the Crisis of the Humanities," *October* 53 (1990): 11−23.

———. "Cultural Studies and its Theoretical Legacies." *Cultural Studies*. Eds. Lawrence Grossberg, Cary Nelson, and Paula A. Treichler, New York: Routledge, 1992. 277−86.

Hebdige, Dick. *Subcultures: The Meaning of Style*. London: Methuen, 1978.

Hoggart, Richard. *The Uses of Literacy*. New York: Oxford University Press, 1958.

Johnson, Richard. "What is Cultural Studies Anyway?" *Social Text* 6, 1 (1987): 38−80.

Lipking, Lawrence I. "The Practice of Theory." *Profession: 1983*: 21−28.

"Literature and Society: Mapping the Field." The Working Group on Literature and Society. *Working Papers in Cultural Studies 4*. Birmingham: Centre for Contemporary Cultural Studies, 1973: 21−50.

McRobbie, Angela. "Settling Accounts with Subcultures: A Feminist Critique." *Culture, Ideology, and Social Process: A Reader*. Eds. Tony Bennett, Graeme Martin, Colin Mercer, and Janet Woollacott. London: Batsford Academic and Education Ltd, 1981. 113−23.

Montgomery, Martin. *An Introduction to Language and Society*. New York: Methuen, 1986.

Nelson, Cary R. ed. *Theory in the Classroom*. Urbana: University of Illinois Press, 1986.

O'Sullivan, Tim, John Hartley, Danny Saunders, and John Fiske. *Key Concepts in Communication*. New York: Methuen, 1983.

Peck, Jeffrey M. "Advanced Literary Study as Cultural Study: A Redefinition of the Discipline." *Profession: 1985*: 49−54.

Poovey, Mary. "Cultural Criticism: Past and Present." *College English* 52, 6 (October) 1990: 615−25.

Prince, Gerald. "Literary Theory and the Undergraduate Curriculum." *Profession: 1984*: 37−40.

Punter, David, ed. *Introduction to Contemporary Cultural Studies*. London: Longman, 1986.

Turner, Graeme. *Film as Social Practice*. New York: Methuen, 1989.

──. *British Cultural Studies: An introduction*. Boston: Unwin Hyman, 1990.

Widdowson, Peter. *Re-Reading English* Methuen: London, 1982.

Williams, Raymond. *Culture and Society: 1780−1950*. New York: Harper and Row, 1966.

Willis, Paul. "Art or Culture? An Inquiry." *Popular Culture, Schooling, and Everyday Life*. Eds. Henry A. Giroux, Roger I. Simon, and Contributors. Massachusetts: Bergin & Garvey Pub, 1989. 131−46.

Willis, Paul, with Simon Jones, Joyce Canåan, and Geoff Hurd. *Common Culture: Symbolic Work at Play in the Everyday Cultures of the Young*. Boulder, CO: Westview Press, 1990.

Winkler, Karen, J. "Proponents of 'Multicultural' Humanities Research Call for a Critical Look at Its Achievement." *Chronicle of Higher Education* (28 November 1990): A5+.

Women's Studies Group, Centre for Contemporary Cultural Studies. *Women Take Issue: Aspects of Women's Subordination*. London: Hutchinson, 1978.

Cultural Studies Courses

Introduction

Michael Vivon

When the composition faculty at the University of Missouri at Kansas City began developing its cultural studies composition program, it encountered an immediate difficulty. Although cultural studies as a critical practice has a documented history, as pedagogical practice it has little documented history and an amazing variety of contents and procedures. The pedagogic essays in this volume are a step in the creation of that history and offer models to other teachers interested in developing courses informed by cultural studies. The essays do not represent the entire range of cultural studies praxis; however, they do represent historical moments in the development of cultural studies as a recognizable practice separate from, for example, social constructionism, writing process, reader response, critical thinking, or any number of other "schools" of teaching. In the same way that teachers say "I'm a process teacher" or "I teach critical thinking," teachers are now overheard saying "I teach cultural studies." Whether we approve of this development is unimportant. It happens and will continue to happen. This naming is one way in which concerned, reflective teachers define themselves and their beliefs. The essays you are about to read illustrate how much room exists within the parameters of cultural studies pedagogy and should help us understand what questions we might ask to understand what our colleagues mean when they say "cultural studies."

Clearly, among the first questions we must ask are those of definition: What do you mean by "culture"? Which culture do you mean? What culture is reflected in your voice as you define yourself? Michael Blitz and Mark Hurlbert begin by asking these questions, among others, and by questioning the role of the academy within the entire culture business. Appropriately, they end their essay with a question: "What set of pedagogies have we packaged and placed on line in an attempt to transmit a view of (our) culture which looks less and less like us — or anybody?" In a way, the remainder of the essays in this collection are responses to that central question.

Another familiar question relates to substance: What is the appropriate content for cultural studies? Once again we find no orthodoxy in the answers provided. Within these pages you will find the focus of cultural study to be remarkably diffuse. The nature of academic discourse. Shakespeare(s). Raymond Carver. The texts of cultural studies. "Let's Makes A Deal." The research paper. *Easy Rider*. Commercials. Gender. Court decisions. The students' own lives. The content of cultural studies is, not surprisingly, as elusive as the definition of culture. The content(s) of cultural studies are the "things" of culture which help shape language, the nature of experience, ideology, and, ultimately within English studies, the production and reception of texts.

If the definition of culture and the content of cultural studies remain elusive, the next question comes unforced to mind: Is there any unifying element within cultural studies—methodology? theory? politics? Once again a certain amount of equivocation is in order. You will discover as you read that our authors practice a wide variety of teaching techniques, that they vary both in how sophisticated they are in their use of theory and in how much they make theory a transparent part of the classroom, that some clearly have a more overt political agenda than others. Despite these differences, however, they share some important features.

They are all sensitive to the culture of the classroom with its special interactions between the authority of the teacher, the institutional apprenticeship of the student, and the problematic authority of the text in relation to the cultures which interact with it. All investigate the role of culture in subjective epistemologies, that is to say, the role of culture in making knowledge for the individual and the groups to which individuals belong. They all intensely explore the social construction of language. They all attempt to establish classrooms in which democratic critique, the critique essential to the concept of participatory democracy, is valued and practiced. They are all teachers, teachers with courage enough to present our readers with historical artifacts, within historical moments, knowing full well that the classes they describe will never exist again; only the processes of cultural studies, also dynamic rather than static, will be repeated.

10

A Course in "Cultural Studies"

Paul Smith

The purpose of this paper is not to make any tendentious intervention — theoretical or practical — into the multiform debates which increasingly attend the rise of cultural studies as a field or discipline within the university right now; nor to argue for or to vindicate any particular approach to cultural studies in the classroom. Rather, what follows is limited to a kind of reportage: that is, I intend to sketch out some of the elements that went to form a particular cultural studies course, one that I designed and taught for the first time in the fall of 1990. Of course, to undertake such a reportage is not so innocent a task as I'd like it to be. Just by dint of the fact that any course is itself an intervention, a rhetorical gesture constituted in a whole set of other rhetorical gestures, a description of it will reproduce certain assumptions and produce particular meanings. Equally, the description of a course is also an intervention of a sort — even an argument of a sort — into a context wider than that of the school in which the course has been taught; in that sense, this essay will probably be understood as an act of persuasion, though I don't fully intend it to be. What I do mean, however, is to contribute to a genre which I'm not sure exists and, if it does exist, whose conventions I'm ignorant of, but whose existence seems to me to be desirable: the genre of essays about the details of our teaching. That is, I don't think that teachers in the humanities can do themselves any harm by breaking out of the almost complete isolation and even fearfulness in which we usually construct our syllabi and conduct our teaching.

Context

The course in question was rather ambitiously, even hubristically, called "What is Cultural Studies?"—rather less to echo the title of Richard Johnson's well-known article and rather more to repeat and perhaps attempt to adumbrate an answer to a question which gets frequently asked at the school I teach at, Carnegie Mellon University. The English department at CMU has had an undergraduate major in literary and cultural studies since 1984.[1] While there are other departmental majors for undergraduates (creative, professional, and technical writing, and possible combinations of those), all majors of whatever stripe currently take an English department, core-course sequence ("Discursive Practices," "Discourse and Historical Change," and "Reading 20th Century Culture"); this innovative core sequence is currently taught exclusively by literary and cultural studies faculty.

Through the presence of this undergraduate structure, the actual existence of a field or discipline called "cultural studies" is more or less taken for granted at CMU by now; and yet the nature of cultural studies—what tasks it sets itself, what methods it employs, what results it claims, and so on—is badly understood, even by those sympathetic to it, and sometimes by those practicing it. Most of all, students beyond the English department seem to have no real sense of what cultural studies might look like. Now, the English Department has traditionally supplied 200-level courses for nonmajors, which have had as their rationale the introduction of aspects of the discipline of English to students outside this department, and indeed outside the College of Humanities and Social Sciences; such courses are offered in part to fulfill nonmajor humanities requirements, and partly with an eye to attracting students into the English department. Traditionally, and even after the establishment of the somewhat radical curriculum of the literary and cultural studies major, such 200-level courses *has* tended to be literature survey courses, courses in Shakespeare, and the like. Thus, they had not really represented an introduction to the dominant cultural studies strand of the English curriculum. So "What is Cultural Studies?" was established at the 200 level, in part as such an introductory course, but also in part as a way of showing that the literary and cultural studies program was confident enough in its own existence to make the effort to explain the nature of cultural studies to the campus.

Course Aims

At the introductory level, then, the course was intended to specify the kinds of approaches and topics, as well as the kinds of theoretical material, that are to be found within the three core courses and within the program's fuller curriculum of cultural studies. The aims that I established for the course were stated on the syllabus as follows:

> Inevitably, in the space of one semester we shan't be able to answer fully the question that the course's title poses. Apart from other considerations, "Cultural Studies" is a field which purports to be able to investigate the cultural formations of any historical period or cultural context, whereas this course by and large restricts itself to contemporary anglophone culture in the North. However, by looking at this narrow cultural and historical range and also at some of the important theoretical texts that seem relevant to it, we shall be able to consider for ourselves some of the central questions and problems that "cultural studies" has formulated about its project. At the risk of prejudicing our discussion of those questions and problems, it might be useful to say at the outset that "cultural studies" is largely concerned with describing and explaining the multiple ways in which both individuals and social groups and their cultural products and artefacts are constructed by, signify within, and also resist the dominant cultural formations of their time and place. To say even this much, however, is already to begin on an explanation of social relations and it will be as well to bear in mind that "cultural studies" is a discourse in and through which all explanations of culture, including those of "cultural studies" itself, are to be questioned.

Three of the main assumptions that I tried to use to inform the everyday working of the course can be read from this opening description: first, the notion that cultural studies can deal with a variety of historically and geographically located cultural formations, though always with a theoretical project in mind; second, that within those formations it is concerned with the construction, signification, and resistance of individual groups in relation to dominant cultural formations; and third, that it is a discipline whose methodology is unsettled, questioning itself and the interdiscipline in which it finds itself. This last point is derived from an expression of Gayatri Spivak's by which I have been struck and which I think must be a crucial premise to the theoretical project of cultural studies: the idea of "the pedagogy of the humanities as the arena of cultural explanations that question the explanations of culture" (Spivak 117).

Syllabus

Each of those above assumptions informed my selection of a syllabus. The first task was to seek what I came during the course to call our "object of study": that is, a time and a place where the construction, signification, and resistance of individuals and groups in relation to dominant culture formations could be read through cultural products and artifacts. And the second, though mostly simultaneous, task was to set a theoretical agenda, that of making a selection of largely theoretical texts which would provide students with what we often like to call a "background" in the literature of "cultural studies".

The first task produced a number of options, which all depended pretty much upon my own levels of knowledge, expertise, experience and, indeed, willingness. From amongst several options I settled upon some aspects of British culture in the last forty years and decided to use Dick Hebdige's book *Hiding in the Light* as a central text and to act as a certain kind of guide through some of the questions of the construction of British culture in that time. Around this text I gathered some others that addressed some of the same questions: some films— *Sid and Nancy, Absolute Beginners, Quadrophenia*, and *Passion of Remembrance*— as well as other readings—pieces from *There ain't no Black in the Union Jack* (Gilroy), and *Resistance Through Rituals* (Hall). Together these texts were to propose a number of different topics, and ways of dealing with, those topics around British culture, within a general project of learning about the relations between sub-cultural subjects and dominant culture.

The second task was to articulate with this cultural moment a number of theoretical texts from amongst those many which might constitute an inchoate cultural studies canon. Part of the issue here was to provide texts which would, in a sense, argue with each other, question each other's "explanations of culture"; and another part was to allow students a familiarity with some of the theory that has histori-cally been of use to cultural studies. With that last point in mind, the first three weeks of the class were dedicated to readings of Freud, Marx, Gramsci, and Althusser. To help with this introduction, we read chapters from *Crusoe's Footprints* (Brantlinger), an account of cultural studies as a discipline (this book didn't seem to help the students much and was subsequently dropped). After that, we began on the Hebdige book, inspissating some of Hebdige's topics with other articles by Adorno ("Jazz"), Bourdieu (*Distinction*), and Benjamin ("Work of Art").

The above texts took the class to mid-semester. Thereafter, we followed the track of Hebdige's book into its final section, which is concerned with the issue of postmodernism and the politics of its productions. Here we began for a short while with *Mythologies* (Barthes), thinking of that book—with its insistence on the usefulness of linguistic and psychoanalytical paradigms for the explanation of culture—as a kind of revision of the more modernist concerns of the first part of the course, and also as an introduction to some of the assumptions that reside beneath Hebdige's text. Then, addressing the issue of postmodernism more directly, we read three essays from *Universal Abandon? The Politics of Postmodernism* (Ross): my own

"Visiting the Banana Republic," Meaghan Morris on Crocodile Dundee, and Laura Kipnis' essay on feminism. These texts, along with Gilroy's and Hall's, took us to the end of the semester, and the syllabus finally turned out as follows:

Week One
> Brantlinger, chapter 1;
> Freud, *Psychopathology of Everyday Life*

Weeks Two and Three
> Marx, Althusser, Gramsci;
> Brantlinger, chapter 3

Week Four
> Hebdige, *Hiding in the Light*
> Adorno

Week Five Bourdieu
> Movie: *Sid and Nancy*

Week Six
> Hebdige, *Hiding in the Light*
> Debord
> Movie: *Absolute Beginners*

Week Seven
> Hebdige, *Hiding in the Light*
> Benjamin
> Movie: *Quadrophenia*

Mid Semester
Week Eight
> Barthes, *Mythologies*

Weeks Nine
and Ten
> Hebdige, *Hiding in the Light*
> Essays from *Universal Abandon?*

Weeks Eleven
and Twelve
> Student Projects

Week Thirteen
> Hebdige, *Hiding in the Light*
> Essays from *Resistance through Ritual*

Week Fourteen
> Gilroy
> Movie: *Passion of Remembrance*

Students and Pedagogy

"What is Cultural Studies?" enrolled seventeen students, most of whom turned out to be seniors in various majors across the university; only three of them were English majors. There were two African-American students and slightly more women than men. These students were, in my view, fairly representative of the kinds of students CMU produces. Although only a couple of them were from engineering, most of them were majors in the school's rather extremely positivistic social science departments or from its vocational and computerized art school. Most of them would have had very little exposure to the kinds of thinking that I take cultural studies to promote.

Given this particular mixture, three consequences immediately ensued. First, with only seventeen students the class could be a seminar with lots of room for questions and discussion; second, with so many seniors the general level of discussion could be quite advanced; and third, the different disciplinary backgrounds of the students would necessitate that some discussion be entertained about the relation of cultural studies to the modes of other disciplines, and it was indeed this discussion that began the course.

For each class' reading assignment I left the students more or less to their own devices, apart from giving them a short description of the reading and telling them briefly what other texts it was intended to engage with and how. The plan was that classes should consist in a general discussion of the readings or of the films seen. Usually these discussions led to my giving a fifteen- or twenty-minute "mini-lecture" in which I attempted to pull together and make connections amongst the various points that had been brought up, while also bringing up issues that I felt had been missed or underplayed. Not all classes actually went that way, however. The main reason for this was that I began each class by asking for questions and comments about the previous class, and the students' interventions there provoked either a longer lecture from myself, or equally often a free-ranging class discussion or argument. Thus, the course could be characterized as being conducted quite informally, oscillating between class discussion and improvised lecturing.

This way of teaching gives students a lot of opportunity to contribute verbally, and it was partly on the nature and frequency of their contributions that I graded the students in this class. Their other main task was to produce a final project. Here again they were more or less left to their own devices, although I encouraged both collaborative efforts and projects in media other than writing. I also monitored these projects from the outset by asking for descriptions and making myself available for consultation out of class. The only other task was an in-class writing assignment where I asked them to summarize in a sentence or two each of the seventeen sections of "Work of Art" (Benjamin). The point of this exercise was to give me a sense of each of the students' grasp of what I took to be the most difficult text in the syllabus.

A Narrative of the Course

Here I can mention only a few of the topics that were put on the table in this course, and I've chosen to narrativize these insofar as they brought up what I take to be important theoretical issues. Again, I'm mostly reporting rather than arguing here. This means that many of the statements here are not fully elaborated or defended but are put forward simply to represent various positions and claims that were discussed in the course. I can only hope that readers do with this narrative what I hoped the students did with its raw material, namely, recognize it as an introductory provocation rather than as a fully fledged set of views about cultural studies. I should also say that the narrative will tend to give a somewhat rosy view of the cohesion of the course, in fact, and because of the style of teaching I adopted, ideas and connections were evidently a lot more ragged in their development than I'll be suggesting.

As I mentioned, the course began with a discussion—deriving from Brantlinger's first chapter on the idea of cultural studies as a response to a crisis or a crisis mentality in the humanities—of the disciplinary place of cultural studies. One remark of Brantlinger's received particular attention: "Most versions of literary theory point in the direction of a unified, inter- or anti-disciplinary theory and practice that, for lack of a better name, is now often called 'cultural studies'" (16). That remark provoked a lot of discussion about the nature of academic disciplines. Particularly, students wanted to know how the field differed from, say, cultural anthropology or even certain kinds of sociology, either in its choice of object or in its methodologies. My response was to suggest that "cultural studies" counters the immobilization in other disciplines of what might be similar objects of study; and also that its methodology is not fixed but rather could be thought of as a kind of metacommentary on assumptions and methods in other disciplines. The fundamental self-authorizing gesture in cultural studies, I claimed, has been the willingness to recognize the political and ideological dimensions of any realm of study as it approaches a particular object. Thus, part of cultural studies "difference" is its insistence that we recognize that all academic disciplines—including cultural studies—function politically and ideologically.

This general introduction was followed by a discussion, through Althusser, of the way in which "subjects" are pulled into place, or interpellated as subjects, not just of the law but of a more generally conceived set of cultural formations and knowledges. The disciplinary question was again brought up here with the claim that in most disciplinary conduct "objects of knowledge" are shorn of their political and ideological appurtenance by being isolated for study. One goal of cultural studies would be to recognize the indefeasible connectedness of such objects of knowledge with each other and with the cultural contexts in which they signify and in which their study signifies, as well as the place of the subject in relation to those objects and knowledges.

The points that I tried to make about the necessarily political and ideological significance of cultural objects provoked a free-wheeling discussion about the literary canon, about the politics of education and study, and of the place and function of the university. In that context it was difficult to avoid—and I didn't try to avoid—proposing cultural studies as in some sense a resistant operation which is designed to interrogate and analyze the elision and annulment of the political functions of the academic. This point was subvented by Althusser's notions of ideology, as they illuminated somewhat a debate the class conducted about the recent attack by the National Association of Scholars on a writing class at the University of Texas.[2] It was at about this time that we decided that Brantlinger's book would not be particularly useful in this course, since neither I nor most of the students had much time for his clear antipathy to the political dimension of cultural studies.

Within these discussions the notion of resistance had emerged in a vernacular way; the term was taken up in the next classes through readings of Freud (*Psychopathology*), selections from Marx and Gramsci, and a continued reading of Althusser. These texts became the occasion for beginning to theorize the notion of resistance. The important point here was to have students begin to think dialectically about the nature of power and dominance (rather than think in the "common sense" antinomies they had brought to the course: consciousness/unconsciousness, state power/individual powerlessness, oppression/resistance, First World/Third World, and so on). Indeed, these classes became increasingly central as the course went on, since throughout I found myself wanting to press quite hard the habit of dialectical thinking; in a sense, it was no unwelcome surprise to me to learn later that many of the students picked this up as the main topic of the course and as one of the centrally defining features of cultural studies.

This elaboration of a notion of resistance and of its dialectical poise was crucial to the class's reading of the first part of Hebdige, with its account of the dialectics of resistance and consent in British punk subculture. The phrase "hiding in the light" in fact became a shorthand way for us to refer to the way in which the "logic of transgression" (Hebdige's words) operates. Hebdige claims that subcultural style "translates the fact of being under scrutiny into the pleasure of being watched" (35). This claim was discussed at length as a potential model for thinking resistance.

Hebdige's chapter on punk and his reading of Sid Vicious opened onto a number of different topics that the class considered quite carefully. Notably, we examined his notion that resistance takes place at the point of representations: the movie about Sid Vicious' life, *Sid and Nancy*, was important here precisely as a kind of belated and recuperative representation of Vicious's own "hiding in the light." The students seemed already highly attuned to the way in which subcultural representations become commodified and to the possibility that this commodification neutralizes them. The class found many instances of this kind of "neutralization" — one African-American student spoke at length about the way in which the image of Nelson Mandela, the colors of Rastafarianism, and, to some extent, rap music have all been commodified and depoliticized both within and without the African-American community.

Central topics here — and ones that would later be picked up in relation to *Mythologies* (Barthes) — were the negotiation and renegotiation of meanings within and between particular discourses, and the processes by which those meanings are culturally hierarchized. Here we found useful Bourdieu's argument about the way in which cultural objects are involved in the production of a formation of "taste" which is stratified according to class formations. We discussed Bourdieu's notion of "cultural capital" — which had been unfamiliar to most of the students in this course, even while it has become a piece of the vernacular for most literary and cultural studies majors. One of the important uses of the term in this context is not only that it enables discussion of class in terms of cultural phenomena, but that it remains closely allied to ways of thinking culture in terms of economics; that is, it remains close to a Marxist tradition and underscores the necessity of understanding the nature of capitalism's role in the production of our cultures. This remains for me a crucial component of any worthwhile cultural studies.

Bourdieu's analysis of taste and class worked well in juxtaposition with Adorno's attack on popular culture in "Perrenial Fashion — Jazz." Students seemed much more sympathetic to Bourdieu than I had expected, partly because of their discomfort with Adorno's dismissive tones. But the two essays together provided a conflictual frame for wide-ranging discussions about art and cultural values, the relations between economic value and cultural values, and about the nature of consumerism. These issues were of topical interest in that we dealt with them at the same time as the Cincinnati art museum was being tried for exhibiting Robert Mapplethorpe's photographs. Also, these texts were being read in conjunction with Hebdige's essays on taste, on the genealogy of the scooter cycle, and on the aesthetics of pop art.

It would have been simple to let discussions of that sort segue into the discussion of postmodernism that ended the course. But my own predilections led me to insist that we spend more time thinking about Adorno's work, following that up with Benjamin's "Work of Art." My aim here was to use those two texts to reaffirm at least a couple of things that I think are critical for cultural studies to foreground: the relation of cultural studies theory to its own history in the Marxist tradition; and a dialectical mode of analysis (that I think is well represented in Adorno but which the students related to more nearly in Benjamin). The half-semester ended with lengthy discussion about the relation of cultural change and the assumption and reassumption of cultural styles to historical crises in capitalism and its processes of "creative destruction" (Schumpeter).

After the midterm break we turned our attention to Barthes' *Mythologies*. A goodly number of his little analyses of cultural objects and his essay on the linguistic paradigms underpinning structuralist thinking were discussed historically. That is, Barthes seems useful in this kind of course, not just to provide engrossing and provocative analyses, but also as a representative both of a particular moment in the history of cultural studies theory and of a particular moment in the history of late capitalism. Barthes' investigation of the first tide of consumerist artifacts introduced for us the vexed question of the periodization of postmodernism: how, that is, postmodernism should be defined — as something resulting from a fundamental shift in the nature of the capitalist mode of production or simply as what one student called "a new and improved consumer product." This is the point in the course where Hebdige's book received the most criticism, students being somewhat less convinced of the "positive potentialities" (217) of postmodernism than he appears often to be. The critique of Hebdige emerged largely from a comparison between his treatment of the rock music phenomenon of Live Aid concerts and Paul Gilroy's treatment of similar issues in his chapter on Rock Against Racism. Hebdige's apparent faith in an almost inevitable and automatic resistance in postmodernist practice seemed seriously threatened by Gilroy's careful explicating of the logic of cultural action.

I want to take some credit for the students' unwillingness in regard to the more optimistic views of the politics of postmodernism, since we had spent a considerable amount of time discussing my own essay, "Visiting the Banana Republic" (Ross, 128—48) — an essay which is by no manner of means a paean to postmodernism or many of its theoretical discourses. That article was intended, however, not just as a counter to what I tend to think of as the quietism of much discussion of postmodernism, but also as a way to open out some of the theoretical and some of the practical issues of cultural studies. That is to say, the article both affirms the global connections that must be thought through in relation to any cultural object of study, and also reaffirms the need for analysis grounded in the history of the mode of production.

This article brought us near to the end of our time, though discussion of it led into some of the most free-wheeling conversations of the semester — notably around the then impending imperialist and racist war in the Middle East. It also articulated somewhat with previous class sessions on questions of race and racism, and feminism and sexism. Those latter issues were in fact continuing motifs throughout the course, and their centrality was reflected in many of the final projects that the students handed in.

This has been, of necessity, a somewhat factitious narrative of the course's progress, and should perhaps be seen as not much more than a partial (in both senses of the word) gloss on the syllabus offered above.

Student Work

The students handed in a quite astonishing array of final projects, many of them done in collaboration with at least one other person, and many of them constituted in whole or in part by nonwritten submissions (art-work, videos, audio tapes). The topics covered included the following: rap music (two female students, one white, one African-American, in a conflictual dialogue); an analysis of the media and government discourse rationalizing the war in the Middle East; a feminist critique of intelligence testing; a paper on pornography (including a powerful suite of posters, in Barbara Kruger style, of pictures from *Penthouse*, overprinted by the student with captions such as "It is only dead flesh"); an analysis of comics drawn and written by women; a critique of ACT UP; a wonderful social history of the sport of wrestling in America; an exploration, via video, of the cultural production of black masculinity in America; and, inevitably enough, a reading of the Teenage Mutant Ninja Turtles.

I was a little surprised that the students' chosen topics were nearly all concerned with America — and with contemporary America at that. On the other hand, it's the case that throughout the course I had continually stressed that the place of the observer was a crucial consideration for "cultural studies," and so their first production of themselves as "cultural studies" was perhaps bound to reflect their place in their own time and culture. I was struck, however, by the sophistication and insistence with which, for the most part, they marked and remarked their own positionality, and by the emergence in their writing of a kind of self-reflexive habit of thought which could almost be called dialectical. Of course, this kind of achievement was unevenly spread across the students, but what was striking was the fact that nearly all of them chose topics where they could either analyze an object of the dominant culture from the point of view of the resistance that it dialectically invokes, or explore a cultural formation or artifact which brought up questions of marginality and the experience of resistance. In nearly all cases, the student work also registered the methodological necessity that I kept foisting on them: namely, the need for both an economic and an historical component to their analyses.

The degree to which any of the students was finally convinced by my claim that the methodology of cultural studies should be unsettled and unsettling is unclear to me. But it seems the case that a certain self-reflexiveness became possible for them as they produced these final projects. Of course, it would be wrong for me to end with any such claim about the success of the course. The degree of success is still not clear to me and, anyway, is probably in most respects a matter for others to judge. In any case, I offer this essay not in order to propose this course as in any way ideal. I mean it merely as an instance of what might get done in a cultural studies slot in the curriculum or as one empirical answer to the as yet unanswered question "What is cultural studies?"

Notes

1. We have also offered graduate degrees in literary and cultural theory since 1986.

2. For our discussion of the NAS's attack on the by now notorious E306 course in the University of Texas Department of English, we relied on accounts given in the Austin student newspaper, *The Polemicist*. 2:1 (September 1990). Copies of their excellent coverage can probably still be had, for a small donation, from *Polemicist*, 504 West 24th #28, Austin, TX 78705.

Works Cited

Adorno, Theodor. "Perennial Fashion — Jazz." *Prisms*. Cambridge, Mass.: MIT, 1988. 119–32.

Althusser, Louis. "Ideology and Ideological State Apparatuses." *Lenin and Philosophy*. London: New Left Books, 1971. 127–86.

Barthes, Roland. *Mythologies*. New York: Noonday, 1989.

Benjamin, Walter. "The Work of Art in the Age of Mechanical Reproduction." *Illuminations*. New York: Schocken, 1969. 217–51.

Bourdieu, Pierre. *Distinction*. Cambridge, Mass.: Harvard University Press, 1984.

Brantlinger, Patrick. *Crusoe's Footprints*. New York: Routledge, 1990.

Freud, Sigmund. *The Psychopathology of Everyday Life*. New York: Norton, 1965.

Gilroy, Paul. *There Ain't No Black in the Union Jack*. London: Hutchinson, 1987.

Hall, Stuart, ed. *Resistance Through Rituals*. London: Unwin Hyman, 1976.

Hebdige, Dick. *Hiding in the Light*. New York: Routledge, 1988.

Johnson, Richard. "What is Cultural Studies, Anyway?" *Social Text* 6:1 (1987): 38–80.

Ross, Andrew, ed. *Universal Abandon? The Politics of Postmodernism*. Minneapolis: University of Minnesota Press, 1988.

Schumpeter, Joseph. *Capitalism, Socialism, and Democracy*. New York: Harper and Row, 1942.

Spivak, Gayatri Chakravorty. *In Other Worlds: Essays in Cultural Politics*. New York: Methuen, 1987.

11

Forming an Interactive Literacy in the Writing Classroom

Cathy Fleischer

I first came to know Sarah in the summer of 1986 when she had just finished her junior year in high school and was participating in a summer writing program for high school students in which I was a teacher. Sarah was one of the "stars" of the program, at least from a teacher's vantage point: she loved to write and spent hours composing, revising, critiquing both her own and her peers' writing. So involved was she with her writing that even when the summer program came to an end and all the students' various writings were handed in (to be published in a book), Sarah was still writing. She said, "I'm going to keep working on [my piece]. I have a copy of it. I'm going to revise it."

Sarah had been writing on her own since she was about twelve, prolifically composing poetry and short stories in out-of-school settings and keeping them in her own writer's portfolio — a box in her closet. She cared passionately about her writing; even as she talked of becoming a professional writer at some point in the future, she already saw herself as an author. By the end of high school, she was confident and compassionate about her writing, always receiving high grades on her writing assignments, while still striking out on her own, both in and out of school, to try new ideas and new ways of composing. At one point, she revealed to those of us who were her teachers that she prefers this kind of writing, as she often feels "a little rebellious when people tell me what to do." Instead, she seeks to write what and how she wants, "not according to someone else's structures."

The Sarah I came to know by the time she was a sophomore in college, when I completed a multi-level study about her and her writing, was the same person in many ways — bubbly, enthusiastic, friendly, and intelligent — but was at the same time quite different, at least in terms of her writing. After a year and a half of college, she'd lost confidence in her writing, rarely wrote on her own, and lacked much of the passion for the written word that once consumed her. She said at that point, "Even when I'm writing, I don't feel like I'm writing." Instead she felt as if she were "fulfilling a requirement...doing something I don't want to do. It's really strange because I've never not wanted to write — *never* — and now, with every paper, I just want to cringe." She continued, "I think it's because I've discovered there are types of writing that I'm not good at, and I'd never entertained that possibility before...I've learned how to be defeatist since I've been here."

What happened to Sarah is a story about how students acquire the kinds of literacies they believe they need to survive in college settings, a story of what the discourses of various academic disciplines seem to demand from their students. For Sarah the notion of "what counted" in these settings had a lot to do with how the writing was formed, with the rules of a game she hadn't yet learned to master, and which she came to doubt she ever would. In Bakhtin's terms, the college forms of literacy became for Sarah a kind of authoritative discourse which remains quite separate from any kind of discourse she knows or understands, what he calls "the word of a father, of adults and of teachers." He continues, "The authoritative word demands that we acknowledge it, that we make it our own; it binds us, quite independent of any power it might have to persuade us internally; we encounter it with its authority already fused to it" (342).

For Bakhtin, the struggle between this authoritative discourse and its dialogical opposite, what he calls an internally persuasive discourse, is an important struggle. Internally persuasive discourse is discourse that arises from our own background and the backgrounds of our compatriots. It enters our consciousness not in the rigid and unchanging manner of authoritative discourse, but rather as "intense interaction, a *struggle* with other internally persuasive discourses" (346).

The interaction between authoritative and internally persuasive discourse is, for Bakhtin, something that is central to one's formation of an individual ideology. He argues that as we begin the "process of assimilating the words of others," an assimilation that is based in a constant dialogue with these various discourses, we begin to formulate our own ideologies (341). Only then can our own voice begin to emerge from this cacaphony of voices to which we are exposed, and only then as Bakhtin says, can "one's own discourse and one's own voice...begin to liberate themselves from the authority of the other's discourse" (348).

When we look at adolescents like Sarah, we can see that they often form their literacy in a kind of battleground similar to the struggle Bakhtin speaks of. Students bring to schools the internally persuasive discourses gained from their own background and experience: the forms and structures of the language of their families and friends, which helps to create a way of speaking, a way of writing, a way of thinking. Once students enter schools, their teachers add to that the authoritative discourse named by the schools as the "correct" kind of discourse. Based in structures often created by schools, this discourse relies on forms which often carry meaning only in school settings; from the five-paragraph essay to the structured research report, such school-sanctioned forms often bear no connections to the means of expression students come to school quite capable of practicing.[1] What Bakhtin calls authoritative discourse could be named as well as a *conforming literacy*, a literacy defined by the school rules and regulations, measured by students' adherence to certain forms and genres. Such a literacy might be seen in contrast to an *in-forming* literacy, the literacy students bring to school settings, whose forms arise from the internally persuasive discourses of their own language backgrounds.[2] The consistent dialectic interplay which naturally occurs between these two, in its most positive moments, helps constantly re-form students' literacy and is important to students' growth in reading and writing. But more often, this interaction is played out in a less positive way in schools, and the interaction truly becomes a battle in which, I believe, students are most often the losers.

Bakhtin's depiction of this struggle and its correlation to issues of literacy helps me understand in some ways what has happened to Sarah and serves as an analogue to help me understand what happens to one kind of student I encounter so often in my college teaching: students who survived, even excelled, at writing in high school while still seeing themselves as authors; students who at one point learned to negotiate the many rules teachers taught them about writing and who still saw their own voice emerging out of the negotiation; students for whom college writing (for a number of reasons) ended that search for a negotiated stance. Prior to her college experience, Sarah, like many of the students I encounter, was a writer for whom the struggle between authoritative and internally persuasive discourses — as well as among various internally persuasive discourses — was a constantly vitalizing presence in the formation of her own literacy. Sarah had learned over the years to take the rules that teachers insisted upon for her writing and to find connections between that discourse and the discourse which arose from her own writing background—gleaned, of course, from an amalgamation of the language of her family and friends. Sarah's individual ideology has been formed in many ways by that continuous and active interplay among these various discourses; even as this interaction has helped her to become a better writer, it helped her become a clearer thinker—someone who could, through her writing, formulate a stance or perspective on the issues she chose to compose. Sarah's writing by the end of her high school years radiated with Bakhtin's heteroglossia: fictive tales interwoven with actual voices from her past and present; arguments tying the stances of other people she'd read and talked with, but written clearly in the words of an independent thinker, even formulaic writing required by specific teachers enlivened with the style and humor that only writers comfortable with their authority can afford to do. In college, however, authoritative discourse triumphed, looming large in her psyche and reducing her confidence in any kind of discourse she saw as her own. College writing for Sarah became an unsuccessful struggle to discover and then mimic the discourse she thought she saw her teachers and her texts using. Sarah came to believe that there was a new set of rules which governed academic discourse and that she must understand these rules and their implied forms in order to write successfully in this new setting. As a result, Sarah's writing came to lack any recognizable voice, instead simply moving between the words and style of the teacher-authority and that of the text-authority, resulting in a composing style which was distanced from Sarah and became, in fact, uninteresting for her even to practice. This distancing coupled with her growing belief that teacher-authorities held the key to how papers should be composed as well as to what truths papers should reveal reached a head her sophomore year with an assigned paper for her psychology class, a paper whose topic she had selected: dream interpretation. Despite her interest in the topic, Sarah immediately distanced herself from the writing of the paper. She explained:

> I'm going to write about dreams and I'm going to take the psychoanalytic approach because my TA sees everything from the psychoanalytic approach to dreams—but, oh well, I'm going to write it that way... I'm really interested in dreams, but the kinds of things I'd want to say are not the things I'm supposed to say in a psych paper.

Sarah still believed that for the discourse to become her own, for it to become internally persuasive and informing, she had to have her own voice struggle with the authoritative voices of her teachers and texts, but she admitted that the ability to join the two voices now eluded her. "You have to know the rules before you can bend them," she told me. "You have to find them...never before have I not known the rules."

This intense and almost blinding focus on Sarah's part toward authoritative discourse, I would argue, began to limit her continuing literacy growth.

If, as Bakhtin tells us, "the ideology of becoming a human being...is the process of selectively assimilating the words of others" (341), we can recognize some of the implications of the problems that Sarah discovered as she tried to find a space for herself and for her words in what she saw as an unyielding authoritative discourse — as we think how this same problem is replayed over and over for the many students we encounter each semester. Sarah is someone who understands that "real writing," writing in which she truly becomes the author, is writing in which she brings to bear her own discourse upon the words of others. Yet, Sarah, who had shown herself capable of this kind of intellectual work, had at this point opted out of writing in both academic settings and beyond; she was disheartened, discouraged, and frustrated. My work with Sarah raised worries for me as well: that as students like Sarah feel distanced from their own in-forming words and come to rely solely on the conforming words of the authoritative school discourse, they will close off any interaction between the two kinds of discourse. And if, as Bakhtin believes, this shutdown limits the growth of their own individual ideologies and their own stance on the world, such an approach to the teaching of writing is tragic.

I believe all of us who are teachers need to take Sarah's rejection seriously and to consider ways in which we can bring together the conforming literacy of the academy and the in-forming literacy of our students' backgrounds. Rather than seeing our classrooms as places where students primarily are introduced to the various academic discourses we are convinced they need in order to survive in college writing, we might do better to imagine our classrooms as literacy sites, as interactive places where students are encouraged to let their internally persuasive discourses, their own in-formed literacies, serve as the basis for their necessary interaction with academic talk and writing. The task as I see it is not to continue to provide introduction after introduction to various authoritative discourses, but rather to create a space in our classrooms where students' internally persuasive discourses are first celebrated and then analyzed as a way into examining what of value might be gleaned from an in-forming literacy and applied to this strange new world of college writing. By beginning to strive toward what we might see as a re-forming literacy, we teachers can help students like Sarah remain authors in their own right — an important first step in their lifelong development as truly literate people.

I'd like to use a course I teach regularly at my university as an example of how an interactive literacy, a re-forming literacy, might take shape in the classroom. First, let me lay out some of the "how-to's" as to the design of the course; then, as Ann Berthoff believes all teachers who share practical measures must do, I'll make you listen to the theory behind the measures.[3] The course, "Intermediate Composition," satisfies a basic studies requirement, and so it is populated with many students who tell me on the first day their reason for taking the course is "because it's required." The course is supposed to have a "Writing Across the Curriculum" focus; many of those who teach the course either adopt an Elaine Maimon approach and teach the history paper, the lab report, the psychology paper, or teach the course as an extended version of introductory comp, which for many is a genre-based approach instructing students in how to write (usually in this order) the narrative essay, the descriptive essay, the persuasive essay, the compare-contrast essay, etc. Both approaches, I would argue, are further versions of the authoritative discourse about which Bakhtin writes. Such approaches, which focus on mimicking some kind of final product, necessarily privilege certain preconceived models of academic discourse. Teaching becomes mostly a product-oriented enterprise with successful imitation of a teacher-determined model seen as the goal. My argument against this kind of privileging is at least twofold: by teaching in this way we assume there is such a single entity as "a psychology report" or a compare-contrast essay, for example, whose form can be taught, an assumption I question; by teaching in this way we also assume that we English teachers really understand the subtleties involved in writing an argument in the physical sciences, for example, an assumption that, at least from my perspective, is false.

In the version of this course that I teach, I instead attempt to look *with* students at what it means to participate in the written discourse of various parts of the academy by introducing them to the notion of language communities in general. We look at language communities in a broad sense, investigating both communities with which they are already familiar as well as communities which present new challenges. In the course description that I hand out on the first day, I explain it in this way:

> As we move from family to friends, from home to school, or from school to profession, the way we talk and write changes. Many scholars of language study believe this happens because as language users who move within a number of communities, we come to understand both the obvious and subtle conventions which surround these distinct discourse communities. In this course we will study the conventions of some of the various discourses which exist at Eastern Michigan University—not so much to memorize the rules and regulations surrounding writing in a particular field of study, but rather to come to understand that conventions shift across place, across course of study, across time. Think of yourself, then, as a detective—as

someone who will learn how to investigate the language which composes certain fields of study in order to see both conventional and nonconventional uses of language and to see how and when rules can be broken.

The course will be divided into two parts. In Part I we will look into patterns of talk and writing with which you are already familiar: the language of your particular family, your friends, your dorm, for example. We will then move on in Part II to investigate the language of this university, focusing on the talk and writing of various disciplines: some of you will investigate anthropology, some psychology, some education, some chemistry, etc., in order to report back to the class on the kinds of talk and writing that go on in a particular field.

By beginning our study of the language of various parts of their own university with the discourse of communities with which they are already familiar, we set the tone for what is to follow. Students investigate their own in-forming literacy and see that the diction, the syntax, and the rhetoric which exist within that literacy are interesting subjects to be studied. As they recognize the connections and disparities among their own familiar communities, they may be able to make better sense out of the less familiar language communities which surround the various parts of the academy: searching for connections among the disciplines even as they look for the identifying features of the disciplines which are of most interest to them. The role of the students in this kind of teaching and learning, then, becomes that of searcher and researcher: students look to their own experiences to make sense of the notions we raise in class and then work to make sense of those experiences in the context of the experiences of others. My role becomes one of reflector as I work to validate their experiences as significant, even as I provide the kinds of prods and pushes necessary to make this kind of inductive teaching a true occasion for learning. Both roles require patience. Patience on the parts of the students as they struggle to fit the form and structure of this class into the picture they've drawn of what a college classroom should be, patience on their part as they learn to consider carefully their own experiences as language users and to see something of value in their memories, stories and encounters with language. This kind of teaching and learning also requires patience on my part as I continually remind myself of the fitful stops and starts that inevitably occur when student talk and writing take center stage to form the text for a class, as I remember each term that the text will vary for each group of students and that the understandings students came to last term are neither the same as nor better than the ones students will eventually come to this term.

Given these caveats and given my recognition that not all groups of students respond in the same time frame to this manner of teaching and this content for teaching, we tend to at least begin each term in the same way. We start with language with which they are already familiar: their home language, their dorm language, the language of their various clubs and groups of friends. Students in this part of the course write about words and phrases which carry meaning only in their families; they then share with their peers the stories which led to the creation of those words, helping us as a class to create a dictionary of terms transferred from their many disparate home communities to our developing one in the classroom.[4] Student-recalled and defined home language takes on a new life in our classroom. As of today, for example, we in my present classroom community know that when someone "quantum-leaps," he or she talks about something totally off the subject (derivation: Donn's mother); we know as well that when someone talks over the head of people, he or she is "wobbling" (derivation: an article in *Reader's Digest* by way of Jennifer's fiance); we also know that next time we see someone doing something ridiculous, we should call him a Larry (derivation: old *Leave It to Beaver* reruns from Jeremy's childhood memories). Next, students expand upon the notion of home language communities to write about language endemic to some community of which they are now a member: Last term Kip told us about the language of cheerleading, stressing the importance of precise use of terminology for safety's sake when cheerleaders perform gymnastic moves; Steve regaled us with the ins and outs of race track talk, preparing us in the language of placing bets and cheering on horses; Amy taught us about "sueders" and "vids," her clique's terms for burned out students and cigarettes, respectively; Jody recreated the syntax and diction of a typical "Incident Report," based in those she often composes in her role as assistant director of her residence hall.[5]

The next section of the course brings us to look at a language community which students all share to some extent and which informs in many ways their learned stance toward writing: the community of classrooms prior to college. At this point we focus specifically on the kinds of reading and writing we all were asked to do in elementary school and high school. Not surprisingly, students generally discover new insights about those experiences as they write, mostly centering on the idea that the freedom and enjoyment they felt toward reading and writing in earlier years disappeared by the time they were entrenched in high school. Many students write about the rules which surrounded writing in high school, raising questions about the importance of five-paragraph essays or rules such as "Never use the word in a paper." Last term we all learned from students who raised these kinds of issues:

Lisa: My senior year of high school I had the hardest writing class that I have ever had...I had to have five to eight paragraphs per paper. Each paper had an introduction, body paragraphs, and a conclusion. The thesis sentence was the same format for each paper also. Every paragraph had to have at least five sentences to it.

Erik G.: In my first four years of high school the worst time of the year was November. Not because it was the beginning of winter, but because that was when my English teacher assigned the dreaded term paper...But the worst part of doing the assignment was not the paper itself, but instead, was doing notecards. On notecards we had to put down information about our topic and where we found this information and we had to do one hundred of these...Mr. Lenox, a shoein for a Fred Flintstone look alike contest, was an ex-college professor and graded so hard even Albert Einstein would not even get an A for a paper. This was because we lost points for incorrect punctuation and spelling. We were forced to always have proper sentence structure or we were doomed for sure. As you can probably see in my paper, I was doomed for life in Mr. Lenox's English class.

Kelly F.: I recall one certain English class in high school that I can't really put my finger on the focus on what we were leaning. Every week we had to write a paper. The teacher would give us the topic and designate either 500 or 1000 words. We couldn't go over or under the limit. I and everyone else found ourselves sticking a "the" here or there and counting the words. Not even realizing what we were writing ... The margins were stressed to perfection. We had to write on yellow pads for the first two drafts and on white for the final. The paper couldn't have notebook holes for frayed edges.

Papers like these always lead to ripe discussions in class; students talk about when and if such rules are useful, why teachers might teach in these ways, how such rules affect their experience as college writers. Keeping in mind their own perspectives on these issues written and spoken about in their own terms, we then look at the opinion of "experts" on the same issues, professional authors who have published books on the same subject: We read selections from Mike Rose's *Lives on the Boundary* and Richard Rodriquez's *Hunger of Memory*, centering our discussions around how our experiences in school were like and unlike those of the professional authors, a discussion about professional texts quite unlike any in Sarah's experience in college. Professional texts in our community are not used as the only authorities; rather they are seen as one authority among many: students too are considered experts on subjects which they take time to consider seriously, and they can thus respond to these texts in the same ways they would respond to the texts written by their peers in class.

At this point I ask students to take on their first formal paper, based in themes which we have raised in class discussion as important. The assignment, deliberately worded in somewhat vague terms, asks them to think about the aspects we've raised about language communities thus far (which vary from class to class) and to tie some of those aspects together to formulate a theme about language and community using their own experiences, the experiences of their colleagues in the class and the experiences of the professional authors we have read. Students are at first quite hesitant to attempt such an open-ended assignment, but the work they produce shows the consideration they have given to the issues we are raising. Last term Kelly M., for example, chose to write a narrative which represented the changes in language teenagers make when talking to parents, grandparents, siblings and friends, concluding that "the type of language used in a family changes from situation to situation. . . Teenagers tend to be self-centered. They lose a sense of closeness with their families. Their independence starts to show through at this age with their families. Their independence starts to show through at this age when it's no longer cool to be buddies with Mom. . .[Their overall tone changes when they talk to their brothers and sisters." Ron took a totally differently slant on the assignment in his paper "It's No Joking Matter." There he reflects on a prank he played on a co-worker in which he phoned the co-worker at work, attempted to talk to him in his best rendition of black English, then surprised this colleague by identifying himself as white. Ron describes his later feelings about this prank:

> Doug. . .cursed my "dumb black dude" performance, and we shared a good laugh. No big deal. Like I said, it was a joke. Or it seemed.
>
> But it is a big deal. It isn't just a joke. It isn't even funny. Instead it is a prime example of how one can abuse and misuse his or her superficial knowledge of a language community. . .Doug was thrown off balance because of preconceptions we shared about the "black dialect."
>
> The amazing thing to consider is how opinions and preconceptions from attitudes about language use. Unfortunately, attitudes often assume a judgmental tone and perpetuate stereotypes. . .[S]o many of our assumptions about language are unfounded, for they are mistakenly based on stereotypes which ignore the inherent value and equality of all language communities.

Continuing our focus on placing students' experiences in language communities at the center of the curriculum, we move on to talk about language communities in the university, particularly in classrooms. Students talk about the reading and writing they have been asked to do so far, as well as the speech that seems to surround learning in the university. After we share these experiences (in the form of a class correspondence and resulting discussion), we again read about the experiences of others. We draw from Rose and from two articles which have proved difficult yet fruitful for students: Bartholomae's "Inventing the University," which raises issues about how students may first need to mimic university language before moving beyond it, and Annas' "Style as Politics: A Feminist Approach to the Teaching of Writing," in which she takes on an essentialist position as she discusses women's experiences as writers in the discourse of the male-oriented university, concluding that there are styles of writing based in gender difference. And again students are able to speak to the notions raised in these essays from a position of authority—comparing what these authors have to say to their own experiences and accepting or rejecting the authors' conclusions based in experiential knowledge. After the end of our discussions linking the professional authors' experiences with their own experiences, students write more formal papers about university language, trying to speak to their own experience in terms of what these professional authors have said.[6] Again, last term one student wrote about her experience on the forensics team and how she has been taught to speak publicly in what Annas sees as a male-oriented, linear style. One student wrote about how spoken discourse varies from class to class, attempting to categorize the differences and to speak about how classes which encourage two-way communication give the students a fuller experience than those which allow only for one-way communication. Another student wrote about the notion of insiders and outsiders in language communities at the university—and about the differences she feels now as an insider compared to her perceptions about the language of academy when she was a high school student. One male student tied in the ideas Annas raised when he discussed his writing projects in a "Philosophy of Women" class: in that class he felt marginalized for the first time, and his writing for that course reflected the lack of authority he felt with the subject matter and the form.

All these pieces lead to the major project of the course, what we call the Ethnography of Writing Project.[7] I lay out here the assignment as the students receive it:

Ethnography of writing project

I see this ethnography project as a way for you to learn about the disciplines you are about to enter as you choose and pursue your major field of study for the rest of your time in the university (and perhaps in your career). As we already have talked about in class, different communities (home, school, dorm, etc.) place different demands upon their writers. Likewise, within the university various disciplines can be seen as different communities, communities whose rules for discourse differ in some subtle and some not so subtle ways.

How can becoming an ethnographer of writing help you learn

about both the requirements for writing in these fields and the occasions when it seems all right to stray from those regulations? What exactly is an ethnography? An ethnography is a written account of a culture: the people who inhabit it, the documents they read and write, the conversations they pursue, the methods of their work, etc. Ethnographers generally enter a community as outsiders; they talk to people, observe them in their setting and study their artifacts as a way of coming to understand that culture "from the native's point of view" (as Clifford Geertz, a leading ethnographer, says). You then write about what you've discovered as a way to introduce other newcomers to that culture, trying hard to capture the richness and depth of the culture you've come to know.

Specifically, you will join with a team of other interested students to uncover the culture of one of the disciplines of this university: chemistry, education, psychology, music, history, etc. You will interview professors and students in this field, you will observe classes, you will read examples of writing—all in the name of uncovering what it means to be a student and a writer in that area of study. The final papers that you write will be directed toward your colleagues in this class, as a way for all of us to learn the conventions (and the straying from conventions) that predominate in your chosen field.

Your written ethnography must include at least these three parts:

1.   Collection and rhetorical analysis of written discourse
      —a section from a textbook (as an example of something written from professor to student)
      —an article from a professional journal (as an example of something written from professor to professor)
      —several student papers from introductory and advanced courses (as an example of something written from student to professor)
2.   Participant-observation in the community
      This could be participating/observing a class in the discipline, a lab, an outside meeting of students...use your imaginations!
3.   Interviews with at least 2 experts
      The reason for these interviews is to uncover more about the kinds of writing demanded by the disciplines, the process writers in this field undergo, the rhetoric of the field. You should interview at least one professor and at least one advanced student.

These papers can be organized in any way you choose, but you must include these three parts, plus a section in which you reflect upon what you've learned. Don't be content just to list what you found from each part; try instead to uncover common themes and integrate the information you discovered to support those themes.

As you can see, our focus in this project is on learning the discourse conventions of various disciplines. Students work in teams gathering materials about a particular discipline, researching in the manner of ethnographers. They become participant observers, sitting in on classes and listening to the oral language which defines a particular subject area. They practice discourse analysis, carefully reading various kinds of writing prevalent in a field of study: textbooks, professional articles, student papers. They become interviewers, questioning professors and students in the field, trying to glean from them the main ingredients of reading and writing in their area. Each student then writes an individual final paper, the thesis and form for this final paper differing even within the same discipline. Last term John composed a narrative of a prelaw student named John trying to learn the language of the law after the confusion which arose from his first class in the discipline. Eric's account of "Accounting Information Systems" practiced what it preached: he prepared his study of the field in the form acceptable for that field, from the table of contents, overview, and body to the type of paper and print and size of margins. Kelly F. constrasted the two key elements she found in history writing (reporting of facts and presenting of opinions) by summarizing the approaches of two professors, each of whom stressed one of those positions in their teaching. Ron showed how literature majors could, with some change in mindset, learn the new scientific language of linguistics. Jennifer explored variations of the lesson plan as taught by different professors, outlined in different journals, and practiced by various teachers, wondering why students are instructed so narrowly when such variety exists. Kevin connected the visual experience of art history to the distinctive style of writing in that field.

These lengthy papers serve as a final text for the class, a text which (like most of the student-written texts for the class) changes from semester to semester. Students study this final text, taking seriously the observations their peers have raised, and then write a summary paper which talks about similarities and differences they notice in their peers' writing about language across these communities of the academy. These papers offer perhaps the most important conclusions of the course as they give students an opportunity to pull together most of the themes we've discussed throughout the semester, but to do so in terms of the texts their peers have composed. For many students these papers seem to lead to the kind of "aha" experience so exciting in education: suddenly the work of a term makes sense. I quote at some length from the papers written last term to give you an idea of what these particular students learned.

Kelly M.: Something universal I found in the papers I read was the progression of intensity. Lower level courses teach the basics. Instructors don't expect the students to recite anything but the facts. But in upper level courses, students are expected to take these facts and apply them with their feelings and understandings to make them work.

...Both Kelly F., Crystal and Eric G. stated similar theories. "Student writing also varies according to course level...As the student develops his historical background, his writing progresses to a more professional level." (Flynn 10). She also said, "The level of history courses also reflects a difference in writing" (Flynn 10). Eric G. stated similar facts in his paper. "The language that is used is very simple in the beginning, but as you advance to higher courses, so does the level of language" (Gorham 1)...

Steve: I thought my topic (accounting) was much different than most of the other students' topics. While researching and writing my paper, I figured my findings were unique. However, after reading other students' papers I came to the conclusion that all majors are different but have some similarities at all levels.

One similarity I noticed is...[e]very field uses the building block technique. Past learnings are always used for present knowledge. Kevin expanded on this thought, "The introductory textbook defines the basic vocabulary of the language which is built upon and expanded in meaning by later courses and texts."...Further down the line, the student becomes an expert. I found that all the journals alienate the novice from the expert in the field...The journals always assume knowledge of the reader and are very informative — if the reader can understand them. Wes backs me up on this by writing, "Higher level courses use less texts and more coursepacks and journals written usually by the instructor or a peer in the field."

John: Much of the learning done in undergraduate work is not ingesting material, but learning to communicate within that field...The point Crystal is making...is a person must learn two things;...a basic knowledge of the material to draw from, and..., the way in which to express that knowledge. The expression of the knowledge is where the papers begin to divide themselves...

If I were to give advice to freshmen entering a university as to how to write and what to expect I would tell them these things. Generally low-level classes want you to start thinking in a certain way. This will gear you to learning and expressing the material in the format your field likes. You will be expected to learn how to express your ideas in this format using a language that is acceptable to this field. In time you will be expected to brave the dark and express your own opinion based on this knowledge you have learned.

Kelly F.: In most cases studied it's evident that all fields create an insider and outsider community in various ways. Perhaps that's why most lower level courses only focus on the basics—because those communities haven't been formed at that level yet.

Ron: I think I have to cover what writing isn't. Having read the ethnographies of writing for management, education, accounting and literature (and considering my own on linguistics), I have come to the conclusion that writing at the university is definitely not some coherent style/format entity to be used at the college level. Style of writing, for instance, varies not only from major to major, but also within majors. Consider how students in accounting and literature approach the "ideas" of their subjects. In accounting, for example, Steve stresses that "accounting writing is very precise and to the point" (1) and is generally free from the "paragraphs, examples, and conclusions" so prevalently found in English classes, where students like Jodi learn to write more interpretively, relying on extended essays to discuss "a more complex language of metaphors" (Jodi 1). I think what Steve's and Jodi's articles illustrate is a tendency in college for writing to become precise and scientific in areas that deal with concrete, rule-bound subjects, while opening up to "essay" writing when dealing with more abstract subjects...

As distinct and various as writing at the college level may be, there is a certain universal trait that makes university writing what it is. It seems as if every field of writing at the university requires a progression of the student to move from the outside of a language community to the inside. It all centers around learning the language and "ideas" of your field. It's a matter of students who have to "learn to write with authority...to state [their] ideas and back them up..." (senior in Jodi's article). No matter what field you go into, you have to learn to write with authority—and that means picking up the jargon, terms and references unique to your field...

As Steve pointed out...the language of accounting majors would baffle any outsider. Languages do that—they baffle outsiders—so too does a lot of the writing. If I've learned nothing else about language and writing, I've learned how powerfully it can separate and create outsiders and insiders.

Steve and Kelly learn that as students continue in a field of study they use more and more of the language of that field as they become increasingly expert in the subject. They see the goal to become professional both in the reading and writing of texts. John adds that the growth one makes in a field has to do with a movement from ingesting to communicating. Kelly's notion expands upon that, believing that the building-block technique relates to the formation of community: you can't move onto communication until communities have been formed.

Ron sees this growth in terms of the feeling of authority and adds some ideas about the potential affects of such authority: the creation of an insider-outsider dichotomy. The students who reached these conclusions, ideas which are reflected in all the final papers I received, show me a kind of thinking about learning which encourages me to continue teaching in this way. For me the kind of thinking they show reflects the notions inherent to the kind of literacy I am continually attempting to promote in my classrooms.

Let me, in summary, try to explain how I think this kind of teaching is different from what Sarah was exposed to — and how I think this kind of teaching and learning leads to an interactive, re-forming sort of literacy.

The first point has to do with selection of content for the course. We study the issue of shifting language communities by beginning with the students' own experiences in the language communities they know: various versions which draw upon their own in-forming literacy. We use their own writing about these subjects as texts for the course, copied and shared with the class. By beginning in this way, students are prepared to read into the notions of language communities put forth by professional authors. They read these professional texts as colleagues-in-arms with these authors, recognizing their own knowledge about the subject under consideration and reading other texts in terms of that knowledge. Student voices are in this way authorized: they understand the message I send that their experience is important, and they begin to read and write about other texts in critical ways, searching for points of agreement and disagreement. Unlike Sarah's experience, these students find a space for their own voices to enter into the ongoing conversation that makes up academic writing. We see this in the most obvious way in the students' approaches to those final papers. Peers' papers are offered as proofs for their theses; in particular, students cite their friends' texts in the same way they cite professional texts.

The second related point has to do with the students' writing. As students write about their own language community, they do so in their own voices. Again, by copying and sharing student texts, we are celebrating not only *what* the students have to say but *how* they say it. Their own literacies, then, are accepted as appropriate ways to relay information. As we then begin to study the literacies which surround academic discourse, students come to see the connections between these and their own writing. They see that there are alternate approaches to writing which are necessary to survive in the university, but, at the same time, they learn there is no such animal as one "academic language." They begin to learn about the variations which exist within the academy and that within particular disciplines authors write in varying ways for varying audiences and purposes. Again, unlike Sarah's experience, these students are learning that there are many ways to write. Because they have come to value their own voices in the context of an academic setting, they search for a way which can tie their own in-forming literacy with the more conforming literacy of the university: a kind of marriage which we hope results in a more interactive literacy than Sarah was able to practice.

Because this is an ever-changing course, its content and context dependent upon the issues raised in students' oral and written texts, it certainly cannot sit as a model, a "how-to" approach which, if adopted, will result in miracles in anyone else's classroom. But, even as I believe there is no single model of the way to promote an interactive literacy, I think my point is clear: if we are to avoid the tragedy of students like Sarah, we must begin to rethink our notions of what counts as literate writing. As teachers of language, of necessity literacy workers, we have an obligation to re-form the notions of literacy that now exist.

Notes

1. The idea that the school forms of communication are quite different from other forms of communication students know has been shown in different ways by different researchers over the years. See, for example, Heath and Cook-Gumperz, among others.

2. For more on the issue of conforming and in-forming literacies, see my essay in Robinson's *Conversations on the Written Word*.

3. Berthoff, in her essay "The Teacher as REsearcher," wisely cautions us against the recipe swapping approach of Exercise Exchanges. She claims that in "my ideal commonwealth, I would order the closing down of the Exercise Exchange; the NCTE would not be allowed to operate it unless they instituted a Theory Exchange. And you couldn't get the recipe unless you went there" (32)

4. I am grateful to Patricia L. Stock of Michigan State University for many of the ideas which help form this section of the course.

5. Each of these short pieces, as well as the others I describe in this section, is photocopied for the entire class. These pieces, named "class correspondences," come to serve as a beginning text for the class.

6. The specifics of the assignment last term were as follows: "Lately we've been discussing issues of the language of the university beginning with our own experiences and then moving into experiences as depicted by Rose, Bartholomae, and Annas. For this paper I'd like you to select a theme about language in the university and discuss it in terms of your own experiences and the experiences of one or more of the authors. It might be a compare/contrast essay in which you compare your experience to one of the author's; it might be a theme essay in which you select a them and support it by your own examples and examples from the texts; it might be a narrative description of your experience with ideas

woven in from on or more of the authors; it could be specifically about writing, reading or talking—or it could look in some way at all three.

The important elements of this paper are these: first, that you mold your ideas into a good thesis that you will try to prove in some way, and, second, that you use as support both your own experiences and the experiences of at least one of the authors we've read."

7. I am grateful to Jim Zebroski of Syracuse University for the ideas behind this Ethnography of Writing Project. Although I have adapted his original assignment to fit into the design of my course, he will recognize many of the ideas and even some of the language of the assignment itself as his own.

Works Cited

Annas, Pamela. "Style as Politics: A Feminist Approach to the Teaching of Writing." *College English* 14 (1984): 360−71.

Bakhtin, Mikhail. *The Dialogic Imagination.* Trans. Caryl Emerson and Michael Holquist. Austin: University of Texas Press, 1981.

Bartholomae, David. "Inventing the University." *When A Writer Can't Write: Studies in Writer's Block and Other Composing Problems.* Ed. Mike Rose. New York: Guilford, 1985.

Berthoff, Ann. "The Teacher as Researcher." *Reclaiming the Classroom: Teacher Research as an Agency for Change.* Eds. Dixie Goswami and Peter Stillman. Upper Montclair, NJ: Boynton/Cook (1987), 28−39.

Cook-Gumperz, Jenny, ed. *The Social Construction of Literacy.* Cambridge: Cambridge University Press, 1986.

Fleischer, Cathy. Re-forming Literacy: A Collaborative Teacher-Student Research Project. *Conversations on the Written Word.* Jay L. Robinson. Portsmouth, NH: Boynton/Cook-Heinemann (1990), 35−48.

Heath, Shirley Brice. *Ways With Words* Cambridge: Cambridge University Press, 1983.

Rodriguez, Richard. *Hunger of Memory.* Boston: David Godine Publishers, 1983.

Rose, Mike. *Lives on the Boundary: The Struggle and Achievements of America's Underprepared.* New York: Free Press, 1989.

12

Issues of Subjectivity and Resistance:
Cultural Studies in the Composition Classroom

Diana George
Diana Shoos

"School Numbs My Buns":

Audrey Horne, *Twin Peaks*

Because cultural studies takes as its subjects of investigation the immediate world of experience as well as mediated discourse, it is very likely to have a major impact on composition classrooms in the next decade. Cultural studies is especially suited to a course like composition, which calls upon students to write about what they remember, what they are currently experiencing, and what they discover through observation, research, and critique. As a critical discipline, cultural studies insists on the relevance of all texts as objects of cultural analysis. It questions the notion of "high culture," especially as the sole domain of the classroom, enabling students to draw upon their familiarity with the texts of popular culture. This is particularly crucial given that, as Mary Poovey remarks,

> ...for most of our undergraduates, the experience of MTV, television, and rock and roll constitutes an important part of the training they have received in how to read before they enter our classrooms. (The freshman class of 1990, you should recall, was born in 1972.) To ignore this and teach only close readings of texts that we

present as static and centered is to risk making institutionalized
education seem even more irrelevant to our students' past experiences
and extracurricular lives than I suspect it already feels. (616)

What Poovey's comment implies is that de-privileging our students'
frame of reference in favor of our own may cultivate the kind of
attitude toward the classroom reflected in Audrey's complaint ("School
numbs my buns"). Thus, it would be easy to say that the aim of placing
cultural studies into the writing course might be to enhance the possibilities of touching on the students' immediate world while also teaching
observation and critical thinking skills.

Yet, cultural studies is not about skills per se at all. It is about
critiquing institutions, especially as those institutions embody power
relations. We would even argue that a course that attempts to use
cultural studies without acknowledging its domain as an interrogator of
institutions is simply a course in pop culture, one in which the "enthusiasm for...popular cultural forms is divorced from the analysis of
power and social possibilities" (Johnson, 42). While such a course may
hold interest for students and faculty, it does not necessarily answer
the call many composition scholars have made for a liberatory pedagogy.
A liberatory pedagogy, as it has been made popular with reference to
the work of Paolo Freire, states as a primary aim the movement
toward a "critical consciousness." For some critics of this pedagogy,
that call for a critical consciousness has seemed to be a call for a
particular politics, and yet, as Freire is quick to point out, sectarianism
has no place in the radical classroom:

> The sectarian, whether rightist or leftist, sets himself [sic] up as
> the proprietor of history, as its sole creator, and the one entitled to
> set the place of its movement. Rightist and leftist sectarians do differ
> in that one desires to stop the course of history, the other to anticipate
> it. On the other hand, they are similar in imposing their own convictions
> on the people, whom they thereby reduce to mere masses...Sectarians
> can never carry out a truly liberating revolution, because they are
> themselves unfree. (11–12)

Part of what this implies for a cultural studies approach to composition is that asking students to become critical readers of their culture
does not mean demanding that they reject that culture. Our role as
educators is not to insist that our students say what we want them to
say or conform to our notion of "political correctness." This is not to
deny that, as individuals and educators, we do take political positions.
However, if we judge our students' work by whether or not they come
to the same conclusions we do, we not only send them conflicting
messages about their own worth as thinkers but also insure our own
failure as teachers. The function of teachers within the paradigm of a
liberatory pedagogy is to allow and encourage our students to become

radical thinkers in the sense of coming of their own conclusions, given a raised consciousness.

This is not to suggest that cultural studies takes no position at all, that it poses as "objective" interpretation. Within the cultural studies framework, students are encouraged to become critical readers of a culture and its popular productions, and to see all texts as culturally anchored. From this perspective there is nothing "natural" about the way minorities, for example, are represented on television or the way teenagers are represented in music videos. To understand that popular art forms emerge partially from cultural conditions is to acknowledge that these forms constitute a mediated reality—a reality that depends upon the interaction of culture, material conditions, and subjectivity.

Freire's notion of the process of subject formation in radical pedagogy is worth mentioning at this point because of the way it can inform cultural studies in the composition classroom. For Freire, the person as subject is opposed to the person as object in that he or she is an integrated, active agent of change in the world:

> *Integration* with one's context, as distinguished from *adaptation*, is a distinctively human activity. Integration results from the capacity to adapt oneself to reality *plus* the critical capacity to make choices and to transform that reality. (4)

This integration leads to a radical subject formation, one in which the subject "perceives historical contradictions in increasingly critical fashion," so that "he is no mere spectator of the historical process" (11–12). The value of Freire's notion of the subject for the composition classroom is that it revises the poststructuralist notion of subjectivity to suggest that the subject is not only constructed (by preexisting social structures such as language, gender, the family, etc.) but that it can actively intervene in the process of meaning making. Freire's subject intersects with a nascent post-poststructuralist subjectivity which implies "desire and transformation," the "discursive self-formation of subjects and political will" (Trimbur, 6). Cultural studies, then, seems to bring together the poststructuralist concept of the subject as produced by discourse with the Freirean subject as agent. In fact, John Trimbur places the concerns of cultural studies right at "the intersection of cultural forms and the reader's subjectivity" (11).

Subjectivity and Resistance

In the classroom, this dual notion of subjectivity is a crucial one for those instructors who face some students' outright rejection of the critical work made possible by cultural studies. For some, cultural studies has led to a kind of war of subjectivities as students and faculty battle over whose subjectivity really counts in discussions of popular culture. However, as teachers we would do well to remember that in a poststructuralist framework, subjectivity is not static but fluid. Readers never constitute a single subject position. Once we accept that, we have already interrupted the notion that such a battle could occur. It becomes easier to allow students not simply a perspective which differs from our own but multiple perspectives in response to different texts or even to the same text.

Take, for example, the case of Cathleen, a first-year student in a composition course designed with a cultural studies base. From the very outset of the course, Cathleen's writing indicated that she was quite capable of distancing herself from advertising texts, while she could get only slight critical distance from television texts. In her first major paper for the course, Cathleen chose an ad campaign for J.C. Penney's Hunt Club clothing. Her analysis points to the similarity between these ads and a current ad campaign for the more upscale and trendy Ralph Lauren line. In that paper, Cathleen tells us,

> Ironically, the expensive Hunt Club clothing is a replica of an even more expensive brand of clothing — Ralph Lauren. Ralph Lauren is worn by the elite who can afford it, and wanted by those who want to appear like they can afford it. Hunt Club compensates for the latter with clothes that are very similar to Ralph Lauren, but are more economical. A secretary on a meager budget, for example, can dress like her lavishly attired boss by buying Hunt Club clothing, rather than Ralph Lauren.

Cathleen's analysis works through this lookalike ad campaign in order to link it with the American consumer's desire to look expensive even though, as she remarks later, "in order to even purchase the more economical clothing, Americans must work long hours." Cathleen points out that these ads sell both prestige and stylishness and feed into "American consumerism — a mindless drive to purchase beyond need."

By the time Cathleen wrote her final major paper for this course, she seemed to understand quite well the role of critique in analyzing popular culture forms. Furthermore, she seemed to enjoy her ability to "see through" these forms. She consistently brought to class additional ad campaigns that furthered discussions of advertising and consumerism. She was a quick and willing participant in both whole-class and group discussions about advertising strategies and how those strategies seemed to mimic what Elizabeth and Stuart Ewen had called "channels of desire" in the book she had read in preparation for her early work in the class. And she began that final paper in a way that seemed directly in line with the kind of critique she had been engaging in all along:

"Cathleen Corelli, come on down!" shouts Rod Roddy in his clear, singsong voice. Hearing my name, I jump up and run down the aisle as the crowd cheers. I take my place in contestants row and wait for one of Barker's Beauties to wheel out the next item up for bid. Remembering the other three bids and believing they are too low, since the *The Price is Right* only features the best of any product, I smartly bid nine hundred and fifty-one dollars — one dollar over the highest bid. Bob Barker announces the correct price, which is well over a thousand dollars, and I leave contestants' row to play a pricing game that promises big prizes. Then I am pulled back to reality — sitting in front of the television set in my living room — as the real first contestant shouts and runs on stage; but I tell myself that someday it will really be me up on that stage. Actually, I would settle for any game show stage as I am a game show junkie, obsessed with watching Americans compete for extraordinary products, some of which they have absolutely no use for.

As Cathleen's paper moves on, however, her enthusiasm for the show and all shows like it seems to overwhelm her critical abilities. She tells us that "*The Price is Right* has taught [her] to be a wise shopper." *Classic Concentration*, *Crossword*, and *Jeopardy* all helped her get into college because through them she learned "a variety of facts and tidbits concerning a broad range of topics." She is, she tells us, a "welcome member on any Trivial Pursuit team," and she has, again thanks to game shows, a quick memory for "names, numbers, and especially directions." "Therefore," she continues, "these games raised my I.Q. while others [*Family Feud*, *Love Connection* and *The Newlywed Game*] enhanced my emotional persona."

On one level, it might be easy to be discouraged about this final paper. If one goal of the liberatory classroom is, as Freire suggests, to move students toward a critical consciousness, Cathleen's paper seems to suggest that she has not attained that goal. In her discussion of game shows, she not only appears to lose critical distance but she becomes an apologist for those shows that, as Alexander Cockburn tells us of *Wheel of Fortune*, represent "a stately mime of capitalism at its best, celebrating that sine qua non of the system, the circulation of commodities." That endless circulation of commodities was precisely what Cathleen had objected to in her discussions of advertising and its appeal to mindless consumption. What, exactly, happened to Cathleen between that first and this last essay? We might turn to Alexander Cockburn here, and then back to Cathleen, to help explain how in that second paper she is perhaps not as far from the mark as it might first appear from these excerpts.

In his discussion of *Wheel of Fortune*, Cockburn contrasts greed ("capitalism at its worst") with the game of winning big prizes and the spectacle of circulating commodities ("capitalism at its best"). Cockburn, who watched an episode of the show being filmed, says this of its participants:

> The competitors I saw were not crazed with greed; indeed, both Mark and Dolores seemed much more excited by the fact that they had won than by what they had won. Dolores referred to her treasures rather disparagingly as "stuff," and was plainly relieved that she would be able to dump much of it on her in-laws. Indeed, she had a positively Brechtian objectivity...as though [she] recognized that it was absurd to have both an RCA and a Sharp video recorder, yet simultaneously accepted the entirely correct proposition that, as presently constituted, American capitalism...can survive only if the consumer buys as many video recorders, microwave ovens, et al. as the home will hold. (148)

Like Dolores, Cathleen understands quite well that this is a game in which the players win silly, even useless, items. She tells us, for example, that "game shows uphold the drive to get something for nothing by awarding [sic] contestants for simply appearing on stage and having a good time. Fully aware of this no-lose situation, Americans appear on these shows for, in the American eye, receiving beyond need is even better than purchasing beyond need." Cathleen even recognizes that she, too, is a part of the game-show mentality. She concludes her paper in this way:

> As an American, instilled with materialistic values, I also plan to take advantage of winning big prizes on simple game shows. If I am a champion, I will win tens of thousands of dollars worth [of] prizes for just a few hours of fun.

Now, Cathleen may not have come to the "positively Brechtian objectivity" that Cockburn notices in Dolores, but she is well aware of what is going on here and how much her own value system has been constituted by these shows and her enjoyment of them. She never gets the distance on these shows that she was able to get on advertising, but that, as well, may be a consequence of quite another facet of her subjectivity, one formed by economic circumstance. Cathleen has grown up in a family that had to pay attention to how much things cost. Her pride in knowing, as she tells us, "that $1.39 is an average price for a medium sized bottle of dishwashing soap," and that she can usually "find an even cheaper price" when she helps her mother with the weekly shopping is not the talk of someone who is simply a good bargain-hunter. She has had to count pennies because she comes from a low to moderate income working-class family and continues to live on a limited income. She understands, as she tells us in that first paper, that much hard work goes into buying even the cheapest clothing. Thus, her easy ability to see through advertising which pushes conspicuous consumption might well be contrasted with her pleasure in playing the games that promise money and expensive prizes for a few hours' fun. The games may play into a desire to, as Cathleen wryly puts it, "receive beyond need," but they do not ask that the recipient pay out beyond resources.

As teachers evaluating the writing of a student like Cathleen, we are faced with several challenges. First, we need to remind ourselves of the often hidden complexity of students' work. As Stephen North suggests, we need to "interpret this writing as meaningful, communicative discourse" and be attentive to the possibility that this discourse inscribes a multiple rather than centered subjectivity (226). Second, we need to recognize the shaping role of our own subjectivity in the evaluation process: Just as important as acknowledging the legitimacy of Cathleen's perspective is understanding our own position as subject in relation to these texts. In other words, in order to appreciate Cathleen's pleasure in the consumer challenges of a game show, we need to account for what may be our own lack of pleasure. It may be, for example, that as baby-boomers who grew up watching shows like *Queen for a Day* (in which contestants had literally to prove their neediness by telling long stories of illness and deprivation), it is difficult for some of us to see the behavior of the recipients of prizes on, for example, *Let's Make a Deal* as more than humiliating, undignified groveling.

What we want to suggest here is that the logical consequence of the concepts of subjectivity which structure Freire's liberatory pedagogy and cultural studies is a radical reformulation of the relationship between teacher and student. In this dialogic framework, the classroom becomes the site of exchange and reciprocity. In such an environment, "Knowledge is not *extended* from those who consider that they know to those who consider that they do not know. Knowledge is built up in the relations between human beings and the world, relations of transformation" (Freire, 109). It would be a mistake to see the discrepancy between Cathleen's first and last papers as a sign of miscomprehension or failure. What the instructor might learn from this final paper is that, for this student at least, pleasure is not incompatible with understanding. Cathleen recognizes her split position with relation to game shows and can even laugh at it. Both the opening scenario she creates and her closing remarks about being an American "instilled with materialistic values" demonstrate a self-awareness and an awareness of the cultural forms in which she participates.

Cultural Studies as Communication and Dialogue

If instructors are to avoid those subjectivity wars we mentioned earlier, they must first face a decision about course content. How do we, as composition instructors using a cultural studies approach, design our classes so that we do not judge our students' positions by how closely they mimic our own? How do we set up true "communication and dialogue," as Freire suggests we must if real education is to take place?

Because cultural studies itself argues that all texts are valid objects of study, there may be a temptation to pick any popular text without much concern over how it might be construed by both students and instructors. By contrast, we would argue that the most effective text that can be used in a course like the one we are discussing is one that offers a kind of cultural and interpretive richness, one in which meaning is unstable for instructors as well as students. This might mean that, instead of choosing texts for which we already have taken a position and which we already find pleasurable, we select at least some materials that are perturbing and perhaps even confusing.

A television program like *Twin Peaks*, for example, is such a text for the two of us at this point because of its ambiguity as well as its status as a widespread pop-culture phenomenon.[1] We emphasize here that this is one of the texts we would choose at this writing because of its richness for us and potential richness for our students. Such choices must be made with specific situations in mind. As scholars, the two of us have written on *Top Gun*, *Northern Exposure*, and *Terminator 2*, films and television programs popular with many of our students. Yet, for one of us to select, for example, *Top Gun* as a primary text for a cultural studies approach would be to close the door on the kind of conversation that ought to take place about these texts. We have already made a statement about the film; we are not trying to work through a position. It would, then, be difficult for us to remain objective as students work toward their own readings of this text.

Thus, in writing here about a particular program, we do not mean to promote the idea of a pop-culture canon that might be developed for a cultural studies classroom. We are asserting that the healthiest critique occurs when everyone involved — instructor as well as students — has yet to take a set position on a text.[2] Certainly, this can happen with any text. We use *Twin Peaks* merely as one example of the kind of cultural, aesthetic, and political complexity that can lead to real dialogic communication in a classroom. Like Cathleen's choice of game shows (a choice her instructor welcomed because she herself was confused by the enormous popularity of these shows), any instructor's choice of text should consider its possible cracks or tensions as places for communication and dialogue between teachers and students, fans and detractors, users and nonusers.

We might begin to approach a text like *Twin Peaks* by exploring this program as a cultural phenomenon. By the onset of its second season, the show's producers, David Lynch and Mark Frost, had pumped the market with such *Twin Peaks* paraphernalia as *Laura Palmer's Secret Diary* and Agent Cooper's tapes to his secretary Diane, the latter enclosed in a book-like container with cover art strongly resembling that of teenage mystery fiction. The concern for popular and commercial success implied by the proliferation of such industry tie-ins was in marked contrast to statements by the show's producers and cast about their expectations for the critical and popular reception of the show. In a cover story for *Time*, for example, one cast member insists, "We kind of like the idea that we didn't get any Emmys...We're not about winning awards; we are about doing what we do. If the Great American public accepts it, fine. If we don't, we still have our core audience. And even if we don't have our core audience, we know we have done it right" (86). That disclaimer, in fact, became a common one for many involved in the show's production, as though this program was to be read only as art and not at all as commerce.

The conflict between *Twin Peaks* as crass commercialism and as the artsy, avant-garde brainchild of maverick filmmaker Lynch is just one of the contradictions which make this text a particularly provocative object of study for the cultural studies classroom. Equally compelling is the show's intertextuality, a complex combination of visual and narrative allusions to classic Hollywood films, other films by Lynch (such as *Blue Velvet*), soap operas, and mystery and detective shows. This intertextuality is an important dimension of the show because of the opportunities it creates for different subjects of different ages, genders and cultural investments to engage with it in myriad ways.

One offshoot of this intertextuality is the ambivalent political stance of the show. The process of reading *Twin Peaks* uncovers important and difficult questions of politics and pleasure how they may or may not intersect. At the center of the show's narrative are such disturbing issues as domestic violence, incest, and drug abuse — often graphically depicted. *Twin Peaks* plays off of the all-too-familiar stereotypes of victimized women, macho abusive men, straight-shooting federal agents, and mysterious, deceitful Orientals at the same time that it complicates, even undermines those stereotypes thereby leaving them open to critique. There are stylistic ambiguities too — within a single episode, the show's tone can shift dizzyingly and unpredictably from overt parody to utter seriousness and back.

Even outspoken detractors of, for example, the program's seeming antifeminist politics admit to being drawn into its world. In a *Ms. Magazine* article Diana Hume George confesses to being "seriously addicted," then explains her own confusion about the program:

> I can see Lynch's work in three ways. All of them scare me. He might be cynically corrupt, exploiting his now vast, gullible, prime-time audience with those secrets he says it's all about. Or I can see

> him as the wise man, the visionary showing us our darkest depths. Or maybe he's really the gifted innocent in touch with, though incompletely aware of, his own unconscious and tapping ours in ways he cannot articulate. (58)

Hume George is here attempting to ask crucial questions of audience reception and mass audience gullibility or resistance. These are precisely the kinds of questions we might want to pose in the cultural studies classroom. Where Hume George's agenda departs from that of cultural studies is that she wants to settle these questions definitively for herself, as well as for others. She succumbs to the impulse we so often feel as academics and teachers to reconcile the contradictions or tensions in a complex text and in the reception of that text. It is this very impulse that cultural studies calls on us to resist, in ourselves as well as in our students. Thus, rather than ask, as does a recent article in *Utne Reader*, why *Twin Peaks* is so disturbing, a cultural studies perspective raises a more basic concern: How is it that this disturbing show is such a compelling one for so many viewers, including those like Hume George who find the politics problematic: Cultural studies suggests that possible answers to such a question are inseparable from a consideration of cultural forms and subjectivity.

Conclusion

In concluding this discussion, we wish to return to the question of what it means, in a classroom situation, to encourage students to critique, to resist. We have claimed that we do not necessarily want students to adopt our point of view or to reject outright the values of the dominant ideology. Yet, in promoting resistance, we run the risk that students will attack the things we love or embrace the things we hate. This is no small concern, especially given the inequitable power relationship between students and instructors, one which is consolidated by the institutional framework of the university. Perhaps the most critical problem becomes how we live up to the ideals of a liberatory pedagogy like Freire's, how we resist falling into old patterns of authority when those are the ones most available to us. A cultural studies approach to composition can give us an awareness of the similarity as well as the difference between ourselves and our students. Like our students, we are drawn to texts which are consistent with our own politics. Yet, like them, not only are we culturally anchored as subjects, but our position as subject is neither centered nor coherent. If the subjectivity of a student such as Cathleen can be engaged in multiple ways by different texts or even the same text, so can our own. In other words, as teachers we cannot ask students like Cathleen to interrogate their cultural pleasures in order to understand their complexities and contradictions without, at the same time, examining our own.

Notes

1. *Twin Peaks* aired on ABC television from the spring of 1989 to spring 1991. It has since been released on videotape for sale and rental throughout the United States. As of this writing, *Fire Walk With Me*, a feature-length film "spin-off" of the series, is in production.

2. Since beginning this article we have written a more thorough analysis of *Twin Peaks*; thus we would no longer use this text in a composition class such as the one we are describing.

Works Cited

Bland, Elizabeth. "Czar of Bizarre." *Time* 1 October 1990: 84−88

Cockburn, Alexander. "The Circulation of Commodities" in *Corruptions of Empire*: *Life Studies & the Reagan Era*. New York: Verso, 1987: 142−49.

Freire, Paolo. *Education for Critical Consciousness*. New York: Continuum, 1989.

George, Diana and Susan Guitar. "Reconstructing Tonto: Images of American Indians in *Paradise*, *Twin Peaks*, and *Northern Exposure*." Paper presented at Conference on Television and Feminist Theory ("Consoling Passions"), Iowa City, Iowa, April 1992.

Hume George, Diana. "Lynching Women." *Ms.* November/December 1990: 58−60.

Johnson, Richard. "What is Cultural Studies Anyway?" *Social Text* 16 (Winter 1986/87): 38−80.

North, Stephen. "Writing in a Philosophy Class: Three Case Studies." *Research in the Teaching of English* 20 (October 1986): 225−62.

Oelette, Laurie, "Is David Lynch Creepier than His Movies?" *Utne Reader* January/February 1991: 14−15.

Poovey, Mary. "Cultural Criticism: Past and Present." *College English* 52 (October 1990): 615−25.

Shoos, Diane and Diana George. "*Top Gun* and Postmodern Mass Culture Aesthetics." *PostScript* Vol. 9 No. 3 (Summer 1990): 21−35.

Shoos, Diane, Diana George and Joseph Comprone. "*Twin Peaks* and the Look of Television." Forthcoming in *Journal of Advanced Composition*.

Trimbur, John. "Cultural Studies and Teaching Writing." *Focuses* 1 (Fall 1989): 5−18.

13

Using Cultural Theory to Critique and Reconceptualize the Research Paper

Kathleen McCormick

i

In *Lenin and Philosophy*, Louis Althusser points out that while the school is the most dominant ideological state apparatus, "hardly anyone lends an ear to its music: it is so silent!" (155). Within the American academy over the last two decades, an increasing number of teachers and theorists have become attuned to the "music" of the schools and the detailed structures within them that carry subtle and not so subtle ideological messages, that thus, in the terms of Althusser's famous metaphor, "interpellate" or hail students to take up subject positions within the dominant ideology. The recognition that the school constructs students as subjects for ideology has led to broad-ranging educational critiques and proposals for pedagogical reform. One thinks immediately of Paulo Freire's "problem-posing" pedagogy (66–74), Gerald Graff's "conflict model" of education (PL 256–62), and Henry Giroux's "critical literacy" (155–72), all of which call for educational practices that teach students how to perceive the interconnectedness of social conditions and reading and writing practices, how to analyze those conditions and practices, and how, to some extent, to take action within and against them. In the last few years, there have also been a number of proposals on ways to use recent literary theory in the classroom.[1]

Few of these, however, have deigned to descend to the mundane micro-level on which ideological struggle functions, that of the textbooks and forms of reading and writing that go on in our classrooms. In this essay, I first use some of the insights of contemporary theory to critique the institution of the research paper as it is described to students in the instructions of some characteristic college textbooks. I will read the instructions less for what they overtly tell students (which may in fact function helpfully) than for their "absences," what is not explicitly *in* the text, but which is nonetheless a part of the ideological situation of the text, what, as Macherey puts it, the text "is compelled to say in order to say what it *wants* to say" (194). I will look particularly for points of contradiction within textbooks because it is there that we may be able to glimpse the ways in which ideology is working to repress the real conditions of cultural production within the curriculum or classroom. While symptomatic analysis of literary and other cultural texts has become commonplace in cultural critical circles in the last decade, it is rarely applied to such humble and apparently innocent "apparatuses" as the textbook, though this is precisely where it is most needed if we are to critique our own practices and to develop alternative ones. These textbooks reveal (while trying to conceal) the fact that the research paper functions almost exclusively as a conservative force, requiring by its very form that students believe in the general coherence of the self, their topic, history, and the current culture.

After analyzing contemporary textbook instructions on writing research papers, I then outline a conception of the research paper from the perspective of cultural studies in which students themselves are taught to do research by following a symptomatic mode of analysis. Since it is impossible, however, to change the ideological function of the research paper without also reconceptualizing particular contexts in which it is taught, I will briefly describe the literary and cultural studies program at Carnegie Mellon University in which I taught for eight years that intellectually and institutionally supported such change during the 1980s. While reform is needed at all levels and while broad curricular revision was undertaken on the undergraduate level at Carnegie Mellon,[2] my primary focus in this essay is the research paper written in the freshman course, "Reading Texts," which I directed between 1985 and 1989. I focus on this course because it is in entry level courses that we reach the most students and help to establish contexts in which knowledge will be produced and received throughout the rest of a student's college career. Thus, while I make summary references to other courses, I will discuss the organization and goals of this course in some detail.

ii

The bulk of current textbook instruction on writing a research paper consists of painstakingly detailed mechanical directions on such matters as how to use the card catalogue, how to take notes on sources, how to access on-line catalogues, how to revise sentences and paragraphs, how to make an outline, and on how to quote and document sources. However useful, such detail works to cover over a glaring absence: there is little if any serious discussion of how students can critically interrogate their sources by placing them in larger cultural and historical contexts, including exploring the ways in which they may be complicit with or work to defy the existing social order, or looking at them in relation to issues of power and privilege. In short, these texts contain little instruction in what Giroux calls "citizenship education," the development of "forms of knowledge and social practices" that make students "critical thinkers" and that empowers them "to address social problems in order to transform existing political and economic inequalities" (9).

Such absences are rich material for cultural analysis. Like the academy itself, the textbook is linked, perhaps inherently, to the residual: major publishers — Norton, Heath, Macmillan, Harcourt, St. Martin's, Little Brown — who control the bulk of the enormously lucrative textbook market are tied primarily to profit and therefore to adoptions. In the mid 1980s, when a group of colleagues and I working in the Carnegie Mellon University literary and cultural studies program managed to persuade D.C. Heath to publish two theoretically innovative textbooks, *Reading Texts* and the *Lexington Introduction to Literature*, we were able to do so at least in part only because we could guarantee that we would use the books at our own university, because we were willing to go "on the road" to persuade other departments to adopt not only aspects of our program but also the textbooks, and because Heath, nervously but not ungenerously, was convinced that our approach — a mixture of reader-centered pedagogy and cultural materialism — was a coming "thing." Nonetheless, at all stages of its production, we were cautioned about not getting too far ahead of the dominant understanding of literary studies, about, for example, balancing innovative teaching approaches with selections of traditional literary texts. We were also instructed to think always of the practical implications of our approach for the classroom teacher. This was, in fact, good advice — even if we profited from it in a sense somewhat differently from the way it was meant. It directed me, for instance, to consider how other textbooks dealt with what I came to see as the necessary micro-level of pedagogy, such as the research paper.

The traditional and still dominant way in which most textbooks describe authoritative sources for a research paper is through the language of objectivism: the best sources are always "accurate" (Veit, Gould, Clifford, 296; Winkler and McCuen, 39) and "unbiased" (Johnson, 70). At times objectivity seems to take on moral and political as well as epistemological significance. Objective sources are described as:

"reliable" (Coyle, 74; Watkins, 251; Johnson, 70), "authentic" (Johnson, 70), and "trustworthy" (Johnson, 72). Sources that are outside the mainstream, in contrast, are "worthless, silly, and misleading" (Winkler and McCuen, 39), "controversial" and of course "biased." Textbooks indirectly link the dominant with objectivity by directly linking bias either with easy targets such as eyewitness accounts of UFOs or with journals that overtly express particular political opinions or special interests.

Such instructions hark back to a phase in the history of the discipline where it was thought that objectivity might accord literary studies some of the respectability of the hard sciences. Of course, not all textbooks offer students the same advice, nor are textbooks necessarily consistent in the advice they give. As I shall demonstrate in this section, some, such as Weidenborner and Caruso, quite traditionally teach students to write objective papers that conform to their sources, while others such as Veit, Gould, and Clifford are committed to teaching students to become independent thinkers and scholars, despite the fact that they too at times lapse into a language of residual objectivism. In developing the *Lexington Introduction* and *Reading Texts*, my collaborators and I became aware of how we were pulled in multiple directions by both contradictory aspects of the residual paradigm and contradictory aspects of our own would-be oppositional approach. As we shall see, it is in part the tensions and points of instability among textbooks—which are reproducing tensions within the larger ideology—that might enable us to envisage the possibility of change. As I look at my and my collaborators' attempts in our own textbooks, particularly in *Reading Texts*, I can see how developments in our outlooks and broader trends in the academy make constant revision necessary.

In recent years, however, while research paper instructions in some textbooks have begun to change in response to reader centered criticism or the process approach to writing, the changes have largely (though not entirely) been cosmetic: in trying to accommodate some of the insights of more student-centered approaches without rethinking basic definitions of knowledge and subjectivity, textbook instructions have often become more conflicted and may reinforce the dominant more silently than previously, because they do so from a supposedly "reformed" perspective.

Indeed, some textbooks—especially those that seem to have added on a few insights from reader-centered theory—are often explicitly contradictory about the distinction between biased and unbiased sources. On the one hand, they argue that sources will always be perspectival or biased, acknowledging that different groups (or at least different individuals) in a society may have conflicting viewpoints on complex topics; yet, on the other hand, they retain the residual assumption that the best sources are unbiased. Spatt, for example contends that sources should be "trustworthy," yet she recognizes that "few knowledgeable people are entirely detached or objective." She goes on to argue that "'bias' is not a bad word, nor is it quite the same thing as 'prejudice'," but then contends that "awareness of bias may weaken your belief in the author's credibility; it is the person who is both knowledgeable and without bias whose opinions tend to carry the most weight" (303). While "bias" might not be a "bad" word at the start of the passage, it becomes increasingly pejorative as the passage develops. Similarly, Johnson writes on one page, "It is impossible to find completely unbiased sources" and on another, "If your subject is controversial, you will want to make sure that you use unbiased sources" (78, 70).

Contradictory statements such as these enable us to glimpse something erupting through the surface, not only of the textbooks, but of the wider ideological conflicts that have produced them, which the textbooks and the ideology itself are trying to repress — that "objectivity" is a constructed category, and that something will appear to be "entirely objective" only from a particular perspective. These texts seem afraid to face the logic of their positions, and this may be because, in the absence of a developed cultural theory, situatedness quickly threatens to become relativism or even subjectivism.

Both reader response criticism and the process approach to writing emphasize the power and uniqueness of the individual reader and writer, but since neither locates the subject culturally or historically, there seems to be nothing to critique the notion that a "powerful individual" could respond in a completely "subjective" manner. So, faced with only the choices of objectivism or subjectivism — the universal or the individual — these textbooks must primarily take the side of the objective in order to guard against the dangers of subjectivism: "Your paper is principally based on your findings from your research rather than on personal speculation" (Veit, Gould, and Clifford, 208). What they do not recognize as an option is that students could move their analysis into the social and historical and thereby situate their own positions, as well as those of their sources.

One current textbook is something of an exception to this, even though it shies away from any culturally based orientation. More consistently than most textbook writers, Lunsford and Connors maintain the stance that "even the most seemingly factual report, like an encyclopedia article, is necessarily filled with implicit, often unstated, judgments" (551). They go on to argue that "there are no neutral facts in the world of meanings", suggesting that students must always query their sources (552). This seems a decided advance on other books that repeatedly lapse into a residual objectivism. But their argument finally is individualist rather than cultural: the reason that "facts" are not neutral is not because they are constructed by discourses in broad ideological contexts, but because they are constructed by unique individuals: "The point is that all knowledge must be interpreted subjectively, by people. As a result, a writer may well tell the truth and nothing but the truth; but he or she can never tell the *whole* truth because people are not all-knowing" (552). Lunsford and Connors thus retain the opposition between objectivity and subjectivity; they simply come down on the side of a reasoned subjectivity.

Most current textbooks, however, try to keep their readers within the dominant not only by sustaining in them a belief that objectivity exists, but also by convincing them that they too will be able to write objective papers. To do this, it becomes necessary to teach students to marginalize or discredit that which threatens to show that objectivity is a culturally produced category rather than a transcendent one. Controversial issues and contemporary issues that lack clear cut answers, therefore, are often treated with suspicion. Students are repeatedly warned to interrogate controversial sources to see if they are "balanced or one-sided" (Walker, 56) or if they "aware of their biases" (Johnson, 70). Further, students are told that a controversial subject may be difficult for them to "consider objectively" because their "preconceptions" may "distort" their judgment (Coyle, 11). Noncontroversial subjects, by implication, are less likely to be biased, and are therefore "safer" for students to choose, despite injunctions by almost all the books to find an interesting topic. The message is clear — topics that would require students to interrogate explicit points of contradiction in the culture, topics that would allow students to examine and possibly critique the cultural means by which forms of knowledge and belief are produced, topics that might enable students to begin to recognize and address seriously forms of injustice and discrimination that exist in our culture are all taboo. Instead, students are often encouraged to use biographical or historical subjects because they are easily defined and limited (Spatt, 272) — that is, one can be more "objective" about them.

Given the importance of distinguishing biased from unbiased sources for the success of the student's paper, one would expect fairly detailed instruction on how students should read and analyze their sources. The instruction, however, is actually quite brief: students are quite uniformly attributed with having an intrinsic ability to distinguish — without training or even explicit instruction — biased from objective sources. This "absence" of instruction in virtually all the textbooks is crucial for a symptomatic reading because it lays bare both the kinds of reading strategies they encourage students to adopt and their underlying complicity with the dominant.

How is the student, presumably just beginning to learn about the topic, to tell a "biased" from an "unbiased" source? Instructions on detecting bias often amount to not much more than whether an argument *sounds* good. Spatt tells the student to "jot down...any rough impressions about the author's reliability as a source" (291–2), but if students are researching subjects like those that Spatt suggests, such as the Berlin Olympics of 1936 or the Battle of Gettysburg, about which they probably know very little, how could they possibly have rough impressions about the author's reliability, or if they did, how could they assume that their impressions were at all "accurate"? Veit, Gould, and Clifford may unwittingly give us some answers. In discussing a passage from an essay by Manuela Hoelterhoff that is critical of Disney World, the authors point out that since Hoelterhoff concedes that Disney World "is almost universally admired" and since she is clearly taking a different position, she has "alerted" readers to her "bias" (170, 171). Is one to conclude that positions in line with the dominant view of Disney World are "unbiased"? While this is hardly the case, it is likely the conclusion that students will draw if they are instructed to detect bias simply by using their own intuition. Perhaps Winkler and McCuen are the most revealing when they come right out and tell their readers to "use common sense" (39). "Common sense" is surely the most unreflective means of passive acquiescence to the dominant that exists — and something that research should help to problematize rather than justify. As Catherine Belsey argues, while common sense might appear to be "obvious and natural," it is in fact "ideologically and discursively constructed, rooted in a specific historical situation and operating in conjunction with a particular social formation" (3). The "obvious" and the "natural," Belsey contends, "are not given but produced in a specific society by the ways in which that society talks and thinks about itself and its experience" (3). Textbooks are able to credit students' common sense with the ability to intuit objectivity only because they have mystified the notion of individual subjectivity, assuming that, as Dollimore puts it, "the individual...[is] the origin and focus of meaning" (quoted in Sinfield 140), and because they have universalized the particulars of their own historical moment.

In addition to using their intuition when reading a text to see if it sounds "balanced," students are also often instructed to test for bias by checking the credentials of authors and the respectability of the publication in which the article occurs. Being told to use and believe various directories in order to determine the "objectivity" of sources encourages in students an even more uncritical acceptance of allegedly objective sources: there is no discussion of how an author or publication gets into — or perhaps more importantly, gets excluded from — one of these indexes. "Objectivity" is invariably linked with the "common sense" of the dominant.

Finally, not only is the procedure for evaluating bias unclearly specified in the textbooks, it is also supposed to remain unvoiced in students' papers: most evaluations — in which students separate "reliable" from "unreliable" sources — are to be done well before they begin writing their papers. That the student's process of evaluating sources is not intended to be seen by the teacher indicates the extent to which it is meant to remain a product of commonsensical intuition rather than critical thinking. For if it became explicit, the student — or the teacher — would have to clarify the premises under which it had taken place, and if those premises came under scrutiny, the whole procedure could potentially fall apart, for the premises themselves would be shown to be constructed, not transcendent.

I have focused thus far on the *reading* instructions students are given for doing research. Now let us turn to the *writing* instructions. By and large, research papers are to follow the same formula regardless of their subject matter. Students are to find an issue which has a clearly delineated mainstream position, but for which there is just enough controversy so their papers can look as if they constitute a decisive and personal choice for a particular position. The student's paper is to be a "discovery" of the objective truth of the dominant, and to qualify as such, it must have three primary characteristics: it must be without contradictions; it must be "objective"; and it must align — and therefore, authenticate — the students' subjectivity with the alleged objectivity of the dominant.

Textbooks, predictably enough, tell students that their final drafts must resemble those sources that they have judged to be unbiased. They must be: "coherent" (Johnson, 177; Spatt 368; Walker, 110; Winkler and McCuen, 89); "balanced" (Veit, Gould, and Clifford, 361; Weidenborner and Caruso, 119); "unified" (Johnson, 177; Spatt, 368; Winkler and McCuen, 89), and "complete" (Johnson, 178; Spatt, 371). A seemingly innocent directive about the paper's *style* is in fact also about a particular way of conceiving of knowledge in the world: by the time of writing, students are expected to be able to neutralize contradictions among sources by using their differences to create a "complete picture."[3] The goal of their papers is to simplify and homogenize, not to study the tensions within a given field of inquiry. Spatt, for example, tells students that they "may decide to exclude those [sources] that do not mesh easily with the others" (291). And even when students are told that they may acknowledge sources that disagree, they are given no instruction on how to analyze *why* the disagreements might exist in the first place: "You may simply report the disagreement, especially if you have no basis for trusting one source more than the others. Or you may choose one source if it seems more trustworthy than the others....Or you might try to verify the fact by further research" (Weidenborner and Caruso, 130–31).

Such directions teach students to believe that, if they know enough, contradictions can always be resolved; contradictions are presented as a kind of fall from objectivity that, paradoxically, need to be gotten rid of before one can discover the "complete picture" about an issue. An alternative view for which I am arguing, however, sees contradictions as a fundamental aspect of human history which ideology works to conceal, simply to make existence more bearable: "In the name of comprehensibility the collective mind invents systems (religions, philosophies, mythologies) that allow it to attain to some notion of coherence" (Dowling, 53−54). From this perspective, far from smoothing over contradictions in the name of a false coherence as it now does, the research paper should interrogate contradictions to reveal the ways in which the dominant represses history, to analyze the effects of that repression, and potentially to reconstruct history from alternative perspectives for different ends.

In addition to being instructed to resolve contradictions, students are also generally told that the persuasiveness of their papers, indeed their very "integrity," depends upon a stance of objectivity: "Lasting persuasion usually depends on a convincing presentation of evidence based on what seems to be undeniable fact" (Walker, 100; see also Spatt, 303, 306; Johnson, 70; Winkler and McCuen, 102).[4] The student's finished paper is, therefore, supposed to be "like" the preferred sources. A symptomatic reading of such instructions would suggest that, despite some claims to the contrary, the goal of the research paper is ultimately knowledge-telling, not the production of knowledge: "Write as if you were passing the information [from your sources] on to your readers" (Johnson, 142). Knowledge is, therefore, something that is transferred or passed on from one source to another − it is certainly not produced by the student.

Finally, what is called "the student's point of view" is often the perspective of one or more of their sources (often those that most represent the dominant position) that the student "chooses" to adopt. Weidenborner and Caruso directly tell students that they should "make whatever modifications are needed" in their own position "to bring it into conformity with the sources" (76). If students speak "in their own voices," it is generally only to repeat the stories they have learned from others: "The paper becomes your message to your readers about the discoveries you have made during your search" (Johnson, 141). Spatt, for example, tells her readers: "In writing about history, you may also have to consider your point of view" (274), but that "point of view" turns out to be someone else's: "If, for example, you set out to recount an episode from the Civil War, you first need to establish your perspective: Are you writing from the Union's point of view? the Confederacy's? the point of view of the politicians of either side? the generals? the civilians? industrialists? hospital workers? slaves in the

South? black freedmen in the North?" (274). While this list of potential perspectives may look exhaustive, it omits the student's—that of a culturally situated eighteen- or nineteen-year-old living in the nineties who may be Hispanic or black or white, residing in the North or South, etc.

As I noted above, some textbooks influenced by reader response criticism and the process approach to writing do not tell students to flatten out differences among sources or take up the positions of their sources. Lunsford and Connors, for example, state that "disagreements among sources can provide particularly fruitful areas to consider and may provoke you to new insights all your own" (559). Veit, Gould, and Clifford, despite other statements to the contrary, repeatedly tell students that "you do not want to be merely a passive consumer of ideas," that "you must be an active, analytical reader and writer," (169), and that "you are fully entitled to think of yourself as a scholar engaged in a scholarly enterprise" (205), and their textbook contains a separate chapter on writing an argumentative research essay in which the student is encouraged to "write an argument of your own" (410). But in the absence of a developed theory of the student as a subject in history, and of an extensive rationale for critiquing one's sources, it is difficult to conceive of how the student is to go about constructing new insights or an original argument. Veit, Gould, and Clifford state that the purpose of an argumentative essay is to "test ideas in a sincere search for truth" (410), implying once again that truths are universal. It is, however, only by recognizing that truths are situated within larger systems of production that students can begin to contextualize their own positions and those of others and that they can develop an argument for the value (not the truth) of one perspective over another.

Imagine students caught within this web of conflicting instructions. They are told to choose an interesting topic, but that it should not be too controversial. They are supposed to be objective, but not too objective. They are supposed to use their own ideas, but to change them if they are not confirmed by their sources. They are supposed to give a complete picture, but they are not supposed to use biased sources. If we ever needed evidence for the poststructuralist emphasis on the de-centered subject, we find empirical confirmation of it in these textbooks.

iii

Giroux argues that any radical political project needs both "a language of critique" and "a language of possibility" (31). Thus, having done a critique of current research paper instructions, I want now to develop an alternative conception of the research paper based on perspectives from cultural studies. The two-part structure of this essay—critique and the posing of new possibilities—is also a vital part of the kind of student research paper I am proposing.

In the mid- to late eighties at Carnegie Mellon, we were fortunate to have had institutional support for a curriculum revision of the English major, beginning with the freshman reading course and proceeding through a set of English core courses to upper level courses. Many courses in our department, therefore, became theoretically focused, though they certainly did not all employ the same particular theories. What most of them had in common was a recognition that every position a student or teacher adopts is theoretically inscribed and that certain issues are of particular interest because they are currently the source of intense theoretical *debate*; that is, an issue is studied in the classroom not because it is of universal or transcendent concern, but because it is seen as significant in our current historical conjuncture.

For a six-year period, we organized our undergraduate curriculum around the concepts of *language*, *history*, and *culture*. The freshman reading course, "Reading Texts," integrated these three concepts and introduced them to our students. When our students proceeded to their sophomore year, they were required to take a common core of courses built on the same three concepts. While our department offered majors in creative, professional, and technical writing as well as literary and cultural studies, all students, regardless of their major, were required to take these courses. The first, "Discursive Practices," was a course in cultural semiotics, which investigated how fundamental systems of language—in the broadest sense, not only in written or spoken discourse—are constitutive of our perceptions, exchanges, and cultural practices. Second, "Discourse and Historical Change" taught students how to read texts from earlier historical formations symptomatically, that is, how to read with historical awareness, to look for the symptoms of a text's ideological battles, and to give language to the tensions and contradictions that the text was struggling to articulate or repress. Finally, "Reading Twentieth Century Culture" explored major theories of culture in the twentieth century, from humanism to cultural materialism, and attempted to read a selection of cultural texts such as poems, novels, films, and plays in relation to these theories.[5] By the time students entered upper level courses, they were thus at least relatively familiar with the basic theoretical concepts of cultural studies.

I turn now to a detailed consideration of the freshman course, "Reading Texts," which provided an introduction to these issues to all students in the College of Humanities and Social Sciences and to many others throughout the university by teaching students to read and write with historical and cultural awareness. The course was designed first to empower students by both validating and interrogating the cultural situatedness of their own experiences. Students were meant to see the liberatory possibilities of recognizing that they are subjects in and of ideology. The course then attempted to teach students a symptomatic way of reading texts of the larger culture and texts from other historical formations. Finally, students were encouraged to develop alternative histories based on their interrogation of their own subject position and their symptomatic readings of cultural and historical texts.

The course was designed to be taught in a dialogic "problem posing" fashion, in which, as Freire argues, "the teacher is no longer merely the-one-who-teaches, but one who is himself (sic) taught in dialogue with the students, who in turn while being taught also teach" (67). Thus, apart from the reading in their textbooks, little if any theory was to be taught directly in class. While some graduate instructors attempted to teach theoretical texts in their courses, this was generally not successful because such texts most often merely intimidated students who found it impossible to argue with them or critique them. The dialogic nature of a class is always lost when texts — whether from the left or the right — are presented according to what Freire calls the "banking system" of education. Instead of presenting theory as doctrine, teachers were asked to construct a series of response statement assignments, in addition to three paper topics, that were to pose problems of meaning, gender construction, historical interpretation, etc., on which students were to write. The students' writing was not only to be read by the teacher and the other students for its manifest content, which often helped the class to articulate particular aspects of the problem being posed, but it was also to be read symptomatically for what it did not directly say, but for what it often unwittingly assumed about a particular issue. One of the assumptions of the course was that students would learn to read texts of the broader culture symptomatically by first reading their own texts in this way.

Although "Reading Texts" was taught in diverse ways by graduate instructors and faculty, its general structure consisted of four parts which I will spell out in some detail in order to delineate one kind of context in which a culturally situated research paper can be assigned and written. The course, first, introduced students to a model of the reading situation that presented reading not as a passive intaking of meaning by a reader but as a complex interaction of the reader, the text, and the larger literary and general ideology. In this first segment of the course, students learned to write response statements that would interrogate the situated nature of their own responses to texts.[6]

In the second section, students were introduced to ways of reading symptomatically in history. In units on anything from *Hamlet* to Abraham Lincoln's freeing of the slaves, students read various critical and historical texts, particularly with contradictory perspectives, in order to help them to develop a sense of difference from the past and to recognize the perspectival nature of history; that is, to recognize that accounts of anything from a literary text to a world event are never neutral, but are always told out of a particular set of values and beliefs. In this section of the course, students were asked to write essays that were to help them learn to read critical and historical texts that often sounded "objective" from a symptomatic and self-conscious historical perspective.

In the third section of the course, students explored the role of language in constituting us as thinking subjects. By reading and writing on extracts from such texts as Raymond Williams's *Keywords* and Susan Sontag's *Illness as Metaphor*, students discovered that meanings of words and concepts, as well as whole texts, change significantly over time as a result of the particular cultural formation in which they are being read, and they began to develop the ability to analyze the ideological situatedness of language itself.

Realizing that language is not objective impinges on students' own sense of their subjectivity. For if language is always value laden, it is impossible to use it for "subjective" or wholly private expression. As Bakhtin writes: "Language is not a neutral medium that passes freely and easily into the private property of the speaker's intentions; it is populated—overpopulated—with the intentions of others" (294). Response statement assignments that asked students first to write what they considered to be a "personal" statement on a topic of their own choice and then to analyze that statement ideologically posed the problem of whether their points of view could be conceived of as either "objective" or "subjective," and brought many of them to at least an incipient sense that their perspectives are what Pecheux call "interdiscursive"—"the product of the effects of discursive practices traversing the subject throughout its history" (Morley, 164). While it is of course impossible ever to "see" fully one's own ideological situatedness, conceiving of the self as an interdiscursive subject rather than a free individual can (paradoxically) enable students to develop greater agency than they might otherwise have had; such a radical reconception of the self may lead students to examine the various discursive practices which have produced them and which both enable and delimit their possible actions.

The fourth section of the course, which focused on reading with cultural awareness, was the culmination of the course, and it worked primarily to develop and deepen students' understanding of many of the concepts and ideas that were introduced earlier in the term. This unit was often organized by having students read various kinds of texts—literary, historical, and popular—which consciously or unconsciously address or embody a particular cultural myth, such as American individualism, success, freedom. Confronting the differences and similarities among diverse cultural texts, students frequently began to glimpse some of the conflicts and contradictions embodied within the myth or institution they were studying. They then often began to explore the relations of power and oppression that underlie these contradictions and that work to repress them. Finally, students were encouraged to suggest ways of rewriting the particular cultural myth they were investigating that might challenge the system of relations that helped to produce it.

It is within this framework, then, that students were given a version of the following research paper assignment:

> Take a current issue in the news, a major myth or a dominant metaphor of our culture, or an American "institution" such as baseball or the Miss America Pageant and analyze the ways in which it has been produced by particular conflicts within the American ideology. What does it explicitly say about our culture? What relations of power, gender, race, class, or nationality does it attempt to hide or repress? Who benefits from this system of relations? Who suffers? Remember to make your analysis specific. Avoid vague platitudes.
>
> What is the function of your analysis? How is your position related to the general ideology? In what ways, if at all, does it constitute an alternative view to the dominant? In what ways is your own position contradictory? What new or different kinds of social relations, if any, does it require?
>
> Read at least six essays on your subject from conflicting viewpoints. Select these essays from a variety of different kinds of journals and magazines. You should not merely summarize these articles in your paper, nor should you necessarily resolve the conflicts among them. Rather, you should attempt to analyze the ideological forces that underlie the positions for which your various sources argue and the implications of maintaining each of those positions. In order to do this, you need to consult texts that are not specifically "about" your topic, but that can give you the historical background necessary to develop a symptomatic analysis of your primary sources. You should at least consult the American history texts we have read in class, and if these seem inadequate, use other histories in order to explore the ways in which your topic is positioned within the larger culture. (Feel free to consult your instructor or other members of the class on this.)

This paper topic attempted to change the function of the research paper from one in which the existing social order was quietly defended to one in which it might be actively critiqued, and it tried to wrench the research paper from the objective/individual paradigm which it generally occupies and into the social and historical. As Sinfield argues:

> The twin maneouvres of bourgeois ideology construct two dichot-
> omies: universal versus historical and individual versus social. In each
> case the first term is privileged, and so meaning is sucked into the
> universal/individual polarity, draining it away from the historical and
> the social — which is where meaning is made by people together in
> determinate conditions, and where it might be contested. (141)

In helping students to develop alternative means of analysis, the course
tried to encourage them to interrogate the ideological assumptions
and the specific power relations underlying the diverse positions they
encountered, as well as the political, moral, historical, and social
implications of maintaining them. Teachers repeatedly emphasized that
this did not involve simply deciding whether sources are "objective" or
"biased," as it may have in other research papers students had written,
for these categories themselves are historically produced, and what
seems "biased" in one social formation may seem "objective" in another.

In requiring students to learn to evaluate their sources ideologically,
the course was not suggesting that they be taught a facile knee-jerk
response to the issues raised to attain some kind of "political correctness." For "political correctness" — when it is more than just a trumped
up accusation by a paranoid right wing — is just another variation on
the old objectivist paradigm: it sees some positions as transcendently
superior to others because they meet certain predetermined ahistorical
criteria. What was advocated, in contrast, was much closer to Giroux's
notion of "citizenship" education or Freire's notion of "dialogic" education. "Reading Texts" was to create conditions by which students
could examine and critique their own place in the cultural contradictions
of our time, and by which they could discover that agency follows only
from a meta-awareness of why (to some extent) one has the beliefs,
assumptions, and habits one does. The goal was never to proselytze,
but to open students' perspectives on the ideological situatedness of their
own positions, and to encourage them to examine the implications — in
relation to such issues as gender, race, and power — of maintaining
those or various alternative positions held by other members of the
class or other authors read in the course.

Despite the guidance students were given during the month in
which they were writing their papers — conferences, in-class short presentations, and discussions of their topics — and despite the work they
did in the rest of the course, most students still easily lapsed into a
residual objectivism when drafting their papers. This is not surprising.
The language of objectivism is, after all, the language for which they
had always been rewarded in the past and which they are most often
required to speak in their other courses. Students who chose topics

that lacked a clearly delineated dominant position (or perhaps where the dominant position seemed too obviously entrenched) and who situated their topics precisely as contestable — indeed, the very kind of topics they are warned against choosing by most textbooks papers — were, however, less likely than others to adopt a stance of objectivism.

Most teachers discovered that students also needed specific — and repeated — instructions on how to evaluate their sources. For, again, despite all they may have learned in this particular course about situating texts in broad cultural contexts, and despite the often probing and detailed cultural analyses they wrote in their informal response statements, the very idea of writing a research paper frequently revived in students objectivist models learned in other contexts that work against the critical and historical process of evaluation required in this course. In the crunch of writing their most extensive paper for the term, most students understandably found themselves wanting to "get it right," to determine the "reliability" of their sources, and to agree with the most reliable of them.

Many students actually became quite proficient at discovering in each other's papers ways that a rhetoric of objectivity cut off social analysis, and they benefited greatly from opportunities to read and critique each other's drafts in class. But nonetheless they often had difficulty developing a different kind of language more suited to cultural analysis — one in which the primary criterion for persuasiveness is an analysis of the historical and social antecedents and implications of a position rather than a pretense to its objectivity. It is perhaps at this point that my students most fully confronted the ideological nature of language. For the language they found most readily available — whether they wanted to be speaking it or not — was the residual language of objectivity. Even when they realized that the language that they — like most of us — have been taught to privilege as "objective" is a product of a particular ideology — and one that impedes historical and dialogic thinking — they nonetheless often found themselves drawn to it because it is easy to speak and because it is generally regarded as powerful. Certainly the textbooks discussed above engender a belief in the persuasiveness of objective-sounding language. Whether or not particular students were ever able successfully to develop a different way of writing their research papers, however, most at least made a significant step in recognizing the ideological imbeddedness of what they had previously thought to be "value-free" writing.

Finally, this research paper assignment also required students to revise their notion of their own subjectivity from something that is supposedly personal and unique to something that is traversed by larger cultural and ideological experiences. Students were encouraged to interrogate — within the paper itself — the contradictory ways in which they, as well as their sources, were situated in relation to the issues they were exploring. This was perhaps the most difficult aspect of the assignment and often the least successful. A number of students early in the course mistakenly assumed that if truth was not regarded as objective and universal in this course, it must then be subjective and individual. Such a conclusion was not surprising given the emphasis in this country on the power of the individual — indeed, a number of the textbooks discussed above emphasized the role of the student's "individuality" (albeit in contradictory ways), and this was certainly the fundamental premise of reader response criticism of the seventies. Further, students are often so used to being told that their own larger experiences are not relevant to school learning, that when they found these experiences being validated in this course, they were loath to want to analyze or critique them in such a way that might have the potential, from their perspective, to once again devalue them.

The tensions surrounding issues of subjectivity and agency often translated into a research paper in which students questioned the ideological situatedness of their sources, but did not extensively interrogate their own positions. I nonetheless consider a paper at least somewhat successful on the freshman level if students are able to take thoughtful stands "of their own" within a many-sided argument and, at the same time, articulate some awareness of how their (and others') views are socially constructed. As Giroux writes, "Knowledge has to first of all be made meaningful to students before it can be made critical" (106). Such a process often just takes time. While the graduate student staff and I tried to construct various assignments throughout the term that would suggest to students that their particular interventions — whether in developing a new reading of a literary text or in taking a stand on abortion — could most effect change if they were historically informed and if they came from a position that interrogated its own ideological situatedness, we were not always successful. Students who went on to take further courses in the English program, however, particularly the core courses for majors, had the opportunity to learn these lessons more slowly and in more detail.

By the time students moved to upper level seminars in literary and cultural studies, they were generally able to confront relatively complex theoretical texts and to engage in fairly culturally detailed and historically self-conscious reading practices. Yet even at the upper level it was still often difficult for students to maintain a sense of their own historical difference from the past and a sense of themselves as constructed subjects. I emphasize this point not in any way to berate our students, but rather to underscore the difficulty of opposing what

Sinfield calls "the two fundamental mystifications of bourgeois ideology": "the projection of local conditions on to the eternal...[and] the construction of individual subjectivity as a given which is undetermined and unconstituted and hence a ground of meaning and coherence" (138, 140).

If the cultural studies movement is to oppose these mystifications of the dominant ideology, it must seriously interrogate the ways in which our own pedagogical practices are so often — even if unwittingly — complicit with the dominant. What we need at this stage of the movement from "literary" to "literary and/within cultural" studies are sustained analyses of even the most seemingly insignificant or "natural" material details of our profession, such as our writing textbooks and our research paper assignments. But, as I hope this paper has suggested, once critiqued, such practices in themselves cannot be significantly changed without our rethinking and then reconstructing the larger web of institutional and ideological forces in which they are produced and which they work to sustain.

Notes

1. See, for example, Robert Scholes, *Textual Power*; William Cain *The Crisis in Criticism*; Dianne F. Sadoof and William E. Cain, eds, *Teaching Theory to Undergraduates*; Maria Regina Kecht, ed., *Pedagogy is Politics*; Douglas Atkins, and Michael Johnson, eds., *Writing and Reading Differently: Deconstruction and the Teaching of Composition and Literature*; Gerald Graff and Reginald Gibbons, eds., *Criticism in the University*; Cary Nelson, ed., *Theory in the Classroom*; special issues of *College English* on psychoanalysis and pedagogy, edited by Robert Con Davis, and on feminism and pedagogy, edited by Elizabeth Meese; special issues of *College Literature* on "The Politics of Teaching Literature" and on "Literary Theory and the Teaching of Literature." Finally, in the area of textbooks, see Gary Waller, Kathleen McCormick, and Lois Fowler's *The Lexington Introduction to Literature* and Kathleen McCormick and Gary Waller, with Linda Flower, *Reading Texts: Reading, Responding, Writing*.

2. See Gary Waller's "Writing Within the Paradigm Shift" for a description of undergraduate curriculum revision.

3. See McCormick, "The Cultural Imperatives Underlying Cognitive Acts," for a discussion of students' perspectives on avoiding contradictions in order to sound "objective."

4. And yet students are also warned against choosing a topic that is too objective. As Weidenborner and Caruso tell their readers, topics with a "single, accepted answer" such as "Why is the sky blue?" are inappropriate because "they have been answered to everyone's satisfaction" (7–8).

5. I explain our core courses in more detail in "Always Already Theorists: Literary Theory in the Undergraduate Curriculum."

6. See *Reading Texts*, chapters 1 through 4.

Works Cited

Althusser, Louis. *Lenin and Philosophy*. London: New Left Books, 1971.

Atkins, Douglas and Michael Johnson. Eds. *Writing and Reading Differently: Deconstruction and the Teaching of Composition and Literature*. Lawrence, Kansas: University Press of Kansas, 1985.

Bahktin, Mikhail. *The Dialogic Imagination*. Caryl Emerson and Michael Holquist, trans. Austin: University of Texas Press, 1981.

Cain, William E. *The Crisis in Criticism*. Baltimore: Johns Hopkins University Press, 1984.

College Literature. "The Politics of Teaching Literature." 17. 2/3 (1990).

College Literature. "Literary Theory and the Teaching of Literature," 1991.

Con Davis, Robert, ed. *College English*. *49.6/7 (1987)*.

Coyle, William. *The Macmillan Guide to Writing Research Papers*. New York: Macmillan, 1990.

Dowling, David. *Jameson, Althusser, Marx: An Introduction to "The Political Unconscious"*. Ithaca: Cornell, University Press, 1984.

Freire, Paulo. *Pedagogy of the Oppressed*. New York: Continuum, 1989.

Giroux, Henry. *Schooling and the Struggle for Public Life*. Minneapolis: University of Minnesota Press, 1988.

Graff, Gerald. *Professing Literature* (PL). Chicago: University of Chicago Press, 1987.

Graff, Gerald and Reginald Gibbons, Eds. *Criticism in the University*. Evanston, IL: Northwestern University Press, 1985.

Johnson, Jean. *The Bedford Guide to the Research Process*. New York: St. Martin's Press, 1987.

Kecht, Maria Regina, ed. *Pedagogy is Politics*. University of Illinois Press, 1991.

Lunsford, Andrea and Robert Connors. *The St. Martin's Handbook*. New York: St. Martin's Press, 1989.

Macherey, Pierre. *A Theory of Literary Production*. Geoffrey Wall, trans. Boston: Routledge and Kegan Paul, 1978.

McCormick, Kathleen. "The Cultural Imperatives Underlying Cognitive Acts." In *Reading to Write: Expanding the Context*. Linda Flower, Victoria Stein, John Ackerman, Margaret Kantz, Kathleen McCormick, and Wayne Peck. Oxford: Oxford University Press, 1990: 194–218.

McCormick, Kathleen, Gary Waller, and Linda Flower. *Reading Texts*. Lexington, MA: D.C. Heath, 1987.

Meese, Elizabeth, ed. *College English* 52.4 (1990).

Morley, Dave. "Texts, Readers, Subjects." In *Culture, Media, Language*. Stuart Hall, ed. London: Verso, 1980: 163–173.

Nelson, Cary, Ed. *Theory in the Classroom*. Urbana: University of Illinois Press, 1986.

Sadoff, Dianne F. and William E. Cain. *Teaching Theory to Undergraduates*. New York: MLA, 1991.

Scholes, Robert. *Textual Power: Literacy Theory and the Teaching of English*. New Haven: Yale University Press, 1985.

Sinfield, Alan. "Give an account of Shakespeare and Education, showing why you think they are effective and what you have appreciated about them. Support your comments with precise references." In *Political Shakespeare*. Ed. Jonathan Dollimore and Alan Sinfield. Manchester, Manchester University Press, 1985: 134−57.

Spatt, Brenda. *Writing from Sources*. New York: St. Martin's Press, 1991.

Veit, Richard, Christopher Gould, and John Clifford. *Writing, Reading, and Research*. New York: Macmillan, 1990.

Walker, Melissa. *Writing Research Papers*. Second Edition. New York: Norton, 1987.

Waller, Gary. "Writing Within the Paradigm Shift: Poststructuralism and the College Curriculum." *ADE Bulletin* 81 (1985):6−12.

Waller, Gary, Kathleen McCormick, and Lois Fowler. *The Lexington Introduction to Literature*. Lexington, MA: D.C. Heath, 1986.

Weidenborner, Stephen and Dominick Caruso. *Writing Research Papers: A Guide to the Process*. Third Edition. New York, St. Martin's Press, 1990.

Winkler, Anthony and Jo Ray McCuen. *Writing the Research Paper*. New York: Harcourt Brace Jovanovich, 1989.

14

"This Could Have Been Me":
Composition and the Implications of Cultural Perspective

Lori Robison

"I did have a lot of difficulty relating to the movie and I did think that it was kind of plotless and out-dated. I understood that they were trying to show an era and I do think they succeeded in doing so, but the movie was boring and therefore I felt kind of pointless. I know the point was to show people without a point or perhaps trying to find one, but I really couldn't get into the movie and that makes it difficult to find value in it. I personally have to be able to relate to something in order to pass a fair judgement, so I'm really looking forward to our class discussion so that I'll be able to have a better understanding of the movie."

The writer of this passage, a student in my first-year composition class, is responding to the film *Easy Rider*. I had presented students with two reviews of the film: an earlier review that emphasizes the film's originality and a more recent one that praises the film though finds it dated. I asked them to consider these two reviews and then to develop their own response to the film. Specifically, I asked the students if the film could be dismissed as merely dated, or if they, as students of the 1990s, could find some way of responding to the film despite the fact that it is so clearly a product of another era. This particular student had trouble, as she says, "relating" to the film, which seems to make her unable to complete the assignment, to respond to the film.

Reading this student and her response as unimaginative or even as lazy would not be too difficult. After all, she has essentially said that she has nothing to say because the film does not engage her, and she has ignored the part of the assignment in which I ask her to consider why the film might not engage someone of her generation. However, I do not think this student was merely ignoring the assignment out of lack of imagination or effort. Instead, I believe she had trouble responding to the film because I asked her to do something in her response that was rather difficult: I asked her to imagine and to describe herself in relation to her culture and, further, in relation to another culture. I asked her, in other words, to imagine her own location within a culture and to see that this perspective did in fact make a difference in her perceptions.

This response was an early assignment in a composition course I taught in the spring of 1990, a course in which culture was both subject and method. As we studied the late 1960s and their impact on our own culture, I continually asked the students to consider the extent to which, and in what ways, their understanding of this topic was influenced by their cultural and historical perspective.[1] As a result of designing and teaching this course, I have become aware of the value of making the implications of meaning-making from within a particular cultural perspective an explicit concern of the composition classroom.

No matter what approach we take to the teaching of composition, the composition classroom is always, as James A. Berlin has convincingly shown, profoundly involved in our understanding of reality: "In teaching writing we are tacitly teaching a version of reality and the student's mode of operation in it" (766). Therefore, he endorses "New Rhetoric" approaches to composition, or those approaches which see writing as a process of constructing meaning, because, as he points out, these approaches can help students achieve a more productive and active "mode of operation" in their world. If we assume that thought is not prior to language and that students construct knowledge through the writing process, we find that as composition teachers we can do more than introduce students to a set of rhetorical tools or a composing process; instead, the student can become "a creator of meaning, a shaper of reality, rather than a passive receptor of the immutable given" (776).

Cultural studies shares with such approaches to composition an awareness of the constructed nature of knowledge and thus a belief that through language we actively shape and create reality. In addition, cultural studies contributes an emphasis on the context in which these meaning-making processes take place, an emphasis which could further enrich New Rhetorical approaches to composition. In defining the New Historicism, a cultural studies approach to English studies, Louis A.

Montrose describes the connection between the social and the linguistic as understood in cultural theory:

> The prevailing tendency across cultural studies is to emphasize their reciprocity and mutual construction: On the one hand the social is understood to be discursively constructed; and on the other, language-use is understood to be always and necessarily dialogical, to be socially and materially determined and constrained. (15)

The mutual dependence of the social and the linguistic, as described by Montrose, allows us to see the student writer, and all writers, as simultaneously enabled and constrained by language. If we again acknowledge that the writing process is the process of coming to thought, to knowledge, and to truth, the writer constructs reality. And yet if we recognize that the writing process cannot occur outside of the social, out of a cultural context, the writer's ability to make meaning is also constrained by his or her cultural situation. Students, then, can productively be seen as the historical subject Montrose defines who has "subjectivity" or "the capacity for agency" but is also "subjected to" or "positioned[ed] within. . . the social networks and cultural codes that ultimately exceed [his or her] comprehension or control" (21). If we see students both as producers and products of their culture, the composition classroom can become a place in which students are not only able to revise the world around them but also to investigate their position in the larger world.

Clearly, the difficulty for the composition teacher is finding ways to demonstrate to students that writing can be closely connected to the world outside of the classroom. Making a cultural issue the focus of the composition course is a first step in helping students see this connection. But, more importantly, the pedagogy of the course should emphasize writing as a process of placing and locating the self within a culture, and it should insure that students are given the freedom and the impetus to discover their cultural situation and its implications through their writing.[2] By saying that the writer both places and locates the self, I want to again evoke Montrose's notion of the subject to suggest a process in which the writer has the agency to place the self and yet is simultaneously and already constrained in a specific location. In such a process students discover their own cultural situation, and yet in making this discovery they find that there are alternative perspectives into which they can write themselves. And these new perspectives do not, of course, allow the students to be free of cultural constraint; they merely give them a new equally constrained position from which to make meaning.

I do not want to imply that students — or any of us, for that matter — can at any given time be entirely conscious of the number of cultural forces under which they are working. Also I want to make clear that I am not suggesting that I merely want students to examine the assumptions or biases with which they begin the writing process. Rather, I am suggesting a reading and writing process similar to the one David Bartholomae describes. He persuasively argues that to become writers students must imagine themselves as writers; they create the self as writer by writing and reading the self into a certain rhetorical position: "The process I have been outlining is not an internal psychological process but a rhetorical act of placement, a way of writing that locates a reader and a text within an institutional setting" (104). Similarly, I am advocating a process of writing and reading that ultimately involves simultaneously finding and placing the self in relation to a variety of cultural perspectives. Creating the self as a writer in my composition class meant writing and reading the self into various cultural situations.

Returning to the student who had trouble responding to *Easy Rider*, I would employ Bartholomae's argument to now suggest that she had difficulty locating herself not only in an institutional setting but also in a historical and cultural one. She begins her response by writing that she cannot relate to the film and implies this is because it is "outdated." She goes on to write about what the film *was* trying to do or to place it back into its own cultural framework—"I understand that they were trying to show an era"—but resorts to her judgement that it was "boring" and, so, "pointless." Finally, she concedes that her problem with it is "personal" and thus perhaps unfair. She shuttles back and forth between past and present judgements of the film, and she is pulled between a response that would emphasize the personal and one that would consider the larger impact of the film. Unable to negotiate through these concerns to come to her own response, she is "looking forward to our class discussion" to help her formulate a response. As Bartholomae points out, beginning writing students often do not have the institutionally sanctioned "counter-arguments or counter-examples until they have been located as writers in a context that makes those arguments and examples possible" (105). Similarly, I believe this student cannot complete the assignment as I requested because she has not located herself or the film within a larger historical and cultural framework. Without an awareness of the extent to which her response is colored by her cultural background or the film itself is influenced by a cultural context, she cannot find the "arguments and examples" to develop a response. Consequently, and more importantly, the assignment remains insignificant for her—it does not allow her any new understanding of her world or her place in it.

While this was typical of many of the students early in the course, I was pleased to see more students, including this writer, find ways to write the self into various cultural locations as the course progressed. I wanted to design a course that would encourage students in this manner and ultimately demonstrate that writing could make a difference in how the writer worked in and perceived the world. Therefore, the topic of the course, the sequence of units, and the writing assignments asked the students to study a cultural issue and, at the same time, reflexively consider the implications of studying culture.

I selected a topic that I thought was complex and broad enough to generate a number of issues for discussion and writing, and yet narrow enough that the students could feel they had achieved a certain level of knowledge and expertise by the end of the course. As I noticed an increased interest in the 1960s in current fashion, advertising, music, film, and television, I became intrigued in creating a course that would explore this cultural fascination with that period. Ultimately, I wanted the students to consider what this interest in another time could tell us about ourselves and about our own culture, and I hoped that a course which challenged students to examine and theorize a cultural phenomenon in this manner would also lead them to other intellectually and socially challenging questions. Importantly, I also believed that this was a topic in which the students' understanding of it would be very obviously affected by their cultural relationships to it. For example, the students are a part of the larger culture that is intrigued by the 1960s, but, interestingly, most of them could not have participated directly in that era. Their understanding of the time, therefore, would come out of its representation through current culture. As children of sixties' students, today's college students may have interesting personal connections to their parents' pasts. Today's students are also aware that they are often unfavorably compared to the students of the late 1960s, who have become exemplary college students for many college educators — who were perhaps themselves college students twenty years ago. Obviously, I cannot name the infinite number of ways that each student could be connected and find connections to this topic, but clearly this is a topic that serves to make these various cultural positions more explicit.

The sequence of units and assignments in the course was also developed to promote the examination of these kinds of connections to the past. I began the course with a unit that asked the students to consider what they knew about the 1960s and from where that knowledge originated. In a first and informal writing assignment, I asked the students to write two self-portraits: one in which they introduced themselves as they are today and another in which they imagined themselves as they would have been if attending college in the 1960s. Essentially, this assignment asked the student to consider the extent to which culture shapes the individual, and the responses were interestingly mixed. A number of students insisted they would have been just the same as they are today in any cultural setting, while others acknowledged that anything from their clothes to their political beliefs might have been quite different. We went on to read some personal reminiscences of college in the late 1960s and a statistical twenty-year study of freshman trends to determine how college students from both eras were being defined. With this unit, I hoped to introduce the idea that our understanding of the 1960s (and, by implication, of ourselves) did not necessarily come out of one source or out of objective fact, but rather was constructed through a variety of conflicting sources and through our own cultural perspective. Thus, for the first major paper I asked the students to reconsider the various pictures of the decade we had examined — their first writing assignment, the reminiscences, and the statistics — not to come up with the "real" picture of the era, but in order to consider what it means to study or define an historical period through such sources.

As the students began to question our accepted definition of the 1960s, we moved on to the second unit in which we tried to understand more about the decade itself by watching two films that were actually produced more than twenty years ago, *The Graduate* and *Easy Rider*, and by reading about and researching events that occurred in the 1960s. I initiated a study of Haight-Ashbury by assigning a number of readings with different perspectives on the implications of young people "dropping out" and moving to San Francisco. I then asked the students to develop group research projects and presentations to the class about an event from the late 1960s that they wanted to learn more about. After introducing the students to Clifford Geertz's notion of ethnographic "thick description," in which "anthropological writings are themselves interpretations, and second or third order ones to boot" (15), I asked that in coming to their own interpretation of the event being researched, the groups of students use a number of different kinds of sources. I suggested the standard materials — newspapers, articles from periodicals, and standard history texts — but I also recommended fictional accounts, photographs, songs, or other artistic depictions. The point here was for the students to collaboratively develop their own thick description of the event, discovering that even sources produced in the era itself did not tell the whole or the true story; these sources merely provided another layer of information. Each source could only contribute an interpretation of the event to the groups' final construction of the event. The paper with which the students concluded the second unit again asked them to reflect on this process of coming to an interpretation of another historical period. I asked the students to reexamine the research project and the other sources we had worked with in this unit to consider how we come to terms with the past from our own cultural and historical perspective.

In the third unit I asked the students to return to the original question of the course and to come to some conclusions about what we can learn about ourselves and our current culture by learning about the past—a question that allowed for some closure and also, importantly, asked the students to consider the value of the course. We watched *1969*, a film produced in 1989, which reflected our own culture and its interest in the 1960s. I asked the students to bring other current representations of the 1960s into class for discussion. After reading and hearing the opinions of some cultural critics, the students wrote a final paper in which they developed their own explanation for today's interest in the 1960s through an interpretation of the cultural representations we had examined together as a class.

I consider this to have been a successful first-year writing class. The students' papers reveal that they became stronger writers over the course of the semester: they convincingly developed their own explanations and interpretations, they drew from sources and ideas from the entire semester, and they seemed very willing to revise or reconsider earlier positions through their writing. And further, many of the students seemed to have found ways to make their writing matter; they wrote papers that suggested that they had explored issues and discovered concerns of profound social and personal importance. I believe that these students became more accomplished writers for a number of reasons. In part, they seemed to have been motivated by a topic that was of interest to them and by the intellectually challenging nature of the issues we considered. And also, I tried to implement a pedagogy that would give them the freedom to discover what they thought about those issues through the writing process. Specifically, I emphasized the entire writing process by commenting on drafts and revisions of papers in a manner that reflected a real interest in content; by assigning informal, ungraded responses; and by setting up writing workshops in which small groups of students read, commented, and discussed one another's writing.

In addition to these pedagogical strategies, students were aided in the process of becoming reflective writers—I would again stress—by the course's emphasis on locating and placing the self in relation to the culture in which they were writing and about which they were writing. Finding ways to understand their own cultural positions gave the students access to a variety of kinds of knowledge—personal, familial, social, political. And these knowledges gave the students the expertise to synthesize issues, to discover how and why they responded as they did to the issues, to reconsider earlier responses, and to write papers of personal and social significance.

A number of students, for example, demonstrate that once they have located the self in a particular cultural moment or situation they become aware of the possibility of other perspectives. One of the first students to overtly reconsider his perspective after becoming aware of his own cultural location wrote this response to *Easy Rider*:

> A major concept in the film *Easy Rider* that I had a lot of trouble with is the concept of just dropping everything and hitting the road on a pair of motorcycles. I just simply could not relate to this kind of freedom. I feel that I have certain obligations to myself, as well as to others. I just could not drop everything and take off. My morals just would not let me do that. I am not saying that I don't wish I could do that. I would love that kind of personal freedom. I guess, in a certain way, I can relate to what these guys did.

I read this student's sense of his morality as an awareness of his cultural placement; morals, as he presents them, are large, overwhelming forces that keep him from doing certain things. This sense of morality won't let him "drop everything and take off," and, consequently, prevents him from "relating" to the film. Significantly, though, once he identifies this morality as a force that influences him, he is able to relate to the film in a new way. Having identified this force, he can seemingly imagine a position out from under that force — a cultural position in which he can imagine enjoying "this kind of personal freedom." In a class discussion of his response, this student made it clear that he still could not envision himself actually dropping out, but he did say that he could now imagine the appeal of doing so. Seemingly, then, he remains in a cultural situation that does not value the actions of the characters in *Easy Rider*, and yet he comes to a new awareness of his own position and thus the possibility of other positions.

Another student, similarly, wrote the following as an introduction to his final paper:

> During our group presentation of Woodstock I was asked, had I been the same age back then, would I have participated in it. I answered no, I would not have been there. Now a month later, after careful thought, I would still give the same reply. I believe in everything that happened, and everything it stood for. I really do not think, however, that I would have grown my hair long, worn ponchos or worn tie-dyes. If I would have done that, I think my father would have disowned me.

This student goes on in the paper to talk about his father, who was the right age but was never "a member of the whole movement." His father, he explains, had values very like those of the counter-culture about which he had been reading, and yet his father did not look or act like a "hippie." The paper goes on to argue that we need not be nostalgic for the sights and sounds of the decade, but rather for the activism and the "love, peace, and brotherhood" that is associated with the 1960s.

Like the student who began to see the appeal of the lifestyle presented in *Easy Rider*, this student comes to an appreciation of other values while remaining strongly attached to his own. In the group research project to which he refers, this student was enthusiastic about the information he had found on Woodstock, and the project seemed to push him into a new understanding of the issues of the course. Reflecting on that project, he finds that he can now value what occurred at Woodstock — "I believe in everything that happened and everything it stood for" — but he still maintains that he would not have participated in it. By examining the values of those in another cultural situation, he seems to have an even better sense of who and where he is.

Of course, it might have been worthwhile to point out to this student that if he really did "believe in everything that happened and everything that it stood for," he really could not know how he would have reacted at the time — he might have been at Woodstock, and he might not have been as concerned that his father would not have approved. But I did not do this because I did not see my job in this final paper as pushing this student into a kind of cultural relativism out of which he could never legitimately imagine or place himself. Instead, I was pleased to see him find a way to formulate a position from which he could engage with a variety of kinds of knowledges. After defining his own relationship with the values of the 1960s, this student, for example, talks about his father in his generation, his relationship with his father, a character in one of the course readings, a theory of nostalgia that was developed by a guest speaker in class, and contemporary social events which this student sees as pointing to nostalgia for the decade and to a new activism. And in the conclusion to his paper, this writer demonstrates that he has found a position from which he can use all of these knowledges; he can move from the class materials, to the larger society, to his own feelings, and finally back again to the society:

> Through studying what happened at Haight-Ashbury, Woodstock, the Kent State Massacre and the emotions that these people were feeling, these kids [the people of his generation] too will start to believe that they can make a difference. These kids will see that a new society does not need to be formed; these feelings already are being felt in our society...I believe that this course has taught me to feel this way. I think that the hippies are not alone and forgotten. The ideas are very much alive today. We have to learn to see through all the nostalgia and get down to the bare emotions of what was taking place. Those like myself must experience these feelings by learning to understand what they were going through and why. I think that people need to evaluate themselves and why they have this interest in nostalgia for the sixties. When they do this, perhaps they will not

need to return back to find the emotion they long for. The emotion is
right there inside of themselves.

Accessing all of these varied knowledges aids this student in writing an
essay that is clearly of personal significance. In this conclusion he
suggests that he has learned something new about himself and about
the culture in which he lives. As he finishes the course, this student
may be in the same cultural situation in which he began the course —
he does not suggest that he could or would become a hippie. However,
having learned something new about his cultural situation, he is able to
write a potential transformation of his reality; he imagines a time when
his peers "will start to believe that they can make a difference."

Another student begins the written portion of her group research
project by very explicitly placing herself in relation to the event she was
researching: "Two months and twenty-three days before I was born
four people who were approximately my present age were shot and
killed by national guardsmen at Kent State University." Interestingly,
she connects herself in two ways to the Kent State shootings. The first
connection is one she cannot change; her birthdate firmly locates her in
a specific historic moment. The other connection is one she has created;
she has placed herself as a college student who shares an age and, by
implication, a perspective with those who were killed. This student,
then, has found a way to write herself into new relationships with the
culture she is studying. She is well aware of where she actually is, but
she can imagine another location — one that gives her a new, more
personal and significant connection to the shootings at Kent State: "I
shudder to think of experiencing something like the Kent State riots,
much less the Kent State 'massacre,' but as I read [about the shootings] I
was very touched. As I read the article I kept thinking, 'had I been
born earlier on July 27, 1950 instead of July 27, 1970, this could have
been me.'"

Finally, I turn to another student who wrote a series of papers that
suggests she also found ways, as the course progressed, to develop new
connections to the culture we were studying, and so, ultimately, to her
own culture. This student begins her first major paper by stating that it
is difficult to ever really know what happened in the past:

> Each of us is molded by the decade in which we grow up, yet each is
> a unique mold which makes its individual contribution to society. By
> piecing together those personal accounts of a particular era we can
> begin to understand what they represent as a whole. Defining the
> culture of the 1960s is difficult when we are unable to reflect upon
> personal experiences. Students in college today have not been subject
> to our nation at war, violent civil rights movements, the strong threat
> of communism and nuclear war, or any of the events that helped

define that era. Therefore, as a student, I am limited to using media in which others have shared their experiences and impressions.

Clearly, this student's understanding of the implications of cultural perspective is very sophisticated; she argues that without experiencing what the students of twenty years ago experienced, it is impossible to understand their perspective, and she is very careful to qualify what the personal accounts can now tell us — we can "piece together" personal accounts to "begin to understand what they represent as a whole." In this first paper, then, this student is very aware of her own cultural situation and the way her own perspective might prevent her from understanding that of another.

She begins her second paper by saying,

Our knowledge of culture is enriched each time we come in contact with a new source of information. We automatically combine previous facts and opinions to formulate our own impression of an era. By this approach, I was able to formulate my own image of growing up in the 1960s.

Though still aware that she cannot get out of her own cultural perspective, the student is able in this paper to engage with the material in a slightly new way; in the first paper she needs personal accounts of others to come to terms with the past, but in the second she seems to have found a way to "formulate [her] own image" of the decade. Without suggesting that this student's papers imply a strictly linear development, I would like to suggest that in her second, and especially her third major paper, this student seems to move out of the relativistic position of her first paper — a position which prevented her from exploring her own connections to the past — to another culture. Her ability to explore these connections is especially apparent in her final paper:

I realize by reading about such events as the Kent State riot that we cannot allow another generation gap to stifle communication. I will implement this knowledge to my own experiences, by respecting the values of other generations, and to one day listen to those opinions of my children...It is crucial that we first examine our personal lives and then join together with society so as to make a difference in an increasingly complicated world.

From her new position of knowledge about events of the 1960s, this student, like the student who writes about Woodstock, is able to pull a great variety of sources and experiences together in her final paper; she goes on in the paper to discuss the Kent State shootings, readings from the course, and her own experiences at an Earth Day celebration on campus. Importantly, her study of the 1960s gives her a new way of looking at her own life and her own society, and this new perspective gives her a way of imagining her world differently; events from the past, the student says, will change her life in the present and into the future.

These student papers raise questions, I am sure, about my own role in the class — about the extent to which my own political views or my agenda for the class may have influenced the students' written work. Though I am tempted to claim that my work in the class was free of ideological perspective, because this claim may serve to legitimate my students' papers and my class, I know that I am, like my students, shaped by my cultural situation; I too have a way of understanding the 1960s. Clearly, through the course design, the assignments, my comments on student papers, and my role in class discussion, this course was infused with my perspective. In fact, I would argue that designing a course in which the instructor's stance is purely objective would be impossible. However, I do not think this means that the students were required to come to my perspective or to answer the questions of the course in one way. On the contrary, the cultural issue on which this course was built provided countless connections to the issue, and thus countless possible perspectives and answers. Though I did not require that my students come out of the course with one particular way of understanding the relationship between their culture and the culture of the 1960s, I did push the students (again, through course design, assignments, comments, and discussion) to find a cultural position from which they could develop a personally and socially meaningful perspective. I am more pleased, for example, that the last student I discussed finds a way in her final paper to make the course materials relevant to her life outside of the classroom than I am that she advocates social activism. Perhaps, then, the distinction I am making here rests on the fact that as an instructor in such a course, I too must be reflexively aware of the implications of coming to know within a cultural context; I must be aware enough of my own cultural position to recognize my influence in the class, and yet by recognizing that I do have a perspective, I too find a way of appreciating other perspective — those of the students.

Notes

1. This course was developed as part of a collaborative pilot project to revise the first-year writing program at Indiana University. In this project a number of courses which focused on a cultural issue were developed. I am indebted to the other members of the committee for their practical and theoretical contributions to the course I describe here.

2. In "Popular Culture as a Pedagogy of Pleasure and Meaning" Henry A. Giroux and Roger I. Simon confirm my sense of the importance of a

pedagogy that allows students to explore these questions: "We are not concerned with simply motivating students to learn, but rather establishing conditions of learning that enable them to locate themselves in history and to interrogate the adequacy of that location as both a pedagogical and political question" (3).

Works Cited

Bartholomae, David. "Wandering: Misreadings, Miswritings, Misunderstanding." *Only Connect: Uniting Reading and Writing*. Ed. Thomas Newkirk. Upper Montclair, NJ: Boynton, Cook, 1986. 89–118.

Berlin, James A. "Contemporary Composition: The Major Pedagogical Theories," *College English* 44 (1982): 765–77.

Geertz, Clifford. *The Interpretation of Cultures*. New York: Basic Books, 1973.

Giroux, Henry A. and Roger I. Simon. "Popular Culture as Pedagogy of Pleasure and Meaning," *Popular Culture, Schooling, and Everyday Life*. Ed. Giroux and Simon. New York: Bergin and Garvey, 1989. 1–29.

Montrose, Louis A. "Professing the Renaissance: The Poetics and Politics of Culture," *The New Historicism* Ed. H. Aram Veeser. New York: Routledge, 1989. 15–36.

15

Cultural Studies:
Reading Visual Texts[1]

Joel Foreman
David R. Shumway

One of the distinguishing features of cultural studies is its intent to expand humanistic studies by including texts in new media and the products of oppressed and marginalized groups. But the point is not to add new works to an old canon or tradition, thus shoring up a monological conception of culture. The cultural studies movement assumes a revised conception of culture which, unlike the Arnoldian one, is not evaluative and which understands culture as a site of struggle and conflict.[1] As such, cultural studies must entail a transformation of teaching practices in English and other departments. Teachers willing to use nontraditional texts in their courses will need both to understand the theory that warrants cultural studies and to develop appropriate methods of textual analysis. This essay is meant to help fill this need by briefly outlining that theory and by illustrating one way that cultural studies may be implemented in the classroom. The activity of reading visual texts that we describe here could be part of a course specifically designated as cultural studies, but it could equally well fit into a more traditional course — introduction to literature, for example — as a way not only to expand the range of texts but also to enlarge the students' understanding of culture.

Following a practice that is now well-established, we use the term "visual text" to refer to any kind of picture: for example, a photograph, an oil painting, or one or more frames from a film or television program. The six visual texts used for illustrative purposes below are editorial and commercial images published in *the New York Times Magazine*, 9 September 1990. By referring to such ads and photographs as texts we indicate that the construction of meaning that takes place when we "read" them requires a complex interpretive process, one that decodes the signs of the visual text in much the same way that the letters and words on the page of a document are decoded. However, the speed and ease with which we consume a visual text tends to conceal the fact that the mind is extremely active in the second it takes to scan the page of a magazine. This facile consumption of visual texts, rather than proof of their superficiality, demonstrates their deep and complex involvement with the culture that produced them. The pedagogical program described below is intended to help students understand this connection.

The teacher's first task is the selection of images to be used for analysis. For our discussion here we selected images from a single issue of the *the New York Times Magazine*. Using an issue of a periodical is a convenient option because students can easily acquire a copy, saving the teacher the effort of reproducing the images. It is also a strategic choice, however, since the relationship of individual images to their context is an important point for analysis. Almost any publication which contains large numbers of images will do as well as the *New York Times Magazine*, although teachers will want to keep in mind that different magazines (e.g., *Playboy, Essence, Sports Illustrated, Cosmopolitan*) will foreground different issues.

A complete analysis of the visual texts we have selected for discussion here would take at least several hours, and probably more with beginning students. Thus the activity we propose is not intended as a single class exercise, but as a course unit, or perhaps as a series of classes distributed over a semester during which students are introduced to cultural studies. The introduction to the activity can usefully take place before the students have been formally introduced to any of the theoretical assumptions of cultural studies. The main objective of such a strategy would be to provide a base for comparison with the insights the students will produce later in the exercise, when the cultural studies content starts to reconstruct the way they look at and interpret visual texts. The goal of the introductory session is for students to grasp the following points:

- pictures are visual texts;
- our apparently effortless grasp of visual texts depends upon complex interpretive processes;
- though apparently superficial, visual texts are deeply revealing cultural products.

One effective method of presenting these ideas is to ask the students to examine the publication and choose images that illustrate them especially well. The ensuing discussion should be directed in a manner that explores and reinforces these notions. It is likely that the students themselves will select for consideration some of the visual texts the teacher wants to use for future sessions. If not, the instructor will want to guide discussion in that direction.

In principle, even a randomly selected sample of visual texts will work, just as a randomly selected group of poems will enable a sophisticated discussion of poetry. We raise this point because there are certain advantages, most notably high interest and motivation, to allowing students to select the visual texts. On the other hand, many teachers will feel more comfortable selecting images in advance and thus having assurance that the class discussions will be as predictable as advance planning will allow.

The group of texts that we've selected from the *New York Times Magazine* indicates first a strategy of selection which foregrounds the most important issues for cultural studies, those of class, race and ethnicity, and gender. Second, our selection emphasizes a diversity of subject matter, formal construction, and overt function. For example, the difference between the photographic subjects of "The Burberry Look" ad and the magazine's cover photo is very useful, as is the different treatments of children in the latter and in the Hofstra University ad "We Teach Success." As we will see, the relationships among the photographs can yield an understanding of the culture that exceeds what can be produced by a single isolated text.

In order to read deeply these visual texts, students will need to be introduced to some specific information and to some concepts. The information we have in mind would be specific to the periodical and to the images which have been selected for the exercise. At the most basic level, students will probably have to be informed about the process and relations of production that resulted in the particular periodical you are using. For example, students may need to be informed that magazines and newspapers generate income mainly by selling advertising, and that ads are increasingly targeted at particular demographic groups by selective publication: ads are published in the magazines which are most likely to reach the desired group and, often, only in particular editions of those magazines which go only to certain regions or even zip codes. Students should be reminded that media conglomerates own most of these publications, and that the interests of these corporations in profits exceed their interest in producing any particular kind of product. It should also be explained that advertising has its own separate system of production, and that the content of particular ads does not normally originate either with the periodical or the company that commissioned the ad. Furthermore, audience analysis is necessary to understand both editorial and advertising images, so information on the readership of the periodical in question should be provided. For example, the *New York Times Magazine* reaches an unusually large number of upper-income readers, who constitute a relatively high percentage of its total readership. This kind of information need not necessarily be provided in advance. It might be more effective to introduce some of it during the course of discussion, but it is necessary for students to learn it at some point if they are to be able to answer the questions we pose later in the essay.

To choose to present the sort of information we have just described involves an interpretation, a decision about what is most significant about the production of the images, but the information itself is more or less a matter of fact. On the other hand, the concepts that cultural studies teaches, the ones which lead us to present these facts rather than others, are rooted in a set of assumptions about culture which are interpretations and are thus contested. Students will not in the main already be familiar with these assumptions, let alone share them. While it is obviously one goal of cultural studies to advance the acceptance of these assumptions, it is not the teacher's job to persuade students that they are true. Rather, all that the program we propose here requires is that students be willing to analyze that material from a particular interpretive perspective. We think that the insight that the exercise will produce will be persuasive enough.

Perhaps the principal assumption of cultural studies is that culture is a site of struggle or contestation. This itself entails a certain definition of "culture," which is itself a strongly contested term. It might be useful to introduce Raymond William's discussion of the term's history (from *Keywords*) which details the main competing meanings. Students will already know that culture can either refer to specific, valorized practices and products such as attending the symphony or a work of Shakespeare, or to the whole way of life of a group of people, for example, the culture of the Eskimo. Cultural studies assumes a kind of combination of the two definitions, taking from the Arnoldian an association of culture with works of art and other representations, and from the anthropological the sense that culture is an aspect of all human societies, rather than attached to only a few superior ones. To this definition, culture as the representations produced by a group, it must be added that these representations bear some relation to the conflicts that structure society and thus that culture cannot be conceived as an organic whole. In the West during the modern era and in the contemporary world as a whole, these conflicts have often been defined by gender, race, and class. There are also conflicts within states between groups that define themselves in terms of nationality or religion, as well as between states which usually are identified with nations.

What it is most important about these conflicts to convey to the students is not that they exist—students will be familiar enough with the reality of conflict—but that in most cases, the conflict exists as a struggle between a dominant and one or more subordinate groups. Thus, culture is structured by a series of hierarchies, male over female, white over black, rich over poor. But this is an oversimplification, since none of these relations, even gender relations, are binary. There are groups which may not be identified as either black or white, and there are various points in the middle of the economic scale that the opposition of rich and poor effaces. Differing sexual identities, including gay and lesbian, fracture the binary opposition of male and female. Furthermore, on the world stage, states and national cultures also exist in relations of dominance. In each of these registers, there will be representations which reinforce the current hegemony and representations which express the interests of those who are oppressed by it.

If the production and distribution of visual or verbal representations were equally available to all members of a society, then we might expect that society's conflicts would be directly and unambiguously played out in them. The interests of each group would under such conditions presumably be clearly articulated for all to understand and acknowledge, if not necessarily respond to or accept. But the production and distribution of representations is controlled by the dominant group, and they use these representations to maintain and extend their hegemony. It is in the interest of the dominant not simply to express their interests, but to behave as if their interests were shared by everyone. In order to convey this impression, the conflicts which characterize social life are best covered up. Under some governments, the production and distribution of representations are controlled directly, with censorship used to prevent any expression of oppositional interest from being circulated. In Western democracies, the decentralized power of corporations and other institutions also tend to limit what is available to see or read. However, such limitation is far from absolute. Oppositional perspectives are allowed to be expressed for a number of reasons, among them that those in power are not themselves unified and that there are profits to be made by exploiting the interests of the oppressed.

Because the media are not absolutely controlled, and more importantly, representations themselves are too polymorphous to be rigorously limited, contradictions to the dominant interests are a part of culture. "The role of *ideology* is to suppress these contradictions in the interests of the preservation of the existing social formation, but their presence ensures that it is always possible, with whatever difficulty, to identify them, to recognize ideology for what it is, and to take an active part in transforming it by producing new meanings" (Belsey, 45−46). Ideology is one of the more difficult concepts on which cultural studies relies.

Students will typically come to class understanding "ideology" only as a system of beliefs and therefore as something which one may or may not have. Everyone has beliefs, they acknowledge, but only some people have systematic beliefs. Ideology, as it has been used in cultural studies, however, doesn't refer to explicit beliefs but rather to "the very condition of our experience of the world, unconscious precisely in that it is unquestioned, taken for granted" (Belsey, 5). Thus all of us, whatever our social position, live in and through ideology. Ideology in this sense is not merely false consciousness, for it always entails both the recognition and the misrecognition of reality. It is one of the aims of cultural studies to analyze ideologies to show what they systematically cause to be misrecognized.

Ideology doesn't operate by directly persuading us to believe this or that falsehood or error. Rather, in Althusser's formulation, it interpellates or hails us. Ideology works by positioning us as readers or viewers in a certain way vis-à-vis the text or picture. When one is interpellated, one feels the obviousness, naturalness, or "common sense" of the message one finds in a representation. The representation itself provides a ready-made place from which such agreement will easily be forthcoming, the "subject-position" which the text assumes for its reader, the picture for its viewer. It is, of course, possible to adopt a different position towards a representation, but this requires that one resist the ideological effects that representation normally has. Cultural studies, for this reason, seeks to explore how different forms of representation position their subjects. Notice that this is not a question of who the real audience for the representation is but of the role that an individual reader is invited to assume.

These assumptions and concepts can be rendered as a set of questions designed to be asked of texts of different kinds. The questions embody what cultural studies typically does with the objects it investigates. In answering the questions with regard to the *New York Times Magazine* images, we have gone beyond the kinds of answers that students themselves are likely to generate spontaneously. The questions themselves could be given to students as study guides or as a small-group assignment. As we have written them below, the questions assume a visual text, but they could easily be modified to apply to texts of other kinds.

The Conditions of Production

Where and when was the text produced?

This may seem like trivial information, but it is crucial to understanding the specificity of the image. Even if the answer is "9 September 90 in

New York," the image becomes historicized. This question makes it clear that the meaning of the image cannot be universal or timeless. To understand "Conde Nast Vietnam," for example, it is necessary to situate the image in relationship to both the Vietnam War and the Reagan era. These historical moments loom large in our cultural memory and general knowledge about them is so available that the way their significance is encoded in the image seems obvious. Moreover, the producers of the image expect it to work as it does because of assumptions, which are usually supported by statistical research, about the anticipated reader's knowledge. As this knowledge base decays, as it inevitably will with the passage of time, the cultural meaning of the text becomes ambiguous, enigmatic, or is lost. As a case in point, consider that history teachers, whose emotions were powerfully engaged by televised images of the first demolitions of the Berlin Wall, were amazed to find their students unmoved by the spectacle. The reason for this emotional discrepancy is quite simple: the cultural and historical knowledge that invested the Berlin Wall images with affective power just wasn't included in the students' memories. It follows that a cultural studies analysis must consider the relevant kinds of information available to the anticipated reader of a given text.

For what purpose was the text produced? For what historical audience was it intended, and how would they have used it?

The demographics of modern media are only the most recent illustration of the fact that all representations are created with specific readers or consumers in mind. And images may assume quite different conditions of consumption. A magazine advertisement is obviously designed to be used by the viewer for a particular purpose, but so is a large painting that takes a museum or gallery as its presumed site of consumption.

Renaissance patrons included themselves in renditions of biblical events not so much as a sign of their religious devotion as an advertise- ment of their social position, wealth, and power. Being represented for public consumption was and is usually a privilege and a resource which tends to amplify and maintain the influence of the one being represented. This is equally true for American celebrities and politicians whose careers rise and fall on their "q" value, the measure of their public recognizability.

Let's consider how these principles work in relation to the ad we will call "classics can swing," which was produced to attract consumers to Barneys New York, a men's clothier. This high contrast black-and- white photo (by Charles Harbutt) covers two pages and highlights the hair of a black musician, his hand, and the strings of a bass. All other distinguishing features are lost in black background or in white circles of light. The slogan "classics can swing. great style ain't stuffy." is situated nearly in the middle of the first page, parallel to the bassist's top hand and roughly where his shoulders would be, if we could see them (32). At the bottom of the page is the logo "BARNEYS NEW YORK" and a list of the company's locations.

The image makes a complex appeal to readers who want to feel both stable and conservative, as implied by the word "classics," but unconstrained by upper-class social convention. This target audience is upwardly mobile, economically advantaged, somewhat knowledgeable about jazz, and insecure about their ability to appear both casual and elegant. Barneys promises to allay this insecurity, thereby fulfilling the reader's desires, by defining the fine line between acceptable and unacceptable fashions for a new elite that's not quite comfortable with its material privileges.

Does the text belong to a genre or to a recognizable product category?

All representation is conventional. We are used to identifying poems as lyrics, lyrics as sonnets, sonnets as Petrarchan because such identifications enable a set of appropriate responses. But we are perhaps less used to recognizing, at least consciously, that images also have genres. John Berger shows how the nude as a genre of painting is repeated in lingerie ads and magazines like *Playboy*, *Hustler*, and *Cosmopolitan*. But ads and photographs themselves have their own genres.

Without conscious reflection, competent magazine readers make generic assignments and thus shape their responses to the complex texts before them. The cover of the *New York Times Magazine* is thus clearly distinguishable from all of the other images we're considering. It falls into the category of photojournalism. The photograph is of "a 4-year-old girl on the porch of her grandmother's house in Bennettsville, S.C." by Nubar Alexanian (4). The child is African-American and she is standing in front of the dilapidated door and storm door of the house. The verbal text is located in the lower left quadrant of the page, and it reads, in white, slightly outlined lettering, "Why Is America Failing Its Children?, *by T. Berry Brazelton*." The magazine's title appears on top in gray lettering and a universal-product bar code at the lower right corner.

Unlike the other texts, the cover photo is not designed to sell a particular product but to draw the reader's attention to a lamentable social condition that needs a remedy. Following the conventions of photojournalism, it's shot in low-contrast black-and-white, and it appears to capture a spontaneous moment from the personal lives of people who are usually not represented.

The other texts, even "My Fair Ladies," the editorial fashion photograph, are much more obviously designed to sell, though other genre distinctions may be made as well. Fashion photography is itself a genre, of which both "My Fair Ladies" and "The Burberry Look" are very different examples. The extreme contrast of black and white in "classics can swing" and the text's deliberate obliteration of the musician's face are signs of yet another genre, art photography. The image is manipulated so much that its expressive qualities dominate its pictorial function. It sells through the set of associations it produces rather than through the representation of a product. By way of contrast, "The Burberry Look" is generically different in at least two ways: first, it fully illuminates, even glorifies, the garments that it represents for sale; second, it participates in the genre of the painted portrait. The model's close-lipped smile, her averted gaze, the bold centrality of her figure all situate the image in the tradition of aristocratic portraiture which can be traced back to the Renaissance. One particular feature is especially notable: the hand that grasps a glove, thereby invoking generic similarities with such typical noble portraits as Titian's 1542 portrait of Ranuccio Farnese or Rembrandt's portrait of a "gentleman with a tall hat," both at the National Gallery. Although such details probably do not register on a conscious level, they are designed to associate Burberry's commodities with the traditions of privilege and noblesse oblige.

Key Features and Their Disposition

What are the key elements represented in the text?

It's important to think of a visual text as an assemblage which has organized various pictorial elements or formal features into a coherent perceptual whole. If the text is well designed, the propriety, significance, and interrelatedness of its constituent elements will be grasped quickly as a total gestalt and its aspect as assemblage will be effaced. But, as time passes after the production of the text and the cultural knowledge of its intended reader decays and changes, the aspect of the text as assemblage is foregrounded in the experience of its readers. So, for example, Elizabethan portraits always strike the modern reader as somewhat bizarre and artificial because of the sitters' neck ruffles. The social significance of this obsolete body ornament is lost, as is the significance of the rings, books, and animals often found in the frame of the Renaissance portrait. All of these elements, rather than contribution to the sense of the picture's unity, stress the artificiality of a defunct sign system.

In an active sign system, like that of the visual texts from the *New York Times Magazine*, such formal features as typography, corporate logos, icons, discrete images of people and other things, and articulations such as hair color, light, clothing, adornments, posture, and a host of others work together to produce visual impact and unified meanings. We have already referred to some of these semiotically active formal features when explaining how genre distinctions affect the reception of a text. Thus the gloves in "The Burberry Look" and the high contrast in "classics can swing" are formal features.

The ability to identify significant formal features is the necessary prerequisite to a deeper cultural reading of visual texts. Let's consider the cover. We notice that there are two doors behind the young girl, who is the major focus of the picture. One, a conventional, wooden front door, has had much of its paint worn away by frequent use; the other, an outer door, has ripped screens and is closed by a spring rather than a hydraulic mechanism. All of these elements signify the subject's economic and, therefore, social position. As for the subject herself, she's photographed from an angle that places her on the same level as the reader; this visual position limits any feelings of superiority and establishes a physical affinity between reader and subject. Her gaze is averted and upward which, in conjunction with a gestural feature (both of her hands hold the bottom of her shirt in her mouth, thus exposing her stomach), suggests emotional discomfort.

In all, the reader feels sorry for this distressed and disadvantaged child, a response which is reinforced and controlled by another textual feature, the caption: "Why Is America Failing Its Children?" The readers who identify themselves as Americans are metaphorically cast in the role of the child's parents and are thus urged to accept some responsibility for her. On the other hand, the caption simultaneously de-personalizes America as an "it" and thus allows readers to maintain an emotional distance from the child's plight. This ambivalent relationship between reader and subject is in one respect a psychological necessity in that it keeps the reader from being compelled to identify with a person that the text defines as a failure.

"The Burberry Look" presents a fine contrast. Here the subject's background is thrown out-of-focus and serves to emphasize the positive features of the central figure. The swirl of carefully coiffed blonde hair and the Northern European facial features invoke a privileged racial type. The calm composure of those features, the gold earring, the trenchcoat, and the colorful hues of the silk kerchief around the subject's shoulders, all work to project a sense of economic stability, social comfort, and good taste. This subject, unlike the little girl before the worn doors, is to be admired and emulated. She is attractive in a way that is in keeping with what is understood as a British tradition of reserve and understatement. Her skin is unblemished, her lipstick only a few shades darker than her cheeks. Her posture suggests the assurance and confidence that are also indices of class. The silk kerchief, the most colorful item in the picture, is worn as a shawl and prominently displays the word "Burberry's." The psychosocial dynamics of this visual text encourage the readers to project themselves into the aristocratic position occupied by the central figure. All that's required is the purchase and wearing of Burberry's apparel.

How does the text organize and define the elements it represents/ figures?

This question encourages students to move beyond the identification of key features to a consideration of their disposition on the page. Another way to phrase the question is to ask What is the significance of the spatial relationships of the elements in a visual text? Consider "Condé Nast Vietnam," a two-page ad for a travel publication. On the first page is a color photograph featuring a fortyish white male in white pants and a florid sport shirt, surrounded by five Vietnamese guerrillas. In the center of the mostly blank opposite page, it reads, "Robert Sam Anson had a better feeling about his second tour of Vietnam. To begin with, it was guaranteed to be round-trip." At the bottom of the page there is more text in smaller type. Next to this text, in the lower left corner, is the magazine's logo, which includes the slogan, "The insider's guide to the outside world." [48–49).

The entire advertisement is designed to pique the reader's interest with an incongruous image, give it a brief, intriguing narrative in the opposing caption, and finally offer an explanation in smaller type. The reader has thus been drawn progressively into the world of the magazine. In the photo, the principal elements are six men who are separated into two distinct visual groups. The first of these is a group of one, an American tourist whose race and clothes distinguishes him from five Vietnamese soldiers. We know the white is a tourist because of the aforementioned shirt and pants, the camera around his neck, the glass in his hand, and the sunglasses pushed back to the top of his head. We know the Vietnamese are soldiers because they carry sophisticated automatic weapons and wear uniforms, helmets, and even camouflaging sticks and leaves. This very powerful contrast is enhanced by the spatial position of the American who is in the actual center of the image as well as the center of the group of Vietnamese.

Given the readers' cultural knowledge of Vietnamese-American relationships, this is a startling image which exists in a contradictory relationship with the many generic images we carry of Americans and Viet Cong. Our expectations are radically reversed. Although the

American is surrounded by the soldiers, he shows no signs of distress. The rich colors in his shirt, the comforting smile on his face, the relaxation suggested by the drink, signify that he is in the center of a protective circle. The familiar way that one soldier rests his arm on the American's shoulder even suggests friendship. Perhaps most important for the ideological analysis that we will pursue in the next section is the fact that two of the Vietnamese are represented as kneeling at the American's feet.

Ideological Structures

Describe the subject-position the text creates for the reader. Do you feel "hailed" by this image? Why or why not?

One way into a treatment of this difficult question is to consider the analogy between subject-position, as we use the term here, and the point-of-view assumed by the representational geometry of a realist painting. The artist's organization of elements in such a painting is based upon a spectator's viewing position outside the frame. In other words, the construction of an image always implies the position from which it will be viewed, as is the case with several paintings Titian designed to be hung on a ceiling thirty feet above the floor. Only if the spectator looks at them from the proper distance is the desired effect achieved; moving closer produces visual distortions that destroy the illusion of perspectival depth.

The subject-positioning produced by ideology is different in that it takes place in psychic rather than physical space. The *New York Times Magazine* images were designed with specific readers in mind and they are expected to appeal to, or hail, readers on very deep affective levels. The design of each image inevitably reflects more than its producers intend, for they themselves are subject to ideologies so much a natural and unthought of part of their conceptual operations that they cannot be aware of, much less control, the inscription of these ideologies in the images they produce. The final effect of both conscious and unconscious forces is the construction of a subject-position that represents the cultural and historical contingencies of the moment.

"Conde Nast Vietnam" is a perfect example. It calls out to a reader who is a member of a nation whose military forces fought unsuccessfully against the Vietnamese. The psychological residue of that experience is a set of discomforting memories. The ad imagines readers positioned in this psychological space and addresses them in a manner designed to soothe. The ad achieves this end by a revision of history that edits and rearranges images, thereby suggesting that those who were ousted from Vietnam have not only been welcomed back but are under the protection of their previous opponents. On one level, foes appear to have become friends. On another, the Vietnamese enemy, victorious in war, has come to see how misguided its policies were. American capitalism, personified by the smiling tourist (a symbol of material abundance and leisure time) triumphs over recalcitrant ideologues who are here converted into travel guides, subservient supporters of the American system. That two of the Vietnamese soldiers squat at the American's feet (they could have been positioned in many other places in the image) fully signifies the ideology of American economic supremacy, a fact or a wish that appeals mightily to most Americans. The text of the advertisement makes sure that this point comes through:

"Bomb craters are now tranquil fishing holes. A U.S. troop ship, a country/western ice cream parlor. In short Vietnam is open for tourism. Former Time magazine correspondent and ex-POW Robert Sam Anson went back to Vietnam for Condé Nast Traveler to find the welcome mat out but the ghosts very much in residence. He met with his former enemies and reflected on their new-found passion for all things American."

Who is the reader for whom this ad performs such work? He is obviously American, but also white and especially not an Asian American. Furthermore, he is wealthy and worldly enough to contemplate — though not necessarily follow through — taking a vacation to a location as exotic as Vietnam. Most importantly, however, he is male. Public opinion polls tell us that American males are far more likely than females to have an investment in rewriting America's loss of face in Vietnam. The weapons and military paraphernalia displayed in the photograph are likely to appeal to the male imaginary which, even in those who consciously oppose war, is constructed in terms of metaphors and images of war. But there is one small detail which, more than any other, shows that this ad positions its viewer as male. The glass which the American tourist holds is decorated with nude female bodies in silhouette. The viewer is positioned to identify with this American who holds in his hand the object of that viewer's desires.

As this account suggests, advertising works by positioning its viewer in such a way that he or she will experience a lack which the advertised product can fulfill. The "Conde Nast Vietnam" ad constitutes a viewer who is the subject of heterosexual desire and who wants to undo America's failure in the Vietnam War, a lack which many other texts in popular culture — for example, the film *Rambo* — have purported to satisfy.

The ideological appeal of the Hofstra ad is somewhat more complex. Why, for example, does an ad that is selling a college education contain as one of its central elements the figure of a boy who is probably in elementary school? And what does his attempt to reproduce a Monet have to do with the "success" Hofstra promises to teach? The answer to both questions lies in an understanding of the subject-position implied in the text. From that position, it is natural to desire to be the best, and such "success" is measured by accumulation of capital. The ad trades on the assumption that cultural capital, as represented by the Monet, is a measure of success, that is, the accumulation of real capital. But this is not the only desire on which the ad trades. The target audience for the ad consists of parents, and it seeks to activate nostalgic recollections of the days when their children were younger, perhaps more manageable, and perhaps more innocent: such a child is a wish-fulfillment for parents of many adolescents. But the child also embodies the romantic ideology of the artist and the creative imagination. The soft hues and blurred outlines used to render the boy and painting emphasize nostalgia and romanticism, and they serve to reinforce the misrecognition that creativity, rather than capital, is the real determinant of success. Thus there are two answers to the blunt question at the top of the page, "What does it take to be the best?" The first answer is explicitly articulated: "Creativity." The second answer is implied by the ad's list of what Hofstra itself has accumulated: Hofstra is in the "top 10 percent of colleges," produces 500 cultural events a year, has a library with 1.3 million volumes, and so forth. The ad thus covertly explains that creativity is in fact not enough and that Hofstra's resources can allow the parents' creative child to succeed. The ad neatly joins the subject-reader's wistful fantasy of the ennobling values of high art with a realistic economic appraisal of the connection between success and the transmission of cultural capital. After all, what the boy-figure holds in his hand is his own reproduction of the Monet, illustrating that what Hofstra promises is the reproduction of the culture rather than its recreation.

What kind of ideological work does the text perform? What social, economic, or political interests does it serve?

The function of ideology is, in Louis Althusser's famous phrase, the "reproduction of the relations of production;" that is, ideology is a conservative mechanism which maintains the shape and orientation of a particular culture with the effect that the class structure of society remains the same (154). Ideology begins its work with newborn humans, which are transformed into social subjects. As they grow up, their acculturation (another word for ideological processing) subordinates them to the complex network of definitions and relationships that is culture. Individuals are thus formed by ideology, achieve their identity through its agency, and thereafter will tend to reproduce that ideology and its cultural matrix through every word and act.

Gender is one of the most elemental structures of identity which ideology reproduces and maintains. In the *New York Times Magazine* images we have chosen for discussion here, gender is pervasive even if it is nowhere thematized. We did not choose any of the more obvious instances of sexual objectification wherein women's bodies, or parts of them, are fetishized. But even the picture of the little girl on the cover of the magazine demonstrates the pervasiveness of gender distinctions. We would find it strange if a child even of this age cannot be easily identified as male or female. It's not a coincidence that the would be Monet in the Hofstra ad is a little boy. We have already pointed out how in the "Condé Nast Vietnam," a particular construction of maleness is both assumed and represented. The two fashion ads assume particular constructions of the feminine, even though both are unusual in the complexity of their representation of gender. "The Burberry Look" is selling social position rather than sexuality, so its image is more identificatory than most fashion ads. The problem for the ad, however, is that the garment it is selling, a trench coat, is not defined as feminine. Thus the ad uses feminine accessories, especially the scarf worn as a shawl, to secure the model's unambiguous gendering.

On the other hand, women in the fashion feature "My Fair Ladies" are undoubtedly constructed as objects of sexual desire. We will focus on the photo (by George Lange) of an African American actress in a silver jumpsuit, which appears on the second page of the story, a piece about opening-night fashions that features actresses as models (79). This picture seems to be an attempt to work against the usual representation of women as such objects while nevertheless remaining within the gender system. The text of the fashion feature tells us that "for four actresses, opening night jitters start in front of the closet, not the curtain." This establishes the ideological interest in reproducing gender constructions by asserting that what is most important to these women is not their work but how to appear (heterosexually) attractive offstage. Thus the women are rendered passive objects of desire in spite of their professional status — which is itself only ambiguously active. The jumpsuit the subject of our photo is wearing reveals her "female" shape even if it does not seem to fetishize a particular part of her body. Her high heels also mark her as an object of desire, but the sequined lunch box she carries, her gender-neutral gloves, and her short hair, all but invisible in the photo, all cut against the norms of the feminine. And the woman's airborne position (a visual pun on her attire) renders her far more active than most models. This play with gender codes suggests that the ideology of gender is secure enough that it can contain many changes that might seem to threaten it.

The ideological work of a text simultaneously reinforces and perpetuates the dominant construction of reality, but to get a full appreciation of this one must do more than read the individual images. In order to illustrate the way ideology constructs social "reality" rather than mere personal "beliefs," the magazine must be read as a whole. Here, our exercise must move beyond the six images we have been reading. To get at the dominant construction of the "feminine," for example, "The Burberry Look" and "My Fair Ladies" texts would have to be contrasted with the more usual depictions of women (and of men) elsewhere in the issue. The conventions of magazine consumption tell us that the ads, pictures, articles, and other elements in a particular issue are discrete and separate units, whole unto themselves. Read in this way, it may seem as though each element of the magazine has its own, separate ideology. An alternative is to consider all of the images in a magazine as related elements in a continuous text. There are three justifications for such an unconventional reading. First, all the images in a given issue of a magazine have been produced within the context of a specific culture and in an identifiable historical moment. Second, the very fact that these images are included in a single magazine indicates that they address the predictable expectations of a demographically defined readership. Third, the physical juxtaposition of the images assures that they will be consumed in proximity to one another and thus stored in related locations in both short- and long-term memory. By reading the *New York Times Magazine* images as parts of a single story (or as pieces in a mosaic), we are able to piece together a much more complex and complete version of its place in culture and ideology.

The juxtaposition of images in a magazine can strikingly reveal cultural contradictions. Consider, for example, the image that follows immediately the one on the cover of the *New York Times Magazine*: a two-page ad for an Estee Lauder perfume called "White Linen." The photograph (credited to Skrebneski) shows a young white woman dressed in a long, white linen skirt and sleeveless blouse, and sporting a broad-brimmed hat and large white belt with a gold buckle. The woman's head is nodded forward and her eyes appear to be closed, yet she has one foot in front of the other suggesting somnambulism. She is posed against a white railing and white pillars on what seems to be the porch of a mansion overlooking a vast landscape of lakes and mountains. The pillars, however, do not support anything but simply end either at the top of the page or in the sky, the latter giving an air of fantasy to the entire scene. It is safe to assume that the woman in white linen is not contemplating "Why Is American Failing Its Children?" Imagine the poor child America is failing, not on the magazine's cover, but *in* the Estee Lauder ad, and you see exactly the contradiction which ideology must constantly work to suppress.

But the juxtaposition of images does not tell the whole story. Selected images can easily be unrepresentative of the kinds of images dominant in the entire issue. The six texts we've been considering seem, on the surface, to represent the racial diversity of our culture. Three of the images represent whites and three represent African Americans. But with the exception of the front page, which depicts one of the poor or underclass, the images efface the reality of economic inequality of the races: the people represented display the signs of cultural and material privileges. In fact they signify class only as a desirable social position. As a result, the conflicts which we know to exist between peoples of different classes and races are repressed in these six images. And in this respect they reinforce the misrecognition that United States is the egalitarian society it claims to be. But the existence of African Americans in three of the six photographs is itself misleading. A quantitative analysis of all of the pictures in the magazine reveals that the more powerful ideology is the superiority of whites. Of the seventy-one separate photographic images in the magazine, only twelve represent non-whites. Most of these are group shots that don't distinguish individuals, while whites are usually shot as commanding single figures. In addition, the whites are models of physical beauty, ease, and conspicuous consumption — visible facts which set the whites in marked contrast to the people of color, a mixture of manual laborers, protestors, and guerrillas. One might say that this is in some ways an accurate view of the material and racial conditions of the world, but that's not the point. Because the whites are represented as objects of desire and emulation, because they depict ideal patterns of material consumption and social class, they work to reproduce in their subject-readers the ideals, desires, and ideologies that are already in place and reflect the past more than a possible future.

Because cultures are dynamic, the ideological activities that reproduce and maintain them must be relentless. Visual texts and other forms of representation play a major role in this effort because they create lacks and instigate desires: for vacations, for clothes, for a certain hair color, for a certain kind of education. To be a desiring subject is to participate in ideology. Objects of desire are never simply attractive in and of themselves: rather they are attractive because of their relations of difference and association with other objects. Images, which depend on these relations to incite consumption of a product, also reinforce the relations themselves.

Ideology is analogous to the genetic code of an organism: it contains instructions for the reproduction of a social order. It positions people within a vertical hierarchy and provides them with the perceptual data needed to signify that position and to decode the positions of others. The maintenance of relations of domination and subordination would be impossible without such instructions as would the unequal distribution of resources they enforce. But just as there is ever the possibility of mutation in the genetic code, so is the ideology always susceptible to rupture and to transformation. By pointing out the work of ideology in covering up the contradictions of the social formation, we can make the visual texts we consume susceptible to new readings. We can understand, for example, that America is failing its children not because of some oversight, but because the social formation is organized to produce profits rather than to assure that all people have an equal chance to live healthy, productive lives. It is the point of the sort of assignment we have described here to help students read their culture critically and thus to produce new meanings that resist ideology. New readings or meanings do not guarantee social change, but they would seem to be at least one of its prerequisites.

Notes

This article grew out of a workshop which was first presented at George Mason University in November of 1989. In that version, designed to illustrate the methods and assumptions of cultural studies to English department *faculty*, a more complex selection of texts from different sources was made. The present classroom exercise was presented at a workshop at a conference, "The Role of Theory in the undergraduate Literature Classroom: Curriculum, Pedagogy, Politics," held at Indiana University of Pennsylvania, 23 September 1990. We would like to thank David Demarest for his helpful comments and suggestions.

1. For extended discussions of the cultural studies movement see Giroux, Shumway, et al.; Grossberg; and Johnson.

Works Cited

Althusser, Louis. *Lenin and Philosophy and Other Essays*. Trans. Ben Brewster. New York: Monthly Review Press, 1971.

Belsey, Catherine. *Critical Practice*. London: Methuen, 1980.

Berger, John, et al. *Ways of Seeing*. New York: Viking Penguin, 1973.

Giroux, Henry, David R. Shumway, et al. "The Need for Cultural Studies: Resisting Intellectuals and Oppositional Public Spheres." *Dalhousie Review* 64 (1984): 472−86.

Grossberg, Lawrence. "The Formations of Cultural Studies: An American in Birmingham." *Strategies* 2 (Fall 1989): 114−49.

Johnson, Richard. "What is Cultural Studies Anyway?" *Social Text* 16 (Winter 1986/87): 38−80.

New York Times Magazine, 9 September 1990.

Williams, Raymond. *Keywords: A Vocabulary of Culture and Society*. Revised Edition. New York: Oxford University Press, 1983.

16

Valmont, the Boutique; Marc, the Gunman; Merteuil, the Feminist:
Some Truly Dangerous Liaisons

Richard E. Miller

> What would be the value of the passion for knowledge if it resulted only in a certain amount of knowledgeableness and not, in one way or another and to the extent possible, in the knower's straying afield of himself? There are times in life when the question of knowing if one can think differently than one thinks, and perceive differently than one sees, is absolutely necessary if one is to go on looking and reflecting at all.
>
> Michel Foucault, *The Use of Pleasure*

A Constellation of Possibilities

Let's begin with a lady's dilemma. There's a full-page ad in the *New York Times* announcing the opening of a new shop in Bloomingdale's and simultaneously the appearance of a lady's dilemma. The ad above the model (who I will discuss in a moment) announces:

Valmont: Catering to the Aristocracy on 3. *Valmont*, a new film by Milos Forman opening nationally November 17th, is now the inspiration for a shop purveying the elegance-as-decadence rococo mode of 18th century France. Embroidered jackets and closefitting tapestry pants. Frilly poet's shirts and lots of lace.

(The ad continues in large letters to the left of the model.)

262

Valmont

Innocent naif, romantic poet, or foppish dandy? A lady's dilemma.

But what exactly is the lady's dilemma here? What is it that she has to choose between? Is the ad proposing the naif, the poet, and the dandy as options for the lady to have or for the lady to be? The model to the right of the dilemma appears on first glance to be a man dressed in pants and a large shirt, but closer inspection reveals that the model is a woman and that this is, on second glance, an advertisement for women's clothing. The model's ambiguity sheds light on the lady's dilemma which appears to be over whether to dress as a naif, a poet, or a dandy.

This is, undoubtedly, a very curious moment, for how is it that Valmont, the seemingly ruthless womanizer from Choldéros de Leclos' *Les Liaisons Dangereuses* has come to pose this dilemma for the ladies addressed by this advertisement? What reading of Valmont and what reading of female sexuality made it possible to imagine that a line of clothing named after a character who devoted his life to ruining women would sell? If this were a line of clothing aimed at men it would be somewhat easier to understand (after all, at one point in my course, one of my male students dropped to his knees and declared Valmont "a god"), but how has it come to be that some (obviously, in this case, upper-class) women are willing to spend $120 to $565 to wrap themselves in Valmont's clothes?

Although one film critic has reported that in Forman's film, "there is no Valmont; he's just the blandly handsome actor Colin Firth, strapping and healthy and rather harmless" (Kael, Nov., 105–6), this is clearly not the only version of Valmont currently available for shoppers to associate with the boutique and its line of clothing: there's also John Malkovich's incarnation in Stephen Frears' successful *Dangerous Liaisons*. Since Forman's film has met with little success, it seems even less likely that his Valmont would be the first Valmont shoppers would associate with the boutique.

My concern at this point, however, is not with the associations these nameless shoppers do or do not make; I want, rather, to mark the activity circulating around the character of Valmont, an activity rife with conflict and contradiction, where a series of texts (the novel, Hampton's adaptation for the stage, Frears' and Forman's filmic versions) have intersected and become affiliated with a specific material practice—the sale of clothes to women. One of the projects of this essay is to try to trace the "affiliative network," to use Said's phrase, that surrounds Valmont in order "to make visible, to give materiality back to, the strands holding the text to society, author, and culture" (Said, 592).

Before I begin discussing how the film itself performs a reading and a revision of the novel and thereby serves to surface some of the current conflicts surrounding the definitions of male and female sexuality, I would like first to draw your attention to the following headline that appeared on page one of *the Pittsburgh Press* on Thursday, 7, December 1989 and to an eyewitness account of the massacre:

Killer of 14 Targeted Feminists

[Leclerc, the gunman] told [the female engineering students], "You're women, you're going to be engineers. You're all a bunch of feminists. I hate feminists!" Leclerc said. My friend Nathalie said, "No, it's not true. We're not feminists." He fired into the group (A14).

You may well wonder what this has to do with issues of sexuality and representation in *Dangerous Liaisons* or with understanding how the film was read and what made those readings possible. I must admit that the connection is not terribly obvious—at least not at this stage—and that it may only achieve at the end of this essay a very tenuous status. For the moment, however, I want only to draw attention to the fact that when Marc Leclerc entered the engineering building and murdered those fourteen female engineering students, his sense of threat and his need for violence became organized around the term "feminist."

Let's let the question of what this has to do with my essay hang for a moment and turn our attention to a review of Frears' *Dangerous Liaisons*, where "feminism" also figures prominently. In this review, Tom O'Brian compares Close's character, the Marquise de Merteuil, with the character of Valmont, noting that:

Close at least has motive, desire for vengeance against men for their dominance over women. Oddly, she doesn't see how private and selfish her "feminism" is, and that women mostly suffer from it (O'Brian, 147).

As O'Brian puzzles over the motivation that drives the Marquise and the Vicomte to behave the way they do, he finds the Marquise's motivation in the term "feminism." While he is careful to put feminism in quotes here, reading those quotation marks become a problem in itself: What exactly is the status of this word at this moment? It seems that O'Brian is equating "vengeance against men for their dominance over women" with "feminism." As I read this passage, O'Brian hasn't deployed the quotation marks in order to call into question this equation of feminism and vengeance so much as he has used the quotation marks to question the Marquise's fulfillment of this definition: the Marquise's feminism is "feminism" because it selects the wrong object for its vengeance (women) and acts alone (no global sisterhood).

How is this possible? How is it that the Marquise can be transformed into someone who is read off as carrying out a "feminist" project? How is it that her punishment and rejection become affiliated with this term? And to return to where we began, how is it that Valmont, on the other hand, becomes someone that women dress up for, someone women wrap themselves in? What is it that allows for his redemption and what terms surround his salvation? And what does any of this have to do with Marc Leclerc, the Canadian gunman, who one witness described as "a Rambo" (and who, we in turn, remember was represented as a tormented vet who had the courage to do jobs no one else would do)? It will be the project of this essay to try to discover what makes the first two readings permissible by situating them within certain discursive practices, and to articulate the possible affiliations between these discursive practices and Marc Leclerc.

The Dropped Sword, the Honorable Death

Since Valmont is a lady's dilemma, let's begin by looking at how Valmont has been constructed within a variety of discursive practices. I'd like to start by returning to the Bloomingdale's ad in order to offer another way of reading the lady's dilemma. What happens if we re-read the lady's dilemma about how to dress and how to appear as the lady's dilemma about how to read Valmont? Is Valmont an innocent naif? a romantic poet? or a foppish dandy? How should the lady dress and behave in response? If this line of questioning seems outrageous, if it appears to offer a series of unlikely, if not impossible, readings of Valmont, then read on, for it may well be that the only way to remain a lady is to restrict oneself to locating Valmont somewhere within the constellation of naif, poet, dandy. Let's see.

David Coward offers a version of Valmont that fits rather easily into this constellation in his review of the film. In discussing the difference between Christopher Hampton's scripts for the play and for the film, Coward notes:

> Hampton restores the [original] ending [to the film] which, in the heavy-duty feminist phrase, restates Laclos's "essentially masculine discourse." Valmont dies an honorable death but Merteuil is destroyed....The result is to make *Dangerous Liaisons* a very moral film indeed (Coward, 251).

Although the resurfacing of feminism should not go unnoticed here, my interest at this point is in drawing attention to Coward's assertion that "Valmont dies an honorable death but Merteuil is destroyed." How is it possible that Valmont, who casually refers to Cecile de Volanges' miscarriage of his own child as a "refurbishment," can, moments later, snatch an "honorable death" from the audience? And what would the moral of such a tale be?

Michael Zorich offers the following reading of how it becomes possible for Valmont to die an honorable death in his essay "Ways of Reading," written in my course "Literature and Ideas." Michael argues that Valmont is presented to the viewer in three stages: first as evil, then as a lover, and finally as "an honor-driven martyr." We pick up his argument at the point where he discusses Valmont's transition from lover to honor-driven martyr:

> This is all portrayed in the scene where Valmont is in [a] duel with Chevalier Danceny. To set the stage we are brought to the scene with an immediate slashing of Danceny's arm thus hinting at Valmont's far superior skills. This is supported by a Valmont rush at Danceny in which Valmont's sword is unraised yet he drives Danceny back as far as he wishes. The reason for this is to make it perfectly clear that this battle even if it were a battle to the death was not a battle which required nor suggested the life be Valmont's. Yet after successive shots of Valmont's sex scene with Tourvel, Valmont decides to thrust himself upon Danceny's sword and end his own life. "Valmont dies an honorable death" as critic David Coward saw it. To make sure the audience makes no mistake that Valmont has died for Tourvel he requests that Danceny deliver a love vow to Tourvel before she dies. This is to prove that Valmont did die because he was killing the only one he ever really loved which is what was fulfilling the requirement of an honorable death (Zorich, 6).

What Michael's explication makes clear is that seeing Valmont's death as honorable requires that his death be linked to love and that it is understood to be voluntary. What we have, apparently, is an enactment of that familiar romantic fantasy where love redeems all, where being in love requires the death of an old self and the birth of a new, and where true lovers are united in death.

Or do we? This reading hinges in part upon the fact that Frears has Valmont drop his sword intentionally. Now, while the symbolic significance of this act is relatively transparent (the "castration equals death" story being almost as tired and familiar as the "redemption through love" story), what is more interesting is Coward's contention that this restores the masculine discourse originally contained in Laclos' ending. If Coward fails to make his method for uniting masculine discourse, death, honor, and castration explicit, he does, nonetheless, invite us to explore the relationship between the story told on the screen and the story told in the novel.

The most obvious difference between Laclos' version and Frears' version of the duel between Valmont and Danceny is that Laclos offers no "eyewitness" report of the event: although it is well within the conventional realms of the epistolary novel to have someone write a letter in such a moment (let us not forget how often and under what circumstances Pamela found it possible to jot down a few thousand words), Laclos conceals from us the actual blow-by-blow interchange of the duelists. In place of Hampton and Frears' swirling meditation, Laclos simply presents Letter CLXII from Danceny to Valmont demanding satisfaction and Letter CLXIII from a previously unknown M. Bertrand to Valmont's aunt, Mme. de Rosemonde, announcing Valmont's death. M. Bertrand narrates:

> I was waiting for M. le Vicomte at his house at the very time when he was brought home. Imagine my terror at seeing your nephew carried in by two of his servants, soaked in his own blood. He had two sword wounds in his body and was already very weak. M. Danceny was there too and was even weeping. Ah! No doubt he must weep; but it is too late to shed tears when one has caused an irreparable misfortune! (Laclos, 408).

Nowhere in the remainder of the novel is there any evidence that would lead one to believe that Valmont killed himself or, rather, allowed himself to be killed. The honorable death of which Coward speaks is not in fact a reading that is suggested by Laclos' text: it is a revision offered by Hampton and Frears.

What's at stake here is not the accuracy of Coward's statement (this ultimately is a trivial matter) but rather the recognition that Hampton's and Laclos' conclusions vary substantially. In order to address the significance of this difference, we need to attempt to place these varying discursive resolutions historically. To begin this process, let's look at how Foucault understands the terms for working out a definition of sexuality and the self during the time that Laclos wrote (Laclos published *Les Liaisons Dangereuses* in 1782). Arguing in Volume I of the *History of Sexuality* that the concept of sexuality began to emerge as a discourse late in the eighteenth century, Foucault speaks of this as the time when the nobility's "symbolics of blood" began to be transposed and reshaped into an "analytics of sexuality." Foucault describes the way the symbolics of blood functioned for the nobility as follows:

> The blood relation long remained an important element in the mechanisms of power, its manifestations, and its rituals...[Blood] owed its high value...to its instrumental role (the ability to shed blood), to the way it functioned in the order of signs (to have a certain blood, to be of the same blood, to be prepared to risk one's blood) and also to its precariousness (easily spilled, subject to drying up, too readily mixed, capable of being quickly corrupted). A society of blood...where power spoke *through* blood: the honor of war, the fear of famine, the triumph of death, the sovereign with his sword,

executioners, and tortures; blood was *a reality with a symbolic function* (Foucault, Vol. I, 147).

Yes, well. Is Foucault right? Is this in fact the way that Valmont's death is configured by Laclos? Is the importance of Valmont's death seen in terms of "blood relations"? The only way to begin to respond to these questions is to look more carefully at the transpositions that occurred in the move from Laclos to Hampton.

With Foucault's emphasis on blood in mind, let's go back to the letter the unknown M. Bertrand writes to Mme. de Rosemonde at the moment of Valmont's death. M. Bertrand's letter continues:

> Tomorrow, after the body is taken away, I shall have seals put on everything and you can rely entirely upon my services. You know, Madame, that this unfortunate event puts an end to the entail and leaves your disposal entirely free. If I can be of any use to you, I beg you will be good enough to send me your orders; I will give all my attention to carrying them out punctually (Laclos, 408–09).

M. Bertrand's kind remembrance of the entail draws our attention away from the actual blood that has been spilled to the blood line that connected Valmont to Mme. de Rosemonde. Having neither husband nor children, Mme. de Rosemonde has no direct heirs. While her intention had been to leave her inheritance to her nephew, Valmont, his death leaves her inheritance "entirely free." Thus, in a stroke, Valmont illustrates both the ease with which blood is spilled and the ease with which it dries up.

Following this train of thought, it is not hard to see how Valmont's death and the extinction of the Rosemonde line might be construed as prophesying the imminent collapse of the aristocracy, a reading which fills the novel with revolutionary content. Richard Aldington argues for just such a reading of *Les Liaisons Dangereuses* in his introduction to his English translation of the novel. Drawing on the fact that Valmont and Merteuil are destroyed in Laclos' version and that the French Revolution was to occur just seven years after the first publication of the novel, Aldington insists that:

> Laclos intended [the novel] as an attack on the upper classes of the *ancient regime*; it was one of the innumerable straws which showed which way the gathering storm of revolution was blowing (Aldington, 4).

He continues this line of reasoning a little further on:

> Laclos saw that a complete reform of the government was the only chance of his gratifying his ambition [to be a *petite naitre*]; as a disciple of Rousseau he was angered by the behavior of the ruling classes; the *Liaisons Dangereuses* was his declaration of war on the *ancien regime*. The book had a prodigious success (5).

While it is not my concern here to refute this reading of the novel as "revolutionary" (nor its twin — the reading of the film as "reactionary"), it is imperative to note how the novel's success serves to problematize Aldington's monolithic reading proclaiming Laclos' revolutionary intentions for the novel. If *Les Liaisons Dangereuses* declared war on the aristocracy, how do we account for its success *with* the aristocracy? For Marie Antoinette's owning a copy?

At any rate, within the confines of the novel's world, Valmont's death certainly is not read in revolutionary terms: it signals, if anything, the re-channeling of wealth within a given class. Though Valmont's passing is mourned by his aunt (and, of course, by the faithful M. Bertrand who would like to have that wealth re-channeled in his direction), Mme. de. Rosemonde does not see her nephew's death as tragic. Made aware of the intricacies of Valmont and Merteuil's machinations through Merteuil's letters, Mme. de Rosemonde can only say: "There is nothing left but to weep and to be silent. I regret to be still alive when I learn of such horror; I blush that I am a woman when I see one capable of such excesses" (Laclos, 421). Her final remarks on the matter, which may well be the "moral" that underlies the entire novel, take the form of advice to Danceny, the only male in the novel who is in a position to pursue a life like Valmont's. She writes: "I would say that if we understood our true happiness we should never seek it outside the limits prescribed by the Laws and Religion" (*ibid.*).

This leads us back to the lady's dilemma that started this entire project, although it's a different lady this time and the dilemma is differently constructed. As Mme. de Rosemonde confronts her nephew's death, she chooses not between the options of innocent naif, romantic poet, or foppish dandy: she chooses between prosecuting the man who killed her nephew in a duel — thereby avenging his death through the only means available to her (the law) — and allowing that man to go free. Mme. de Rosemonde chooses the latter option and Danceny chooses to go to Malta and take religious vows. Mme. de Rosemonde's decision suggests that, in the end, she read Valmont's fate as deserved: she mourns his passing, but she does not speak of his salvation through love.

Now if, broadly speaking, we can say that Valmont's death gets appropriated and deployed in Mme. de Rosemonde's reading as an illustration of why one should stay inside the law and religion, and that to stay in such a place serves to protect the symbolics of blood of which Foucault speaks, what are we to make of the fact that Mme. de Rosemonde's final moral reading and M. Bertrand's final economic reading are erased in the film? Again, what interests me is not speculating on why these readings were erased, but rather focusing on what filled the discursive space once occupied by these readings. To return to

Foucault, if he is correct about the broad transitions comprising the history of sexuality, we should expect to find this discursive space filled by an "analytics of sexuality."

Hampton's move to fill this space with Valmont's dropped sword suddenly takes on a new significance if we read this moment as reconfiguring Valmont's death within a psychological discourse. In this way, the novel's aristocratic enactment of the tyrant's justice, where evil is punished by death, is revised within a bourgeois discourse that allows for forgiveness in the film. Death is still required, but within the film the swords and blood allow one to read Valmont's death in terms of his attempt to redefine his own sexuality. In "Sexuality, Memory, and Symbolism," Steve Forrester reads Valmont's death in the film explicitly within these terms. Steve writes:

> In [the duel] Valmont's pride and ego demand that he win and he starts with a well trained attack and he cuts Danceny. Then he changes his sword. After he changes swords his style of fighting changes. This change is brought about by the combination of a change in his sexuality and his memory of his emotions for Tourvel.... The combination of these two things makes him not as aggressive in the sword fight. After he loses some of his aggressiveness he ends up falling on the ground and he cuts his arm with his own sword. While on the ground he examines the wound which symbolically represents him being cut by his own sexuality...[Ultimately] he realizes that he cannot live with this change in his sexuality especially since he is now a lover and the person he loved he can no longer have. This realization is what causes him to give up his sword and his life (Forrester, 7–8).

Steve's essay illustrates how the dropping of Valmont's sword can be placed within a psychological framework, one which allows Valmont's choice of death to be configured as a redefinition of his sexuality. It is exactly this redefinition, we will see, that allows Valmont to be reborn as a boutique in Bloomingdale's.

The revision of Valmont's death in Frears' version suggests that Valmont serves as a site where the current contradictions that inform the problematics of (no doubt, straight, white, first-world) male sexuality are being worked out. Where Laclos felt no such need, it has suddenly become necessary to save Valmont at the end of the twentieth century. Indeed, Kael's review, cited earlier in this essay, suggests that with Forman's version the palliation of Valmont appears to have been completed. This compulsion to save Valmont is driven by something like a crisis over sexual identity, for what can a man (Valmont) be if not a lady-killer? The only other options offered, at least within the discourses available in this film, are innocent naif (Danceny), romantic poet (Valmont, reborn) or foppish dandy (Belleroche).

The Marquise de Merteuil, speaking the unspeakable

If we read along with the film and with Coward, accepting the depiction of Valmont's death as honorable, what of Valmont's opposite: Is the Marquise, as Coward suggests, "destroyed"? What are we to think of this woman whose name is revealed in the film only at the moment of Valmont's death, this woman so often, and so curiously, linked with feminism in the previous reviews? What makes her so unspeakable?

J. Samon offers the following extraordinary description of Glenn Close's appearance and assessment of her character:

> Miss Close (pregnant during the shooting) looks like an albino Indian head on top of a pile of melting wax — pale wax with an archipelago of freckles on its billows...Merteuil is, in short, a saccharine harridan (Samon, 55).

While the offensive power of this review increases exponentially as one moves through it, beginning with the initial marked use of "Miss," then proceeding to the (incorrect) parenthetical assertion of pregnancy,[1] and so on, word by word, to the end, I want to focus on Samon's final judgment that Merteuil is a "saccharine harridan" in order, ultimately, to rephrase the questions that opened this section. A harridan, from the French *harridelle* meaning "gaunt woman" (!), is variously identified as a vicious, scolding woman (American Heritage) and as a haggard, old woman, a vixen, a strumpet (O.E.D.). One assumes that Samon's use of "saccharine" here is deployed to comment further on Close's acting and her failure to embody the main character from what Samon calls "one of the most awesome novels ever written" (*ibid.*). Who, then, is this Marquise, who is at once so unspeakable and yet speaks (at least as Samon articulates it) so scoldingly? Who is this respected member of the aristocracy who is simultaneously a haggard strumpet?

R.A. Blake's reading of the end of the film offers some insight into who the Marquise is in Frears' film. Although his narrative starts off discussing both the Marquise and Valmont as artificial, somewhere in the middle of his reading Valmont drops out, so that, in the end, as with Coward's reading, it is only the Marquise who gets punished:

> As the opening titles roll, both the Marquise...and the Vicomte...are being dressed and powdered by their attendants. Life for them is one of appearances and artifice. At the end, after Paris society has at last become revolted by the effects of her cynical machinations and publicly humiliates her, the Marquise sits alone at her dressing table slowly removing her garish makeup. At last, evil is punished by the cruelest of all torments: the truth. (Blake, 88).

What is this truth that Blake speaks of? And how is it punishing the Marquise? If it is the truth that life is not appearance and artifice, it seems peculiar that the opera society would be able to announce such a truth: after all, all the other people in the opera house, all those who are hooting the Marquise, are wealthy, layered in makeup, entertained by performance. So, how is it that a society depicted as sheer artifice can expel one of its members on the grounds that the member in question is artificial? Doesn't this make a truth out of hypocrisy and the celebration of such a truth itself hypocritical?

If Blake's notion of truth seems somewhat enigmatic, a formal means of punishing whose content is not named, it is nonetheless clear that his reading of the Marquise is that she is "the embodiment of pure evil" (Blake, 89) and that she has been duly punished by the end of the film. While it is striking that the Vicomte is allowed to disappear from this equation, so that he once again somehow manages to escape being read off as evil, what is even more striking is the way in which truth is understood here to represent the cruelest of all punishments. It's odd that Blake seems satisfied with this distribution of justice. Given the instrumental role the Marquise has played in arranging Cecile's "deflowering," the duel between Valmont and Danceny, and the destruction of Mme. de Tourvel, given that she is "pure evil," how is it possible to construct her as sufficiently punished at the end of the film as she sits before her mirror removing her makeup? This question is intended to verge on the offensive (since so many of the reviews strive for the same): How does this ending in any way satisfy the lust for vengeance hinted at in the various reviewers' configurations of the Marquise as feminist?

Comparing Frears' fate for the Marquise with Laclos' begins to provide some answers to these difficult questions. In the novel, Letter CLXXV from Mme. de Volanges to Mme. de Rosemonde begins to detail the extent of the Marquise's punishment:

> Madame de Merteuil's destiny seems at last accomplished, my dear and excellent friend; and it is such that her worst enemies are divided between the indignation she merits and the pity she inspires. I was indeed right to say that it would perhaps be fortunate for her if she died of her small-pox. She has recovered, it is true, but [is] horribly disfigured; and particularly by the loss of one eye. You may easily imagine that I have not seen her again; but I am told she is positively hideous (Laclos, 428).

Laclos turns a rather different portrait of the Marquise towards the reader at the end of his novel than the one Frears offers his viewers at the end of the film: Laclos shows a pox-marked, one-eyed monster. He is not finished with her yet, however. Mme. de Volanges goes on to recount the Marquise's defeat in the courts, her subsequent financial ruin, her midnight escape from her creditors. And even though this is the last letter in the novel, Laclos' punishment of the Marquise continues beyond the novel's last line: in the editor's note (written by Laclos) following the final letter, the readers are informed:

> Private reasons and other considerations which we feel it our duty to respect, force us to stop here.
>
> For the moment we cannot give the reader the continuation of Mademoiselle de Volanges' adventures nor inform him of the sinister events which completed the misfortunes or the punishment of Madame de Merteuil (Laclos, 430).

Although she is physically disfigured, destitute, and homeless, something quite literally unspeakable awaits the Marquise after the novel's completion, a punishment never named or described: the sequel promised here was never written. The Marquise dissolves into thin air, suspended in the realm of potential punishment. Has she, one has to wonder, joined that other Marquis off in the mountains?

If the punishments doled out in the two texts differ so substantially, can the crime of Laclos' Marquise be the same as the crime of Frears' Marquise? In the film, Valmont hands Danceny a blood-soaked packet of letters from the Marquise, saying, "When you've read them, you may decide to circulate them" (Hampton, 73). While we do not know that exact content of the letters Valmont hands over, we know that whatever they say, they are sufficient to the task of having the Marquise expelled from society. There is no reason not to assume that the letters detail the basic outline of the film itself, tracing the Marquise's plot to corrupt Cecile first through the Vicomte, then through Danceny, then through the Vicomte and Danceny. If one accepts the Valmont's romantic transformation, it seems less likely that any of the letters he includes in the packet discuss Mme. de Tourvel, but whether he did or not has little bearing on the fate of the Marquise: she simply encouraged him, in this instance, in an affair of his own design. Listing the Marquise's "crimes," it becomes clear that they all involved words: she is being punished for duplicity. The Marquise has not physically done anything (obviously this is a function of her "lack"): she has only made it possible for certain deceptions to take place. For this crime, the film is satisfied with expelling her from society (and even her expulsion is ambiguous, since her wealth remains intact): the film finds it unnecessary to deprive her of all her money, her home, her looks.

Laclos, on the other hand, is quite specific both about which letters Danceny chooses to publish from the packet and what happens to the entirety of the correspondence between the Marquise and the Vicomte. Danceny publishes just two letters from the Marquise: one of his own choice detailing the Marquise's seduction and humiliation of a man who had set out to seduce and humiliate her (this adventure is not included in the film); the other at Valmont's request. Danceny honors Valmont's request and publishes this long letter from the Marquise detailing how it is she came to be the kind of woman she is because he felt "it was rendering a service to society to unmask a woman so really dangerous as M. de Merteuil and who, as you can see, is *the only real cause* of all that passed between M. de Valmont and me" (Laclos, 418, emphasis mine). This letter serves as the basis for the following dialogue between the Marquise and the Vicomte in the film[2]:

Valmont: I often wonder how you managed to invent yourself.

Merteuil: I had no choice, did I? I'm a woman. Women are obliged to be far more skillful than men. You can ruin our reputation and our life with a few well-chosen words. So of course I had to invent: not only myself but ways of escape no one has ever thought of. And I've succeeded, because I've always known I was born to dominate your sex and avenge my own.

Valmont: Yes; but what I asked you was how.

Merteuil: When I came out into society, I was fifteen. I already knew that the role I was condemned to, namely to keep quiet and do what I was told, gave me the perfect opportunity to listen and pay attention: not to what people told me, which was naturally of no interest, but to whatever it was they were trying to hide. I practised detachment. I learned how to look cheerful, while under the table I stuck a fork into the back of my hand. I became a virtuoso of deceit. It wasn't pleasure I was after, it was knowledge. I consulted the strictest moralists to learn how to appear, philosophers to find out what to think and novelists to see what I could get away with. And, in the end, I distilled everything down to one wonderfully simple principle: win or die (Hampton, 25–6).

What is it about the position that the Marquise espouses here that is so threatening that it not only justifies her expulsion from society but also her financial downfall (the success of her case, we are told, depended on "a great deal of favor" lost as a result of the revelation of her "adventures" [Laclos, 426])? That is, Danceny and Mme. de Rosemonde are very careful not to reveal anything that the Marquise has said about or done to Cecile de Volanges, Mme. de Volanges, or Mme. de Tourvel, thus her crimes, as society receives them through her two letters are: (1) defeating a known libertine at his own game and (2) revealing her own survival strategies. We have, in short, something of a paradox: the society of Laclos' novel knows less about the Marquise's affairs than the society of Frears' film, yet the punishment exacted on the Marquise is much greater in Laclos' world than in Frears'.

While this assessment is true enough, it does not, in itself, help us to understand exactly what the Marquise has revealed in these two letters that justifies her punishment in either the novel or the film. A possible explanation as to what is so threatening about the letters can be found in Irigaray's discussion of masquerade:

> I think the masquerade has to be understood as what women do in order to recuperate some element of desire, to participate in man's desire, but at the price of renouncing their own. In the masquerade, they submit to the dominant economy of desire in an attempt to remain "on the market" in spite of everything. But they are there as objects for sexual enjoyment, not as those who enjoy.
>
> What do I mean by masquerade? In particular, what Freud calls "femininity." The belief, for example, that it is necessary to *become* a woman, a "normal" one at that, whereas a man is a man from the outset. He has only to effect his being-a-man, whereas a woman has to become a normal woman, that is, has to enter into the masquerade of femininity. (Irigaray, 133–34).

The Marquise's speech in the film and her Letter CLXXXI from the novel can both be read as pronouncements of her awareness of the masquerade involved in becoming a woman. While the Marquise refuses to place herself "on the market" explicitly, (she states in both the novel and the film that she's had a number of opportunities to re-marry and has refused them all), she nonetheless is still forced to renounce whatever "her desire" might be: far from gaining access to something that might be construed as "feminine pleasure," the Marquise declares, "It wasn't pleasure I was after, it was knowledge" (Hampton, 26).

But is this position one that is to be understood as essentially "feminist"? Does this explain what made it possible for so many contemporary reviewers of the film to link this pre-Revolutionary woman with feminism? While the passage from Irigaray offers an argument about the status of women from a feminist perspective that has certain affinities with the Marquise's autobiographical account of her emergence in society, this is not the same thing as asserting that the Marquise actually embodies a feminist position, at least not as defined by Irigaray. A reader or reviewer interested in making such an assertion would have to return to Irigaray's insistence that there is no element of choice involved in the adoption of the masquerade and thus that there is nothing either explicitly or implicitly feminist involved in the adoption of the masquerade. Within Irigaray's taxonomy, the interim strategy for a woman to assume, in order to gain access to pleasure, is mimicry, which allows a woman to see the ways in which discourse works to exploit her and to strategically exploit that position in turn. To engage in mimicry is to move towards a feminist position; it is, I would say, to engage in critiquing, among other things, the masquerade. The question stands at this point: In recognizing and articulating the masquerade of womanhood, has the Marquise moved to occupy a position of mimicry? Is that what she is being punished for?

Whether the Marquise "really" is or isn't a feminist within Irigaray's taxonomy is not our concern here, however, but rather how the Marquise came to be read as a feminist by so many reviewers. It seems safe to say that it was not the implicit assertions about the impossibility of female desire resonating in the Marquise's speech that allowed her to be read off as a feminist (there is nothing in any of the reviews cited, at any rate, that would suggest such a definition of feminism is in play). It seems more likely that the Marquise was seen as a feminist because of her insistence that being a woman involves the necessary invention of a self in the service of male desire. In other words, while knowledge of the masquerade does not, in itself, constitute a feminist position for Irigaray, it seems to have sufficed for many of the viewers of the film.

The Politics of Reading

Throughout this discussion I have tried to restrict myself to recording and problematizing the discursive formations both in and around *Dangerous Liaisons* and *Les Liaisons Dangereuses*. My goal all along has been to try to trace the outlines of what Raymond Williams defines as the workings of hegemony: "the central, effective and dominant system of meanings and values, which are not merely abstract but which are organized and lived" (Williams, 383). That is, my concern has been with looking at some of the material effects that have followed upon the original production of *Les Liaisons Dangereuses* (a movie, a boutique, a handful of film reviews, some student essays) not to come to a better understanding of the text but rather to read readings of the film and the novel as sites where the some of the fundamental problematics of contemporary culture are exposed and explored. In the process, reading Valmont as the villain redeemed through love and the Marquise as the duly punished feminist have emerged as ways of working through current problematics of sexuality. Clearly, neither of these readings is politically neutral: both can be seen as working in the service of a variety of ideologically conservative projects.

These are not, however, the only readings possible for the film. Although I have yet to discuss any responses to the film that work against these "dominant" readings of the film, I would like, at this point, to look at two instances where these "dominant" readings are challenged, beginning with a review that calls into question the ready identification of the Marquise and feminism. Pauline Kael writes:

> There are times when the Marquise — a happy widow — sounds much like a modern, "liberated" woman. This is basically faithful to Laclos, who reads like a feminist if you don't pick up on the nuances. . . In both the novel and the film, the Marquise is liberated to lie and scheme, and her primary motive is vicious, vengeful jealousy. . .
>
> The Marquise is actually the opposite of liberated: she is one of the most formidable examples of hell-hath-no-fury-like-a-woman-scorned in all literature. Childless, of course, she's woman the destroyer. . .a power-hungry, castrating female as conceived by an eighteenth-century male writer (Kael, Jan., 78).

While Kael works to separate the notion of the "liberate woman" from visions of the "power-hungry, castrating female," the sheer number of reviews that link these two images show how difficult this task is. It should not go unnoticed that in order to take on this task, Kael has to suppress the f-word. Instead, Kael calls on "liberated," concealing the very term that names the concept she wants to recuperate. (I leave interpreting the significance of Kael's deployment of the quotation marks in this moment to the reader.) And yet, what status does feminism have if it can only be recuperated and erased simultaneously? And what does its embattled status within this discourse tell us about the culture(s) deploying the term in this way?

Before going on to look at a reading that works against the dominant reading of Valmont, I'd like to contrast Kael's move to represent and then challenge the dominant reading of the Marquise with Peter Travers' tactic in his review of the film. Travers writes:

> You can read *Liaisons* as a metaphor for modern political aggression, a feminist tract, or an attack on the Thatcher England (the Prime Minister "would be very, very good as the Marquise," Frears has joked). Better to simply enjoy this spellbinder for what it is: a seductively, scary, savagely witty look at the unchanging way of the world (Travers, 17).

Travers' review works to mask its ideological content by transforming *Dangerous Liaisons* into a story about the "unchanging way of the world," a masking accomplished by erasing the historical specificity of the film (it speaks its word, ever the same, across the expanse of time) and by cartooning all other readings as overtly political and therefore opposed to pleasure. Who, one wonders, is going to produce the readings Travers imagines? Who is going to see this as a film about "modern political aggression"? The characters are completely uncon-cerned with politics and, despite the fact that Hampton moves the story up to the summer of 1788, the immanence of the revolution is never alluded to. A feminist tract? As we've seen, it would be more accurate to see this as a tract against feminism. An attack on Thatcher England? Such a reading would only occur to someone who knows Frears' other work, while Frears himself seems to call such a reading into question with his joke. The joke aside, the very fact that American actors play the leading roles in the film makes the connection with England, at the very least, less automatic.

My point here is not to argue that these readings are impossible, but to expose a general problem that arises when discussing actual receptions of films: because Travers reads this as a film about the unchanging way of the world, he cannot propose alternative readings with any seriousness. And yet, Travers' cartoon version illustrates that dismissive, totalizing responses can just as easily be found among those critics who imagine themselves laboring for The People and those employed by *People* magazine. Both camps — those who espouse the view of Hollywood as producer of ideologically pure, timeless products and those who espouse the view of Hollywood as the producer of purely corrupt ideological products — have failed to understand the complex workings of hegemony and that, as Raymond Williams expresses it, "no mode of production, and therefore no dominant society or order of society, and therefore no dominant culture, in reality exhausts the full range of human practice, human energy, human intention" (Williams, 386). Both camps have also failed to consider adequately Jameson's critique of current shouting matches about postmodernism when he states that "the point is that we are *within* the culture of postmodernism to the point where its facile repudiation is as impossible as any equally facile celebration of it as complacent and corrupt" (Jameson, 425). Once the concept of hegemony is sufficiently problematized, the necessity of developing a theory of reception that recognizes and articulates the contradictions and complexities that arise in the reading of a film becomes manifest.

I would like to close by looking at a way of reading the film that begins to address these complexities, a way of reading that takes pleasure in the film while, nonetheless, working against its impetus. Returning, once again, to the dual, we return also to Michael Zorich's essay, picking up his argument at the point where he has just completed his explanation of how Valmont made the transition to the "honor-driven martyr":

> It is a beautiful story of sin, love and honor [the one of the honor-driven martyr, that is]. It is a shame it holds less water than a fork when the text is turned on itself...To turn the story on itself is to question the fact that a man, who has spent his whole life of royalty playing deceitful games that utilize the most erotic of strategies uncon-ditional upon the degree of innocence of the victims involved, is able to fall in love so easily.

[Michael proceeds to argue that Valmont remains evil throughout the entire story, re-reading the scenes where changes in his character "supposedly" occur. A problem, however, arises when it comes to explaining why Valmont drops his sword in his final scene: If he hasn't changed, what leads him to do this?]

> This is a question that seems unanswerable apart from the love and honor explanation. Valmont was in a war with the marquise and he considered himself too good to lose. He is in love with himself and he is the only one he would die for. His only regret is that to win the war he is no longer able to play his game and enjoy the fruits of his labor, women. This is all very clear when one follows the process of thought going through his head throughout the fight. His first two memories are of women in bed, Tourvel in particular. These memories remind Valmont of what he is giving up to win this war, sex with woman. These thoughts are chronologically moving and when Valmont closes his eyes to remember for the third time we need not see his thoughts. Followed chronologically he is thinking of when he says, "when will you start writing again?" This reminds him of why he is there in the first place and thus he thrusts himself onto Danceny's sword. The only thing Valmont loves more than conquering women in bed is himself...Further in the end not only does his well worded pledge to Tourvel avoid the words "tell her I love her" but also he pulls out the proof against the marquise, her letters to him. Here we find love was not his motive, it was the destruction of the marquise to win the game that he was interested in (Zorich 6–9).

Note the way that Michael defines his project as "turning the text on itself" and then proceeds to rigorously read against his initial reading of the film. The result is not a simple reversal of the initial reading or the casual adoption of an ironic perspective, but an effort to read both the film's manifest content and what the film conceals ("when Valmont closes his eyes to remember for the third time we need not see his thoughts"). Reading this concealed space, this blank that confronts the audience when Valmont closes his eyes the final time, Michael unravels the romantic recuperation of Valmont, exposing the core of narcissism that drives the Vicomte to act as he does. Reading in this way, Michael is able to step outside the constellation of readings that cast Valmont as naif, poet, or dandy to argue that he actually remains evil throughout the film.

There are two obvious reasons to object to the presentation of this essay as exposing the complexity of the workings of hegemony. First, it was produced in a class I taught. Second, it is being contrasted with brief excerpts from movie reviews, where the discursive conventions and the imagined audiences vary significantly. Thus, it seems that any effort to represent this essay as working against the dominant discursive practices has to be fundamentally flawed from the start. While these objections seem reasonable enough, the imagined conclusion is not where I'm headed. The problem arising at this moment is, actually, much greater than the fact that I've offered the work of one of my own students to show a reading of the film which none of the reviews either offer or account for: I want to claim that the existence of such a reading, although it was produced within and for the institution in response to institutional requirements, attests to the fact that "no dominant culture...exhausts the full range of human practice." This does not mean that Michael's rejection of the romantic recuperation of Valmont is fundamentally counter-hegemonic, or revolutionary, or even political in any of the ways suggested by the *People* review; rather the status of Michael's reading at this moment is that it resides both inside and outside the "dominant culture." It demonstrates, for this reason, that the real work to be done in cultural studies, in general, and in composition classrooms devoted to cultural studies, in particular, is the development of a sufficiently complex reading of dominant culture to account for this possibility. That, however, is the work of another paper. For the moment, it suffices to point to the results Michael claims for this work:

> From Gadamer we can understand that the easier it is to accept what is being presented, or situations in which we tend not to question, the harder we should strive to exploit the power we as readers possess. This power of interpretation that the two interpretations of Valmont has exposed needs to be used in all situations in which we are subjected to others thoughts. It acts as a machete in a jungle of rhetorical truths. It has the power to free us from the shackles of bondage produced by the iterators and sustain our free standings in the world (Zorich, 11).

In a classroom environment where interpretations were produced, negotiated, and challenged by the students and teacher together, Michael found a way out of the morass that results when class occurs under the banner of "everyone's entitled to their own opinion." Here Michael speaks earnestly about what can be achieved when readers are imagined as active producers of meaning rather than passive consumers of propaganda. If you are suspicious that Michael's exuberance is a necessary pose given the institutional distribution of power that informs the teacher-student relationship, doesn't such a suspicion arise from a certain despair about what can be achieved in the classroom? About what can be claimed for praxis? Isn't Michael expressing the same sentiment, the same desire, that resonates in the Foucault quote that opens this essay? Why be suspicious of Michael and not Michel?

Marc

My goal has not been to produce yet another paper that says reading is complicated, that the way we do it depends upon our specific historical context, another paper that falls into the abyss of indeterminacy, but rather to try to demonstrate the ways in which discursive practices and material practices are affiliated. We have seen, for instance, how the material practice of opening a boutique called Valmont, (which can be understood as writing a particular reading onto the face of the world), is affiliated with the discursive practice of representing the male as redeemed through love, a, perhaps familiar, working through of the problematics of maleness in terms of the binary opposition, libertine or poet. We have also seen how certain material practices found in the academy can come to be affiliated with discursive practices that serve to problematize reductive definitions of hegemony. But can I, or should I even dare try at this point, to link the discursive practice uniting Merteuil and feminism found prevalent in the film reviews with the actual material practice of a certain Canadian gunman? I do feel they are affiliated, but I don't want to appear to trivialize the death of real women in the real world by relating their deaths to certain filmic practices, nor do I wish to appear to suggest a cause and effect relationship betweem film and the world. My intention in bringing Marc Leclerc into this essay is to suggest something that may seem fairly obvious by this point — namely, that the representation of feminism as the vengeful domination of men by women is a living, breathing discourse in contemporary culture, one that surfaces somewhat benignly in the move to define the Marquise as a feminist and assumes a much more violent form in the Canadian's actions. It is the same discourse that speaks in both moments.

Notes

1. Edmund White, getting the facts right, describes Close as follows: "She has to sit on a taboret rather than on a chair because her gown is so full. She's just had a baby, so she's filling out her low-cut bodice with maternal splendor" (White, 54).

2. I quote the film and not the novel for two reasons: (1) Letter LXXXI in the novel, which is the source for the dialogue, is over eight pages long and (2) the dialogue accurately represents the kind of information the Marquise reveals in Letter LXXXI.

Works Cited

Aldington, Richard. "Introduction." in *Dangerous Acquaintances (Les Liaisons Dangereuses)*. Laclos, Choderlos de. London, Boston and Henley: Routledge and Kegan Paul, 1979.

Blake, R.A. "Winter Lite." *America*, February 1989: 88.

"Bloomie's Diary: Week in Preview." *New York Times*, 12 November 1989: Y5.

Coward, David. "A Conspiracy of Nobles." *Times Literary Supplement*, 10 March 1989: 251.

Forrester, Steve. "Sexuality, Memory, and Symbolism." Unpublished student essay written in fulfillment of the requirements for Lit 037, December 1989.

Foucault, Michel. *The History of Sexuality, Volume I: An Introduciton*. Trans. Robert Hurley. New York: Vintage Books, 1980.

———. *The Use of Pleasure, The History of Sexuality, Volume II*. Trans. Robert Hurley. New York: Vintage Books, 1986.

Hampton, Christopher. *Dangerous Liaisons, The Film*. London/Boston: Faber and Faber, 1989.

Irigaray, Luce. *This Sex Which Is Not One*. Trans. Catherine Porter. New York: Cornell Univ. Press, 1985.

Jameson, Frederic. "The Politics of Theory: Ideological Positions in the Post-modernism Debate." Reprinted in *Contemporary Literary Criticism: Literary and Cultural Studies*. Eds. Robert Con Davis and Ronald Schleifer. New York: Longman Inc., 1989: 417–27.

Kael, Pauline. "The Current Cinema." New Yorker 27 November 1989: 104–7.

———. "The Current Cinema." *New Yorker*, 9 January 1989: 78–81.

"Killer of 14 Targeted 'Feminists.'" *Pittsburgh Press*, 7 December 1989: A1, A14.

Laclos, Choderlos de. *Dangerous Acquaintances (Les Liaisons Dangereuses)*. Trans. Richard Aldington. London, Boston and Henley: Routledge and Kegan Paul, 1979.

O'Brian, Tom. "Seduction with a Vengence: Frears' *Dangerous Liaisons*." *Commonweal*, 10 March 1989: 147.

Said, Edward. "Reflections on American 'Left' Literary Criticism." Reprinted in *Contemporary Literary Criticism: Literary and Cultural Studies*. Eds. Robert Con Davis and Ronald Schleifer. New York: Longman Inc., 1989: 579–94.

Samon, J. "Review of Dangerous Liaisons." *National Review*, 4 February 1989: 54–55.

White, Edmund. "Before the Revolution." *Premiere*, January 1989: 50–54.

Williams, Raymond. "Base and Superstructure in Marxist Cultural Theory." Reprinted in *Contemporary Literary Criticism: Literary and Cultural Studies*. Eds. Robert Con Davis and Ronald Schleifer. New York: Longman Inc., 1989: 377–90.

Zorich, Michael "Ways of Reading." Unpublished student essay written in fulfillment of the requirements for Lit 037, December 1989.

17

Deconstruction for Cultural Critique:
Teaching Raymond Carver's "What We Talk About When We Talk About Love"

Peter Carino

For many academics trained in the decades when formalism and humanism held critical sway, deconstruction once elicited fear and loathing. For most, this is no longer the case. Some have ignored deconstruction, others have embraced it, becoming deconstructionists themselves, and still others have dabbled in it to find additional approaches to reading and teaching. Whatever the case, the term "Yale Mafia," once used pejoratively to designate such American proponents of deconstructive theory as de Man, Hartmann, and Miller now seems almost comic. No longer do we find articles in nonacademic publications quizzically attempting to define deconstruction for the general public while implicitly attacking it as some airy theory concocted by rarefied academics to claim that nothing means anything. Its shady past behind it, deconstruction has not only achieved respectability but also has established itself as a powerful way of seeing language. Indeed, deconstruction has become almost a synonym for poststructuralist thought, with Derridean premises informing feminist, Marxist, reader-response, new historical, and cultural criticism, as well as rhetorical theory in composition studies.

The work of such explicators of Derrida as Jonathan Culler, Vincent Leitch, and G. Douglas Atkins has done much to clarify deconstruction, if in a simplified way, as their detractors claim, for those of us in the rank and file of teachers of literature. A smattering of publications in the 1980s have addressed the question of deconstruction in the classroom, but it is unlikely that deconstructive pedagogy is widespread in undergraduate literature courses, particularly those for nonmajors.[1].

What do undergraduates in such courses have to learn from deconstruction? Given the deceptive use of language in advertising, politics, and media, deconstructive assumptions about the tenuous relations between signifiers and signifieds, the blurring of boundaries between seemingly binary oppositions, and the power of individual words to evoke whole systems of signification can contribute to empowering students as readers of culture as they attempt to situate themselves within it. Simply put, deconstruction can equip students for cultural critique. Raymond Carver's "What We Talk About When We Talk About Love," the title story of his 1981 collection, proves an apt text for achieving this objective. I would like to present a deconstructive pedagogy for this story, but before doing so, I will briefly sketch the deconstructive tenets that inform it—logocentrism, *differance*, violent hierarchies, and supplement.

Theory: Deconstruction and cultural critique[2]

Logocentrism, a powerful notion in Derrida's critique of Western philosophy in *Of Grammatology*, questions Aristotle's faith in the power of language to represent truth. As Sharon Crowley interprets it, logocentrism rests upon "a self-sealing argument regarding the representative relationships that exist between the minds, the world, and language" (3). From a logocentric perspective, one can believe in absolute truth, in foundations, in grounds on which figures can be judged, for that which is present in the world can be re-present in words and in the mind. Such an absolute becomes the center of a structure of thought and a system of signification. This center, from a logocentric perspective, is immune to analysis since to analyze it would presuppose a new center and structure. Human beings schooled in the humanistic tradition desire a center, whether it be the "*I*" that constitutes self and being, a Platonic ideal, the word of God, or a belief in capitalism, for it accords the sign presence. We often see the effects of this desire when students reify or "naturalize," to use Roland Barthes's term, a belief that is culturally constructed: for example, racism is a fact of life, liberals favor increased government spending, conservatives lack compassion, abortion is murder, and the like. Whatever the belief, logocentrism bestows the status of presence, presence which marginalizes that which it excludes.

This presence, Derrida argues, is possible only because of differance.

Derrida coins the word *"differance"* from the French verb differer, which can mean both to differ and to defer. Differance simultaneously establishes and undermines the presence of the sign, for the signifier is recognized only because it surfaces from the Sausserian system of differences which enables language. It enjoys no presence on its own. At the same time, the signifier defers presence of the signified, complicating the notion of sign, of representation.

Because of differance, the hierarchical relations of binary oppositions — for example, presence/absence, man/woman, conservative/liberal, and so on — can be collapsed and reversed. In the speaking/writing binary, for instance, speaking is privileged as presence, but although writing marks the absence of speaker and thing, it is a presence as we read and can remain a presence long after the writer is dead. Western philosophy, Derrida argues, privileges presence in what he calls a "violent hierarchy," violent because to establish one term of any binary opposition — whether it be good/evil, love/hate, presence/absence — is to do violence to the second term, which makes the first possible, which enables the presence of the first by its own absence. Differance, of course, has powerful implications for establishing authority in literary studies when we consider as violent hierarchies such binaries as writer/reader, literature/criticism, teacher/student. Beyond literary studies, developing students' abilities to recognize and deconstruct violent hierarchies helps free them from the prejudices imposed by such culturally inscribed binaries as self/other, white/black, male/female, capital/labor, American/foreign, rich/poor, to name a few.

The second term in a binary opposition becomes for Derrida the supplement. The supplement adds to the first term, but coming from the French verb *suppleer*, which can mean to substitute as well as to supplement, the supplement, Derrida writes, "adds only to replace" (145). In bringing the supplement to bear, reversing the hierarchy, we now do violence to the initially privileged and present term. Of course, the notion of the supplement can be invoked again to restore the original hierarchy, and invoked ad infinitum as we find ourselves in the play of differance. In short, we know the privileged term, acknowledge its presence, by that form which it differs and by that which it defers.

But how does deconstruction enable cultural critique? Indeed, deconstruction is often criticized as apolitical while cultural studies is sometimes criticized as too political. But linkage is evident, though hardly neat, if we consider Stuart Hall's "Cultural Studies: Two Paradigms," an attempt to define the critical practices of the Birmingham school. Hall's definition, however, resists definition, substituting for closure "reinforcing antagonisms" (72) between culturalist and structuralist models of signification. In the culturalist model, largely attributed to Raymond Williams, Hall traces Williams's opposition of a "social" notion of culture as practices, as lived experience, and a "documentary" notion of culture as description, as discourse. Hall concludes that for Williams "'Culture' is not a practice; nor is it simply the descriptive sum of the 'mores and folkways' of societies...It is threaded through all social practices, and is the sum of their inter-relationship" (60 Hall's emphasis). Against this paradigm, Hall places structuralist models of Levi-Stauss and Althusser. While the culturalist and structuralist models converge in that both subvert a "base/superstructure" metaphor that privileges material reality, lived experience, over language and ideology, Hall contends that the structuralist model, because of its grounding in Sausserian linguistics, asserts "the conception of 'men' as bearers of the structures that speak and place them, rather than as active agents in the making of their own history" (66); that is, as imbricated in ideology, in language.

Opposing culturalist and structuralist paradigms, Hall traces in both a problematizing of binary notions of culture as material reality and culture as discourse. Thus, he images cultural studies deconstructively, according neither model presence, deferring neither as absence, eschewing synthesis for a play of difference in "the terrain marked out by those strongly coupled but not mutually exclusive concepts culture/ideology" (72). This play is not apolitical play for its own sake, the academic parlor game critics of deconstruction often see in it, but, as Frost said of poetry, "play for mortal stakes."

All this seems heady stuff for the undergraduate classroom, but in learning to think deconstructively students discover that meaning is not absolute, not readily there in experience, not in the text, or in the teacher's mind to be apprehended and banked to be returned on the test. Rather, meaning is tenuous, questionable, always already subject to interrogation — culturally constructed in, as Williams argues, "a field of mutually if also unevenly determining forces" (qtd. in Hall, 61). This is not to say that anything goes, that sheer relativism reigns, but that any position must be aware that in conferring presence it privileges certain statements while marginalizing others.

Such awareness is certainly valuable in a culture in which advertisements confer presence on gym shoes, soda pop, beer, or presidential candidates as centers of signification soliciting the formation of social structures and individual identity. You are your shoes, say the Nike ads; you belong to the Pepsi Generation; your nights belong to Michelob; and you live in a kinder, gentler nation brought to you each day by high technology and advanced capitalism. Admittedly, this representation of the student's plight may be somewhat exaggerated; however, students learn a valuable lesson when they begin to decenter the constructions by which culture attempts to define them. A deconstructive perspective on Raymond Carver's "What We Talk About When We Talk About Love" can help teach this lesson.

Practice: Teaching "What We Talk About When We Talk About Love"

Positing and problematizing culturally held definitions of love, Carver's story interrogates a word which humanist culture generally upholds as the most gratifying and ennobling of human emotions, but which is emblazoned on T-shirts, coffee mugs, bumper stickers, and other such bric-a-brac of mass culture. The story's plot recounts two married couples, one in their late thirties, the other in their early forties, both on their second marriages, sitting around a kitchen table drinking gin and attempting to define love. As afternoon moves into evening, and sunlight into darkness, they discuss definitions of love in terms of spirituality, violence, passion, chivalry, transience, endurance, and parenthood, to name a few. The driving figures in the discussion, and the heaviest drinkers, are Mel McGinnis, appropriately a heart surgeon, and his wife, Terri. The narrator, Nick, and his newlywed wife, Laura, serve as foils. often trying to placate the McGinnises' anxieties about the discussion, while attempting to maintain the security of their own love. In sum, the story, as Arthur Saltzman points out, burlesques Plato's (117), but Carver's version disallows closure on Platonic ideals. As the story ends, the four, benumbed from the conversation, sit silently in the dark of the onsetting evening as Nick hears the "human noise" of everyone's heart beating.

As a noun clause, the title of the story announces itself as a presence. Like a dictionary entry poised before its definition, the title stands at the threshold of the narrative suggesting that we need only read on to attach the signifier of title to the signified of the story, and the signifier of the story to the signified of experience to apprehend the sign, to know what love is. Simultaneously, the noun clause defers meaning in that it lacks predication, lacks the verb that would connect it to the narrative, that would lead to predication, to meaning. Thus, the title plays on our logocentric desire for a center, for the word that would fill the absence it suggests, the word that would tell us what we talk about when we talk about love.

The story's multiple perspectives on love, however, create indeterminacy, inviting a deconstructive reading that decenters culturally validated but naively simplistic definitions. To lead students to this reading, the story first can be read from a formalist perspective that centers a definition of love as lasting and satisfies the students' logocentricity, their desire for the authoritative word. Near the end of the story, Mel relates the tale of an elderly couple brought to the hospital where he works, after they have been near fatally injured in an auto wreck. Suffering multiple fractures, bruised organs, and internal hemorrhaging, both pull through after a team of surgeons labors all night to save them. Two weeks later both have regained consciousness but are confined to body casts from head to foot. When the old man tells Mel he is depressed not because of the accident but because the casts and bandages do not allow him to turn his head to see his wife, Mel is astonished. "Do you see what I'm saying?" he pleads to his three listeners (151). Mel, at this point, is his most emphatic, seemingly elevating this version of love above the others.

Added to Mel's emphasis, references to the two couples' previous marriages can be appropriated to construct a binary hierarchy in which the longevity of the old couple's marriage is placed on opposition to the brevity of those of the younger couples. In other words, the binary opposition permanence/impermanence establishes a hierarchical relation with permanence as ground against which to judge the impermanence of the relationships of the younger couples. Consequently, the story can yield a determinate meaning that reinforces the cultural cliché that love is forever, implicitly exposing the inferior love of the younger couples' transient marriages in the past and brief marriages in the present. With the old couple's love privileged as meaningful center, we can construct a unity and closure that seemingly accounts for the story's movement from sunlight to darkness and for the younger couples' final response, placing them as William Stull does in a paradigm often attributed to Carver's work before *Cathedral*: characters suffer a state of "anxious isolation, enervation, and stasis" (2).

Students generally seize on this reading, for it provides a momentary stay against confusion in its logocentric delivering of "the word" on both the story and love, comforting them with a meaning they can give back on the test and perhaps an answer to their own questions about love. In accepting this reading, they happily situate themselves in a system of signification that values longevity and permanence in love, and unity, closure, and determinacy in literature.

But such a reading is a misreading, for the story's multiple perspectives on love generate a polysemy that undoes any attempts to establish a centered definition that would render all other examples supplemental. If lasting love is conferred this status, then the old couple can be dislodged as the privileged center when we consider that the story opens with a definition of a love that exceeds that longevity of theirs. Remembering five years he spent in a seminary, Mel concludes that "real love was nothing less than spiritual love" (109). To assume a religious perspective in which spiritual love continues past death is to reverse the old couples' position in the binary permanence/impermanence. No longer is their example the center guaranteeing love as presence; rather it is another supplement to the now centered spiritual love. This move, of course, arrives back at logocentrism, establishing a system with religious precepts—spirituality and love of God—as its center. Like the first reading, if we accept this one, it again allows us closure if we attribute the final state of the characters to a failure of spirituality in a contemporary world of gin and darkness.

This second reading is also attractive to students, particularly those of religious faith. However, many protest that spiritual love is a different kind of love: as love of God, it is not of this earth. With this response, students are beginning to think deconstructively, beginning to problematize the relationship between signifier and signified, for, if love can admit kinds, a center cannot hold against the supplementary contentions of the multiple possibilities for definition offered elsewhere in the text.

At this point, I ask the students to choose one example of love, besides the old couple's, that would enable a satisfying definition independent of the faith required for the privileging of spiritual love. Most select the relationship between the narrator, Nick, and his wife, Laura. Unlike all other examples in the story, Nick and Laura's love is not the topic of an extended conversation. It surfaces, rather, in Nick's thoughts of her and in his comforting physical gestures, a touch on the wrist, a kiss on the hand, in the face of Mel's loud and anxious discussions of love. These gestures, however, are mocked by Terri as newlywed lust that will cool with time, and Nick validates her mockery by histrionically kissing Laura's hand. Pushed to describe this love, students generally conclude that it is normal love. Normalcy, of course, is one of our most comfortable centers, right up there with common sense, for it establishes order, indeed, a norm, a word with its roots in the Latin for carpenter's square, rule, pattern, precept.

Against this norm, class discussion turns to a love designated abnormal. Early in the story, Mel and Terri argue about whether the behavior of Ed, her lover prior to her marriage to Mel, constitutes love. In one sense, Ed literally dies for love, or at least of love. While living with Terri, he beat her up and "dragged [her] around the living room by [her] ankles" all the time screaming declarations of his love (138). When Terri leaves, he drinks rat poison, which fails to kill him but attacks his gums, leaving his teeth standing out "like fangs" (139). After continued threats of violence to Mel fail to win Terri back, Ed shoots himself in the mouth but lives three days with his head grotesquely "swelled up to twice the size of a normal head" (142). Terri attempts to sum up his tale of woe, arguing, "It was love...Sure, it's abnormal in most people's eyes. But he was willing to die for it. He did die for it" (142).

In most student's eyes, the violence of Ed's love and its grotesque results disqualify it as a definition they would endorse, but in their rejection they must also reconsider romantic definitions of love as that which endures until death or that which is worth dying for. When pushed to examine Ed's behavior further, students who will not describe it as love will concede that it illustrates passion, an attribute called into question in Nick's introduction of Laura and their supposedly normal love:

> Laura is a legal secretary. We'd met in a professional capacity. Before we knew it, it was a courtship. She's thirty-five, three years younger than I am. In addition to being in love, we like each other and enjoy one another's company. She's easy to be with. (141)

Even students who are not very skilled interpreters can recognize the flatness of Nick's measured, reasonable, even business-like tone here. Obviously this is not the rhetoric of the sonneteer. They met in a "professional capacity." Any passion they may have enjoyed in the development of their love is undercut by the formal and Victorian connotations of the word courtship. Their ages are offered like statistics, and the only reference to their love is dropped into a transitional phrase, as if an aside, before Nick remarks their easy companionship. Their occasional gestures of affection notwithstanding, Nick's description makes it easy to picture them bicycling or reading the Sunday papers together but difficult to imagine them in bed.

Placing Nick and Laura's love against Ed and Terri's, we can establish additional binary hierarchies: normal/abnormal, reasonable/passionate. In establishing them, however, we must realize what we exclude as the supplement comes to bear on our choices. While the calm of Nick and Laura's love is preferable to Ed's violence, theirs certainly lacks the intensity of his. Of course, both of these oppositions — normal/abnormal, reasonable/passionate — can be reversed, but in the reversal the full presence of love would again elude us, erasing the desirable aspects of Nick and Laura's love, the harmony implicit in the reasoned calm which seems undesirable when it is present at the expense of passion and intensity.

Added to these readings, subsequent discussions of chivalric love, parental love, and friendship leave students uncomfortable, agitated, annoyed, for they begin to suspect, if they haven't before now, that neither the story nor the teacher is going to define love for them. They thus begin to see that whatever example we choose, whatever definition we examine, if we center it as that which structures all else in the story, we must hold at bay the supplements that contend not merely to add to our center but to replace it. Having problematized the sign, the class, like humankind in a fallen world, can not return to a state that would recover the word as incontrovertible presence. Put more concretely, we cannot establish meaning without recognizing our own role in its establishment and the cultural biases that inscribe our roles.

One might argue that a deconstructive perspective on "What We Talk About When We Talk About Love" renders the story far more depressing than it should be. With meaning decentered in favor of indeterminacy, the characters' final state, like ours in the classroom, can be attributed to their inability to articulate what they talk about when they talk about love. However, neither the story nor the state of its interpreters need be depressing at all. As Saltzman notes,

> Rating the quality of the consolation that remains at the end of the story depends upon to what extent the elusive, unpredictable, hazardous process of love compensates for the skewering of the romantic ideal (upon which the discussants can not agree anyway). In the darkened room, silent save for the "human noise we sat there making" (154), perhaps these moments together, deeply imbued with shared sensibilities, make up for the antagonisms, the regrets, the flirtations, the spilled gin. (120)

Saltzman's reading raises the possibility of consolation for both the characters and Carver's readers. The final state of the characters parallels that of the agitated class, and while the characters may console themselves in their shared sensibilities, the students can find affirmation in sharing authority for making meaning.

Addressing the question of authority in Carver's fiction, Michael Vander Weele offers an interpretation of the situation of author, reader, and text that raises the possibility of what a deconstructive pedagogy can achieve:

> Carver regularly situates his characters so that they realize the need to move from a more passive willingness to an active, discoursed will. But they seldom accomplish this movement. The responsibility for such a failure is not described by Carver. It may be social, referring to the anonymous social influences of our institutions, or, despite the social influences, it may be personal...It is likely both. Carver concerns himself less with the cause and more with the failure of language in this movement toward an examined and discoursed will. That failure, the title of Carver's second major collection of stories makes clear, is a failure of *our* language as well: *What We Talk About When We Talk About Love*. The "we" of the title is part of a complex social discourse between author and reader. It refers to us, implicates us as readers equally with author and characters. (113–114).

In Vander Weele's description of the characters' need to move from "passive willingness to an active, discoursed will," too many of us will recognize our students. Students cannot achieve an active discoursed will in a logocentric classroom. Like Carver's characters, or Beckett's Pozzo and Gogo waiting for Godot, they sit suffering their own failure of language, waiting for the teacher as center to deliver the word on another center, the author, waiting for the presence by which they themselves unwittingly will be rendered an absence. A deconstructive pedagogy, in contrast, situates students, along with author, characters, and teacher, within the *we* of "What We Talk About When We Talk About Love," affording them authority and forcing them to take it.

Conclusions: Talking About More Than Love

Deconstructive pedagogy, of course, can be uncomfortable for students accustomed to logocentric pedagogy, for it reverses the traditional hierarchies of author/reader and teacher/students. To reverse these is neither to say that the story is meaningless nor to encourage students to conclude that no one knows what they talk about when they talk about love or literature. Rather, the indeterminacy yielded by the reversal enables students to realize that when they, or we, attempt to define love, or any other problematic concept, that judgments are made, that authority is seized, that truth is constructed, not discovered — a proposition that advertisers and politicians appear to know.

Admittedly, this pedagogy does install a deconstructive indeterminacy as the privileged center. However, the students can opt for a reading that would decenter indeterminacy and replace it with the romantic ideals evident in the examples of the old couple or the monk. But having been exposed to deconstructive pedagogy, they will make this move self-reflexively with increased awareness of the move itself and the position it delivers. They may come away with a definition of love or a reading of the story that they are comfortable with, that they are willing to defend; however, they will not see love as a transparent signifier but as a locus of signification where various attitudes, emotions, and cultural prejudices about human relations struggle for hegemony.

With meaning thus problematized, students will be better equipped as they negotiate a postmodern culture described by Jean Baudrillard, in his *Simulations*, as "hyperreal." In the culture of the hyperreal, the endless capabilities of technology to reproduce objects and of mass media to proliferate images have subverted the process of signification to the extent that" [t]he very definition of the real has become: *that of which it is possible to give an equivalent reproduction*" (Baudrillard's emphasis, 146). In the culture of the hyperreal, the signifier, through multiple reproduction, becomes self-referential, an image more present, more real, than its signified. Take Coca-Cola, for example. Granted, it exists materially as a sweet, brown carbonated beverage that we can ingest, but it becomes hyperreal in the perpetual reproduction of either its trademark script or the block-lettered "Coke" in advertisements, on signs, on bottles, on cans, on a complete line of clothing. The diffusion of the signifier here (which is always already split as Coca-Cola and Coke) renders the material substance supplemental, collapsing the slash between signifier/signified — between representation/reality — until the multiply reproduced signifier constitutes more of our experience of the product than the thing itself. That is, the profusion of media images of Coca-Cola constitutes its reality, reducing its material essence to a copy, or to use Baudrilliard's term, a simulacrum.

Although not much is at stake when we consider soft drinks in the culture of the hyperreal, the media reduction of experience to simulacrum, to second-order status, has powerful implications politically and economically. From a naively logocentric perspective, one might argue that politics and economics are separate entities that can be differentiated and placed in binary opposition, but in the culture of the hyperreal

> propaganda and advertizing fuse in the same marketing and merchandizing of objects and ideologies. This convergence of language between the economic and the political is furthermore what marks a society such as ours, where "political economy" is fully realized. It is also by the same token its end, since the two spheres are abolished in an entirely separate reality, or hyperreality, which is that of media. (Baudrillard, 125)

While the hyperreal culture of media collapses binaries, thus problematizing meaning, it also reinscribes them to marginalize other choices, to exclude them from the hyperreal. If we return to Coke, on the one hand, its incessant media blitz subsumes all other brand names to the point that Coke becomes the generic name for cola; on the other, its opposing term is not beverages other than colas but Pepsi, the only other cola which can marshal media power to contend with Coke's. The established binary Coke/Pepsi is, of course, a simulacrum, for experience tells us we can drink something else if we choose. What is at stake here is not a choice of drink but the power of media to produce a simulacrum of choice where little exists because other possible choices have been excluded from the reinscribed binary. This power may appear innocuous enough when applied to soft drinks, but consider, as Baudrillard does, public opinion polls on political candidates. The binary logic of the polls disallows alternatives, reflection, further, discourse, reducing public opinion to a statistical simulacrum of reality that, in turn, becomes reality as campaign contributors and voters are influenced by the polls: "It is no longer necessary that anyone *produce* an opinion, all that is needed is that all *reproduce* public opinion." (Baudrillard's emphasis, 126).

Lest this all begin to sound like some Pynchon-esque conspiracy, consider that in recent years major advertising agencies have been paying large consulting fees to anthropologists, ethnographers, and semioticians to lend their expertize to marketing campaigns (Blonsky;

Kanner; Miller and Tsiantar). Consider further the words of the chairman of a billion-dollar advertizing agency, writing for the agency's house organ:

> Too often we hear — and ask — "Are we talking about the product, or are we doing imagery?" It's the wrong question. Everything is imagery...We don't really remember the facts, the figures, the classic copypoints of the strategy. What we do get is a net impression, a sense of what the brand is about. This is what we call imagery...Every brand creates through its advertising a brand imagery which in a very real sense is the consumer's only perception of the brand. The brand image, above all else, is the brand reality. (Blonsky, 507)

Couple this rhetoric with what we know of political "spin doctors" and a logocentric pedagogy becomes not only naive but damaging to students.

A deconstructive pedagogy, in contrast, empowers students to interpret the constant bombardment of signs which daily form public opinion and reinforce ideology. Alerted to the tenuousness of meaning and the interrelationships between culture as lived and culture as signification, students begin to become aware of possibilities for opposing the culture as it speaks them. Granted this is a tall order. However, by learning to think deconstructively students are more likely to reflect on their positions, to discover the structures forming public opinion and their own. This is not to say that teaching Carver's "What We Talk About When We Talk About Love" will render students proof against mystification but that through their engagement of the story's multiple tracings around one of our most powerful cultural signifiers, they will begin to see that what we talk about when we talk about love, or politics, or commodities, or any other aspect of experience is an occasion for interpretation, an occasion for the "human noise" that keeps our hearts beating in the dark.

Notes

1. For theoretical overviews of deconstructive pedagogy, see Barbara Johnson's "Teaching Deconstructively" and James Raymond's "What Good Is All This Heady, Esoteric Theory?" For a specific example of classroom application, see Irene Goldman's "Feminism, Deconstruction, and the Universal: A Case Study on *Walden*."

2. Theoretical discussion in this section is a composite of material from Derrida's *Of Grammatology* and the works of the following explicators of Derrida: Atkins, Culler, Crowley, Leitch, Selden.

Works Cited

Atkins, G. Douglas. *Reading Deconstruction: Deconstructive Reading*. Lexington: University Press of Kentucky, 1983.

Baudrillard, Jean. *Simulations*. Trans. Paul Foss et al. New York: Semiotext(e), 1983.

Blonsky, Marshall. "Endword: Americans on the Move: a Dossier." *On Signs*. Ed. Marshall Blonsky. Baltimore: Johns Hopkins University Press, 1985.

Carver, Raymond. *What We Talk About When We Talk About Love*. New York: Knopf, 1981.

Culler, Jonathan. *On Deconstruction: Theory and Criticism after Structuralism*. Ithaca: Cornell University Press, 1982.

Crowley, Sharon. *A Teacher's Introduction to Deconstruction*. Urbana: NCTE, 1989.

Derrida, Jacques. *Of Grammatology*. Trans. Gayatri Chakravorty Spivak. Baltimore: Johns Hopkins University Press, 1976.

Goldman, Irene. "Feminism, Deconstruction, and the Universal: A Case Study on *Walden*." *Conversations: Contemporary Critical Theory and the Teaching of English*. Eds. Charles Moran and Elizabeth F. Penfield. Urbana: NCTE. 1990, 120–31.

Hall, Stuart. "Cultural Studies: Two Paradigms." *Media, Cultural and Society* 2 (1980): 52–72.

Johnson, Barbara. "Teaching Deconstructively." *Writing and Reading Differently*. Eds. G. Douglas Atkins and Michael L. Johnson. Lawrence: University Press of Kansas, 1985. 140–48.

Kanner, Bernice. "Mind Games." *New York* 8 May 1989: 34–40.

Leitch, Vincent B. *Deconstruction: An Advanced Introduction*. New York: Columbia University Press, 1983.

Miller, Annetta and Dody Tsiantar. *Newsweek* 27 February 1989: 46–47.

Raymond, James C. "What Good Is All This Heady, Esoteric Theory?" *Teaching English in the Two-Year College*. 17.1 (1990): 11–17.

Saltzman, Arthur M. *Understanding Raymond Carver*. Columbia: University of South Carolina Press, 1988.

Selden, Raman. *A Reader's Guide to Contemporary Literary Theory*. Lexington: University Press of Kentucky, 1985.

Stull, William L. "Beyond Hopelessville: Another Side of Raymond Carver." *Philological Quarterly* 64.1 (1985): 1–15.

Vander Weele, Michael. "Raymond Carver and the Language of Desire." *Denver Quarterly* 22.1 (1987): 108–22.

18

Composing a Post-Sexist Rhetoric:
Introductory Writing Instruction as a Cultural Production

Alan W. France

Most institutions of higher learning have adopted by now some official policy to eliminate sexist language from discourses of knowledge and administration. Drawn from sources like "NCTE Guidelines for Non-sexist Language," such policy statements recognize, at least implicitly, the role of language in reproducing social realities. At the university where I teach, the president has circulated a pamphlet, *Guidelines for Avoiding Gender-Biased Language in University Communications*, for "the purpose of emphasizing the University's commitment to equal opportunity for all." In the introduction to this document, he "discourages any use of language that reinforces stereotypes or inappropriate attitudes concerning gender roles" and mandates that" [a]ll official University communications, either written or oral, shall be free of gender-biased language."

Those of us who take these aims seriously are perhaps entitled to scepticism about the depth of commitment to social change implied by calls for the elimination of sexist language. Nearly everything we know about the history of language, after all, suggests that changing social practices drive linguistic change and not the other way around. Nevertheless, following Antonio Gramsci, we might consider the ideology of "equal opportunity" as one of those "concessionary" moments when "[w]hat was previously secondary and subordinate...becomes the nucleus of a new ideological and theoretical complex" (195). For while it is easy to complain of institutional duplicity and cynicism, an official policy against sexism might well provide the nucleus for progressive curricular and even institutional change. It is toward that end that I want to explore one way to help implement — or at least take advantage of — official initiatives against gender-biased language.

The representation of "stereotypes and inappropriate attitudes" in language perpetuates asymmetries of social power and opportunity. This much *Guidelines* explicitly concedes by linking its commitment to nonsexist language to its affirmative action policy. If language represents inequities, then, the necessary next step is to examine the cultural sources of gender-biased language: the material inequities signified in and reproduced by discourse. *Guidelines* proscribes the generic use of "man" and male pronouns, use of gender-coded occupational terms, and patronizing references to a stereotypical world of logical men and emotional women. It mandates parallel *language* for men and women. Yet everything we know about linguistic change suggests its dependence on social and material change. The word "sexism" describes a condition of social subordination, a material world where occupations *are* typically gender-coded and women (and men) *are* stereotyped.

To integrate university initiatives on nonsexist language into the curriculum, therefore, we must design courses that examine the cultural construction of gender inequities in the material and imaginary world our students actually inhabit. Such a program is primarily rhetorical because it involves, in Walter Beale's words "the process by which social ideals and constructions of reality are given voice and emphasis in historical situations" (633). Introductory college writing courses, where most students are initiated in rhetorical practices, seem the ideal place to incorporate fully the mandates of university policies into the curriculum. By teaching students how to investigate the rhetoric of gender representations in the media they consume, introductory composition instructors can deepen students' understanding of how culture attributes differential meaning to sexual identity.

Such a "post-sexist" rhetoric requires the exercise of moral authority and a political commitment to change. But even without serious institutional commitment to social change (which in any case seems utopian), liberal gestures can underwrite curricular reform. As Patricia Bizzell puts it, "An argument against sexism can make use of values concerning human equality and fair play that even some sexists may hold" (672). The openings provided by university initiatives like affirmative action and nonsexist language (and a number of others under rubrics like critical thinking, ethical implications of knowledge, and ecological responsibility) can be cited to authorize the critical study of culture as the practice of rhetoric.

Institutional initiatives against gender-biased language seek to promulgate change by adding one more category of rules to the bulging current-traditional handbook. This emphasis on propriety obscures the relationship between language and society. To integrate proscriptions of gender-biased language into the curriculum, we will need to "teach the conflict" (in Gerald Graff's words) between egalitarian ideals and actual social practices. The introductory composition course is the ideal laboratory to examine the social practices that manifest themselves ultimately in linguistic differences of worth, power, and freedom. Before I get to a description of the composition course as laboratory for cultural studies, however, I must acknowledge the political realities that circumscribe writing instruction.

As Linda Brodkey's experience at the University of Texas illustrates, a serious program of cultural studies — one that moves from platitudes to politics — can expect to encounter resistance in most academic settings. If the study of the rhetoric and reasoning of civil rights law can be characterized as George Will has, as "political indoctrination supplanting education," institutionalizing the study of gender inequities must remain utopian.

But integrating cultural studies into introductory writing programs also violates dominant theoretical orientations of rhetoric and composition as a field of knowledge. As James Berlin has argued, self-expressivist and cognitivist rhetorics organize the writing process in specifically ideological ways: they focus attention on the writer as the maker of meaning and privileged interpreter of his or her own experience. In other words, they ignore the cultural subjectivity of individual meaning and experience. But because the writer is already an engendered subject, she or he cannot — without a critical (i.e., political) theory of cultural formation — get outside culturally ascribed identities of self and other. Annette Kuhn describes self-identity in our culture this way: "Subjectivity is always gendered and every human being is, and remains, either male or female...Moreover, in ideology gender identity is not merely absolute: it also lies at the very heart of human subjectivity" (52). Asking the writer to reflect on her gender or to discover a solution to the "problem" of sexism will leave untouched the ways the writer herself is constituted as a subject of her own ideology.

If, however, institutional and ideological resistance to gender studies in the composition classroom might be side-stepped, subverted, or — as we might hope — legitimated by liberal values of equal opportunity and fair play, a course integrating the cultural study of gender with rhetoric and composition might be shaped by the following principles.

A Pedagogy for Composition as a Cultural Process

Before turning to the specifics of a post-sexist writing course, I want to outline four general principles that might help integrate cultural studies with instruction in composition. Such a course would be dialectical (e.g., politically oppositional), inquiry-driven, cross-disciplinary, and multichanneled.

The first principle for teaching writing as a cultural practice is that discourse is inherently dialectical and, therefore, political. As Volosinov put it, "Any real utterance, in one way or another or to one degree or another, makes a statement of agreement with or negation of something" (80). Composing a post-sexist rhetoric begins with the recognition that sex is valued differently and that these differences are reproduced, not merely synchronically by language (e.g., the gender specificity in English of singular pronouns), but by cultural media: verbal discourse, written texts, electronically produced images, and combinations thereof. Media organize the raw data of experience into social and historical narratives about being female or male. These narratives are sexist in that they attribute unequal public capacities and worth to women and men. There is no way to avoid politics here: to confront social inequities in public discourse for the purpose of redressing them is an overtly political activity. Because most of our students share the dominant patriarchal narratives that underlie gender-biased language, professing a post-sexist rhetoric places the teacher in conflict with his students (see Bauer). Engaging students in a rhetorical mode that goes against the cultural grain requires, as Susan Jarratt argues, "overtly confrontational feminist pedagogies as a progressive mode of discourse in the composition classroom" (3). Teaching dialectically, however, does not mean imposing dogma. A political engagement with students is not merely "an extension of the politics of the left," against which Gerald Graff cautions (64). Nevertheless, the pedagogy described here openly confronts not only the existence of social inequity but also a much more volatile issue: how the individual comes to recognize the self in a dominant or subordinate subjectivity.

The second principle for a post-sexist writing course requires that composing grow out of inquiry. In practical terms, this means that research into the cultural intertext must replace "readers." Anthologized readings, no matter how well selected or sophisticated, no longer belong organically to the primary economy of the cultural production. Like a bunch of cut flowers, they have been harvested and consciously arranged for purposes more or less removed from their original rhetorical contexts.

Wherever possible, the pre-texts of student writing should be "primary" sources; research should be as much as possible like field work. Student-inquirers should use "secondary" sources, but they must be active construers of knowledge, consciously constructing interpretations to explain the meaning of social life to themselves and others. This focus on composing as an act of interpretation, of making new texts out of the always already extant cultural pretext, subverts the traditional research project: writing as the assemblage of cut-and-paste "term papers" that mimic the dissemination of authorized knowledge in institutional hierarchies. Instead, it gives the students the "textual competence," in Scholes' words, the critical and interpretative independence to be active participants in their culture rather than its "insensitive dupes and victims" (21, xi).

A third principle of composing as a cultural process follows from an inquiry-driven pedagogy: writing and research are cross-disciplinary. Questions of cultural production cut across traditional disciplinary boundaries, but they require answers in the various academic vernaculars of knowledge. In the course of investigating the construction of gender, students borrow as much as possible from the knowledge, nomenclature, and methodologies of the human studies: classifications of social organization, ethnographic methods of observation, functionalist approaches from structural anthropology, mass communications theory, techniques of film and literary criticism, historiographic conventions of explanation, concepts from religious studies, and much else. In so doing, students learn to respect disciplinary knowledge as tested resources, valuable to their own rhetorical ends rather than as monolithic embodiments of universal truth. Thus, the post-sexist investigation of gender provides a natural interface between the introductory writing course and academic discourses across the curriculum.

The fourth and final principle in taking a cultural approach to the composing process recognizes the centrality of the electronically reproduced image in representational acts. The texts from which students construct their gendered narratives of self are no longer—if they ever were—primarily written. The performance of "pertness" in women or "aggressiveness" in men (the parallel use of which, in their adjectival forms, *Guidelines* proscribes as gender-biased) is a complex social behavior much easier to model pictorially than to describe in words. A post-sexist writing pedagogy borrows from the applied grammatology of Gregory Ulmer the notion of "scripting," according to which composition becomes a "multichanneled performance": the image can be translated into written text, while writing can become the "screenplay" for enactment (xii–xiii). The transcription of moving or print images, which for our students are the basic medium of cultural currency, in the same act composes an interpretation and stabilizes the text in letters, facilitating rhetorical analysis. It might be noted as well that studying the imaginary, as always potentially scriptable, cultural performances, revives the oratorical and elocutionary dimensions of rhetoric, which are usually absent from contemporary concepts of communication.

Syllabus: Writing, Intermedia, and Inquiry

The syllabus that follows was developed for a required, second-semester composition course, in which students are expected to learn the techniques of library research, the use of secondary sources, and the conventions of academic discourse. These objectives, I hope to show, are quite compatible with inquiry into the cultural formation of gender, the foundation on which a post-sexist rhetoric must be constructed. The syllabus is divided into four segments: Parts I to III require about three weeks each and are devoted to methodology; Part IV, consuming the final seven weeks of the semester, applies methods to a major research project.

Part I: The Basics of Academic Inquiry

Assignment 1: Summarizing a Written Source. Read the textbook chapter on summarizing sources. Then, using the online catalogue, find an extended definition of "culture" and summarize it.

Assignment 2: Synthesizing Two Sources. Read the chapter on writing a simple synthesis; then find and summarize an extended definition of "gender." Review your definition of "culture" (Assignment 1) looking for similarities that connect the two concepts. Finally, write a synthesis in which you establish the primary relationships between the concepts of culture and gender.

Students work individually on the first two assignments. They familiarize themselves with the library and its various systems of information storage and retrival, the note-taking process, the determination of what counts as a scholarly source, and the basic interpretive skills of paraphrase and citation necessary to retextualizing written sources. At this stage, they also work on the grammatical, stylistic, and rhetorical refinement of their own writing. In Part II, the focus shifts from individual to collaborative investigation as students work in groups of three to four to develop the critical abilities by which knowledge is constructed socially.

Part II: Dialogue and Knowledge-Making

Assignment 3: Comparison and Critique of Sources. Using individual summaries and syntheses of written sources, each group will construct its own definition of "culture" and "gender." Group definitions will build on — and add to — individual summaries and syntheses, first, by comparing and evaluating and, second, by refining, illustrating, and elaborating them. Group definitions must include a complete annotated bibliography of sources considered by its members.

Assignment 3 is pivotal to the production of a post-sexist rhetoric for two reasons. First, without carefully articulated definitions of culture and gender, students will find it impossible to resist their own ideology. Students begin with assumptions about the world and their relation to it that are the common epistemic property of mass youth-culture. In Moffatt's words, their "sense of generation"—their situation in society and history—"comes to them through popular music, the movies, TV, and certain mass-market magazines"; and their understanding of culture "only marginally modifies their fundamental individualism" (32, 151).

In this context, the teacher of cultural studies must struggle constantly and vigilantly to keep one set of signifiers, here "the cultural reproduction of gender," from slipping into the dominant cultural discourse, according to which individuals recognize and voluntarily accept or reject sex roles. To anticipate my conclusion, the dialectical tension between these competing structures of reality is pedagogically healthy: its negotiation demands real intellectual discipline. The give-and-take of conflicting interests, out of which the "obvious" takes shape, recreates for both teacher and student the very process by which history has organized our world for us. And this dialectical relationship prevents what critics on the right call political indoctrination—although it does insist that students confront the ideological blind spots of their enculturation, which would not otherwise be visible to them.

A second reason for insisting on the negotiation of precise definitions for the propositional terms driving inquiry (culture and gender) is pedagogical: learning, as Bartholomae and others have insisted, requires learners to "reinvent" the known. Recitation was the formal means by which students reinvented knowledge when knowledge was conceived of as static. In an age of information overload and ethical brown-out, we must involve students in helping to determine what should count as knowledge. As Reither and Vipond argue, writing and knowing are "profoundly collaborative processes" (862), and collaborative inquiry is therefore the best approach to giving students the critical distance from which to reconsider the "realities" of the media they consume. In Assignment 3, students appropriate an approach to knowledge by defining the terms of their investigation into gender and media.

Part III: Doing Field Research

Assignment 4: First, read the assigned chapters [on library reserve] in Michael Arlen's *Sixty Seconds*. Then select a full page ad from a men's or women's magazine—one that suggests a story to you. Finally, write a script for converting your ad's image into a short play, complete with descriptions of setting, props, and characters as well as stage directions and dialogue.

The basic objective of this assignment is to sensitize students to the fact that images are *re-presentations* of imagination, not windows on reality. The Arlen text, an ethnographic study of the production of AT&T's original "Reach Out and Touch Someone" campaign, provides an inside view of how these representations are constructed. By re-materializing the social production of image/text, the assignment requires students to address what John Trimbur has called "the rhetoric of deproduction" (80), the discursive practices by which, first, propositions are divorced from the objects and artifacts to which they refer and, second, the contingent and culturally mediated nature of this reference is erased. The result is our students' faith in the existence of an objective reality mirrored by an unproblematic, univocal language (80–82). The scripting of a text's production helps to reestablish its links to the material conditions of its production. (Arlen makes these links most palpable.)

In the following assignment, the process is examined from the opposite direction: the class applies the ethnographic technique Geertz calls "thick description" to the film *Working Girl*. Students formulate a specific question from a list of suggestions focusing attention on the representation of gender in the film (see Appendix A). We spend several class periods analyzing the means by which the cinematic narrative works to create an image of man and woman in the world it constructs. Each student contributes evidence gleened from the focal perspective of the question she or he has selected.

It should be noted that performing a close reading of a film text is no easier for students than discerning nuances in written texts. Visual details pass unnoticed, and much class time must be invested in close analysis ("thick description") of frozen frames.

> Assignment 5: The Narrative as Image. Using evidence from your own "field notes" and those of other class members, explain how Tess's story in *Working Girl* creates an image of what women or men are like.

Part IV of the syllabus, "Representation of Gender in Visual Media," brings together the textual competencies developed in the previous five assignments. Students select a film, television series, or set of print images as the topic of the final research paper. They form research and editing groups based on medium and genre. During the final week of classes, these groups will summarize and synthesize their research for a desktop publication, "Studies in Gender and Media," which I distribute to students at the final exam. The research project is presented in the following terms:

> Assignment 6: In examining the construction of gender in the particular visual "text" you have chosen, remember that images — whether still

or moving — are *re*-presentations of the physical world (including human sexual differences) and of the society that produces them. The patterns that we see in media are not nature itself but culturally coded interpretations of what nature "is like." The meaning is not already there; it has been put there.

In determining *what* has been put into your text, you will be looking for the answer to the question: Anatomy aside, how are men and women different in the world constructed — "imaged" — by...[your text]?

The research paper reporting your investigation of gender and visual media must contain four parts (not necessarily in this order):

1) An extended definition of "gender," drawn from at least two written sources, in which you clearly distinguish it from sex.

2) A thesis statement clearly articulating the conclusion(s) of your study (for example, "In...wo/men are represented as...").

3) A discussion of "representation" in the medium you have chosen, based on a minimum of four sources (two of which must be scholarly), which will support your textual critique and analysis.

4) A detailed explication of gender (using "thick description") as represented in your text, carefully deployed in support of your thesis.

Two Writers Composing a Post-Sexist Rhetoric

Most students first encounter rhetoric as young adults in an introductory composition course. Either explicitly or implicitly they are pointed to a discursive space and taught how to situate themselves in relation to texts, theirs and others, and the field that social reference texts occupy. The reproduction of orthodox individualism, learned at home, in the schools, and in the media, requires an introductory rhetoric that constructs the writer as an autonomous arbiter of reality, capable of "saying no" to gender-biased language as well as saying yes to the conventions of academic discourse. Reigning expressionist and cognitivist rhetorics teach students to construct just such a relationship between self and "audience."

A post-sexist rhetoric, by contrast, insists that both writer and audience share a cultural subjectivity that has effectively "naturalized" gender. Because of these blind spots (which might as well be called ideological), the focus of inquiry must shift from the world, where women and men are the way they really are, to the media which recreate the naturalness of the way things really are. To illustrate this, I want to discuss briefly the inquiry into representation of gender conducted by two students who worked through the syllabus described above.

Terri's research paper, "Sex-Role Stereotyping in Children's Cartoons," examined the construction of gender in children's television programming. After defining gender and discussing its relationship to cultural media, Terri reviewed the scholarly literature, choosing Richard Levinson's 1976 content analysis of Saturday morning cartoons as the point of departure. She then presented her own research, the "field work" she had done in the "Saturday morning ghetto" (as Levinson phrased it) of children's cartoons.

On two consecutive Saturdays, Terri taped episodes of programs including *Josie and the Pussycats,*, *Scooby Do*, and *The Flintstones Comedy Hour*. She then transcripted the representations of males and females in her pictorial texts, focusing in particular on "changes [since Levinson's 1976 study] in the ways that television cartoons portrayed female characters." At first, she hypothesized that the cartoons would reflect the progress toward equality that she believed had taken place in the last fifteen years. "What I found was that women were given more freedom to do things, other than be maids and housewives, than they had in the 1970s, but their relationship to the male characters was still the same." In one episode of *Josie*, for example, Valerie (the program's only black) "engineered the major rescue by programming a robot to become an ally against the villain." Valerie piloted the group's spaceship, but she was the only female character observed at the controls of a vehicle: "Females rarely drive any vehicle when males are available."

The most common relationships between boys and girls in the cartoons Terri studied were romantic: "Not much has changed since Olive Oyl." Polly, of *Sweet Polly Purebread*, fell into the clutches of a villain and required rescuing by the hero, as did Melody in *Josie*. When not in need of rescue, the girls in the cartoons often plotted to "catch" or "trap" boys. Terri describes three instances that occurred during the two-hour observation. Other major preoccupations of females included "nagging, complaining, wanting things, or in the case of Alexandra [on *Josie*] just talking until someone put a bag over her head." In her conclusion, Terri wrote: "The sex roles in the cartoon programs continue to emphasize tradition and sexism. Young people are not likely to gain any insight into the new roles and perceptions that many women have of themselves or want for their daughters today."

In "The Quiet Inner Strength of Women: *The African Queen*," Shawn examined John Huston's classic film as a representation of the "common belief that women have the inner strength and endurance to hold men, families, and societies together...in such a way that the male is never made to feel inferior or put down by this strength of a woman." The Hepburn character, Rose Sayer, is "the perfect role model for women to act as men's social crutch." Shawn analyzes in detail the mediary role Rose plays, first between her unctuous missionary brother and the two-fisted, hard-drinking Charlie Allnut (Humphrey Bogart) and for most of the film, between Charlie and the vicissitudes of their journey downriver.

Shawn's reading focuses on the position of the protagonists in relation to each other and to other characters. She diagrammed a number of pivotal scenes in addition to transcribing the dialogue, voice, expression, and gesture. In one scene, for example, Rose hits on the idea of making torpedoes to blow up the German boat *Louisa*:

> The camera stays on Charlie as he laughs and tells her that she is being ridiculous. But then she becomes excited and begins to move forward and gesture with her hands. She wrinkles her forehead in a puzzled way and asks him questions about how to make torpedoes which he knows the answers to. Once he is convinced by her that the idea will work, she then becomes stern and ladylike again. Her face relaxes and she moves to the background again.

In sequences like this, Shawn locates the representation of woman as "social crutch," as she calls it: "Rose exudes strength and courage that she cleverly gives to Charlie...by optimism, small compliments and feminine gestures of helplessness. This is shown most clearly in her movements forward and back in the scene."

Resolving the Conflict in Gendered Representation

Terri and Shawn both put their fingers on the representational pulse of gender-biased stereotypes proscribed by their university's official policy against patronizing and stereotypical references to women. *Guidelines* admonishes: "Avoid the stereotypes of the logical, objective male and the emotional, subjective female. Women should not be portrayed as helpless nor be made the figures of fun or objects of scorn." The female figure in childrens's cartoons Terri studied is "the little woman," and Shawn's Rose Sayer character is certainly "the better half," both expressions labelled biased terms by the *Guidelines*.

Cultural studies, nevertheless, do not produce epiphanies. The post-sexist pedagogy described here offers students an alternative means of constructing experience of gender, an opportunity to re-think in a disciplined way their relationship to the world, reimagining experience as subject to history and culture rather than as a series of objective choices made by autonomous individuals. The writing instructor can show students how to resist dominant cultural formations like gender; but he or she cannot overcome students' inherent acquiescence in them. The instructor can open up the discursive space—a post-sexist rhetoric—for a critique of dominant narratives of gender; but students can be counted on to resist significant revisions of their own personal stories.

I have advanced the claim that the pedagogical attempt to compose a post-sexist rhetoric is inherently dialectical because it assigns students to resist their own cultural subjectivity. The other pole of the dialectic is the students' resistance to this assignment. Dale Bauer has pointed to the "critical tension" that the politically committed feminist teacher inevitably faces in the classroom. In their inquiry into the representation of gender, my students felt compelled to resolve the tension between their ideology of equal opportunity and the assymetries of power and worth they discovered and documented in their research.

Student resistance to the subjectivity of gender — their determination to resolve the conflict between the equalitarian discourse of American individualism and the pervasive evidence of inequities — employs a number of recurring and interrelated rhetorical strategies. These strategies, doubtless familiar to regular readers of student writing, include the doctrines of *separate* (but equal) *spheres*, the public sphere for men, the private one for women; of *social meliorism*, according to which things were bad in the past but are getting better; and of *demenology*, the belief that social inequities are the result of a few bad people or institutions, which can be distinguished from "society." I would like to discuss in a little more detail two other rhetorical moves that subvert more directly a post-sexist pedagogy: *vulgar realism* and *naturalization*.

Because students occupy a still largely uncomplicated world of commonsense dualism, they have difficulty distinguishing between representation (which is constructed) and reflection (which implies a direct access to nature). In spite of the careful exercises in definition prescribed by the syllabus, they often use the concepts interchangeably. In a study of how representation of women on television programs "reinforce[s] our definition of gender," a student concludes:

> Because television needs to be realistic, sometimes it goes too far and isn't representative of our society. On TV, women that have important executive jobs can stay late at work and don't worry about a family when, realistically, most women do have to come home to a family.

Even though the student announces the influence of the media in reinforcing gender, as he puts it, he still holds onto a naive realism according to which television must reflect or keep up with objective social changes (from *The Donna Reed Show* to *Growing Pains*) but not get too far ahead and thereby "misrepresent" the "real" reality of women's changing roles.

Terri's study of children's television programs resolves the conflict between her ideology and her evidence in much the same way: her own text constructs a world fully formed and independent of its linguistic representation. We can glimpse this strategy in her judgment about the cartoon's not offering children "any *insight* into the new roles and perceptions that women have of themselves or want for their daughters today [emphasis added]." Terry creates a world for the new roles and perceptions, accessible by "*insight*," thereby circumventing the biased, stereotypical representations of sex in the "old" world of childrens' television.

In the concluding sentence of her research paper, Terri claims that her study has "raised serious questions about television's *accuracy* of sex role representations [emphasis added]." She has finally shifted the problem from the inertia of cultural reproduction — which she herself identifies in the stereotypical representations of the cartoons — to a simpler reality that television programming ought to reflect more *accurately*. Terri has thereby harmonized the dissonance between her evidence of inequality and her faith in the "reality" of social equality.

The strategy of *naturalization*, the collapse of distinctions between culture and nature, takes *vulgar realism* one step farther. Anything that goes on in the world students refer to as reality is *natural*. As a result, they have a hard time distinguishing between sex, patently an objective characteristic existing in the "real world," and gender, a cultural formation that ascribes meaning to biological identity but is a quality of subjective experience. Without a clear concept of cultural subjectivity, students often represent gender as a behavior "learned," by observation and mimesis, from "society." Gender is thereby reduced to a set of objective characteristics that the subject must consciously learn to match with her or his physiology. And if gender is learned, it can also be mis-learned. In the course of defining gender, a number of students speculated that homosexual identity was a willful, voluntary decision to learn the wrong, the *unnatural*, gender-role.

This ideological impetus to naturalize and to intentionalize gender pervades Shawn's paper; it is always ready to help her subvert her attempt to understand the film as a cultural production. There is a constant tension between her sense that she is watching the subtle replication of androcentrism (woman as "social crutch") and her re-presentation of Rose's "quiet inner strength" as a reflection of woman's *natural* responsibility for social cohesion. At one point, she observes that the "classic" status of the film tells us something about what Americans "really believe about relationships." Elsewhere, she wonders if she isn't "reading too much into" what "could just be a story about two people." Her paper is marked by numerous signs of the epistemic struggle between two modes of explaining sexual identity: the autonomous and the cultural.

In her conclusion, Shawn finally resolves this dialectical tension. *The African Queen* becomes "a remake of what we all know as the real world." The discursive space, opened up by the assignment, is closed again, laying to rest the problem of social inequity by *naturalizing* the woman's performance as "social crutch" and as mirror of male egoism.

The pedagogy outlined here introduces students not only to the conventions of academic research and writing; it also introduces them to the study of culture. Our students, like most Americans, lack a theory of subject-formation. They explain their experiences to themselves in terms of autonomous individuals freely choosing their identities, as they might fashion themselves from the copious outlet malls of consumer capitalism. The work on composing a post-sexist rhetoric is a first step in overcoming this deeply ingrained cultural narrative of autonomy and autogenesis. And it is the first step as well to eliminating gender bias from university discourses.

Appendix A

Suggested questions to guide research into the representation of gender and media:

Who looks at whom, and how? What does the camera's position—our eye—focus attention on? What is left at the margins or not pictured at all (and why not)?

What contacts—eye or touch—are made? By whom? Under what circumstances? With what response?

Who speaks, to whom, in what tone? Who curses, cries, screams, laughs, etc.?

How are people physically positioned in relation to each other and to objects? What gestures, "body language," is displayed?

Who smiles, glowers, etc.? Are these expressions coded as "natural" or manipulative?

Who refers to the body, whose body, and how? Who grooms, under what circumstances, and how?

What's the costume: dress, ornament, jewelry? What physical objects (or props) are characters associated with?

Who takes their clothes off and under what conditions? How do clothes enable or restrict action?

What activities do the characters engage in or avoid? What are their goals? And how do they try to accomplish them?

Who's good at what task? Who's incompetent, bumbling?

What work do the characters do? How do they get things? What is their (apparent) relationship to the world outside the camera's eye?

What do the characters desire? Fear? Value?

What's funny, to whom and why?

Works Cited

Arlen, Michael. *Sixty Seconds*. New York: Farrar, Strauss, and Giroux, 1980.

Bauer, Dale M. "The Other 'F' Word: The Feminist in the Classroom." *College English*. 52 (1990): 385–96.

Beale, Walter H. "Richard M. Weaver: Philosophical Rhetoric, Cultural Criticism, and the First Rhetorical Awakening." *College English*. 52 (1990): 626–40.

Berlin, James. "Rhetoric and Ideology in the Writing Class." *College English*. 50 (1988): 477–94.

Bizzell, Patricia. "Beyond Anti-Foundationalism to Rhetorical Authority: Problems Defining 'Cultural Literacy.'" *College English* 52 (1990): 661–75.

Graff, Gerald, "Teach the Conflicts." *South Atlantic Quarterly*. 89 (1990): 51–67.

Gramsci, Antonio. *Selections from the Prison Notebooks*. Ed. and trans. by Quinton Hoare and Geoffrey Nowell Smith. New York: International, 1971.

Guidelines for Avoiding Gender-Biased Language in University Communications. West Chester University.

Jarratt, Susan C. "Feminism and Composition: The Case for Conflict." *Contending with Words*. Ed. Patricia Harkin and John Schilb. New York: MLA, 1991. 105–123.

Kuhn, Annette. *The Power of the Image: Essays on Representation and Sexuality*. London: Routledge & Kegan Paul, 1985.

Moffatt, Michael. *Coming of Age in New Jersey: College and American Culture*. New Brunswick: Rutgers University Press, 1989.

Reither, James A. and Douglas Vipond. "Writing as Collaboration." *College English*. 51 (1989): 855–67.

Scholes, Robert. *Textual Power: Literary Theory and the Teaching of English*. New Haven: Yale University Press, 1985.

Trimbur, John. "Essayist Literacy and the Rhetoric of Deproduction." *Rhetoric Review*. 9 (1990): 72–86.

Ulmer, Gregory L. *Applied Grammatology: Post(e)-Pedagogy from Jacques Derrida to Joseph Beuys*. Baltimore: Johns Hopkins University Press, 1985.

Volosinov, V.N. *Marxism and the Philosophy of Language*. Trans. L. Matejka and I.R. Titunik. New York: Seminar, 1973.

Will, George. "The New Campus Hegemony: Every Academic Activity Must Reform Society." *Philadelphia Inquirer*. 7 September 1990: 27.

19

Reteaching Shakespeare

Mark Fortier

1

The subject of this essay is Shakespeare and cultural studies. In 1990, while teaching cultural studies and puzzling over exactly what it was I was teaching, I adapted an aphorism from Marshall McLuhan: Cultural studies is anything you can get away with.[1] Given the contingencies of forming the alliances necessary to institute and maintain a cultural studies program, perhaps the only workable limitation would be to say that cultural studies practices a broadly defined cultural materialism. There is more to say about the variety and provisionality of cultural studies as an interdiscipline, but to begin with cultural studies and Shakespeare have no essential relationship, so I cannot provide or point to *the* relationship between the two. What I want to do is begin to map points in a certain possible relationship, points which can be read as discrete possibilities or as a direction of change in the relationship, a change which, taken to the extreme, takes cultural studies away from English studies or literary studies, and perhaps inevitably away from Shakespeare.

The vector of this change begins with the question of the text— actually with the new questioning of the text. *Political Shakespeare, Alternative Shakespeares, Shakespeare and the Question of Theory, Shakespeare Reproduced*: through deconstruction, new historicism, feminism, psychoanalysis, Marxism, the Shakespearean text has been subjected, first on the margins and increasingly towards the center of English studies, to a renewed questioning. This questioning undermines the traditional responses, which used to be read off the surface of the text, undermines authorial intention and the unbroken continuum of civilization and truth, which used to unite the timeless Shakespeare and the timeless reader. This questioning overlays the text with histories of power, language, gender, subjectivity, race, and class in such a way as to question the hermetic independence of the text, so that the English scholar must now also be historian, philosopher, psychoanalyst, political scientist. With the new questioning the text is no longer trusted as it once was, no longer independent of either context or strategies of reading.

If to know the text alone is no longer enough, the new editing questions with increased urgency whether it is possible to know the text at all: Gary Taylor, Stephen Orgel, and Jonathan Goldberg argue that the knowable text, the certain text, has become a figment of the scholar's longing. Any way the new editor turns — to manuscripts, to books, to the lost foul papers — she or he doesn't find the authoritative but only the traces of a phantom. As Jonathan Goldberg has said, given the contingencies of theatrical production, what Shakespeare really wrote or meant may never have existed; the singular text, the correct text, the original text, like the author itself, is a phantom of desire only realized in variation.

The Shakespearean text, as it crumbles and fades, is framed by disciplines and data of increasing toughness. Nowhere is this more evident than in certain renewed interests in theatrical history. Stephen Orgel has pointed out the truly mind-boggling cuts that Shakespeare's texts seem to have routinely suffered on the late Renaissance stage: A *Hamlet* without "To be or not to be," *The Winter's Tale* without the statue scene, *Henry V* without the choruses. On the stage Shakespeare's text gives way to the play of performance and the times. David Wiles, in *Shakespeare's Clown*, shows how Shakespeare's text, or even the play produced from that text, did not constitute the entirety of the theatrical event. The central element, in the theatrical event, but not by any means the only element, is not the drama text but the multifaceted relationship between the play and the afterpiece, between Shakespeare's drama and Will Kempe's jig. The text, already rendered uncertain by new readings and new editing, is now understandable only in relation to the entertainments it was paired with, and these are almost never known.

And yet we remain at this point, with all this questioning of the text, within the realm of the text, within the circle of English studies. John Donne wrote that a heresy could arise from something as seemingly inconsequential as a preposition (78). But orthodoxies can be seen in a preposition, too. In a work such as *Shakespeare Reproduced*, with all its variety of new readings, there is a tellingly repeated structure in the subtitles of the essays: "class-gender tension *in The Merry Wives of Windsor*," "femininity and the monstrous *in Othello*," "gender and rank *in Much Ado About Nothing*," "subversion and recuperation *in*

The Merchant of Venice." Not *The Merry Wives of Windsor* in class-gender tension, or gender and rank alongside of *Much Ado About Nothing*, or subversion and recuperation beyond *The Merchant of Venice*: Shakespeare's text remains the privileged object of study, in a way which perhaps defines and delimits the possibility of literary studies. Similarly, Jonathan Goldberg, when undermining the possibility of a decidable text for *Romeo and Juliet*, finds in the image of Rosaline a textual incorporation of textual undecidability, thus returning to Shakespeare's text its position as privileged object of reflexivity and insight. Even a work such as David Wiles' *Shakespeare's Clown*, which uses social and theatrical history to undermine the independence and privilege of the Shakespearean text, falls back ultimately on the foresight of the dramatic script—the jig is always an outgrowth of possibilities latent in Shakespeare's play: "Of course, we cannot ever say that the jig is moving in a direction which Shakespeare has not himself pointed to in his scripts" (56). Why not? I suppose because we still believe in, are disciplined by, the infinite expansiveness and foresight of the drama text, of Shakespeare as author. Once again there is something symptomatic in the title of Wiles' book: Why is Kempe Shakespeare's clown? Why such proprietary privileging? Is Kempe Shakespeare's clown any more than Shakespeare is Kempe's playwright?

If the reprivileging of the text is an almost inevitable (re)turn of the new textual questioning, that is, if this turn serves as a founding principle of the new English studies, this need not be true of cultural studies, which would question the text without the need to reprivilege it. Within the realm of the text, when Shakespeare's text is no longer the privileged object of study, textual rewriting and reprocessing of Shakespeare in all its forms—exegesis, editing, adaptation, citation, parody—can come to the fore. Once outside the study of the text in the narrow sense, new areas of study open up. Theatrical practice, editorial practice, academic practice, critical practice, publishing practice. Cultural studies would not merely engage in new versions of these activities, but would pull back to make them a part—and no small part—of the object of study. As Terry Eagleton writes in the afterword to *The Shakespeare Myth*, "Shakespeare is today less an author than an apparatus." Shakespeare is not only a set of literary texts from the late sixteenth and early seventeenth centuries but "an entire politico-cultural formation" in the world around us (204).

Gary Taylor has suggested a name for this new "subject": "Shakesperotics." Shakesperotics "embraces everything that a society does in the name. . .of Shakespeare." Shakesperotics as defined by Taylor, is a much bigger subject than literary studies can manage:

> But in order to interpret what a society does in the name of Shakespeare,
> you have to know what else that society does. You can hardly recount

> the history of the theatre, of publishing, censorship, journalism, education, morality, sex, without becoming entangled in the complex entirety of their host society, its economics, politics, ideology, its total social and material structure. And so a history of Shakesperotics becomes, inevitably, a history of four centuries of our culture. (6)

Taylor's work, given the inevitable limitations of anyone's ability to complete such a task and given Taylor's specific literary, academic, and high-cultural slant, is hardly this history. Taylor avoids a more broadly cultural engagement with Shakespeare, especially in its more "trivial" but important and pressing manifestations in popular and mass culture. This remains true of much cultural study of Shakespeare. Michael Bristol's *Shakespeare's America, America's Shakespeare*, although it begins with Charlie the Tuna (15), elsewhere rarely strays from the likes of Emerson, Harry Levin, and Stephen Greenblatt.

The Shakespeare apparatus, the Shakespeare industry, Eagleton writes, "interlocks with almost every structure of late capitalism" (207). In other words, Shakespeare is the name of something which continues to have a political effect in our own day. Graham Holderness writes, "Shakespeare is, here, now, always, what is currently being made of him" (xvi). For instance, in Britain Shakespeare continues to be an effective and pressing ideological state apparatus, disseminated through such industries as tourism, broadcasting, publishing and education. Of course, the situation in the United States is different, and the effects of the Shakespeare apparatus must always be seen in national or local terms. A specifically Canadian study, for instance, might explore issues in its neocolonialist cultural mentality and focus on the Stratford Festival as an entire sociocultural and economic event, or on Northrop Frye, whose strictly literary analysis of Shakespeare's texts as works expressing universal truth (or at least universal or epochal literary truth) might be symptomatic of a continuing blindness to the specifics of Shakespeare in Canada. At any rate it remains important to hold tenaciously to national and local differences in the institutionalization of Shakespeare, a point which I make in light of the following example.

As is the case of all aspects of the Shakespeare industry, new areas of production quickly burgeon to produce massive amounts of material. Shakesperotics is already a minor boom area, and one of the latest works in this field is Michael Bristol's *Shakespeare's America, America's Shakespeare*, which I mention above. Bristol, like Holderness, Taylor, and other cultural students of Shakespeare, sees Shakespeare as a complex institutional reality, which cannot be studied through textual analysis, and assumes that this institutional and social life of Shakespeare is what really matters. He is interested in the way Americans have been "Shakespearized" — as Shakespeare has been Americanized — made into seemingly autonomous subjects within a bourgeois economic dispensation. Although Bristol pulls up short of envisioning such a thing, the point is to search out a new sociocultural dispensation and to put Shakespeare at the service of this.

There is one curious aspect of Bristol's book, however. The book was funded by a research stipend from the Social Sciences and Humanities Research Council of Canada and by financial assistance from the Graduate Faculty and Department of English at McGill University in Montreal where Bristol teaches (ix). Although there is a passing allusion to previous studies of Shakespeare in "North America" (10), the footnote in support of this lists no studies of Shakespeare in Canada or Mexico — although England is mentioned (213–14). Nor is any absence noted. Finally, Bristol undertakes a substantial critique of Northrop Frye's work on Shakespeare, but the only institutional affiliation listed for Frye is his having delivered the Brampton lectures at Columbia University in 1963 (174). This effaces Frye's long tenure at Victoria University in the University of Toronto. I believe that Canadians should have the right to claim their own villains without having them co-opted by the forces of American imperialism. Bristol notes that even within hegemonic Shakespeare there is a radical potential held in reserve. Bristol's own cavalier attitude toward Canada shows that even within radical Shakespeare there is the power to sustain hegemonic values.

One aspect of the Shakespeare apparatus that is of central importance to reteaching Shakespeare is teaching Shakespeare. Once again, as Don E. Wayne and Walter Cohen in *Shakespeare Reproduced*, Alan Sinfield in *Political Shakespeare*, and David Hornbrook in *The Shakespeare Myth* have shown, the import of teaching Shakespeare is not the same in all places. Cohen argues that Shakespeare studies form "the cutting edge of academic criticism in the United States" (18), but only at elite conferences, in scholarly journals, and in large research universities.[2] Elsewhere Shakespeare studies often remain the castle keep of academic feudalism. In Britain Hornbrook notes a strange new twist: while Shakespeare plays a progressively smaller role in the education of the working class, the elite in British "public" schools continue to be well-versed in their bardolatry. Hornbrook argues that the exclusion from Shakespeare studies goes hand in hand with an exclusion from access to the managerial class (154). Not surprisingly, no one has as yet clarified the specific role that Shakespeare plays in Canadian education.

In *Shakespeare Reproduced*, Margaret Ferguson questions the potential of Shakespeare studies as an effective oppositional strategy and shows that the forces for containing the subversive power of radical Shakespeare studies are truly formidable (274). Similarly, Gary Taylor reflects upon the complicity of radical projects, including his own work with Oxford University Press, with hegemonic structures:

> Like IBM and the Berliner Ensemble and the [Royal Shakespeare Company], OUP can afford to experiment, because its risky innovations are subsidized by its safe market leaders. The Oxford editors, too, can afford to experiment, because they know that the global power and prestige of OUP will be mobilized in support of their experiments. Their shocking edition is empowered by and, in turn, empowers the multinational business interests of Oxford University Press, just as Eagleton's Marxist monograph is underwritten by and underwrites the capitalist family firm of Basil Blackwell Ltd. (321)

The glib sense of the almost inevitable subversion of subversion aside, there is strong reason to suspect that institutional and cultural hegemonies make it next to impossible for Shakespeare studies to really be on the cutting edge of anything.

I'd like now to return to the point I made at the beginning of this paper: the variety and provisionality of cultural studies as an interdiscipline, the important local flavor of any cultural studies program. The very notion of reteaching Shakespeare seems to be based upon a somewhat limited and generalized notion of cultural studies as an outgrowth of English studies or literary studies, which take for granted the importance of teaching Shakespeare both in the past and in the future. So far this paper too has been based upon the idea that cultural studies starts in English studies, even if it takes flight from there. At Trent University, where I taught cultural studies—and which, it is important to note, has one of a very few cultural studies programs in Canada—the program is staffed largely by disaffected English professors, although philosophers, art historians, sociologists and political scientists are also represented. But at Trent the relation between English and cultural studies is not so much like that of a parent and a child as it is like a particularly rancorous divorce. This has meant that cultural studies, having severed its ties with English, has had to make new allegiances elsewhere. When I arrived at Trent I spent several months wondering why there were no common links between English and cultural studies, why they didn't show up for our events and we didn't show up for theirs, but then I realized that in the absence of such links cultural studies had forged connections with other newer departments, such as native studies. Now the department dreams of alliances with comparative development studies and women's studies. Such alliances will take cultural studies further away from English studies, and some possibilities will thereby be lost, but new possibilities will arise.

One of the possibilities that may be lost is the possibility of reteaching Shakespeare. This is not necessarily a bad thing. There is no reason to think that Shakespeare will be important to the projects of all cultural studies programs in their localized distinctiveness. It may be that, firstly, at least in Canada and the United States, Shakespeare is no longer all that important as a cultural and social force, and secondly, that an oppositional or even relevant, educational practice might be better off setting its sights on other subjects. When Gary Taylor writes, "Within our culture, Shakespeare is enormously powerful" (411), he is glossing over any number of questions and specifications: who is the we in "our" culture? What is culture? What is the duration of the present in "is"? In what ways is Shakespeare enormously powerful and in what ways is "he" not, or no longer, enormously powerful? It may be that in certain circumstances Shakespeare must go from near deity to nonentity; that, in the face of more immediate concerns, Shakespeare is just another dead cultural worker.

2

Since I first began to work on this paper, much about my own localized circumstances has changed. For the 1990–91 academic year I moved from a position in Trent's cultural studies program to a position in Trent's English department. One of the interesting opportunities that arose from this move is that I was allowed to offer a fourth-year seminar in Shakespeare studies. And so the line of flight, which might have taken me further away from Shakespeare, made at least a temporary loop, and I found myself working once again not beyond but in, or on, Shakespeare.

The course I offered was an outgrowth of the positions I outline in the first part of this article. Here is the course description given to students:

"*Shakespearean Contexts*." The course will explore the way Shakespeare's work is appropriated by, and functions in, different historical, social, and cultural contexts.

The first quarter of the course will be concerned with Shakespeare's "original" context. We will explore the relations between Shakespeare's plays and Elizabethan-Jacobean England. Issues to be dealt with include the status of the author/playwright, the literary/theatrical mode of production, censorship, theatricality and power, historiography and national identity, the relation in the theatrical event between elitist and popular elements, the role or absence of women in the theatre, the structuration of the audience.

The second quarter of the course will jump to late 20th century Canada to look at the Stratford Festival. We will attempt to generate a cultural understanding of the festival and the style of Shakespeare it produces. This will entail the analysis of videos of Stratford productions and perhaps a field trip to the festival.

The third quarter of the course will examine recent trends in the academic appropriation of Shakespeare: the new editing, new historicism, cultural materialism, feminism, "Shakesperotics."

> The fourth quarter will turn to recent adaptations or recontextualizations of Shakespeare by Edward Bond, Charles Marowitz, Heiner Müller, and Ann-Marie MacDonald. We will end by comparing Shakespeare's *Henry V*(s) to the film of Kenneth Branagh.

In a concession to tradition, respectability, and the primacy of the text, each quarter of the course would focus on a Shakespearean work: the first quarter on the second tetralogy, the second quarter on *The Taming of the Shrew*, the third quarter on *King Lear*, the fourth quarter on the play(s) corresponding to that week's adaptation.

Trent's English department is not the most progressive; the course I was offering had very little resemblance to what has been offered here in the past. When I met the students for the first time in September I was so bold as to declare that what I was presenting to them was really a cultural studies course in disguise, that it was about understanding rather than appreciation and that impressionistic responses to the text would not do. Within two weeks my twelve students had dropped to eight, although part of that might have been due to the normal shakeout at that time of the year.

Three years of English studies at Trent had not really prepared many students for the work I was asking them to undertake. Because there are so many fourth-year students in English, however, the course was virtually closed to students from other departments, specifically interested cultural studies majors who had done this kind of work before. In large part, therefore, this course functioned for most of the students taking it as an indoctrination into something they found alien and even mind-boggling. But, if not prepared in certain ways, these students were bright and more than capable of interesting and unexpected contributions.

How did the course progress? The first part of the course was less successful than I might have hoped. I don't think I really succeeded in instilling a very sophisticated sense of history into the students. English students are traditionally unsophisticated in their understanding of the past, which they tend to think of as full of people like themselves, only without microwaves. It is difficult for them to get their mind around, say, the author function as an historically specific situation. One thing that became apparent was the importance of feminism as an access point to a changing understanding of Shakespeare. The majority of English students at Trent — and likely many other places — are women, who therefore constitute the most visible oppressed social group. Therefore, it was easiest to introduce new ideas when they were relevant to questions of gender. This continued to prove true in later parts of the course.

The second quarter of the course, dealing with the Stratford Festival, produced much more lively results. Trent is part of the archipelago of southern Ontario universities which sends yearly pilgrimages to Stratford, so that only one student in the course had never experienced the festival firsthand. Looking at Stratford in a new light was, therefore, interesting and constructively unsettling. The local reading of Shakespeare also played into endlessly troubling and complex questions of Canadian culture and Canadian nationalism. Since *The Taming of the Shrew* was the text on which we were focusing, questions of sexual politics also came to the fore. This section of the course generated several interesting papers, including two, titled "Shakespeare in Canada: Who Gave Him a Passport?" and "The Timing of the Shrew," which were sophisticated analyses of Shakespeare as a historically contingent formation (Holloway; Holmes).

After the December holidays we returned to study trends in recent criticism. Here I realized the effect that the students' future plans had on their interests. I had designed the course, it seems to me in retrospect, as if it were to be given to a group of future graduate students; however, I was actually teaching more education students than future Ph.Ds. The more esoteric the criticism, the less excitement it generated. World events conspired in this, too. The students found it particularly futile and pointless to be reading Stephen Greenblatt's "Shakespeare and the Exorcists" on the very eve of the Gulf War. That was, perhaps, due in part to my inability to draw the necessary connections. Once again, feminism proved more engaging, as did, strangely enough, the nuts and bolts of recent editing practices. The education students were always sifting through the material to discern whatever could be used to stimulate the teaching of Shakespeare in high school; they were wary of whatever they thought high school students would only find confusing or needlessly deflating.

As for the adaptations, Ann-Marie MacDonald's *Goodnight Desdemona (Goodmorning Juliet)* drew the most enthusiastic response, which is not surprising: it is Canadian, feminist, funny, and accessible. All in all, as the course wound down I thought of it as a beginning or a partial success. Although the students had come a long way, I don't think I began with a sufficient understanding of the kind of preparation they originally brought to the course.

Meanwhile, I was also part of the team which teaches Trent's second-year Shakespeare survey course. Here, more than anywhere else, I came to understand the conflict of paradigms at work. It was good, I believe, for the students in this course to witness the debates not only over what Shakespeare means, but what Shakespeare is and whether we should care. I see my voice in this course as the one which wrenched Shakespeare out of the past — or more often out of a timeless present — and cast it into play in the world around us. The night the Gulf War began I was accosted in the street by a small group of drunken gay bashers: it felt as if I was experiencing male thuggery on both the global and local levels. The next week I lectured on *Othello*, which was suddenly very clearly a play about war and male sexual violence. My lecture on *The Tempest*, called "Brave New World and New World Order," treated the play as a moment in the history of technology and imperialism which leads not to the ability to conjure a tempest at sea but to Operation Desert Storm. Lectures like these may be given again sometime, although these particular lectures were too profoundly enmeshed in the events of early 1991. These lectures as such are not to be repeated, which is as it should be. The work continues.

Notes

1. McLuhan writes, "Art is anything you can get away with" (132–36). My variation is intended to stress the strategic and contingent element in McLuhan's statement, somewhat as in Marx:

> Men make their own history, but they do not make it just as they please; they do not make it under circumstances chosen by themselves, but under circumstances directly encountered, given and transmitted from the past. (97)

2. Trends change quickly in academia and I don't think Shakespeare studies are the cutting edge anymore. The cutting edge is now probably postmodern studies, science-fiction studies, postcolonial studies, gay studies, or something even more recent which I don't even know about.

Works Cited

Bond, Edward. *Lear*. London: Methuen, 1983.

Branagh, Kenneth, dir. *Henry V*. Renaissance Film Company, 1989.

Bristol, Michael D. *Shakespeare's America, America's Shakespeare*. London: Routledge, 1990.

Cohen, Walter. "Political Criticism of Shakespeare." Howard and O'Connor, 18–46.

Dollimore, Jonathan and Alan Sinfield, eds. *Political Shakespeare: New essays in cultural materialism*. Ithaca: Cornell University Press, 1985.

Donne, John. *John Donne and the Theology of Language*. Eds. P.G. Stanwood and Heather Ross Asals. Columbia: University of Missouri Press, 1986.

Drakakis, John, ed. *Alternative Shakespeares*. London: Methuen, 1985.

Eagleton, Terry. "Afterword." In *The Shakespeare Myth*, see Holderness, 203–8.

Ferguson, Margaret. "Afterword." In *Shakespeare Reproduced*. see Howard and O'Connor, 273–83.

Frye, Northrop. *Northrop Frye on Shakespeare*. Ed. Robert Sandler. Markham, Ontario: Fitzhenry and Whiteside, 1986.

Goldberg, Jonathan. "'What? In a Names That Which We Call a Rose': the Desired Texts of *Romeo and Juliet*." 24th Annual Conference on Editorial Problems. Toronto, 5 November 1988.

Greenblatt, Stephen. "Shakespeare and the Exorcists." Parker and Hartman 163−87.

Holderness, ed. *The Shakespeare Myth*. Manchester: Manchester University Press, 1988.

Holloway, Susan. "Shakespeare in Canada: Who Gave Him a Passport?" Unpublished paper, 1990.

Holmes, Trevor, "The Timing of the Shrew." Unpublished paper, 1990.

Hornbrook, David. "Go Play, Boy, Play": Shakespeare and educational drama. Holderness 145−59.

Howard, Jean E. and Marion F. O'Connor. *Shakespeare Reproduced*. New York: Methuen, 1987.

MacDonald, Ann-Marie. *Goodnight Desdemona (Goodmorning Juliet)*. Toronto: Coach House Press, 1990.

Marowitz, Charles. *Measure for Measure. The Marowitz Shakespeare*. New York: Drama Book Specialists, 1978. 181−225.

Marx, Karl. "The Eighteenth Brumaire of Louis Bonaparte." *Selected Works*. Karl Marx and Frederick Engels. London: Lawrence and Wishart, 1968: 95−180.

McLuhan, Marshall and Quentin Fiore. *The Medium is the Massage*. New York: Bantam, 1967.

Müller, Heiner. "*Hamletmachine. Hamletmachine and other texts for the stage*. Ed. Carl Weber. New York: Performing Arts Journal Publications, 1984. 49−58.

Orgel, Stephen. "Acting Scripts, Performing Texts." 24th Annual Conference on Editorial Problems. Toronto, 5 November 1988.

Parker, Patricia and Geoffrey Hartman. *Shakespeare and the Question of Theory*. New York: Methuen, 1985.

Taylor, Gary. *Reinventing Shakespeare: A Cultural History from the Restoration to the Present*. New York: Weidenfeld & Nicolson, 1989.

Wiles, David. *Shakespeare's Clown: Actor and Text in the Elizabethan Playhouse*. Cambridge: Cambridge University Press, 1987.

Notes on Contributors

James A. Berlin is Professor of English at Purdue University. He is a former elementary school teacher, former Director of Composition at the University of Cincinnati, and former director of the Kansas Writing Project. He is the author of *Writing Instruction in Nineteenth-Century American Colleges* and *Rhetoric and Reality: Writing Instruction in American Colleges, 1900–1985*. His recent work has explored the relations of rhetoric, cultural studies, and the classroom.

Michael J. Vivion is Associate Professor of English and former Director of Composition at the University of Missouri at Kansas City where he coordinates the High School/College Credit Program and the Greater Kansas City Writing Project. He co-authored *The Writer's Circle* (St. Martin's), *Houghton Mifflin English 9–12*, and has written articles on teaching composition and literature which have appeared in journals such as the *Arizona English Bulletin, English Journal,* and *English in Texas*. He believes that the conversations on cultural studies must be expanded to include teachers throughout the grades who have thus far been excluded from the dialogue.

Anne Balsamo teaches cultural studies and feminist studies of science and technology at Georgia Institute of Technology as part of a new program in science, technology, and culture. She is coordinating an SCE project on Cultural Studies and Pedagogy. Her current research focuses on the relationships among the body, technology, and gender.

Michael Blitz and C. Mark Hurlbert just can't stop collaborating. Their articles include "Utopia Notebook," "Rumors of Cgange: *The* Classroom, *Our* Classroom, and *Big* Business," "The Institution('s) Lives!" "Anarchy as a State of Health," "Toward a Poetics in the Age of Intersubjectivity," and "To: You, From: Michael Blitz and C. Mark Hurlbert, Re: Literacy Demands and Institutional Autobiography." They also edited *Composition and Resistance* for Boynton/Cook Heinemann. They are currently working on a book about the rhetoric of the academic institution.

Linda Brodkey is Associate Professor in the Department of Literature at the University of California, San Diego, Where she is Coordinator of the Warren College Writing Program. She is the author of *Academic Writing as Social Practice* and a number of articles on writing theory, research, and practice.

Peter Carino earned his Ph.D. from the University of Illinois and is Associate Professor of English and Director of the Writing Center at Indiana State University, where he teaches writing, rhetorical theory, and American literature.

323

He has published two basic writing textbooks in addition to articles on writing centers, composition pedagogy, and American literature.

Christine Farris is an assistant professor of English, adjunct professor of Women's Studies, and Research Coordinator of the Campuswide Writing Program at Indiana University. She has published articles on the relationship between composition theory and practice, training new teachers, and writing across the curriculum. Hampton Press will be publishing her new book *Subject to Change: New Composition Instructors' Theory and Practice.*

Cathy Fleischer is an assistant professor of English at Eastern Michigan University where she teaches courses in composition, literacy, and pedagogy. She has recently published "Reforming Literacy: A Collaborative Teacher-Student Project" in Jay L. Robinson's *Conversations on the Written Word.* She is also a 1992 recipient of the James Britton Award for Inquiry in the Language Arts.

Joel Foreman is an associate professor in the English Department at George Mason University. He is currently writing a select cultural history of America in the 1950s. Most of his previous publications have taken the form of television documentary. His subjects include William Styron, Carlos Fuentes, and Stanley Fish.

Mark Fortier's main area of interest is the study of Shakespeare in a changing context. He is a member of the English Department of Victoria College at the University of Toronto.

Alan W. France teaches writing and directs the introductory composition program at West Chester University. His essay included here is part of a longer work entitled *Composition as a Cultural Process.* He gratefully acknowledges the collaboration of Karen L. Fitts and his composition students.

Diana George is an associate professor in the Humanities Department at Michigan Technological University. Her work has appeared in *College Composition and Communication, English Journal, College Teaching,* and, most recently, *Post Script.* She is co-editor, with Nancy Grimm and Ed Lotto, of *Writing Center Journal* and co-author with John Trimbur of *Reading Culture.*

C. Mark Hurlbert (See Blitz above.)

Alan Kennedy is Head of the Department of English at Carnegie Mellon. His most recent book is *Reading Resistance Value: Deconstructive Practice and the Politics of Literary Critical Encounters.* He is working on a book tentatively called *Committing the Curriculum and other Misdemeanors.*

Kathleen McCormick, is Associate Professor of Literary and Cultural Studies at Carnegie Mellon. She is currently completing *Reading: Cognition, Institutions, Ideology* (Manchester University Press) and is one of the editors of the forthcoming MLA volume *Approaches to Teaching "Ulysses."* Her monograph *Multiple Pleasures in Reading: "Ulysses," Wandering Rocks, and the Reader* (Edwin Mellon Press) is also forthcoming.

Richard Miller is completing his Ph.D. in Critical and Cultural Studies at the University of Pittsburgh. His current project involves combining his interest in composition theory, pedagogy, and popular culture to interrogate popular reading practices.

Donald Morton teaches critical theory at Syracuse University, where he was director of the humanities doctoral program from 1974 through 1983. He is the author of *Vladimir Nabokov*, and his work on postmodern thought and contemporary institutional practices has appeared in *MLN, boundary 2, Cultural Critique, Social Text,* and other periodicals.

Richard Penticoff was a graduate student at the University of Texas at Austin when this essay was written. He is now an assistant professor at the University of Idaho.

Lori Robison, a doctoral candidate at Indiana University, has designed and taught a number of first-year writing courses. Currently she is writing her dissertation, which examines the cultural, political, and gender implications of post-Civil War local color literature.

Delores Schriner is an assistant professor and former director of composition at Northern Arizona University. She has published in *College Composition and Communication, Computers and Composition,* and *Arizona English Bulletin.*

Diana Shoos is an assistant professor of French and Visual Studies in the Humanities Department at Michigan Technological University. She co-edited with Diana George "Reading Images," a special issue of *Reader: Essays in Reader-Oriented Theory, Criticism, and Pedagogy* in which their article "The Culture of the Bath: Cigarette Advertising and the Representation of Leisure" appears. Shoos and George are also co-authors of "*Top Gun* and Postmodern Mass Culture Aesthetics" which recently appeared in *Post Script*. Shoos' work on film has also appeared in *Literature and Psychology.*

David Shumway is Associate Professor in the area of Literary and Cultural Studies in the English Department of Carnegie Mellon University. He is the author of *Michel Foucault* (1989) and of *Creating American Civilization: A Genealogy of American Literature as an Academic Field* (forthcoming).

Paul Smith is Coordinator of the Literary and Cultural Studies Programmes at Carnegie Mellon. He has published widely in the areas of literary and cultural theory, film, art, pedagogy, and on other related issues. He is author of *Pound Revised, Discerning the Subject* and a forthcoming book called *Clint Eastwood: A Fantasy*. He also co-edited *Men in Feminism* with Alice Jardine.

Phillip E. Smith, II. is Associate Professor and Chair of the English Department at the University of Pittsburgh. He is the co-author and co-editor of the recent edition with commentary of *Oscar Wilde's Oxford Notebooks: A Portrait of Mind in the Making*; he also writes and teaches in the areas of Victorian and modern literature and science, drama, and the teaching of English studies.

Mas'ud Zavarzadeh teaches critical theory at Syracuse University. He is the author of *The Mythopoetic Reality* and *Seeing Films Politically*. His texts on postmodern critical theory have appeared in *Film Quarterly, Rethinking Marxism, Cultural Critique, boundary 2, Telos,* and other journals.

James Thomas Zebroski teaches undergraduate and graduate courses in writing and rhetoric at Syracuse University. He received three degrees from The Ohio State University, having taught in the public schools and at colleges in Ohio, Texas, and Pennsylvania. His research on the psychosocial theory of Lev Vygotsky and composition practices complements his work on M.M. Bakhtin. Of current importance to him is making sense of the ways his working-class, ethnic heritage has composed him and his writing.